VICTORY DAY

VICTORY DAY

Winning American Independence

★ ★ ★

The Defeat of the British Southern Strategy

★ ★ ★

KENNETH SCARLETT

Charleston, SC
www.PalmettoPublishing.com

Hardcover ISBN: 978-1-68515-476-9
Paperback ISBN: 978-1-68515-477-6

Front Cover: Victory Day Etching, Continental troops led by General Nathanael Greene liberating Charlestown, SC on December 14, 1782. Image courtesy of South Carolina Historical Society Archives, Reproduced and enhanced from The History of South Carolina, 1922, Simms.

Back Cover: British Evacuation of Charlestown, SC, via the harbor, December 14, 1782, 1898, painting by Howard Pyle, image courtesy of Delaware Art Museum/Bridgeman Art Library.

TABLE OF CONTENTS

PURPOSE, FOUNDATION, AND ACKNOWLEDGMENTS

Filling in the Gaps of Our Untold Revolutionary History

In the Information Age, the study of history has an opportunity to become more scientific. I am a researcher with leadership, domestic security, and organization consulting experience who enjoys historical investigation and root cause analysis related to the events of the American Revolution. Applying intelligence analysis techniques to original sources left in darkness for centuries reveals an untold story about the conclusion of the Revolutionary War and achieving independence many Americans may find enriching on the doorstep of our nation's 250th anniversary.

I have had the honor of leading many fine people in civilian and military organizations, in research, in the field, during domestic security operations, and in business. Our teams performed analyses and interventions in time-critical, high-stress situations with businesses or lives at stake. I draw upon these military and intelligence skills and my experiences in Joint Forces Operations Command as a liaison officer when analyzing historical correspondence in the Revolutionary War from a concept of operations and common operating picture perspective. Analyzing command correspondence and supplementing that analysis with additional research, on-site investigation, and local interviews, as if the described threats and opportunities are present or emerging at that very moment, leads to some remarkable findings. Using now-accessible primary sources, this research methodology reveals previously unknown aspects about the war's final phase and ending in the Lower South that have been left vacant for over two centuries.

According to Pulitzer Prize recipient Gordon Stewart Wood, the Revolutionary War was "the most radical and most far-reaching event in American history," if not world history. The American success in achieving independence from fighting that war made democracy and capitalism the global standard for ethical and prosperous governance. Yet there is insufficient scholarship that adequately explains when and how the war ended successfully enough to achieve the political goal of collective, sovereign independence for America. Original command correspondence to write the closing chapter of the war was thought to be lost or not accessible. Historians had to work with whatever information was available to them at the time of writing.

That situation changed when firsthand correspondence by Southern General Nathanael Greene, whom George Washington and the Continental Congress tasked to liberate the South from British occupation, became available to all researchers around 2005. This time-capsule correspondence now enables military-minded historians to reconstruct the events that likely produced independence for all the colonies in rebellion. Researchers can now see command decisions' cumulative effect on civilian, political, and diplomatic relations in a clearer light. The expertly transcribed correspondence of *The Papers of General Nathanael Greene* is "the missing link" of the latter stages of the Revolutionary War. These papers, Greene's command center hub of communications, connect events and strategies to the center of the decision wheel that drove the War for American Independence to a successful conclusion in the final phases. The final phases of the war consisted of two parts: the convoluted British trek to Yorktown originating in Charlestown, South Carolina (now Charleston), which ended in defeat for one British army, and the complex Continental counterstrategy to liberate the entire Lower South from two more British armies over the next fourteen months after Yorktown, concluding with the British surrender of Charlestown. The successful completion of both campaigns in succession earned enough respect at the European negotiating tables for the world order to concede independence to the United States and recognize the new nation governed by a popularly elected set of state governments represented by a single confederation. The preeminent correspondence found in *Greene's Papers* is an excellent resource for deconstructing the evolution and winning of the American Revolution from its chief strategist and Southern theater commander. Greene's battlefront communications cast a whole new light on the war's later stages.

Greene's Papers reveals that the War for American Independence, in its final phase, was about territory possession, pushing the British military machine entirely out of the South and holding on to liberated territory by popular consent while reconstituting state governments loyal to the confederation. I study military history by examining moment-in-time correspondence, troop movements, prime directives, standing orders, and primary threats while combing through other internet-accessible resources to get a sense of leadership behavior profiles, organization hierarchies, chain of command, leadership training and experience, strategic plans, logistics, the means to get things done, the methods to get things done, the "teams" responsible for the execution, areas of operations, the operational outcomes, and the consequences or rewards of leadership. Sometimes I find the underlying cause of how things came off by studying the orders, stated objectives, places, facts, cultures, metrics, constraints, and personalities. Sometimes I piece together the highest-probability scenario based on the known facts after checking out the area of operations, terrain, and physical evidence collected at the sites and proceeding with the most likely story—like an intelligence estimate.

At all times, I think about troop sustainment and fighting fundamentals. Force security, potable water, food, protein, shoes, gunpowder supply, firearms, firepower, horses, horse feed, shelter, blankets, terrain, weather, and health were fundamental to combat capability. My research methods differ from traditional academic research methods in that I do not always seek quotes from institutionally approved sources to defend hypotheses and provide intellectual balance but instead, look at where the chain of events and facts lead as if I am constructing a situational analysis at critical moments in time with lives at stake. The end product resembles a military situational report describing the common operating picture delivered to a general's staff.

Besides dog-earing my thirteen volumes of *Greene's Papers*, I have consulted over two hundred additional books and sources, visited numerous battle sites, interviewed legacy residents, and received briefings of ground-penetrating radar results. The cool thing about historical research nowadays is one can find out through internet open sources what events occurred and what the outcomes were, so the significant challenges are finding out why they happened, how they fit into a larger operational plan, and how those events affected war fighting strategy during the Revolutionary War and diplomatic world decision-making going forward. If one looks hard enough, first-person accounts that "connect the dots" of the territory control strategy that ultimately liberated the South and significantly influenced the granting of independence can now be found. As a result of current-day information accessibility, an updated history of the final thirty-one months of the War "for" American Independence, such as *Victory Day*, can be written.

The Information Age, ushered in thanks to the World Wide Web, now provides access to the many eyewitness accounts of what happened in the South during the War for American Independence. Many of these contemporary accounts and command reports—"the war in action," so to speak—were almost impossible to access during the analysis process until the last fifteen years. Past historians were left without a broad spectrum of primary sources from leaders in the know. While this book relies heavily on operational interpretations of the papers of General Nathanael Greene, the papers of King George III, Washington's papers, John Adams's papers, Henry Clinton's memoirs, and Robert Howe's papers reveal the magnitude of the war in the South from the leaders calling the shots. Their activities unveil how the defeat of the British Southern strategy resulted in independence. In addition, now-accessible first-person accounts enable the development of realistic situational analyses to fill the gaps between local histories and the strategic war in action while avoiding an overdependency on propagandized British newspaper articles and homogenized postwar testimonials from British field commanders who can be placed at the scene of war crimes. The effect of Lower South territory possession on the world order deciding whether America would be granted her independence has come to light for those who wish to see the connection.

The "last miles" of the road to independence have been obfuscated for centuries. The British confiscated many printing presses in their seven-year tour de force across America, so postwar Patriot accounts had to run the editing gauntlet of London publishing houses for years to come if they were to see the light of day or profit. Many reports were written in genteel King's English designed to minimize British atrocities, enhance reputations, avoid pro-plaintiff libel lawsuits, and avoid criminal arrest on charges of sedition by the Crown. (Daniel Webster did not publish the first American dictionary until twenty-three years after the war, and freedom of speech was not protected in the United States until 1791. Britain does not have First Amendment freedom of expression to this day.) Given the traditions of the time, former British commanders were likely given the courtesy of "commenting" on manuscripts before printing to avoid libel claims and obtain their promotional endorsements—not unlike the process American publishers employed after the Vietnam War to put a good face on things.

Using their language mastery, the British had a penchant for expressing their misdeeds and leadership failures in the most gratifying light after the war. They were well acquainted with the practice of *damnatio memoriae* to exclude the memory of people from historical records who were regarded as traitors or enemies. Exploiting their control of postwar publishing, the British government blamed "lukewarm Loyalists," an uncontrollable internecine war in progress, and fragmented Native American allies for their failures to put down the colonial rebellion and conquer America. The closer truth is that there was a complete ethical breakdown across their military chain of command emanating from "the Divine Power of the King" and driven by Britain's War Ministry to punish the Southern colonies for their rebellious disloyalty. This preferred policy of punishment was compounded by each field commander's insatiable quest for self-glory at the expense of coordinated strategy and operational unity of effort. Not only did poor ethics and uncivil treatment of civilians drive the majority to the Patriot cause, but British commanders also spent more time outwitting each other to gain favor with King George and his ministry than they did on cooperatively conquering America. Nonetheless, he who controlled the publishing houses and wished to remain in business printed the postwar narratives compatible with the government's storyline.

But those are bygone days. We can know more now than our ancestors could because of accessibility. No longer does one need to rely on British-approved accounts or their spin-offs, or on physically combing through libraries and taking notes inside high-security archives and special collections just to get a notion of which events are connected and theorize about their strategic objective or commander's intent. Nor does one have to depend on local lore or the carefully word-smithed postwar accounts from America's oppressors such as British commanders General Alexander Leslie, Lord General Cornwallis, Lord Francis Rawdon, Lieutenant Colonel Banastre Tarleton, Lieutenant Colonel Alexander Stewart, and Lieutenant Colonel Nesbit Balfour, mindful of their legacies and postwar careers in the king's service. Nor does one have to depend on disinformation and propaganda printed in the British and British-American newspapers of the time. The correspondence containing the facts from both the leaders defending and prosecuting the War for American Independence as it was happening is now out there for everyone to see the big picture, the links between the regional actions, the strategies and counterstrategies in action, and the net outcome of a series of operations. Hence, the British occupation of the Lower South can now be observed with a more comprehensive lens in the context of a global war in search of a political solution with America hoping to be granted collective independence if they kicked out all the king's forces and all the king's men.

Analyzing Greene's theater command correspondence from different military, political, commercial, and diplomatic leaders circa 1780 through 1783 reveals that South Carolina was the epicenter of a world war that would decide the fate of sovereign independence for America and the future of kingdoms, democracy, and the wealth of nations in the Western world for centuries to come. Militarily, the war on the ground hung in the balance during this time, so Congress sent their best military leaders to take back the Lower South after Britain conquered most of the region. Britain emphasized its importance by sending its best armies and commanders to reannex "their" Southern provinces by force. If as few as two Southern provinces remained occupied when Britain considered ratifying the peace proposal put before Parliament in February 1783, the likelihood of passage without reducing the size of the thirteen-state confederation would have been unlikely given the slim nine-vote margin. Such territory possession would have also argued for offering only home-rule "independence" within the empire to non-occupied states, not sovereign and collective independence for all thirteen. The colonies would have likely been split based on territory possession, similar to the North and South Korea solution adopted at the end of the Korean War.

The British precedent for rejecting overgenerous, preliminary peace treaties when ground had not been lost had been established by King George II and Parliament's William Pitt in 1758. The Crown's leadership disavowed the Convention of Klosterzeven agreement, reached during the Seven Years' War, and continued fighting despite the peace treaty. Britain would not surrender lands their armies occupied.[1] Territory possession would also decide the collective independence question in America twenty-four years later.

In 1782, Britain had recently granted Ireland home-rule independence within the empire, so there was no historical precedence or political appetite for acceding the rebellious thirteen colonies' collective nationhood. Unlike Ireland, British forces had been completely pushed out of the South, culminating with the hard-won liberation of Charlestown in December 1782. Granting only home-rule government within the empire and selling it as "independence" was not a credible counterproposal option for Parliament to advance with archenemy France at the head of the negotiating table as America's steadfast ally, financier, and power broker with the final say-so. France was committed by alliance agreement to signing a peace accord only after Britain recognized the United

States, in part or whole, or Britain's armies conquered the colonies or defeated France. Peace negotiators Henry Laurens, Benjamin Franklin, John Adams, and John Jay would not take less than genuine, collective independence after Continental allied forces completely liberated the Lower South without foreign help. The Carolinas and Georgia, and the city-states of Charlestown and Savannah, were freed after Yorktown, so there was no sound argument for British negotiators to stand on to carve out a few states from the thirteen-state confederation recognizing two separate governments. If the Lower South territory had not been completely liberated, the European community would have likely imposed a two-country solution. Instead, the only British troops remaining in "their provinces" were isolated on the Manhattan peninsula and areas off mainland New York when Parliament voted to concede independence in exchange for peace with France, Spain, and the Netherlands. All the other territory in America had been lost.

Britain's great armies had been completely pushed out of the Carolinas and Georgia in the fourteen months after Yorktown, so Parliament had no leverage to stake a counterclaim on those states. The royal governments in each Lower South British province had also been forced out. British troops had surrendered the American economic metropolis of Charlestown. The Southern Continental Army escorted the last British troops in the South to their withdrawal fleet in Charlestown harbor—not unlike America's evacuation of Saigon, Vietnam, about two hundred years later, which ended that war. Equally important, all thirteen states had operating governments seated in each of their respective capital cities confederated under Congress at a crucial decision-making point in time for an up or down Parliamentary vote. The United States had stuck together to complete the ouster of all the British armies occupying the Lower South, so British negotiators could not carve out a few provinces with a European side deal or wink. France would remain faithful to the United States. The cease-fire, merchant agreement, and forced British withdrawal from Charlestown persuaded the majority of Parliament to ratify the preliminary peace proposal because there was no better way to settle a war gone global about to get worse.

Conceding independence to America opened the door to a British peace settlement with France, Spain, and the Dutch. General Marquis de Lafayette was about to sail from Spain with a large multinational fleet and amphibious army to join Washington in assaulting New York and then Canada after capturing Jamaica, which significantly influenced Parliament's timely decision to ratify the signed peace proposal. With the completed removal of British troops from the South in December 1782, Greene's Southern army could join Washington in a coalition attack on New York City should the enemy insist on remaining there.[2] A British surrender of New York after losing the entire South and Jamaica would smell like blood in the water for France, Spain, and the Netherlands to invade England while Lafayette attacked Canada. The war was no longer about squashing a colonial rebellion: the British Empire was at risk.

Unbeknownst to many, South Carolina was the key to winning the Revolutionary War and settling Britain's global war. Out of seven Gold Congressional Medals of Honor awarded to military commanders by the Continental Congress, five recipients served in South Carolina. Two Gold Medals were awarded for battlefield action in that province: General Daniel Morgan at Cowpens and Major General Nathanael Greene at Eutaw Springs. In addition, two Silver Congressional Medals were awarded to Continental commanders Colonel John Edgar Howard and Lieutenant Colonel William Washington for executing a double envelopment under fire in South Carolina that changed the course of the war at Cowpens. In his *American History* interview titled "Rethinking the Revolution," best-selling author and historian John Ferling stated that "the war came much closer to ending short of a great American victory than many now realize." Based on the now-accessible records from the top leaders on both sides, I contend that the time from the British capture of Charlestown in May 1780 to the liberation of Charlestown by the Continental Army in December 1782 may well have been *the thirty-one months that won the Revolutionary War*, with South Carolina as the pivotal epicenter.

The colony of Carolina was named after British King Charles II, as was the South Carolina provincial capital city of Charlestown. South

Carolina's two main inland ports, Dorchester and Camden, were named after British lords. Besides a close cultural connection with the mother country, Charlestown was the focal point of British trade in the Lower South both directly and interconnectedly with the West Indies.[3] South Carolina's vast network of navigable rivers originated in the western mountains and connected to an intercoastal waterway. These rivers efficiently carried vast quantities of furs, skins, rice, indigo, ginseng, tea, mica, hemp, flax, and many other natural resources by small boats to the coastal capital city of Charlestown for export anywhere in the world. Before the war, renowned botanist William Bartram chronicled South Carolina's vast natural resources. He identified hundreds of plants, minerals, and animals of significant interest to his London patron and potential trading investors.[4] Commerce was doing so well Britain passed the Currency Act of 1764 in large part to void South Carolina's successful currency, which had supplanted the pound sterling in the colony. John Adams, who helped negotiate the peace and independence deal between the United States and Britain, wrote to Congress in 1777 about this prosperous, resource-rich economy: "South Carolina seems to display, a spirit of enterprize in trade, superior to any other State."[5] John Adams knew leveraging a restoration of trade with the Lower South would "sweeten the pot" for the British just enough to squeeze a majority of votes out of a Parliament tired of a seven-year colonial war bankrupting their economy. As an alternative to a crippling tax on their own subjects to continue the war, Britain's much-needed trade with South Carolina would likely continue if the peace proposal was ratified.

South Carolina's unique system for generating wealth was brought to the attention of European powers at the onset of the Revolutionary War by Adam Smith's 1776 best-selling book *The Wealth of Nations*. Smith's new global economic model became the guidebook for emerging capitalist societies eager to increase their wealth and power without suffering the administrative costs of a centrally controlled economy. Carolina's thriving financial system that maximized the productivity of capital was precisely the return-on-capital engine every European nation coveted to achieve global supremacy, access to markets, and supply chain dominance. In

Smith's terms, South Carolina had bountiful *Land* and massive amounts of Black enslaved *Labor*, complemented by vast amounts of independent contractor *Labor* in the form of itinerant and Native American traders. This enormous infrastructure of Labor was actively "harvesting" the perpetual bounty from the Carolinas and Georgia and efficiently transporting these bounties through an interconnected system of waterways down to Charlestown onto ships and to awaiting European customers. This system enjoyed the collaboration of planters, mechanics, traders, and merchants to keep it running smoothly.

The South Carolina economy was further boosted by large upcountry trading posts, such as Fort Granby and Fort Ninety-Six, where traders and Native Americans could bring in furs, skins, and other goods from the country's interior to exchange for finished goods and arms. According to Adam Smith's new theory, such a powerful economic engine would generate massive wealth for any nation that could factor this "free trade" out to the highest bidder, putting the world's preeminent "invisible hand" in their pockets. In 1775, South Carolina exported over 579,000 pounds sterling worth of goods (about ninety-five million sterling today), led by rice and indigo, while importing only 6,385 pounds sterling (about one million sterling today) worth of goods from Britain.[6] This ninety-five-to-one return on capital did not go unnoticed by European monarchs jockeying for global supremacy. Possessing South Carolina would almost certainly guarantee the future wealth and power of the nation that governed it.

Besides the implications of Mr. Smith's "radical" free-market economic model on military priorities, nineteenth- and twentieth-century historians telling their stories of the Revolutionary South had minimal access to first-person, Revolutionary leadership correspondence in their pre-internet world. The whys, hows, and connections of events synthesized into a larger context were often indiscernible and left disconnected. One specific example is the clandestine activities of Continental general Charles Lee. His serial duplicity significantly affected the actions of both armies throughout the war. However, his pattern of perfidy was not evidentially validated until the mid-nineteenth century and is still largely ignored if not entirely excused. Lee's treasonous activities, documented in his handwriting, significantly change the historiography of the Revolutionary War.[7] Ironically, turncoat Charles Lee was the father of the core Southern Strategy that doomed the British conquest of America. Tracing his duplicitous activities and strategy advice to the Crown's war planners is crucial to understanding the course and outcome of the war.

Other examples of missed connections reside in the numerous accounts describing the Revolutionary War through a myopic New England lens, unable to see Britain's obsession with the Lower South in general and South Carolina in particular. Britain's first amphibious invasion of the colonies was launched against South Carolina on June 28, 1776, at the First Battle of Charlestown, locally known as the Battle of Sullivan's Island, Palmetto Day, and Carolina Day. The Declaration of Independence was approved in a unanimous voice vote by Congress on July 2, four days after the Patriots defeated the Crown's massive invasion force at Charlestown, probably before word of the victory reached the entire assembly. However, the Declaration became more than a floor vote agreeing to Thomas Jefferson's wording after fifty-six members of Congress officially signed the document on August 2, ostensibly putting their individual lives on the line and unifying the thirteen colonies in the cause of independence. Without the Charlestown victory in the showcase and personal signatures affixed to the document, the Declaration would appear to the world of monarchs like wishful thinking from semiautonomous, New England–based rebels, marketing themselves as the "united States Congress." The Declaration became a legal document after signatures were affixed. If the British had won the First Battle of Charlestown, an unsigned Declaration of Independence would have lacked the credibility necessary to launch a successful revolution.

"State" representatives authorized to sign the document by their respective legislatures had more than an entire month to discuss the importance of the British defeat at Charlestown before making their fateful decisions. While some historians are dismissive about the American victory at Charlestown as the deciding factor that prompted *all* states to unify in signing the Declaration around John Hancock's daring signature, the indisputable fact is that the signing of the Declaration transformed the rebellion from scattered armed conflicts against taxation and imperial aggression to an internationally recognized, ethical war for independence Americans believed they could win. Whether all the thirteen states would have authorized their representatives to personally sign an open letter of rebellion without proof of military competence is a question for the angels. The Patriot victory at Charlestown, at the very least, gave the independence movement confidence and unity.

Combined with the forced British evacuation of Boston by Continental forces earlier in the year, the defeat of the attempted British invasion of South Carolina at the mouth of Charlestown harbor in June 1776 added considerable gravitas to the signed Declaration when read at home and abroad. The rebellious colonies had proven they could beat the Crown's professional army and navy led by their best commanders. The Charlestown victory was proof positive that the words "Don't Tread on Me" were more than an empty bluff from handfuls of commercial rabble-rousers who did not want to pay taxes. It proved that the thirteen-rattle rattlesnake had a deadly strike when attacked. The 1776 Battle for Charlestown resulted in the first American victory over the British Empire in the Revolutionary War and the first battle victory for America's armed forces.

Another such illustration of New England centeredness involves textbook forgetfulness about South Carolina Continental Congressman Christopher Gadsden, the inspirational leader of the War for American Independence. Gadsden ignited and fueled the rebellion from start to finish. In the February 11, 1766 edition of the *South-Carolina Gazette and Country Journal*, Gadsden was credited with emblazing "Aut Mors Aut Libertas" or "Liberty or Death" on American minds in his column protesting the Stamp Act. Operating under a veil of secrecy, Gadsden's men conducted a successful armed assault against British forces in November 1765 during the Stamp Act crisis, resulting in the capture of Fort Johnson, which guarded Charlestown harbor. According to historian John Drayton, Gadsden's army of 150 men held the British soldiers' prisoner, raised the triple crescent Gadsden flag, and turned the fort's powerful cannons on the British sloop commissioned by Parliament to deliver their tax-stamped papers. Gadsden's actions forced the removal of the embossed paper from South Carolina shores, thereby informing Parliament's decision to rescind the act or face insurrection in the colonies.[8] The British could have hung Gadsden and his Sons of Liberty for their actions. John Adams, Sam Adams's second cousin, wrote in his diary during the Second Continental Congress that Gadsden was the most committed to the American cause of anyone in attendance.[9] Gadsden has been referred to as the "Sam Adams of the South" rather than calling his mentee Sam Adams the "Christopher Gadsden of the North." Gadsden was one of the earliest leaders in the Sons of Liberty movement, meeting with countryside "mechanics" as early as 1765 under the Charlestown Liberty Tree near his wharf. "Don't Tread on Me" Gadsden likely radicalized Sam, who was ripe for the job, during the First Continental Congress—not the other way round.

Christopher Gadsden portrait, courtesy of the *Charleston Museum*, Charleston, SC.

More importantly, the story of how the main American objective of the war, *sovereign independence*, came to be is habitually conflated with Cornwallis's surrender at Yorktown. The reality was the Southern Continental Army and its allied state militias had to liberate the capital port cities and capture all the territory in the Lower South during the fourteen months following Yorktown to win at the negotiating table. *The Wealth of Nations* author Adam Smith introduced his friend Richard Oswald into treaty discussions in 1782 to begin serious negotiations only after the British armies in the Lower South were painstakingly forced to retreat into the South Carolina low country around Charlestown and the liberation of North Carolina and Georgia was accomplished. Britain's evacuation of their last foothold in the South at Charlestown was impending. Oswald was a leading Scottish slave merchant who allowed the American delegation to insert the proposed issue of sovereign independence in the November 1782 Provisional Treaty that would eventually make its way to Parliament in February 1783 for a binding up or down vote. Adam Smith introduced Oswald to Prime Minister Lord Shelburne, who had recently assumed overall responsibility for negotiating a co-lateral peace pact with the United States diplomats. Lord Shelburne was a friend of Adam Smith and a disciple of Smith's new free trade model. After Oswald began informal peace talks with Benjamin Franklin and agreed to recognize America's diplomats, the subject of political independence was finally admitted into a provisional proposal guided by Oswald's hand in exchange for a most favored trade agreement with the US.[10] With the last British troops in the South scheduled for withdrawal from Charlestown and attempts to drive a wedge between America and France unsuccessful, time was running out. Shelburne stated his general objective in September 1782: "Peace is a desirable object, but it must be an honorable peace, and not a humiliating one dictated by France or insisted on by America." Washington wrote Greene on September 23 about the negotiation stalemate, quoting Benjamin Franklin: "They are, says he, unable to carry on the War and too proud to make peace."[11] The longer the war dragged on, the greater the humiliation of a lost war hung in the British air unless one could argue it was not a lost war by blurring the end.

Meanwhile, back in Charlestown, a temporary merchant agreement was being actively negotiated between sides to soothe the economic sting of a final British withdrawal from the southern colonies. The consummation of a merchant agreement signaled the Lower South's willingness to continue trade with Britain rather than shut them out in favor of the French, Spanish, and Dutch. In the end, Shelburne's objectives were met. British forces were escorted from Charlestown tensely but peacefully with a "peace with honor" slogan on their battle-weary lips. The vengeful torching of Charlestown countered by an all-out battle was averted, and five fleets of British ships set sail to separate parts of the world—Jamaica, Saint Augustine, West Florida, England, Nova Scotia, New York, and Saint Lucia. After all, Britain needed Carolina's vast supplies of raw materials for their domestic and West Indies economies to thrive again.

Economics is usually the root cause of war and peace. An unantagonistic withdrawal from Charlestown pleasing to the British merchant class proved necessary to curry just enough favor with the king and sway a few more Parliament votes in time for the preliminary peace proposal debates. The Crown's decision to consider trade for genuine independence, in keeping with Smith's economic principles, was likely decided after three stars aligned: Lord Shelburne became prime minister, Richard Oswald agreed to Benjamin Franklin's proposal that the subject of independence would be a condition for commencing bilateral negotiations, and Charlestown's liberation was imminent. Some trade with Carolina was better than no trade, and for the French and friends to get it all would humiliate the proud empire and depreciate Great Britain's economy. Nature's circular trade winds blew efficiently from England to Charlestown's doorstep.

The former president of the Continental Congress, Henry Laurens, was injected into the peace negotiations to hammer out enslavement business issues with Oswald, his old slave-trading partner. Richard Oswald had negotiated Ambassador Lauren's release from the Tower of London by pledging his fortune as a bond. There were thousands of enslaved refugees whose status was contested, which had to be adjudicated. Tragically, peace negotiators missed the opportunity to free all enslaved Black persons in America with the stroke of a quill. John Laurens, Henry's pro-emancipation son, was dead and could not lobby his father to end the evil institution. The prospect of the South rebuilding and England getting their rice, indigo, furs, raw materials, and capital gains from the enslavement trade would find no alternative. The notorious slave trade was the primary economic engine for the resource-poor empire. Oswald was one of the chief purveyors of kidnapped human beings from Africa to America. After their enslavement in the Carolinas and Georgia, those Blacks produced huge quantities of indigo and rice for export back to England. British trade with the southern colonies, now states, had to resume, but only if the proud empire could walk away with their heads held high and tell America's "civil war" story their way. Appearances always mattered to the Crown.

After Oswald's and Lauren's insertions into the formal bilateral talks, American colonies not in British possession would be recognized as independent of Britain in a new "provisional" treaty proposal in exchange for trade rights subject to Parliament's ratification. The order to withdraw the surrounded and disintegrating British forces in Charlestown, the last king's forces south of New York City and surrounding areas, had already been issued. The immense withdrawal armada, pieced together from all points across the Atlantic, had been ordered to sail. It was time for King George to acquiesce on the issue of real independence and for Parliament to agree to the peace deal before the French could plug their money and trading merchants into Carolina's lucrative economy as the king's occupation forces departed and Charlestown became a free port. To pass the moment would risk the national security of Britain.

War rarely has a predictable ending. The second British invasion of the South, which began in December 1778, was directed by the ministry offices at Whitehall, London—two thousand miles away. Britain's war ministers and Parliament were greatly influenced by merchants such as Richard Oswald. Merchants, the economic backbone of island Britain, were eager to put Smith's ideas into practice by capturing the "super-Walmart distribution center" of Charlestown with its built-in supply chain, deepwater port, river "superhighways," and economic synergy with the West Indies. Perhaps this explains why "more battles and skirmishes were fought on South Carolina soil [over two hundred] than any of the other thirteen colonies."[12] Charlestown was vital as a military base for snuffing out the rebellion in a land offensive going northward. Its possession was economically crucial to Britain's commercial class sitting in Parliament.

The war to capture and hold Charlestown and South Carolina was a top priority of the British War Ministry for the future wealth and power of their nation. If Parliament could not raise taxes on the colonists to pay off their debts, they would milk the Lower South's fat cow with their shipping merchants and fixed prices. By militarily occupying Charlestown's international port trading center, transferring plantation and enslavement "ownership" to Loyalists, and controlling South Carolina commercial river routes by force, the British would have their cake and eat it too. Certainly, they could run things better than upstart colonial dandies.

The Continental Southern Army commander, Major General Nathanael Greene, spoiled their Southern Strategy master plan. General Greene directed the American counterstrategy to take back the Lower South after the British conquest in 1780. Regional historians have repeated, often quite accurately, local battle stories without having access to British objectives, European intrigue, intelligence reports, overarching military strategies, and command intent. Without access to such information, the negotiating importance of territory possession and operating state governments was not evident. Looking at battles and skirmishes in isolation obscures the interconnectedness of events and the big picture. Moreover, battlefield wins and losses, as scored by European standards of the time, do not tell the bigger story of achieving strategic objectives. Contributing to yesteryear's myopia were the typical portrayals of the war as North centric, further obscuring Greene's insurgent war to defeat Britain's omnipotent Southern Strategy Campaign.

The full array of evidence reveals the war became South centric, especially if one demarcates along the Delaware River, as those who fought it did. Few regional historians from yesteryear had access to King George's, Nathanael Greene's, or George Washington's papers and correspondence to get a strategic operating picture of what was going on across the military, political, diplomatic, and economic landscape to connect the battles and strategies across the Southern colonies with independence negotiations. Oft repeated, Johnson's *Reminiscences of the Revolution in the South*, published in 1851, comes to mind, while *Partisans and Redcoats*, published in 2001, interprets the two and one-half years of the Southern conflict as "America's First Civil War" won by a "chain" of mostly unaided partisan victories that resulted in Cornwallis's surrender at Yorktown, which resulted in independence. The depopulation strategy of British occupation forces inciting fratricide to expand their control amid a scarcity of manpower is easy to misconstrue as a "civil war" in the absence of information to the contrary. Unfortunately, both works were published before full access to Commanding General Greene's overarching war-theater correspondence became available and treasure troves of internet search engine material became accessible. Without these new resources, the likelihood of seeing an interconnected world war decided in the Lower South by a planned Continental strategy of dispossessing the occupying British armies of territory while earning the population's trust was practically impossible.

Regional stories about the Revolutionary War in the South have much merit. They well highlight the British conquest of Charlestown, the "partisan war," the Battles of King's Mountain and Cowpens, the Race to the Dan River, and the triumph at Yorktown. However, many accounts leave one to think that the entrenched British armies decided to abandon the Lower South fourteen months after Yorktown because the surrender of Cornwallis's army in Virginia was enough to decide the war. Now that Major General Greene's previously cloistered military records are publicly available, the detailed activities of the Southern Continental Army and state militia allies during the "lost" post-Yorktown period show otherwise. This newfound primary-source evidence does not invalidate previous historical perspectives; it mainly fills in the long-lost documentary gaps to reveal the complete story and conclusion to the Revolutionary War.

In addition to the detail found in Greene's papers, contemporary correspondence from other top leaders is now readily accessible to conduct fact-finding research to fill in the historical record. The list includes Commander in Chief George Washington; King George III; Congress; the presidents of Congress; the British Ministry; Parliament; British generals Clinton, Leslie, Carleton, and Cornwallis; the Comte de Vergennes; the Marquis de Lafayette; John Adams; Thomas Paine; Benjamin Franklin; and Lord Shelburne—decision-makers running the war and attempting to negotiate a desirable end to it. Their correspondences disprove the Yorktown end-of-the-war theory, as do the facts on the ground, diplomatic records, and the substantial time lag until a cease-fire and formal treaty occurred.

The big story becomes clear based on now-assessable primary-source evidence: Major General Nathanael Greene's Southern Continental Army prevented the British Empire from conquering the Lower South. Of equal importance, Greene's forces drove out the British armies occupying the Carolinas and Georgia with essential support from state militias through an insurgency strategy consisting of "defeat by a thousand cuts" rather than relying solely on set-piece battles. This book explains how Greene liberated the occupied, populous low counties in the Lower South after Yorktown to "win" the War for American Independence. He methodically pushed Britain's armies into their coastal garrisons by a series of many small engagements, special operations, rapid troop movements, Loyalist conversion initiatives, and enemy desertion incentives. Unable to sustain themselves without host-nation support and unable to break out, the British armies of occupation evacuated or surrendered each garrison under military pressure, one after the other, culminating with the evacuation of Charlestown. Britain's extraction of its surrounded armed forces from their Southern Army headquarters in Charlestown, South Carolina, marked the end of Britain's prosecution of their war against America. General Greene successfully depleted and dislodged the two British armies occupying the Lower South after Yorktown.

In addition, Greene's correspondence shows he established operating elected state governments loyal to the national Congress to repatriate those states back into the confederation as he was liberating them. He also prevented a governmental vacuum that non-confederation power seekers or foreign agents would have likely filled to create separate fiefdoms or affiliations. In the final analysis, General Nathanael Greene was responsible for clearing the Lower South of British troops, making the Carolinas and Georgia safe for democracy to function, and proving to the world that America could defend itself without foreign alliances if granted nationhood. These outcomes were essential lynchpins for the colonial-world powers to unanimously consent on the point of sovereign independence in diplomatic negotiations.

Hence, examining the original correspondences describing the vicious war in action from and to the commanding general of the South, his chain of command, and numerous leaders of the time casts an illuminating light on the war's final phase in the Lower South. This voluminous evidence shows that the conclusion of the ground war that prompted the ratification of independence by Parliament took place in Charlestown, South Carolina—fourteen months after the great Yorktown triumph liberated Virginia. Complete liberation of the South was necessary for collective independence negotiations to succeed. In contrast, the Yorktown end-of-war theory battles an inexhaustible array of timespan, territory possession, and diplomatic implausibilities, unresolved for over two hundred years.

Greene's Papers fills in the missing gaps about the necessity of pushing all British forces and their royal governments out of the Lower South to win independence after Yorktown. The papers are, in intelligence language, "raw correspondence"—initiated and dispositioned at theater headquarters by Major General Greene. Military experience in leadership, military-civilian joint operations, joint forces operations, logistics, military doctrine, mission tasking, mission execution, command correspondence, after-action reports, and intelligence analyses lend a kind hand to interpreting Greene's ofttimes secret correspondence. The archaic language nuances, writing courtesies of the day, and sometimes coded messages within a message require careful deconstruction, as does following the individual chains of correspondence back to their sources, while being mindful of the constantly evolving and interdependent tactical, strategic, civilian, political, and diplomatic situations. Traditional academic research methods are employed throughout this book; however, the trajectory of this book follows Nathanael Greene's contemporaneous correspondence over less-reliable secondary and reminiscent sources repeated over the years.

While these methods may tempt academic criticism leveled at balance and interpretation, I invite readers to peruse the papers for themselves to see the actual reports and intelligence from those who were running the war. As one who has experienced detention in an occupied country, I have observed the reality that an occupying soldier's everyday duty is to maintain control by aggressively crushing civilian and insurgency resistance. Instant death, brutality, torture, and turning the population against one another are the primary tools of successful occupation. Intellectual balance criticizes why I was in the occupied country in the first place rather than allowing the harsh reality of the situation to speak for itself. Balance tends to sanitize the cold, hard truth of a ruthless occupation by a foreign army that is ordered to "pacify" the population at their pleasure and rewarded for doing so. If history is about accurately reconstructing what happened in the past, original correspondence from decision-makers in the center of the action to defeat a punitive war of occupation should take precedence over gratuitous intellectual balance that blurs our history.

Many significant historical gaps were left empty or explained away for so long the full story takes a while to digest. Professionally organized and published, General Greene's theater-command communications give voices to the leaders directly involved in managing the war as they were attempting to survive it, tame it, and win it. Their writings characterize the war in the Lower South with more urgency and importance than yesteryear's interpolations composed in their absence.

For example, past historians described the "devastating fall of Charlestown" in 1780 as a likely death knell to the war for collective independence but rarely mentioned the reverse effect after its valiant liberation. Few historians ascribed the same importance to the Patriot liberation of Charlestown in December 1782 as the final blow to the empire's Southern Strategy master plan to crush the rebellion, restore British rule, and deny independence to the declared United States or any part thereof. Few knew about Britain's secondary plan to partition and retain the Lower South to eviscerate the confederation after Yorktown.

The final fourteen months of the war in the Lower South received scant attention or note of importance even though this final phase of the war likely decided complete American independence, defeat, home rule, or a splitting of the thirteen colonies.

According to one expert who reviewed this manuscript, "Most address 1780–1781 and give only passing mention to the fourteen months after Cornwallis's defeat at Yorktown," as if the numerous battles and skirmishes of 1782 did not happen. During the "lost" year of 1782 and the two months prior, the British conducted countless military operations to retain and expand, if possible, their territory control. Besides using their superior military forces, they constantly schemed to maintain possession of the Lower South, even offering the Southern Continental commander, General Greene, any title and position he liked if he would become a turncoat and lead an army for the Crown to "form Georgia, No & So Carolina into a Kingdom …similar to that of Ireland."[13] When the British could not beat him militarily, they attempted to bribe him, kidnap him, and assassinate him to retain possession of the Lower South's economically valuable and populous port cities with Charlestown at the center. King George himself instructed his ministry to negotiate separately with South Carolina and Georgia to keep them in the empire. All the British hopes of keeping the colonies came down to militarily holding the low countries of the Carolinas and Georgia, or at the very least Charlestown, until a separate deal could be negotiated with those provinces or a conciliatory treaty could be signed in Europe, subtracting some Lower South territory from the agreement.

The margin for victory for all thirteen states to collectively "win" independence was so slim George Washington referred to it as "little short of a standing miracle" in his farewell address to his troops.[14] Two months after the fall of Charlestown, the Provisional Peace Proposal was placed before Parliament. At that time, British troops no longer occupied territory in the South with which Parliament could insist upon retaining a province or two. Operating state governments, militarily protected by Congress's Continental troops true to the national cause, possessed the capital cities in all thirteen states, including those in the Lower South.

Getting history right is essential to learning its lessons. Two of the early American versions of the Revolutionary War were heavily influenced, if not heavily edited, by British publishing entities to avoid libel and to successfully sell into the United Kingdom's mass market without running afoul of King George and Parliament.[15] Dr. David Ramsay's and Pastor William Gordon's accounts, published by British printing houses, are recognized as "having borrowed heavily" from the *British Annual Register* rather than drawn from their original manuscripts. Two critical investigations of Revolutionary War histories published by Oxford University Press found that "no fewer than nine of the histories of Revolution…have now been found to be plagiarized" from the *Register* accounts of unknown authorship rather than originating from authentic accounts.[16] Fortunately, contemporary correspondence to fill in the blanks is now accessible.

Why there are so many pseudo histories of the last thirty-one months of the war is unclear. King George's tolerance for going off script could be one explanation. Thomas Paine made the mistake of publishing his unapproved manuscript *The Rights of Man* in England after the war, which earned him a seditious libel lawsuit and a warrant for his arrest. William Gordon's London publisher refused to print Gordon's original manuscript until it was "fixed" for British audiences, in part to eliminate accounts about British "cool barbarities" and possible war crimes in the Carolinas and Georgia. Gordon's original manuscript was never published, while Ramsay's unapproved history was banned in Britain due to accounts of "British murders and villanies." Lack of written evidence makes for plausible deniability. George Washington politely "regretted" that Dr. Ramsay's published version "did not take a more comprehensive view of the war." Ramsay was imprisoned in Saint Augustine after the British captured Charlestown in 1780, so his viewpoints of the prosecution and defeat of the British Southern Strategy Campaign were not firsthand or privy to command information. What does seem clear in examining the landscape of remembered histories is that these British-approved narratives innocently carried on through the years obscure the crucial final phase of the war in the Lower South that achieved both peace and independence.

The British were much more receptive to a "civil war"-ending storyline where Cornwallis's second-in-command, O'Hara, offered his sword to the distinguished French General Rochambeau after a protracted American-assisted siege at Yorktown with light casualties. In their series of wars with the French, a gentlemanly capitulation to another European power was nothing to be ashamed of. The storyline of the mighty British Southern armies withdrawing from the civil-war-stricken Carolinas and Georgia due to security priorities elsewhere was politically palatable. National pride would not hear of an outnumbered, navy-less, unpaid, and ragged Southern Continental Army and allied partisans made up of farmers and tradespeople cornering Britain's finest professional forces in the Lower South capital port cities. Under the duress of military dissolution, "evacuation" became the preferred term and method of not admitting defeat.

The national park at Liberty Square in Charlestown, South Carolina, is where the last British forces in the South left America to end the Revolutionary War. This massive withdrawal played out as the final catalyst for Parliament to approve independence for all thirteen states.[17] Fourteen months after Yorktown, a cease-fire agreement between armies was finally reached in Charlestown on the eve of evacuation, setting the stage for Britain to formally end the prosecution of hostilities against America. The numerous post-Yorktown battles, skirmishes, deaths, territory acquisitions, and hard-fought capital-city liberations in the Lower South produced the desired result. The Southern Continental Army and their allied state militias heroically persevered to the end. Two months after the British evacuation from Charlestown, Parliament reluctantly ratified the Provisional Articles of Peace, which acceded independence to the United States.

The Liberty Square National Park evacuation site overlooking Charleston Harbor is similar to another forced British evacuation site earlier in the war, Dorchester Heights, Boston. The forced evacuation from Boston in March 1776 is commemorated by a grand white marble tower and an engraved stone marker prominently displayed atop the heights.

The inscription begins "Driving the British from Boston required months of grueling work on the part of the colonists." Gunpowder to sustain the siege was supplied by South Carolina, according to historian Mrs. Saint Julien Ravenel. Noteworthily, the total number of British troops and refugees evacuated by the British Empire from Boston in 1776 and from Charlestown in 1782 is about equal. The Boston liberation became a Continental military model for expelling the British from America by controlling the countryside surrounding the population centers the redcoats occupied.

Similarly, the last British troops occupying the Southern states evacuated from Gadsden's Wharf (present-day Liberty Square) in Charlestown on a cold December day in 1782, after months of being denied access to food from the countryside. The evacuation was covered by over 130 of His Majesty's ships positioned for battle in the harbor and chaperoned by America's best Continental dragoons following a negotiated cease-fire and merchant trade agreement. This climactic event finalized the withdrawal of over ten thousand surrounded British regular troops, Hessians, Loyalists, refugees, and enslaved Blacks from the Charlestown peninsula. To scale, about the same number of British troops who surrendered at Yorktown withdrew under duress from Charlestown. The historical painting that adorns the back of this book depicts the British evacuation to their warships in the Charlestown harbor, effectively ending the war.

The cost to see things through to the victorious end was high. In addition to thousands of post-Yorktown casualties, hundreds of forgotten Patriot prisoners died from starvation and disease aboard British prison ships in the Charlestown harbor. On December 14, 1782, at today's Liberty Square, the final liberation of the Southern states took place, marking the end of organized fighting between the British and Continental armies. The joyous aftermath of this final victory is depicted in the historical etching that adorns the front cover of this book. The documented significance of this site cannot be overstated: Liberty Square is America's Revolutionary War National Victory Site.

There is much ambiguity about when the War for American Independence ended. The confusion may stem from George Washington not singling out a specific day recognizing Revolutionary War Victory Day. According to Dr. John Ferling, "during his presidency Washington neither commemorated any epic battle of the Revolution nor asked Congress to designate a date for remembering…'the brave men…who fought' so that the 'nation might live.'" He did not make any national speeches as president about the epic conclusion of the war in the Lower South that sealed the deal for independence, even though he made some inferences during his presidential tour of Charlestown-area battle sites in 1791. However, in one of his letters to General Greene, Washington predicted that the liberation of Charlestown would be the tipping point for Parliament to recognize America's independence.[18] From a postwar nation-building perspective, Washington faced the dilemma that recognizing the fall of Charlestown as "America's Victory Day" could have unjustly diminished the numerous sacrifices in the long chain of heroic links in every state that together attrited the British into finally quitting their war against America and reluctantly granting her independence. It would have also drawn attention away from the more critical founding values espoused in the Declaration of Independence he wanted all Americans to embrace. Building national unity by living those values prioritized singling out one long successful siege against the British Southern Headquarters in Charlestown. The deciding victory was made possible by the cumulative effect of all the other battles and sieges across the United States that came before it. Washington wisely left the designation of America's Victory Day to future generations, like the present.

The complete story about war's end languished in obscurity until the University of North Carolina Press published the last volume of *The Papers of General Nathanael Greene* in 2005. This release concluded an extensive twenty-nine-year organizing, transcription, and decoding effort by expert forensic historians. Over 600 letters between General Greene and General George Washington are now accessible, 100 letters to and from Francis Marion, 130 to/from Thomas Sumter, and over 200 to/from "Light Horse" Harry Lee, one of the greatest light-cavalry commanders in American history. Greene's letters also include those to and from the various presidents of Congress (his bosses), John Adams, Thomas Jefferson, the Marquis de Lafayette, French General Rochambeau, Alexander Hamilton, British generals Clinton, Leslie, Carleton, and Cornwallis, state governors, state militia commanders, his field commanders, and numerous other dignitaries. These letters reveal the regional, national, and international coordination and goings-on from the battlefront that led to winning the war. Greene's papers have been meticulously transcribed, decoded, translated, dated, chronologically arranged, and indexed by subject matter. Previous secret intelligence and critical spy networks are now revealed. The preservation of this Revolutionary treasure trove borders on miraculous given the travels and dangers the trunks containing this correspondence endured over many years. Vital first-person evidence from Southern Command headquarters, now available, details the military strategies and operations in action that resulted in the liberation of the South and the birth of our nation.

There is little scholarship on the British occupation of Charlestown from 1780 to 1782 or how the city's liberation became the lynchpin that ended the war. Charlestown was the British Southern headquarters, where the military held control over paper, ink, and printing presses. Therefore, British-leaning perspectives dominate the documentary landscape and historians' footnotes. *Greene's Papers* provides a comprehensive American version of the war in the South left in the dark for more than two centuries.[19] Reminiscent of the Rosetta Stone discovery, which reframed Egyptian history, over half of the thirteen volumes involve correspondence in the Southern theater of operations with Greene as commanding general reporting directly to George Washington and the president of Congress. These papers are eyewitness accounts, a chronological guidebook, and a key to decrypting how America achieved her independence by defeating Britain's Southern Strategy based in Charlestown. I contend that one of the most critical thirty-one-month periods in the history of Western Civilization was widely unknown until the publication of *The Papers of Nathanael Greene*, containing over eight thousand pages of original correspondence involving over six thousand documents detailing the prosecution of the war, came to light.[20] While some may disagree with the operational interpretations and the effect of territory possession on diplomatic negotiations, we now have authentic, first-person resources to see Revolutionary history from the victor's perspective. Thank goodness for the Information Age to illuminate our way back into the Age of Enlightenment.

The Information Age presents an opportunity for historians to become more like research scientists to improve historical accuracy. As more and more original sources and archaeological evidence become available, this new information can be analyzed to clarify and update the richness of our Revolutionary story, especially in the South, where numerous records went missing. When new facts and newfound truths become known, the historical record can be updated like other fields of science. The challenge is whether collective wisdom can set aside illusionary truths.

Accessibility to contemporary, primary sources has changed the game of historical research. Truth is now accessible to everyone who dares to follow the facts wherever they lead. As more primary source is discovered, we get closer to the truth if we admit those new facts into the record and resist dismissing them because they do not conform to yesteryear's repeated assumptions. Facts can also be established through advances in ground-penetrating radar, which produces reliable physical evidence that significantly changes our understanding of where, how, and in what sequence battles occurred. Also, analytical intelligence methods generate reliable connections that complement traditional research techniques. Means, motive, and opportunity tied together are decisive evidence in a court of law. Using multiple research methods allows us to see that two or more things can be accurate at the same time and that one truth does not necessarily void another. Since events in war rarely stand in isolation, newfound sources enable us to make connections previously obscured.

For instance, a battle story can be true, and its planned strategic intent can also be true, and the impact of both on diplomatic negotiations can also be true. Dismissing possible connections irrespective of probability logic often misses the point of discovering what happened and why one event likely caused another event to occur. Significant events during wartime rarely occur in isolation or the light of day, so all firsthand accounts are essential to connect the tactical war on the ground to their strategic intent and their effect on political decision-making. Tracking who was driving the war from above and for what purposes often leads to high-probability, common-sense connections that are, in fact, true. Using various scientific methods to analyze command decisions enables researchers to connect the political, economic, social, military, and diplomatic dots essential to discovering the truths about our great Revolutionary history.

For example, great commanders will "lose" a battle by another nation's standard to gain the strategic or psychological advantage that eventually wins the war. Nathanael Greene commented to John Adams that his papers, when published, would reveal "measures which led to important events and the reasons for these measures."[21] Commanders' strategic intent, when the goal is sovereign independence, is to take possession of the country and keep it, not to chalk up technical battle wins for newspaper headlines.

Britain learned this lesson in the Revolutionary South, and America learned this lesson in the Vietnam War. Celebrated battlefield victories and body counts don't win wars if the "victor" does not maintain possession of the region. Holding surrounding territory forever as the result of a battle is usually more important than possessing the field at the battle's end. The Battles of Guilford Courthouse and Hamburger Hill taught the astute general that tactical victories that produce disastrous strategic defeats lose wars. Hence, piecing together military and political correspondence from top leadership and linking it with actual events into a probable strategic narrative enables us to view history more accurately through a wider lens focused on long-term outcomes rather than who possessed the battlefield immediately after the battle. Winning territory and keeping it was the primary military objective of the final phase of the Revolutionary War, not temporarily pushing the enemy off a battlefield. Achieving the military aim of ridding the South of multiple British armies of occupation and their allied Loyalist militias enabled America to achieve its political objective of collective independence and nationhood.

Thus, *Victory Day* is a story about winning the Revolutionary War based on the best available evidence to date I have found and reasoned. It is about the brilliant execution of compound military strategy and the intelligent use of light cavalry and "flying armies" in a lightning-fast war replete with numerous sieges. It is about bringing order and conclusion to a war that had sunk to the lowest levels of barbarity and inhumanity. It is about ethically winning over hearts, minds, and territory that would add up to winning the Lower South, and with it, American independence. *Victory Day* is about dedication, duty, and sacrifice in the face of unspeakable horrors and nearly impossible odds. I challenge that as more international records, contemporary accounts, previously secret intelligence, and physical evidence become available, this story should be updated or amended, like any other field of science.

Victory Day, and the final phase of the war to get there, is one of the most important chapters in our nation's history. However, this story is simply a framework for avid students of history to consider a more comprehensive, interconnected picture of the War for American Independence and dig deeper. The internet enables everyone direct access to the same first-person information to see the testimonial history of things for themselves. The South had numerous political and military heroes of all skin colors, religions, and nationalities that rival or, in some cases, exceed those that monopolize textbooks. There are many unsung Patriot African Americans, Native Americans, and women who are obscured in history waiting to be researched and recognized. Continental officers John Laurens and Nathanael Greene worked hard but unsuccessfully to obtain consent from the Carolina and Georgia legislatures to recruit enslaved Blacks into the Continental Army as a pathway to manumission, if not across-the-board emancipation for all Blacks. Both men viewed the war as an opportunity to abolish the British institution of slavery imposed on her colonies by offering each "property owner" one thousand dollars per individual released from bondage to serve in the Continental Army with pay, as authorized by Congress, subject to each state's legislative approval.[22] General Nathanael Greene might have been America's greatest general, second only to George Washington. Other great heroes such as Christopher Gadsden, William Moultrie, Francis Marion, Andrew Pickens, William Washington, Harry Lee, Anthony Wayne, Thaddeus Kosciusko, Rebecca Motte, and the Marquis de Lafayette were indispensable to the United States becoming a sovereign nation by their heroic leadership in the South. Please get to know their ethical profiles in courage that collectively won the freedoms we enjoy today, like free speech.

Throughout this book, I refer to Revolutionary sites that still exist. Charleston and South Carolina is full of them. There are over seventy-five Revolutionary War–era houses still in existence in Charleston that have individual stories to tell, in addition to British-built government buildings and period churches. Visit these places where many significant events occurred, study the people who put their lives on the line for united independence, and put yourself in their situation under foreign occupation. Ask your research libraries' boards to create passport research networks and omni-index their Revolutionary War archives for ease of remote accessibility. Ask board members to update their business models to make historical research more fun, living, and inclusive. Please encourage them to host yearly and collaborative open-enrollment "What's New?" Revolutionary War symposiums, showcasing their archives, artifacts, and yearly breakthrough research to switch all Americans on to our brave birth. As General Greene once said: "Learning is not virtue but the means to bring us in acquaintance with it."

In the Information Age, we can all be inclusive historians building upon each other's work to accurately reconstruct the multidimensional past and debate its lessons. Because of instant accessibility to a worldwide range of primary sources, newcomer historians can pursue research beyond general reference books housed in the libraries of academia. Besides exploring new information made possible by the internet of things, iconic places like Charleston's British-built Exchange and Provost building, the Powder Magazine, Liberty Square, Charlestown's Liberty Tree marker, Marion Square's Horn Work remnant, Rebellion Road, McCrady's Tavern, Henry Clinton's and Nathanael Greene's headquarters, and Middleton Place still exist for you, the curious historian, to eyewitness history and see what others missed. Attend the next Victory Day reenactment and see William Washington's regimental flag displayed by the Washington Light Infantry dressed in their historic uniforms—"the only Revolutionary War flag from active service still borne by a unit of the US Army." Witness the War for American Independence for yourself and share it widely with others.

Our history belongs to us all. British prime minister Winston Churchill, who emphasized the importance of never giving up to tyranny, also warned that "the most thoughtless of ages" would emerge from forgetting the past: "Every day headlines and short views" would rule popular thought. Our distinguished national characteristics of unity, freedom, justice, honor, duty, mercy, and hope were imperfectly founded during America's incredible quest to achieve independence from a foreign power and tyrannical king. This history deserves to be scientifically updated based upon the best available information and logic so we can understand the world's ways and know what to do when our personal and national moments of truth arrive. Our authentic Revolutionary history reminds us of our core values, where we came from, and what we can be together if we learn from our past—e pluribus unum.

With my purpose stated, I wish to acknowledge and thank those Patriots, civilian and military, who gave everything to bring our nation into existence. I hope this book inspires everyone to follow their example of selfless service to others. Great warriors are always prepared to fight, but the greatest warriors achieve bloodless victories that endure.

I also thank those heroes who work in national security, particularly those who keep their noses out of domestic politics. There are many of you out there who work silently in a collective effort to keep us safe, 24-7/365. You save lives, avert disasters, and achieve bloodless victories every day, of which the public never knows. Thank you.

I wish to especially thank those great Patriots who work in Joint Operations Commands and Joint Force Headquarters around the world. Always on duty, always ready with a response plan, always prepared to do whatever it takes to counter any enemy. You are always thinking, "One Team, One Fight." You serve with professionalism and a focused purpose to keep us safe. You are America's silent sentries that preserve the hard-won victory of independence. Thank you for bringing your best every day.

I also thank the great professors at the Citadel Military College for dedicating their lives to training future leaders to keep America safe.

The original tabby Citadel, where the school takes its name, guarded the Charlestown entrance during the Revolutionary War. General Mark Clark, former Citadel president, US secretary of state, and WW II theater commander and intelligence oversight report chairman, once wrote, "The art of leading can be taught, and it can be mastered." General Walters and the Citadel professors make that concept a reality with every cadet and student. Their diligent work weaves together the ethical leadership fabric that keeps America strong and free.

The Citadel teaches that honor, duty, and respect are timeless traditions that enable earnest students to become great leaders and achieve great victories. One can see the evidence of these characteristics in graduates, especially those who choose to serve our great nation. Major General Nathanael Greene, commander of the Southern Continental Army, often told his officers, "Respect breeds honor." This is the Citadel way.

I thank the university scholars and my academic friends who diligently reviewed my manuscripts and provided expert advice. Dr. Nic Butler, "Charleston's historian" and the best research historian and author I know, has been a great inspiration. I have incorporated most suggestions in this published version. I was flattered by the compliment that *Victory Day* could be "a valuable contribution to reading lists in undergraduate and graduate courses in the history of the Revolutionary War." Peer review and academic critique are very humbling experiences.

I would also like to thank my deceased mother, Margareta Gabriel Benvenuto Scarlett, who read to me every day as a preschooler, emphasizing, "Do not think you can't; always think you can." My abilities as a reader caught the attention of a Harvard professor taking a year off to teach miscreant high schoolers, Dr. Susan Miller, who took me under her wing and taught me how to write before her tragic death. I hope this book will not disappoint either.

Lastly, but most importantly, I thank my wife and chief editor, Deborah, for more than I can express in words. If I am any sort of a good leader, it is because she believes in my better angels at times when I am not so sure. I dedicate this book to her.

Punishment has more the appearance of resentment and persecution than a common measure of justice

Nathanael Greene equestrian statue. Courtesy of the National Park Service, US Department of Interior, Stanton Park, Washington, D.C., H. K. Brown, artist.

Major General Nathanael Greene, Southern Continental Army commander, 1780-1783

INTRODUCTION

War Is a Beast No One Knows for Sure

Victory Day—Winning American Independence is about the last thirty-one months of the Revolutionary War, with particular emphasis on the final phase after Yorktown. This book brings to light the successful Southern Continental Army military strategy, which resulted in taking back the Lower South from British occupation and explains how the completion of that militia-allied campaign to completely oust multiple British armies was fundamental to creating a negotiating advantage for American diplomats that ended the war and awarded the thirteen colonies their Independence. This updated history of the Revolutionary War is based on long-lost first-person correspondence from the American military, civilian, political, and diplomatic leaders running the war.

Victory Day connects the war in the North with the war in the South. It explores the importance of lesser-known battles, rapid troop movements, and the importance of territory possession supported by the local populations to hold it. It also explores the importance of conducting an ethical war based on America's founding values to see the war to a successful conclusion. This book explores the activities of a documented traitor who unintentionally changed the course of the war to one America could win. It describes the management of the war as it was happening, beginning at the First Battle for Charlestown in 1776 and extending to the time the British captured Charlestown, South Carolina, in May 1780 and then to their forced departure on December 14, 1782—the thirty-one months that won the Revolutionary War. The book acquaints readers with the possible options and decisions various command centers were faced with at critical moments. It explores the value of timely and actionable intelligence and counterintelligence to defeat armies of conquest and occupation. Above all, *Victory Day* tells the story of America's forgotten journey to collective, sovereign independence against almost impossible odds.

In the year 1780, South Carolina was the epicenter of a world war that would decide the fate of democracy and monarchs for hundreds of years to come. Britain's finest armies, led by their finest generals, invaded and completely conquered a mostly wild and densely forested land inhabited chiefly by Europeans, enslaved Africans, Great Wagon Road settlers, roaming traders, and diverse Native Americans.

The Southern British Army commander, General Lord Cornwallis, destroyed two Continental armies sent to stop the British conquest of the Carolinas. He armed Loyalist militias, built an interconnected network of military forts—from the Pee Dee to the Piedmont—and negotiated alliances with the Cherokees and Creeks. "Rebels" were ordered immediately hung if they did not bend to the will of the Crown's conquistadors. State-sponsored religion was installed, freedom of the press was outlawed, martial law was established, guns and powder were confiscated, freedom of assembly was banned, property was seized, plundering was rampant. British authority was ruthlessly upheld through fire and sword. Continental currency became almost worthless. Citizens were forced to sign allegiances to the Crown or became instant outlaws. With no viable currency, no Continental Army, and no elected government, the revolution and quest for liberty were all but over for the Carolinas and Georgia. Virginia and Washington's army outside New York were slated as the next targets to be conquered.

Victory Day follows the progressive undoing of the British mission to conquer America. Particular attention focuses on the final phase of the war—the roles poor British leadership and unethical conduct played in shifting public sentiments toward a victorious outcome for the Americans. The book explores how being ethically true to the cause enabled General Nathanael Greene's compound military strategy to succeed.[23] As British occupation troops became isolated and undermined, they were forced from their Lower South forts and garrisons, region by region, back to their coastal bases. The completed liberation of the Carolinas and Georgia, combined with the installation of democratically elected state governments, resulted in the British Parliament's ratification of a peace proposal recognizing sovereign independence for all thirteen colonies. While Yorktown was a great American and French siege success that opened a narrow path to achieve political autonomy, the war did not end there. Ridding Virginia of British troops created an opportunity for Southern Continental forces and their state militia allies to liberate the rest of the South from ensconced British occupation if they fought long and hard. The world still had to be turned right side up after Yorktown by completing a war of territory possession without foreign help.

After the victory at Yorktown, all eyes became focused on the Lower South in general and Charlestown, South Carolina, in particular. Charlestown was the colonial South's largest city and the fourth largest in America. This city-state, cosmopolitan metropolis, and international trading center, the economic crown jewel of America, was occupied by Britain's foremost troops. According to *The London Magazine* in an article before the war, "It is a market town, and the produce of the whole province is brought to it, for sale or exportation. Its trade is far from being inconsiderable for it deals near one thousand miles into the continent." Displacing the British from their Southern army headquarters in Charlestown, without French help, after clearing British regular, Hessian, Provincial, and Loyalist troops from throughout the Lower South was hard work yet to be done after Yorktown if independence were to be achieved.

The American rebellion did not stand a chance without French assistance. Approximately 90 percent of the arms and gunpowder used by Patriot forces at Saratoga were secretly supplied by the French.[24] Congressional solvency and rebellion credibility emanated from the French alliance. The French provided the navy, hard currency, munitions, siege cannon, technical expertise, and troops that enabled the Franco-American siege of Yorktown to succeed. The iconic Trumbull oil painting *Surrender of Lord Cornwallis* depicts the French army on one side and the Continental Army on the other—both wearing French-made uniforms and bearing French-made weapons. France's alliance and recognition of the declared "united States" established political legitimacy for Congress, both domestically and internationally. Congress instantly became the official, European-recognized, overarching government body duly representing all thirteen states in the eyes of the world powers. This recognition likely discouraged individual colonies from leaving the confederation and from another kingdom carving out a few colonies at the negotiating table to settle the global war. The value of Congress's overarching political representation and promise to provide Continental Army protection to each state was substantial enough to bind the colonies together. The Declaration of Independence, signed by all thirteen states, gave the "General Congress" power to represent them on the world stage as "the united states of America."

The reality was that the United States received so much help from the French between Saratoga and Yorktown, America teetered on becoming a client state the French could claim. After Yorktown, the war shifted focus from a Franco-American military campaign to a four-faceted military, political, diplomatic, and economic campaign against the British. Yorktown set the stage for the war to enter this complex final phase necessary to achieve independence. The final phase had to be adroitly and ethically managed over the next fourteen months to take back British-held territory and effect a British political capitulation on the point of *sovereign* independence for all the states. The Lower South was actively in play to be traded away by self-appointed European mediators (Russia and Austria) eager to take a bite out of America in exchange for not attacking or declaring war against Britain. A military stalemate after Yorktown would put pressure on Congress to abandon the Lower South in exchange for receiving independence recognition for the other nine colonies. Britain would be positioned to negotiate separately with both Carolinas and Georgia, still under their influence if not control.

Without a Continental Army–led final phase, the British would have had little reason to abandon the populated coastal areas in the Carolinas and Georgia, where large plantations and capital port cities generated immense wealth. After Yorktown, the British intensified their incitement of internecine and Native American warfare, enticed turn coating through bribery and promises of power, worked to keep state representatives in exile, and worked to prevent elections which would invalidate their legal claim over "the king's" Lower South provinces at the negotiating table. With no national army counterforce to keep the British Army from reacquiring territory or to militarily pressure them out the Carolinas and Georgia, those provinces would have likely been excluded from independence-granting discussions at best or traded off to another European monarchy at worst. Britain had not lost their Lower South colonies from the European perspective of things.

After Yorktown, the Lower South still had to be won to achieve sovereign independence for all thirteen confederated states. British forces occupied the three coastal capital cities of Wilmington, Savannah, and Charlestown, which all stood guard over their profitable ports of trade. These three garrisons provided mutual support under the assumption that only one city could be attacked at a time; British troops could be quickly transferred from one fort to another by their powerful navy. To counteract that strategy, the Continental Army would have to manage the ground war of territory possession like a concurrent tightening of three large nooses encircling the capital cities in the Lower South simultaneously. This "asphyxiation strategy" of the final military phase involved encirclement, containment, debilitation, and attrition. This strategy often involved vicious fighting in pressing in each circle while challenging enemy breakouts and foraging operations. Control of the countryside and forests was imperative to success.

In South Carolina and Georgia, the Americans faced an entrenched enemy determined to retain "their lower British provinces" and their precious trade centered in Charlestown and Savannah. While Yorktown had little economic trade value, the Lower South capital cities with their thriving ports had plenty. Those cities had to be liberated by Congress's army if collective American independence was to be conceded by Britain.

However, the immense task of capital-city liberation, if achieved, would produce only half the solution to win independence. Installing operating state governments loyal to the United States confederation was crucial to providing proof to the world powers that America could rule itself without devolving into anarchy like most rebellions. Even if the military liberation of the Carolinas and Georgia could be accomplished without a navy or foreign assistance, the task was immense. The undertaking required reassembling exiled governors and state representatives in each state and then holding supervised elections without one or more states abandoning the confederation. Someone would have to entice representatives to return, guarantee their safety, help them gain quorums, hold official sessions and announce elections, provide guardianship of elections, publish results, seat the newly elected representatives, and ensure that regular government administration ensued. Proof of these operating governments would have to be conveyed to Congress and to the American peace delegates in Paris for them to make a legitimate claim for each state's inclusion in the collective independence package. Without installing operating state governments loyal to the confederation in conjunction with the British ouster, the Lower South states would be ripe for another nation or self-proclaimed ruler to seize power and establish a separate government.

The final phase of the war after Yorktown encapsulated the entire struggle for American independence. Conducting an ethical war true to the congressionally stated values mattered. Winning civilian hearts and minds mattered. Keeping the confederation together mattered. Every battle, skirmish, troop movement, and Loyalist negotiation mattered to incrementally win territory and keep it. Resurrecting the exiled state governments in North Carolina, South Carolina, and Georgia required a gentle guiding military hand and unwavering resolve. It required gaining widespread support in the liberated territories to ensure each state remained within the confederation. Playing a patient game of encirclement until the only collapsing circle left was around the besieged Charlestown garrison took ongoing support from the other states, Continental and militia teamwork, elected state government cooperation, and relentless fortitude.

Only sound leadership would hold an unpaid army together while keeping state militias and politicians cooperative and holding conspiracies at bay. All the trials and tribulations encountered from being at war for six-plus years came down to fourteen months of methodically shrinking British-held territory until the only choices left for the British forces and friends bottled up in Charlestown were to dissolve, starve, surrender, or evacuate the South forever. Winning the final phase of the war on the ground reached its climactic conclusion at Charlestown on December 14, 1782, with both sides poised for a horrendous battle between their best national troops.

The human cost to finish out the war after Yorktown was high. Thousands of Patriots were bankrupted, maimed, or killed while finishing the job to achieve independence. Hundreds of soldiers perished aboard British prison ships in Charlestown harbor from disease and neglect.[25] Blacks suffered terribly. Many enslaved Blacks died of illness and overwork as they were ordered from one plantation to the next to produce enough food to maintain British and Loyalist troops. Many other enslaved Blacks were directed to the building of fortifications and servicing the British. Many others were promised their freedom only to be sold by unscrupulous British officers in the West Indies.[26] Many spied for the Patriots to turn the tide of the war. Many Black persons served as loyal bodyguards, confidants, orderlies, and companions to Patriot leadership while enslaved. Many others died while fighting for one side with the prospect of freedom dangling in the air. Black participation in the war was ubiquitous.

The same was true for the thousands of Loyalist and Tory refugees who flooded into a makeshift shantytown around Charlestown as the battle lines closed in around the low country. They were prohibited from entering the city and had to fend for themselves in makeshift camps. Cherokee and Creek tribes, incited into the fighting by embedded British officers, conducted numerous raids and gathered for a massive offensive. As a result, these nations suffered Patriot counteroffensives that displaced their Piedmont settlements and devastated their populations. In the Lower South area of operations, the human cost of the final fourteen months of the war was substantial. The British tried everything in their brutal playbook to defeat the Patriot offensive to oust them.

Described in a larger context, the Revolutionary War was a means to decide the political dispute of independence between a confederation of declared states along the east coast of North America and the British Empire. The king and Parliament would have to relinquish their claim to rule over their colonies for the United States confederation to "win." The only way to pressure King George into abdicating his right of sovereignty over America was for the United States military forces to push British troops and their allies out of the thirteen colonies so His Majesty would have no claim. The liberations would have to be accompanied by establishing operating governments in each state committed to representation by the national Congress and then appealing to Britain to grant collective independence to the united thirteen states in exchange for trade rights with the new nation and France, Spain, and the Dutch calling off a world war against them. Thus, winning the War for American Independence all came down to territory possession by Congressional forces with the consent of area residents.

The great hope was that if the military could secure all the states and keep them united within the national confederation, the war could be won. With the country liberated, King George and Parliament would eventually find themselves in a political, economic, diplomatic, and national security quandary: granting across-the-board independence to all thirteen states was the best choice among a host of worse options or doing nothing. Continental Army possession of all the states, empire-threatening international pressure from America's allies, intolerable economic pain, and destabilizing political forces all had to align to create a multidimensional dilemma for Britain to make such an undesirable choice. Benjamin Franklin's slogan summed up the fundamental American mission : "We must all hang together, or, most assuredly, we shall all hang separately."

On an even larger scale, the War for American Independence ultimately decided whether government by the people would have a place in the world monopolized by monarchies. Reestablishing and protecting elected state governments loyal to the confederation while the enemy possessed those states in the Lower South was a catalyst for achieving the consent of the governed, achieving collective independence, and giving democracy a serious audition on the world stage. Never in human history had a military general initiated the peaceful transfer of power to multiple elected bodies when unilaterally assuming a position of an emperor was the easier option. General Nathanael Greene's restarting and protecting exiled elected governments in the Lower South states completed the new nation and changed the world forever—right side up.

Completing the war on the ground for territory possession in the Lower South made Britain's international diplomatic puzzle and their internal political crisis solvable only by the king and the Parliament cooperatively granting independence to America. The colonial rebellion against taxation had escalated into a world war solvable only by conceding sovereignty to the declared "united States." In the final analysis, granting collective independence to their American colonies in rebellion became the only solution to untying the Gordian knot strangling the British Empire.

Winning wars is about achieving objectives, not achieving battlefield possession. Battles are necessary for generals who are not clever enough to achieve strategic goals without engaging the enemy, bringing one to realize that the tenacity of the Patriot forces staying in the field to see the war to its conclusion is unsurpassed in American history. The territory the British had conquered in the Carolinas and Georgia had to be reclaimed. The resolve of wearing down the enemy, depriving the enemy comfort and food, and confining them to undersupplied and disease-stricken cities equaled or exceeded the courage of not only those who withstood close-range cannon fire from His Majesty's Navy at the first battle for Charlestown in 1776 at Fort Sullivan but also those soldiers who followed Washington and Greene on the "Victory or Death" blizzard mission to Trenton on Christmas Day that same year. Many of the Continental and militia troops present at other battlefields throughout the war were there in the Lower South during the final phase to finish the task of completely pushing the British out of the region. They risked, and many sacrificed, their lives fighting for another fourteen months after Yorktown to oust British forces from North Carolina, then Georgia, and then South Carolina, culminating in the liberation of Charlestown.

The final act had to be written just right for the seven-year play to end well for America. The Southern Continental commander, Major General Nathanael Greene, facilitated a Loyalist merchant agreement and sent his best cavalry general to negotiate a cease-fire agreement and then have him carefully escort the last British troops below New York onto their covering ships without incident. These measured actions communicated respectful civility across the ocean to the British Parliament, dispelling any notion that Patriots were raging mobs unworthy of ruling themselves, as often characterized in the British press. Greene's political, economic, diplomatic, and military moves likely saved Charlestown from destruction. He kept both armies from a headlong, cataclysmic battle that would have likely renewed the war rather than ended it. Finishing the job of ousting the grand British Armies of occupation from the South left nothing for the British kingdom to accept but a timely diplomatic proposal before them, which granted sovereign independence to all thirteen colonies in exchange for peace with France, Spain, and Holland and continued trade with America. "Peace with honor," from their point of view.

Sir Peter Parker's attack on Fort Moultrie courtesy of the *Colonial Williamsburg Foundation.* Museum purchase. James Peale, Pennsylvania, 1782-1791. Oil on canvas.

I.
THE BRITISH EMPIRE STRIKES AMERICA

"The tree of liberty must be watered with the blood of tyrants and patriots."
—Thomas Jefferson

Britain's first military target in their war to extinguish the American rebellion and reestablish royal authority across the thirteen colonies was Charlestown, South Carolina. General Sir Henry Clinton, General Lord Charles Cornwallis, and seven regiments of British soldiers, along with the recently exiled royal governors from both Carolinas, arrived off the coast of Charlestown about June 1, 1776 aboard about fifty ships in an armada commanded by Commodore Sir Peter Parker. This impending attack would commence Britain's declared war against "His Majesty's American Colonies" in revolt.

General Clinton's published mission was to "support the Loyalists and restore the authority of the King's government" in the South. King George had written the royal governor of South Carolina, Lord William Campbell, assuring him that troops would arrive shortly and South Carolina would "be the seat of the war" to subjugate all the colonies. General Clinton's specific orders from the king's War Ministry in London were "to restore legal government in the southern colonies, with the assistance of the well-affected inhabitants." Acting on the king's authority, the ministry ordered that an army be assembled in Cork, Ireland, and combined with units evacuated from Boston, Massachusetts, at the rendezvous point of Wilmington, North Carolina. Lord Dartmouth drew up the initial plan in 1775.[27] When all was ready, an amphibious attack on Charlestown would be launched from the Wilmington port with the express mission to capture the city and conquer the South. Commodore Parker would be responsible for assembling a fleet to transport General Clinton and his troops, plus about six months' supply and about ten thousand muskets and rifles to arm "the King's friends" who would assist in putting down the rebellion. The planned invasion of the South, to be headquartered at Charlestown, was technically a joint military operation with Clinton in command of ground forces and Sir Peter Parker commanding naval forces.

Charlestown was the largest city in the South and the most prosperous city in Colonial America. The capital city of the province of South Carolina began its long rise to prosperity in the 1600s after King Charles II granted eight lords proprietors' ownership of the Carolina coastal areas. By the 1770s, the city was an economic nexus that shipped vast amounts of rice, indigo, furs, and animal hides transported there by South Carolina's extensive and far-reaching network of rivers. Rice and indigo plantations worked by many thousands of enslaved Blacks dominated the Low Country landscape around the city. Charlestown's western trade stretched hundreds of miles into the interior of America, while her shipping looped along the Eastern Seaboard, the West Indies, and to England. The port-city capital was located on a peninsula surrounded by a towering brick wall flanked to the east by the Cooper River and on the west by the Ashley River. Charlestown resembled a European walled city-state complete with a network of canals running through it and long wharves extending out into the Cooper River. The harbor offered good maneuverability for warships, but troop landing areas were rife with quicksand-like pluff mud and razor-sharp oyster shells inhospitable to a seaward ground assault. The King's Highway was the only road from the mainland into Charlestown. The entranceway into the city was protected by a gate, moat, drawbridge, and imposing brick-and-tabby citadel or horn work. Nicknamed Little London, the city streets were lined with Trafalgar-style lanterns, lit by lamplighters every night. Charlestown and the Low Country towns around King Charles's namesake were connected economically and culturally to Britain.

Early in 1776, General Henry Clinton received a secret letter from Sir William Howe, commander of British Expeditionary Forces in America, ordering him to "get possession of Charles Town." If Charlestown could be captured quickly and used as a base of operations to put down the rebellion in the South, organized resistance to the Crown across America would crumble. While making preparations, Sir Peter Parker received intelligence that the fort on Sullivan's Island, guarding the north side of the narrow entrance into Charlestown harbor, was unfinished and vulnerable.[28] Sullivan's Island was approximately four miles long and about one mile wide at the most extreme shores. The island was situated about six miles by water from the city. It was known to the British navy as a slave refugee center after the royal governor of Virginia, Lord Dunmore, offered freedom to enslaved people who would escape "rebel owners" to join His Majesty's troops. About five hundred Blacks were encamped there awaiting their turn to sign onto passing British ships in December 1775 when they were captured by militia troops and presumably reenslaved.[29] Sullivan's Island offered an excellent staging area for the fleet to attack Charlestown and a secure base of operations for invasion ground forces.

Parker's first warships arrived in May to begin blockading Charlestown harbor and gather intelligence. The primary British plan of attack was to place a landing force on Long Island (now Isle of Palms) of approximately 2,200–2,500 top-rate soldiers commanded by General Henry Clinton, who would cross Breach Inlet at the first ebb tide and land on the northeast end of Sullivan's Island. From that beachhead, Clinton's force would neutralize Patriot entrenchments under the command of Provincial Colonel William Thompson. Once Clinton neutralized those entrenchments, he would march his troops southwest about three miles across the island and assault the unfinished backside of Fort Sullivan with cannon and mortars. Once Fort Sullivan was captured, Commodore Parker's warships would proceed unmolested into Charlestown harbor to demand the city's surrender or have them face bombardment and destruction.

Sir Peter Parker was an experienced Royal Navy sea captain born in Ireland. In 1772, King George III knighted Parker after Parker had served with distinction in various wars. He was also experienced in amphibious assaults, having participated in the capture of Belle Ile off the Britany coast. He was chosen in 1775 to command a fleet to go to Cork, Ireland, to load soldiers and supplies and then continue to Wilmington, North Carolina, to rendezvous with soldiers evacuated from Boston and militia from North Carolina to prepare for and conduct an amphibious assault on Charlestown, South Carolina. General Henry Clinton would serve as co-commander of the operation in charge of ground forces. Parker had command of about twelve warships and forty supply and troop transports, crews, and royal marines of an unknown number. To prepare for the invasion, he had sent two sloops to inspect the islands along with the water entranceways into Charlestown Harbor in May.

General Henry Clinton was second-in-command of British forces in the colonies under General Robert Howe. Clinton was about forty-five years old and an experienced regimental commander with successful combat experience. He served with Continental General Charles Lee in Europe in the 1760s. As a youth, Clinton lived on Long Island, New York, and became a member of the Provincial militia, so he was experienced with American culture and militia tactics. In his first assignment in Boston, Clinton became noticed for his recommendations to fortify Dorchester Heights and his two-pronged attack plan on Breed's Hill, which together could have secured Boston if implemented. His second-in-command was Lord Charles Cornwallis. Clinton had 2,200–2,500 fully-equipped regular and provincial troops under his command supported by two armed schooners, fifteen armed flat-bottom boats, about ten armed transport ships, and two hospital ships.[30] He commanded roughly 2,900 professionally trained soldiers, including attached seamen and marines.

With the British fleet positioned off Folly and Sullivan's Island blockading Charlestown harbor, Continental general Charles Lee took command of the Patriot forces on June 9, 1776. The militia forces from South Carolina and North Carolina, totaling about 3,700 men, had assembled under order and request from South Carolina president John Rutledge to oppose the expected British attack. Congress voted to send an additional 1,200 Virginia Continentals, of which about 800 arrived just before Lee took overall command. He dispersed these forces to defend about five fortified areas on James Island, Sullivan's Island, and the Mount Pleasant mainland in addition to the walled city of Charlestown.[31] General Clinton's forces would outnumber any single Patriot fortification they chose to attack.

Before General Lee arrived on June 6 and 7, Sir Parker and General Clinton sent demanding messages to South Carolina president Rutledge. Clinton's "Proclamation" forewarned "the deluded people ...to return to their duty to our common sovereign [King George] ...offering, in his Majesty's name, free pardon to all such as shall lay down their arms and submit to the laws." He also "required" all congresses and associations dissolve or "they will answer the contrary at their peril."[32] Sir Peter Parker followed with a demand of his own: "The purport is to demand Fort Johnson [surrender] upon pain of having the town burnt."[33] The British demands implied that refusal to submit would result in the burning of Charlestown and the execution of those who refused to surrender. President Rutledge refused both requests.

In his demand note, Peter Parker's emphasis on Fort Johnson was a likely attempt to focus Rutledge's attention away from adequately preparing Fort Sullivan across the narrows. The Crown's military leaders often employed this distraction strategy, called "the art of the feint," before concentrating their attack in a weaker area. British advance forces had already landed behind Sullivan's Island, which indicated the attack would be focused there rather than Fort Johnson.[34] President Rutledge continued to focus on strengthening Fort Sullivan and ordered Colonel William Thomson to attack enemy advance forces on Long Island from Sullivan's Island. Continental General Charles Lee arrived in Charlestown on June 9 to assume overall command. Shortly after that, General Lee ordered the abandonment of strategic Fort Sullivan.

Charles Lee was one of the most controversial Continental generals of the war, second only to Benedict Arnold. Nicknamed Boiling Water by the Mohawk, Lee at best suffered from uncontrollable temper episodes and at worst sought opportunities to hand the British a revolution-stopping victory, through clever intrigue, where he would emerge as the brilliant savior of Britain's American colonial empire. Some who knew him referred to Lee as selfish, bad-tempered, lacking courage, and having bad morals.[35] Although he had a history of fighting in several armies and wars, Lee had been on retired half pay from the British army for the prior twelve years when Congress offered him a commission. He was an excellent self-promoter who spoke at least five languages. Lee became noticed by coming to America in 1773, buying an estate in Virginia on credit, and marketing himself as a military expert who could lead the rebellion-minded Patriots to stand up to the British army. He was a prolific pamphleteer, letter writer, and gambler. Lee used his aristocratic language skills and world knowledge to convince semiliterate Americans and members of Congress that demanding the right to self-governance was justified, and the Americans could win a war with Britain if it came to that. "It is most certain that men may be smartly dressed, keep their arms bright, be called [British] regulars, be expert in all the antics of review and yet be unfit for real action," he wrote convincingly in American newspapers. His erudite writings and superb education mesmerized Americans, propelling him to center stage in the lead-up to war with Britain.

While some historians refer to Charles Lee as a "place hunter," he referred to himself as "the whole show," which one might attribute to narcissism. After Lee visited Mount Vernon twice in 1775, George Washington became convinced that Lee would be an exemplary, if not trustworthy, Continental general. Washington could learn the classics of literature and tactics of European warfare from him. Lee also had the rare experience of combating partisan warfare in Europe, so he probably knew how the tactics of *petite guerre* could defeat the linear British war machine. King George III purportedly promised him a generalship, a promise he did not fulfill. Lee and Washington had served in the French and Indian War under General Braddock, so Washington likely felt a camaraderie with Lee that needed little stimulation. Plus, the immense international prestige and propaganda value Lee would bring to the American cause could not be ignored.

British and French newspapers acknowledged that the revolution had become more than a mob insurrection led by amateurs once Lee was admitted into the top echelon of Continental Army leadership. Lee brought instant military credibility to a disorganized colonial rebellion no European nation could endorse. Washington recommended Lee to Congress, and despite Congress's trepidation, they appointed him a major general on June 27, 1775. When Banastre Tarleton read in a British newspaper of "his treachery" pursuing a Continental commission while still on British army half-pay, Tarleton reportedly proclaimed in a very public English tavern that "he would see his head on the end of a pike for it." Charles Lee had finally received the general promotion that King George III had promised him, albeit in an enemy army.

Major General Charles Lee was appointed the first commander of the Southern Department of the Continental Army in early 1776, despite never having commanded a regiment. Congress tasked Lee to go to South Carolina to prevent the British from capturing Charlestown and basing their expeditionary operations there to conquer the South. Before receiving this assignment, Lee met with British general Sir Henry Clinton in New York on February 4, 1776, "in a chance encounter."[36] The British Ministry of Defense at Whitehall in London had already chosen Clinton to command the first British invasion of America at Charlestown. Lee had been assigned by Washington and Congress to develop a plan of defense for New York City at that time. General Lee wrote to General Washington dismissing his meeting with Clinton as a coincidental encounter while at dinner with his old friend Royal Governor Tryon of New York. Lee's letter to Washington reads as though word of the meeting with an enemy governor and military commander had leaked out and Lee was covering his tracks. The exiled royal governors Lord William Campbell of South Carolina and Josiah Martin of North Carolina were also in the neighborhood of the meeting, if not at the dinner.[37] In the same letter to Washington, Lee passed on intelligence to Washington that General Clinton intended to collect reinforcements at Cape Fear, North Carolina (Wilmington), near Moore's Creek on his way to assault Charlestown and invade the Carolinas later in the year. This information, which appears to justify Lee's fraternizing with the enemy by gaining intelligence, would prove vital in limiting the scope of Clinton's June 28 attack on Charlestown.

Four months after meeting with General Clinton and his company in New York, General Lee took command of Continental and militia forces in Charlestown on June 9, 1776. It did not go well. Lee looked over the area, inspected the troops, and determined that Charlestown was indefensible against the power of the approaching British armada. "Lee must puzzle everything he meddles in…" according to a Briton who knew him. Lee argued that Fort Sullivan "could not hold out half an hour, and the platform was but a slaughtering stage." He ordered the fort to be abandoned, which, if obeyed, would enable Parker's armada to sail through the narrows into Charlestown harbor unopposed except for a few cannons at Haddrell's Point.

Lee's plan was for the primary defense of Charlestown to take place from behind the city's walls under the command of Continental general Robert Howe of North Carolina. Moultrie's men would reinforce Mount Pleasant at Haddrell's Point, whose strategic importance of protecting the Mount Pleasant mainland from British troops was superfluous if Parker's fleet gained the harbor. With Fort Sullivan abandoned, Lee would likely be limited to opposing Parker's nine warships (three hundred guns) admitted into the port with the crippled brigantine *Comet*, the twelve cannons aboard the schooner *Defense*, the twenty-eight guns at White Point battery, and twelve guns at Gibbes Wharf. Such a battle would destroy the city at worst or would result in Parker's warships retreating from the harbor at best. The most likely outcome would be the destruction of the *Comet* and *Defense*, the neutralization of White Point battery (Broughton's Battery), and the decimation of the walls around Charlestown, followed by a landing of ground forces on the peninsula to capture the city if surrender had not already taken place.

Fortunately for America's fledgling rebellion, Colonel William Moultrie refused to abandon Fort Sullivan. South Carolina president John Rutledge asserted that Moultrie was not to vacate the fort. Rutledge would not allow Lee to confuse Moultrie's simple plan to keep the British from gaining the harbor most believed would succeed if left intact. Moultrie's key officers, Lieutenant Colonel Isaac Motte and Major Francis Marion, stood firmly with their commander. Rebuffed in his attempt to have the strategic Fort Sullivan and cannons vacated, Lee redirected the bulk of enslaved workers completing the fort to building a pontoon-like bridge to the mainland as a rapid escape route for Moultrie's men. Colonel Moultrie maintained that building such a bridge would be of more advantage to the enemy to attack the fort from the mainland than to his men. Despite Moultrie's recommendations, the floating bridge was built, and during testing, it sank.[38] Using whatever human resources were left available, Moultrie continued work on the fort, helpless to prevent Lee from ordering six thousand pounds of scarce gunpowder to be moved off the island. Moultrie would have to make do against the onslaught of up to eleven of His Majesty's finest warships with only twenty-one suitably aligned cannon behind palmetto logs, enough powder for thirty-five rounds per gun, and an unfinished fort.

Colonel William Moultrie was the commander of Fort Sullivan. Appointed by President Rutledge, Moultrie was a wealthy planter and the son of a doctor. His combat and military leadership experience came from the Cherokee War in 1760. Moultrie was also the Second South Carolina Regiment commander and manned the fort with the Fourth South Carolina Regiment of Artillery. His total command consisted of 413 men and thirty-one cannons ranging from nine- to twenty-six-pounders.

Opposite Fort Sullivan across the narrows on James Island, Fort Johnson protected the main entrance to Charlestown Harbor. Fort Johnson's foreboding, medieval-looking walls and sixty heavy cannons towered over the narrow, navigable waters on the south entranceway into the harbor. Provincial colonel Christopher Gadsden and Charles Pinckney, a future framer of the US Constitution, commanded the fort. Flanking Fort Johnson was Hyrnes Battery, which was manned by about

110 Black artillerymen and three three-pound cannons under the command of Captain Thomas Pinckney. General Clinton reconnoitered Fort Johnson but determined that a successful ground assault on Fort Johnson would be extremely difficult, if not impossible. Ships could only pass Fort Johnson in a single file along the southern water passageway into Charlestown harbor. The British derisively named this passageway Rebellion Road on their maps. The fort's enfilading batteries would destroy any unwelcome ships as they slowed to navigate a turn or ran aground. Across the entranceway into Charlestown harbor to the north lay Sullivan's Island, where ships could pass through at high tide out of the range of Fort Johnson's cannon if their harbor pilots knew how to avoid the mazelike sandbars.

Fort Sullivan flew a flag with a color field of indigo blue bearing a white crescent in the upper corner next to the staff and inscribed with the word "LIBERTY." The fort was constructed of palmetto logs and sand, which could absorb or repel most cannonballs without splintering death like common wood forts. The British fleet could attempt to sail past Fort Johnson in single file to get into Charlestown harbor, which was sure to fail, or they could land their invasion force on the north end of Sullivan's Island and march south to capture the unfinished Fort Sullivan from the landside. With Fort Sullivan subdued by General Clinton's ground forces, Sir Peter Parker's eleven warships, totaling about three hundred cannons, could wait for the right tide and wind to sail unopposed through the narrows, out of range of Fort Johnson's guns, into Charlestown harbor. Haddrell's fort would be leveled as the ships passed Mount Pleasant. Once in Charlestown harbor, Sir Peter Parker would order the city's surrender, or he would unleash the fleet's guns. The newly commissioned HMS *Acteon* would spearhead the attack, equipped with secret, high-velocity cannons designed to blow apart the most substantial walls.

On about the ninth of June, General Clinton began landing the First and Second Brigades of British regulars on Long Island to prepare a base camp for an assault on Sullivan's Island. Elements of Brigadier General John Vaughn's First Marine Brigade and the Royal Highland Brigade, consisting of approximately 70 men, had been reconnoitering on Long

Island since about June 1. The initial landing of Clinton's regulars was effected by about fifteen armed flat-bottom boats and lasted through the stormy night until the morning of the tenth. Clinton's entire force of about 2,500 men was in place by about June 22.

General Clinton made repeated attempts to cross the inlet, named Breach Inlet, which separated Long Island from Sullivan's Island. Clinton's force faced hot late-June temperatures, shadeless deep sands, swarms of mosquitoes, alligators, damp gunpowder, rusting weapons, unpotable water, poisonous snakes, pools of putrid water, and no game. Dehydration and dysentery were accompanied by the onset of mosquito-related illnesses of malaria, yellow fever, and dengue fever. Clinton's hospital physician described the conditions: "The most insufferable I ever felt, not a breath of fresh air stirring…every hundred yards a swamp with putrid standing water in the middle, full of small Alligators, a black cloud of Mosquitoes everywhere, and no place free of Rattle Snakes…Crocodiles are very frequent and large in these places; we killed one nine feet long which attacked a soldier."[39] Since fresh food and water were nonexistent on the island, both had to be brought in from the supply ships offshore. Troop health management likely became all-consuming. As a result of these conditions, offensive combat capabilities deteriorated quickly.

About six days into the progressive landing of troops, on June 16, Clinton ordered his army to march across Breach Inlet and attack Thompson's fort at zero hundred hours (midnight). The currents between Long Island and Sullivan's Island were swift and deadly—capable of sweeping good swimmers out to sea. At a moonless low tide, some areas were less than three feet deep but interspersed with deep sinkholes carved by strong currents.[40] Clinton could only cross a maximum of eight hundred fully kitted men in fifteen flat-bottom boats at one time, depending on the tides and cannon or rifle fire they were receiving from Thompson's elevated fort. The banks on both sides of the breach were reportedly steep, with deep, poor-footing sand on both sides and razor-sharp oyster shells. This topography created a situation where the boats could not be loaded or unloaded with men directly from the beach. As fully kitted men waded toward their assigned boats, they could be subject to stepping into a sinkhole, being swept away by the fierce currents, or becoming unable to pull themselves into a boat. As boats began making it to Sullivan's Island's shore, one could expect they would be landing amid Patriot-set bonfires at best or falling into the water while wading ashore at worst. Their powder would be damp, and there would be no possibility of retreat after landing. The stark reality was an uphill bayoneted charge without cover against entrenched positions and enfilading fire. Thompson's expert riflemen and cannon crews firing grapeshot would have silhouetted targets to fire upon at close range. Conducting a boat crossing of the inlet at night to effect an uphill assault under fire was fraught with the potential for high casualties, if not total failure.

Clinton's alternative plan was to march his army across Breach Inlet at low tide to conduct the assault on Colonel Thompson's entrenchments on Sullivan's Island. Because his strike force reported that a crossing was "not practicable," Clinton canceled the mission. General Clinton wrote the following dignified report: "An attack on Sullivan's Island from Long Island would be rendered extremely hazardous from the many natural impediments attending it." One can only imagine 2,200–2,500 fully kitted troops attempting to march across Breach Inlet in the night conditions described. The operation was likely a humiliating disaster.

With General Clinton's forces stuck on Long Island, a new plan was developed. Commodore Parker would simply sail past Fort Sullivan while blowing it to pieces. Besides his mortar ships being able to lob exploding charges over the fort walls, Sir Parker had secret weapon cannons on the HMS *Acteon*, which, he was assured, could penetrate the walls. Success was almost inevitable, given the combination of cannons on his men-of-war and frigates and his marines ready to launch a frontal assault on the fort.

Simultaneously, General Clinton would lead his men across Breach Inlet, assault Colonel Thompson's outnumbered troops on the northern end of Sullivan's Island, and quick march down to the southwest end of the island to attack Fort Sullivan's unfinished rear. Fortunately for Fort Sullivan's 413 defenders, Clinton's army could not cross Breach Inlet on June 28 either. Colonel William Thompson's Breach Inlet defenders comprised about 780 Carolinians and Catawba Native Americans, augmented by about 700 Continental Virginians.[41] According to Lord Cornwallis's account, his assault force was repulsed by "crocodiles," dangerously deep and swift Breach Inlet waters, and accurate rifle and cannon fire from the state militia and Continental forces. Some troops under Cornwallis's command were veterans of the bloodbath at Breed's Hill in Boston and wished not to repeat it against Thompson's fortifications. In the end, the British mission to capture Fort Sullivan by attacking the backside of the fort by land failed again. Clinton could not get his forces across the inlet onto Sullivan's Island with Colonel Thompson's men in the way.

Meanwhile, on the other end of Sullivan's Island, Sir Peter Parker brought up nine warships into the narrows at approximately 10:00 a.m. to destroy Fort Sullivan in a frontal bombardment. An old sailor saying is "When the land commands the sea, everything is screwed up," which foretold the day. Unknown to Sir Peter, the navigation buoys had been moved toward the midchannel sandbars during the previous nights. Colonel Christopher Gadsden had led a special operation mission some nights before to burn the lighthouse on Morris Island so it could not illuminate the straits. The buoys could then be moved at night undetected.

Nevertheless, Commodore Parker was so sure of his success in reducing the fort and capturing Charlestown and the Carolinas that he had the royal governors from both Carolinas on board his flagship, HMS *Bristol*. Plus, he had on board his fleet of fifty ships about ten thousand stands of arms to distribute to Loyalists and Native Americans across the Lower South.[42] He was still expecting General Clinton to simultaneously assault the backside of Fort Sullivan when his cannonade commenced. Sir Peter Parker was unaware that Clinton did not want to pay the butcher's bill crossing Breach Inlet, or, according to Clinton, "he did not receive the expected signal to attack" from Commodore Parker.

Poor coordination, bad luck for the British, and resolute bravery from the Patriots would have their day. First, His Majesty's bomb ship *Thunder Bomb* fired excellently targeted mortar rounds into the fort's powder magazine, doing no damage. Sometime after that, the mortars aboard the ship became dislodged from the deck platform and were rendered useless. Then the HMS *Acteon* became entangled with two other warships. It became grounded on the middle ground sandbar (near present-day Fort Sumter) without firing a single shot from her high-velocity cannon. Moultrie's sharpshooters neutralized the fleet's foretopmen and their grapeshot-firing swivel guns on the mainmasts from firing down into the fort. Dutifully following the relocated buoys, Sir Parker's pilot guided the warships to a less-than-ideal firing range for Parker's cannons but a perfect range for the cannons on elevated parapets in Fort Sullivan facing the ships. Notwithstanding, the commodore anticipated that the South Carolina royal governor Lord William Campbell would be seated in the capital city by the end of the day.

But that was not to be. Lord Campbell was seriously wounded in the heat of battle, resulting in his eventual death. Commodore Parker had the indignity of having his knickers blown off before ordering his fleet's uncovered withdrawal. The retreat was very timely because the Patriots were running out of scarce gunpowder for the second time. Strangely, while winning the battle, Lee sent an order to Moultrie directing him if his ammunition (gunpowder) became exhausted to "....spike your guns and retreat with all the order you can" instead of sending the messenger boat with more gunpowder.[43] The fort's flag post was shattered by cannon fire, causing the Liberty Flag to fall into the sand outside the wall. With some combatants thinking that the colors had been struck, the firing slowed until Sergeant William Jasper jumped through an embrasure under heavy enemy fire, rescued the flag, tied it to a cannon sponge staff, and replaced it on the parapet.

Firing resumed until about 3:00 p.m. when the fort ran out of gunpowder. Fort Sullivan's guns fell silent for more than an hour, but Moultrie and the defenders still did not retreat, and the British, beset with casualties, did not launch a frontal assault by boat. Francis Marion led a mission to obtain two hundred pounds of powder from the Patriot ship *Defense*, stationed in Stop Gap Creek behind the fort during this period. He was likely accompanied by his enslaved orderly Oscar "Buddy" Marion, who remained loyal to both Marion and the Patriot cause throughout the war. Shortly after Oscar and Francis's successful resupply mission, Governor Rutledge sent another five hundred pounds of powder by boat from the city accompanied by a note of encouragement to Colonel Moultrie: "Do not make too free with your cannon. Cool and do mischief." Since Clinton's ground forces were out of position to thwart the resupply missions, Moultrie's steadfast defenders resumed their defense of Charlestown.

General Lee watched what he could of the smokey battle from the mainland near Mount Pleasant opposite Charlestown, reportedly crossing over during a lull in the action. The Charlestown city peninsula, defended by Continental General Robert Howe's North and South Carolina troops, would have likely been the next target of the British fleet if they ran the Fort Sullivan gamut. Lee could point to Moultrie and Howe if Fort Sullivan and the city fell.

Strangely, General Lee exchanged compliments with General Clinton, in writing, before Sir Henry's and Peter Parker's attack.[44] During the battle, Lee instantly dismissed a low-risk, high-reward plan presented to him to launch a small boat assault to capture crippled British ships and turn their guns on the enemy, covered by Fort Sullivan. By the end of the day, the British had fired about twelve thousand rounds and shot at the fort that Colonel William Moultrie refused to surrender to the British or abandon under General Lee's two orders to do so. Moultrie's unfinished palmetto-trees-and-sand fort absorbed and deflected the most lethal ordinance the King's Navy could deliver. Sometime after 9:30 p.m., firing from the fort subsided when the remnants of His Majesty's assault fleet retired out of range.

His Majesty's forces were still not done. At about six o'clock the following morning, Clinton ordered his troops across Breach Inlet in their flat-bottom boats after suffering "the disadvantages of having been eighteen hours under Arms up to their knees in a Swamp and nothing to eat or drink at the time…they swore they would not fire till they could bayonet the Yankees as they called their Rebel Enemies, the common men are highly exasperated against the provincials, they say it is not fair fighting, their aiming their rifle Barrel guns."[45] There is no explanation why Sir Peter Parker did not support Clinton's final crossing attempt with a devastating cannonade on Colonel Thompson's entrenchments from his idle warships. There are two versions of how the last inlet crossing attempt was thwarted on the twenty-ninth. The first version, corroborated by several accounts on both sides, reported that the British troops received such a destructive fire from rifle and cannon fire in two attempted landings, "which prevented General Clinton from fording the inlet, and not the depth of the water."[46] Clinton contradictorily reported to Lord Germain that he aborted his final attempt because he ordered his "small armed vessels to proceed toward the point of Sullivan's island, but they all got aground." Clinton could not acknowledge publicly that a group of amateur citizen-soldiers half his size and dangerously low on powder had kept the king's best troops at bay. With a force upward of 2,500 top-rate soldiers, General Henry Clinton could not land any of his troops on neighboring Sullivan's Island over four weeks to capture Fort Sullivan.

The astounding defeat echoed across the colonies and Great Britain. South Carolina's vice president, William Bull, wrote, "When the administration [British Ministry] gets an account of the action of Sullivan's Island, they will be devilishly at a loss, how to dress it up in public." Three of Britain's best commanders, Sir Peter Parker, General Henry Clinton, and Lord Charles Cornwallis, were sent on their way. Their inglorious retreat was commemorated annually by Charlestown's Saint Michael's Church bells ringing out the tune of "Three blind mice, see how they run."[47] A London newspaper printed a scathing song after the trio's defeat titled "A New War Song by Sir Peter Parker," mockingly critical of both Parker and Clinton and their contemptuous reports to the king of "the cowardly Yankees" who "stood so stiff" at the mouth of Charlestown harbor. This sardonic song likely made the rounds in English taverns posting casualty lists of lost loved ones. General Clinton reported minimal casualties from severe illnesses and combat injuries for the entire month of June despite horrendous health conditions, numerous crossing attempts under fire, and reports to the contrary. The operations maps he sent to Whitehall inaccurately showed about a two-mile distance between Long

Island and Sullivan's Island when American maps of the period showed fewer than one hundred yards.[48] General Cornwallis cited infestations of aggressive "crocodiles" in Breach Inlet that prevented the British crossing despite the fact none were known to exist so far north of the equator since before the Ice Age. Official British reports would minimize their defeat by characterizing the invasion attempt as a half-hearted trifle to cannonade a small harbor fort before commencing their subsequent invasion of New York. The news of the Declaration of Independence spreading across Europe complemented the news of the British debacle at Charlestown arriving simultaneously. Both Parker and Clinton would return to England to defend their defeat. King George knighted General Clinton in exchange for not publishing his account criticizing Parker. Irrespective of nuanced reports, fallacious maps, and story-spinning, Sir Peter Parker would blame the army for the failure, and General Clinton would blame the navy for the empire's defeat so that neither would have a spot on their record.

For the Americans, it was a total victory. The American resolve for liberty was forever instilled in the hearts of Patriots because of the bravery of Colonial William Moultrie and his 413 men defeating the world's most powerful navy in a face-to-face cannon duel on June 28, 1776, and the courage of Colonel William Thomson's and Continental Colonel Peter Muhlenberg's regiments defeating the world's best army on June 28 and 29. After the battles, Sergeant Jasper received President Rutledge's sword for his act of courage in saving the Flag of Liberty, and the Continental Congress awarded Colonel Moultrie a generalship in the Continental Army, making him the highest-ranking officer from South Carolina. The Second South Carolina Regiment was inducted into the national Continental Line. General Charles Lee accepted overall credit for the gallant victory and became forever known as "the Hero of Charlestown."

Lee's puzzling plans for the defense of Charlestown, if not challenged, would have likely delivered the city to the British. Moultrie's insistence on defending the narrows from Fort Sullivan so irked Lee he ordered Colonel Francis Nash of the First North Carolina Regiment to take command on the morning of the twenty-eighth so Nash would follow his orders to abandon the fort.[49] Miraculously, Parker's attack commenced before Moultrie could be relieved of command. Lee was aware that the British fleet would have maneuverability once in the harbor after passing the abandoned Fort Sullivan. Parker could land troops directly on Mount Pleasant after cannonading Haddrell's Point into rubble. After that, Sir Peter Parker could form a battle line in the harbor to broadside the city into submission. The *Acteon's* high-velocity cannon would have pummeled Charlestown's fourteen-foot-high brick walls, making surrender the practical alternative to the city's destruction. Lee also ordered Moultrie to remove two six-pound cannons from Colonel Thomson's fortifications on June 21, before British troops assembled for a crossing on the twenty-second. General Clinton did not attempt to cross the inlet after the same cannon Lee had curiously ordered removed the day before fired upon his readied troops.[50] There will always be a question if Lee had secretly collaborated with Sir Henry Clinton, his old British army comrade, to "open the gates" to Charlestown by abandoning Sullivan's Island and Fort Sullivan. Lee had "coincidently" met with Clinton in New York months before the attack—a meeting where the royal governors from both Carolinas, aboard the flagship HMS *Bristol*, could also be placed. At least six of Lee's orders, if carried out, would have likely resulted in an American defeat: abandoning Fort Sullivan before the British fleet arrived, replacing Colonel Moultrie with Colonel Nash to abandon the fort, redirecting the work on the fort's unfinished back wall to a failed barrel bridge connecting to Mount Pleasant, removing ample supplies of gunpowder from Fort Sullivan, issuing two orders to abandon Fort Sullivan during the battle, and ordering the removal of two cannons from Fort Thompson. Charles Lee's puzzling behavior would affect the course of the war again in both the Northern and Southern areas of operations.

Besides Colonel Moultrie not playing the fool at Fort Sullivan, the Highland Brigade defeat at Moore's Creek, North Carolina, four months before the Battle of Charlestown, significantly limited the scope of Clinton's invasion plan to conquer the Carolinas. Clinton had no indigenous ground force to collect Loyalist volunteers and attack Charlestown from the landward side to create a two-front offensive. The intelligence

Lee provided to General Washington about Clinton's plan to rendezvous with the Highland Brigade in Wilmington to augment his attack on Charlestown made its way to the Continental Army commander in eastern North Carolina. As a result of receiving the information Lee furnished to Washington, Continental Colonel James Moore issued orders to Richard Caswell and his Patriot militia force to intercept and destroy the Royal Highland Emigrant Brigade.[51] On February 27, 1776, Caswell's Patriot force destroyed the Loyalist forces at Moore's Creek that Clinton was counting on to augment his attack on Charlestown.

The Highland Brigade, made up of hearty Scots dressed in kilts and armed chiefly with broadswords, was an integral part of Sir Henry's plan to capture Charlestown and South Carolina. General Clinton's plan called for arming the 1,500-man Highland Brigade properly when they rendezvoused at Moore's Creek, appointing them with regular officers, and using the brigade to assault Charlestown by land while he attacked from the sea. Unfortunately for Henry Clinton, the sword-wielding brigade was cut to pieces as they charged headlong at entrenched rifle and cannon positions shouting, "King George and broadswords." On March 12, two weeks after the Highland Brigade's defeat, Clinton arrived in Wilmington to discover his ground attack force was nonexistent. He had planned for them to march down the King's Highway from Wilmington to South Carolina and launch a coordinated attack with him on Charlestown. Clinton's plan instantly became one-dimensional. He had no local ground force to conduct surveillance, gather intelligence, and recruit local Loyalists, enslaved runaways, and spies. He could not coordinate with the Cherokees and Creeks filtering down from the upstate or up from Georgia. Nor could he conduct disrupt-and-destroy operations or begin siege operations against the city. Clinton would have to go it alone.

Whether General Lee was covering for his dubious meeting with General Clinton and Royal Governor Tryon and friends by including seemingly unactionable intelligence to Washington cannot be proven. What is certain is the information Lee provided to Washington gained from his "coincidental" meeting with British General Clinton on February 4, 1776, severely limited the scope of Clinton's offensive on June 28. The

Highland Brigade Clinton counted on to join his attack on Charlestown was destroyed due to Lee's intelligence getting into the right hands. Thus, Moultrie's plan to defend the Charlestown narrows succeeded, and the bravery of the Patriots at Fort Sullivan and Breach Inlet defeated General Clinton's professional army and the world's most powerful navy in the first Patriot victory of the war. Britain and Europe were stunned, while America was elated. In his newspaper articles months before the battle, Charles Lee was correct in his assertion that the American colonies united could defeat Britain's professional military forces. He was lionized for making his prophesy come true.

The British would try again to insert a duplicitous Continental general into the head command position in Charlestown. Three years later, in the summer of 1779, British intelligence officer Major John Andre propositioned then Continental General Benedict Arnold to request the Charlestown command to coincide with the upcoming British offensive to capture the city. Andre wrote, "Could you obtain the command in Carolina? The rest you must understand."[52] Arnold would be rewarded with two guineas a head for soldiers surrendered up to the number of five or six thousand. Arnold turned down Major Andre's proposal, choosing to betray his soldiers at West Point rather than Charlestown.

On the same day of the June 28 British defeat at Charlestown, the Crown suffered another setback in their plans to nip the rebellion gone revolution in the bud. In New York, one of George Washington's elite Life Guards involved in a conspiracy to kill or kidnap Washington and other key commanders was hung in front of assembled Continental troops. Counterintelligence by John Jay uncovered the plot just before it went operational. Some historians have identified the architect of the conspiracy as the New York royal governor, William Tryon, whom Charles Lee had dinner with in February.

For the moment, news of the great Charlestown victory spread throughout the world and ignited "The Spirit of '76" into a bonfire. The republic of the United States suddenly came into being. Militiamen from across the colonies streamed into New York to oppose the next expected British assault. On July 9, about forty Patriot soldiers and sailors pulled down the two-thousand-pound gilded-lead statue of King George III in New York City, near Battery Park, in an act of unity and repudiation of the king's governance. Lead from the statue was melted into much-needed bullets to prepare for the expected British assault there. The collective political will to resist the Crown's plans to conquer America received the boost it needed. According to esteemed Harvard professor of history Dr. Edward Channing, "It is entirely conceivable that rebellion would have never turned into revolution" if the British invasion of the Carolinas had succeeded. [53] Spurred on by the great victory at Charlestown, representatives from all thirteen states emerged from the shadows and signed the Declaration of Independence on August 2, 1776, thereby committing their "Lives, Fortunes and sacred Honor" to achieve political independence from Britain.

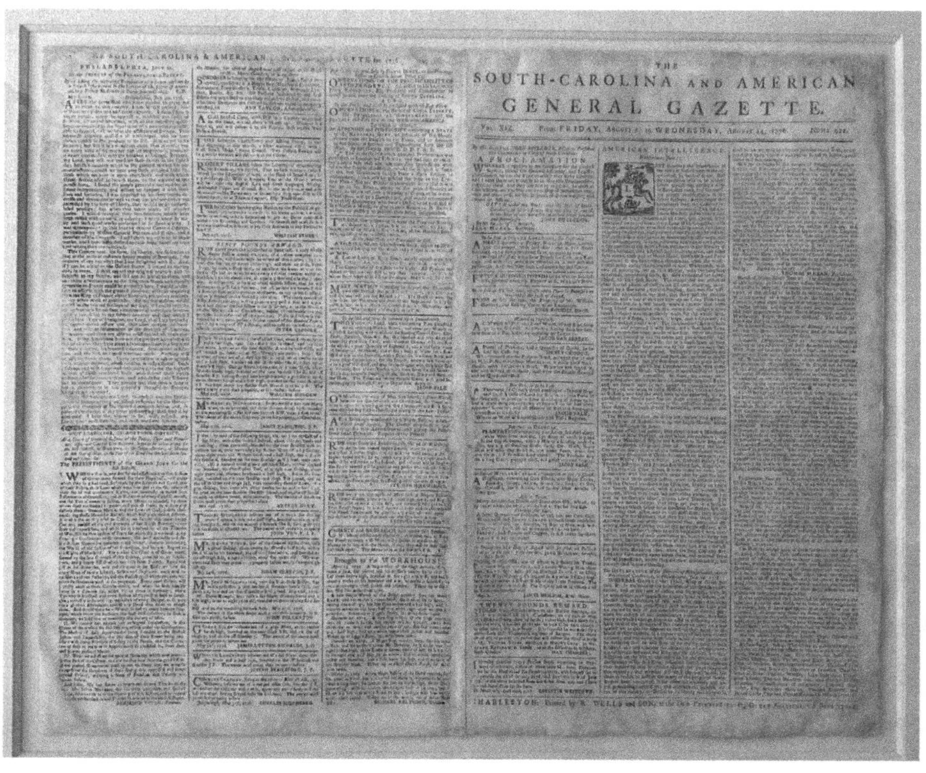

THE
SOUTH-CAROLINA AND AMERICAN
GENERAL GAZETTE.

A PROCLAMATION

AMERICAN INTELLIGENCE.

Declaration of Independence PHOTOCOPY OF THE *South Carolina and American General Gazette* NEWSPAPER, AUG 2–14, 1776.
IMAGE COURTESY OF THE POST AND COURIER FOUNDATION ON PERMANENT LOAN TO THE CHARLESTON LIBRARY SOCIETY'S SPECIAL COLLECTIONS.

II.
CHARLESTOWN'S IMPACT ON THE DECLARATION OF INDEPENDENCE

The Right Cause, for the Right Reason, at the Right Time, Fought the Right Way

Many historians argue about the point of no return in America's pursuit of independence from Britain. The defeat of Britain's attempt to invade America at the First Battle of Charlestown crossed the Rubicon. There was no turning back.

Released to the world on the heels of the Charlestown victory, the Declaration of Independence instantly undercut the mission of British forces sent to America to reseat the king's royal governors. Nathanael Greene, a Continental general on George Washington's command staff, had recommended to his Rhode Island congressman about six months before the Charlestown victory that the Continental Army and the united colonies needed Congress to issue a formal "declaration of independence." On January 4, 1776, from Continental Army Headquarters outside Boston on Prospect Hill, Greene wrote Congressman Samuel Ward Sr. proposing the Continental Congress issue such a formal declaration: "Permit me... to recommend...a declaration of independence, and call upon the world, and the great God who governs it, to witness the necessity, propriety, and rectitude thereof."[54] Greene stated his reasons were that the idea had become prevalent; it would stop payments and shipments of goods to Britain, open the ports to free trade, and inspire the troops. The troops would no longer toast or cheer the king but Congress and their united "States."

Greene also emphasized the importance of catering to a possible French alliance by adopting an independence declaration. On October 23, 1775, he wrote, "The French never will agree to furnish us with Powder as long as there is the least probability of an Accommodation between us and Great Britain."[55] The colonies did not produce gunpowder to fight a sustained war. By General Greene advancing the idea to Congress of formally declaring independence months before Britain's amphibious attack on Charlestown, South Carolina, the congressional political body had ample time to debate the necessity of adopting such a declaration when the time was right.

After the British defeat at the mouth of Charlestown harbor, the timing was right. The Americans united had proved they could win. Congress had sent some of its best troops and who they thought was their best commander to oppose the British attack they predicted was coming to South Carolina. They simultaneously set Thomas Jefferson off on a writing mission to draft a declaration of independence in early June. On June 28, 1776, without a navy to speak of, the Provincial troops, Catawba Native Americans from South Carolina and North Carolina, and Virginia Continentals took the brunt of a major British assault and won. The king's best army and naval forces were properly bloodied and neutralized into a forced withdrawal, taking their shell-shocked royal governors with them. Charlestown suffered no damage. Recognizing the full wrath of the empire was about to take wind, representatives from across the colonies knew there was no turning back from an all-out war to achieve independence. King George and his ministry would not be in a forgiving mood after being humiliated at Charlestown. With an independence draft at the ready, it was commitment time for the revolution and for politicians across the colonies.

The moment of truth had arrived. On July 1, before hearing news of the British defeat, Delaware, New York, Pennsylvania, South Carolina, and Georgia would not approve the "declaration of Independence" without edits, according to Thomas Jefferson's account.[56] The next day, all the states representatives approved the revised version.

After the victory at Charlestown, General Nathanael Greene wrote to Governor Cooke of Rhode Island on July 22, 1776, from his command center on Long Island, New York, emphasizing the importance of the American victory. "General Lee has given General Clinton a cleaver snubbing. It almost amounts to a total defeat....Our people behaved with great spirit." The citizen-soldiers at Sullivan's Island had handed the politicians the victory they needed. The time for united political leadership to make a world statement as a nation had come. The alternative to banding together to keep the king's forces out of the colonies was to submit to being a conquered people without a political voice. Failing to act inside such a window of opportunity would be a choice in itself. On August 2, 1776, more than one month after the American victory at Charlestown, representatives from across all thirteen colonies found the political will and united resolve to sign the Declaration of Independence in Philadelphia.[57] As a result of their political bravery, the rebellion instantly escalated into a united war for independence the world could respect and the Americans could affectionately call the Glorious Cause.

On August 4, 1776, Major General Charles Lee ordered all Continental soldiers to assemble at the Liberty Tree in Charlestown at 3:00 p.m. on August 5 to hear a reading of the Declaration of Independence sent from Congress.[58] The next day, Major Barnard Elliott read the declaration to all the Continental troops not on duty in the Charlestown area, at the approximate location of 80 Alexander Street, site of the Liberty Tree. The reading was followed with a sermon by Reverend William Percy and enthusiastic musket volleys. Reverend William Tennent stated that the event was the "most important epocha in the history of South Carolina, & from this day, it is no longer considered a colony but a state." On August 6, special readings took place for the Provincial soldiers, enslaved persons, and citizens at Fort Johnson and Fort Sullivan, who together had defeated the world's most powerful military. Their brave victory reinforced if not inspired all thirteen colonies to declare by signature their independence from Great Britain as one "united States."

The Declaration of Independence would become the higher purpose and central tenet document that would steer the war. The founders' intentions were for military commanders to conduct an ethical war for American independence in keeping with the principles espoused in the declaration. This ethical framing would prove decisive in winning the war.

The success of "The American War for Independence" would depend on ethics. The idea of fighting an "ethical revolt" as the overarching strategy was formalized at the onset of hostilities with Britain. Ethics refers to "a social, religious, or civil code of behavior considered correct, especially that of a particular group, profession, or individual."[59] A year before the Declaration of Independence, in support of the Battles of Lexington and Concord, the Second Continental Congress issued the Declaration on the Causes and Necessities of Taking Up Arms to provide a context for justifying war, or *jus ad bellum*. This document was publicized and distributed across the colonies after ratification on June 6, 1775. The Declaration of Causes explained the ethical rationale for a call to arms across the colonies to oppose British occupation.[60] This document explicitly stated the virtue ethic that "Government was instituted to promote the welfare of mankind," while the British Parliament sought only to ignore "truth, law or right...to effect their cruel...purpose of enslaving these Colonies by violence." The document further explained the rights-based ethic that the British government had taken upon themselves to declare that only they had the "right to make laws to bind us in all cases" without recourse. Their soldiers "have butchered our countrymen, have wantonly burnt... houses, seized our ships and confiscated our provisions." Not only did this *jus ad bellum* establish a moral high ground for unified resistance, it likely prevented moblike, lawless bloodbaths delegitimizing this colonial rebellion early on and dooming any chance of success. Ethics in principle became the foundation for building a nation out of a visceral rebellion.

Immediately after the Declaration of the Causes and Necessities of Taking Up Arms was published, the Continental Congress established the Articles of War on June 30, 1775. These articles stated the justice in going to war, or *jus in bello*, and outlined the ethical conduct expected of armed forces serving in any capacity to repulse the occupation of British troops and their allies.[61] Article XII was essential in establishing a clear ethical guideline for treating inhabitants of the continent with respect. John Adams described this ethical code of conduct as "the policy of humanity." Congress realized that often wars were won or lost based on the treatment of civilians and gaining the consent of the governed. Article XII specified that it was the duty of army officers to enforce the respectful treatment of all civilians. Ironically mirrored in the established British Articles of War, this ethical code would prove to be the difference between independence and a quashed, moblike colonial rebellion that alienated world opinion against a government by the people forevermore.

In response to the Declaration of Causes, King George III issued the Proclamation of Rebellion on August 23, 1775. This proclamation officially declared war on the colonies.[62] The King's declaration of war was not the outcome the Continental Congress expected or wanted. After waiting a year without positive results for the king to "cool off," the Founding Fathers formalized the ethical perspectives articulated in the Declaration of Causes into the Declaration of Independence. Following several drafts and a unanimous vote on July 2, 1776, to accept a final wording, The Declaration was finally signed by all thirteen states' representatives on August 2, 1776.

In the Declaration of Independence, the signers explained they were decent men and clarified their reasons for breaking bonds with Britain—they were not committing wrongdoing by respectfully asking for a separate and equal relationship.[63] Their list of grievances attached to the Declaration of Independence described Britain's violations of colonists' economic and human rights, their oppressive military occupation, and the disregard of established laws by the king's appointees in America—against its citizens. By the end of August 1776, the world's major newspapers had printed the Declaration of Independence for all to read.[64] This announcement was distributed worldwide, as an open letter of sorts, to establish the legitimacy and branding of a new, virtuous government of the people dedicated to serving the needs of citizens throughout the thirteen *United States of America*.

This global public relations announcement detailed the ethical high ground from which all hearts and minds of good men and women would be enlisted to defeat the world's most powerful army. The declaration made clear to European nations that this was a defensive pursuit, not an offensive pursuit that could threaten them. It enfeebled the British propaganda campaign, which characterized the rebellion as crazed mobs perpetrating a violent colonial insurrection against a loving King and the established order of civilization. It opened the door for Britain's enemies to join the new nation in their just war against unreasonable oppression. The declaration also publicized that the "united States," as a civilized nation, would fight to expel British troops if the king did not recognize America's independence and withdraw his forces. Moreover, the Declaration of Independence created an instant ethical dilemma for Britain's politicians and generals: treat the insurrectionist rebels as traitors who deserve only punishment and capricious violence or treat them humanely and honorably as enemy combatants deserving of respect within the established articles of war? To their detriment, the empire never resolved this dilemma.

III.
MORAL HIGH GROUND: BRITISH AND AMERICAN ETHICAL DIFFERENCES

King or Conscience?

The declaration emphasized British and American ethical differences in the treatment and governance of people. The Second Continental Congress decided early in the war that America would be founded on virtue and rights-based ethics theories derived from John Locke's philosophies of self-government, liberty of conscience, natural rights, and the common good.[65] These ethical ideals, which contained the "goodwill" tenets of freemasonry and freedom of conscience, were expressed in the Declaration of Causes and continued in the Declaration of Independence. Intellectual thinkers who focused on the natural rights of man, such as Voltaire, Immanuel Kant, and Sir Francis Bacon, also greatly influenced congressional thinking when drafting these documents. The common thread of these influences was expressed in the rights-based assertions that "Life, Liberty and the Pursuit of Happiness" endowed by the Creator trumped the sovereign rights of King George III.

Conversely, the British required ethical conduct reflective of egoism and deontology.[66] This thinking emanated from the king's divine authority traditions and phalanx-style war fighting based on solid-mass infantry formation firing and bayonet charging in unison—instant obedience without conscience. (Baron de Steuben commented that the difference between European soldiers and American soldiers was Americans would always ask why before they would obey.[67]) Two different ethical doctrines would prove decisive in the upcoming winner-take-all fight for the Lower South and thus American independence: authoritarianism and obedience to the will of monarchy, or the other, founded on liberty of conscience, government by the people, consent of the governed, and the pursuit of happiness.

The origins of the ethical code embraced by Congress at the onset of hostilities came from a combination of sources. Thirteen signers of the Declaration of Independence were Freemasons. Paul Revere, the Marquis de Lafayette, Benjamin Franklin, Nathanael Greene, and George Washington were active Freemasons. "Washington never willingly gave independent command to officers who were not freemasons," according to one historian.[68] Freemasonry was a worldwide fraternal organization whose members subscribed to a code of conduct based on truth, service, and goodwill toward others, always promoting the happiness of humanity. The Declaration of Independence expressed these principles as the rights of "Life, Liberty and the Pursuit of Happiness." As a Freemason, breaking these codes was not permissible. About 1,162 Masons occupied leadership positions in the Continental Army.[69]

Masonic lodges were also the learning laboratories for elected self-government. Secret lodge meetings became networks for planning and financing the war. Mason lodges across America often served as bases for insurgent operations and secret intelligence operations against the British occupation. The Boston and Charlestown Tea Parties were conducted by recessed Masonic lodge meetings to ensure that individual identities would never be betrayed.[70] French-based lodges, such as the Parisian Masonic Lodge of the Nine Sisters, to which Benjamin Franklin belonged, were instrumental in promoting the idea of an "international humanity" across the Atlantic. The French general the Marquis de Lafayette bestowed General Nathanael Greene with a Freemason Medal, which was awarded to fellow Freemasons who embodied the codes of freemasonry. Greene wore the medal throughout the war in the South.[71] The Freemasonry code contributed to the ethical blueprint and Continental Army code of conduct that enabled the War for American Independence to succeed.

Religion also contributed to the ethical foundation needed to win people over to the Glorious Cause. The British reimposed their state-sponsored religion after conquering an area, which created instant conflicts of conscience and resistance. The primary author of the Declaration of Causes, John Dickerson, was likely influenced by his Quaker religion. Quakers believed that all people should be treated equally. They opposed anything that harmed or threatened them, and they placed great reliance on conscience, not force, as the basis for morality.[72] The Southern Army commander, General Nathanael Greene, was raised in the Quaker religion, as was his "public information officer," Thomas Paine. In the American retreat from New York, Greene encouraged his then aide-de-camp Paine to author a morale-boosting essay, *The American Crisis*, to keep Patriots from losing hope. Later in the war, Paine helped persuade Patriots in the Lower South to persevere to finish out the war until all British troops were expelled from America and Independence was granted. He wrote the ethical phrase, "An army of principles can penetrate where an army of soldiers cannot," which inspired many Patriots to support the Continental policy of moral treatment of civilians and prisoners in the face of the enemy's barbarity.

Similarly, Baptists contributed to the conscience-based founding credo. Baptist preacher Richard Furman produced sermons and pamphlets undermining the biblical basis of King George's divine right referred to in Romans 13: "Consequently whoever rebels against the authority is rebelling against what God has instituted." Furman asserted that it was the duty of all people to fight against the king to achieve independence and support a "God-like" representative government of the people. His preaching emphasized that rebellion is not a rejection of the king's "lawful authority" but an affirmation of God's power to have men live by a "liberty of Conscience." Furman traveled throughout the South preaching with a thousand-pound price on his head issued by British general Cornwallis.[73] Furman's pamphlet, calling on Patriots to take up arms against the Crown, was the religious version of Thomas Paine's "Common Sense." These pamphlets communicated Congress's rights and virtues-basis ethics as the basis for the rebellion. During the time of British occupation in the South "that tried men's souls," Richard Furman helped convince inhabitants that resistance against the king was the Christian thing to do, while Thomas Paine provided a series of essays motivating the public to "defeat the powers only God should have."

Presbyterians played a significant role too. Presbyterian preachers used their pulpits to convince their flocks that rebellion was the correct choice. The British stereotyped Presbyterian religious dissent with rebellion and labeled their churches "houses of sedition." Major James Wemyss burned a Presbyterian church and persecuted Presbyterian congregations throughout South Carolina, which influenced the Scots Irish across the Lower South to take up arms against Crown forces. Joseph Galloway wrote about the Presbyterian national amalgamation of the independence movement. Presbyterian churches and congregations were a threat to the conquering British.

Ethics of conscience practiced in the Quaker, Baptist, and Presbyterian religions, combined with the introduction of religious free choice by Congress, significantly influenced citizens and aided Patriot recruitment. These tenets shifted the American rebellion from outraged tax and occupation protests to a higher ethical ground of free conscience of belief. With support from major religious groups, Congress rejected British state-sponsored religion (Church of England) in the declaration. They ethically positioned the independence movement to religious free conscience rather than mandatory worship and compulsory tithing.[74]

Art fills in the rest of the ideological and ethical foundation upon which the war would be conducted. Joseph Addison's *Cato, a Tragedy* was a popular play before and during the war, with the themes of individual liberty versus government tyranny, republicanism versus monarchism, and the harsh struggle to keep one's beliefs about freedom in the face of death. The Continental Army's Liberty or Death motto, first espoused by Christopher Gadsden and then Patrick Henry, was used as the password during Trenton and Hammond's Store (*Cato*, Act II, Scene 4). The first apprehended American spy, Nathan Hale, and General Washington himself, quoted text from the play.[75] *Cato* supplied compelling examples of virtue and rights-of-man ethics, the inspiration and basis for Continental Army conduct.

From the British perspective, ethics were clear. Self-interest as the ethical foundation for colonial rule, or egoism, was not to be questioned. Soldiers obeyed orders in the spirit of deontology and enjoyed the spoils of war. Their orders came from the divine authority of the king, obediently pushed down through the chain of command. Two quotes from King George summarize his commander's intent in dealing with the colonists: "A traitor is everyone who does not agree with me," and "Once vigorous measures appear to be the only means left of bringing the Americans to a due submission to the mother country, the colonies will submit." Thus, traitors or insurrectionists to the Crown received the harshest possible treatment, including assault, torture, plundering, death, and home burning as decided by the king's loyal officers in the field. British officers followed the chain of command to General Clinton, who took his orders from Secretary of State Lord Germain and Prime Minister Lord North.

The prime minister was responsible for the general war strategy, figuring out how to finance the war, and keeping Parliament informed. Lord North also reported directly to King George III, who was one of his childhood playmates. Troops swore to obey King George's commands, and according to the traditions of a strong monarchy, only the king could begin wars, grant independence, and end wars.[76] Therefore, the king's orders were always "ethical" and reigned supreme. King George's political quest was to return England to a strong monarchy. Ruthlessly squashing the American rebellion would likely advance his cause.

Ethical dilemmas created by the duty to follow orders at the expense of conscience were not the only contexts for immoral British conduct. Many of the British officers assigned to the South lacked moral standing. Historian and Revolutionary War veteran David Ramsay was personally subjected to British cruelty while imprisoned. He wrote about the British officers posted to the South, stating, "Low ethical quality of officers plus institutionally corrupt policies resulted in horrible atrocities against both friend and foe."[77] Hessian soldier Arthur DeBardeleben testified that "the weight of duty to the King" was "contrary to my principles."[78] Rewarded unethical behavior multiplied into widespread slaughter and plundering. Promotions were based on "pacifying the countryside" by harsh subjugation and barbarity. Twenty-six-year-old Lieutenant Colonel Banastre Tarleton inspired his subordinates by emphasizing that terrorizing inhabitants was a "point of duty," and he would "carry the sword and fire through the land", punishing the treasonous rebels and destroying their farms and livestock. Rewarded unethical behavior multiplied into unrestrained barbarism that would cost the Crown potential supporters and alienate the Loyalists they expected to help them conquer the South.

Poor ethics extended throughout the British regulars' ranks. British officers would have their soldiers whipped if they hesitated to follow ruthless orders against civilians. The famous British poet Lord Tennyson would characterize these ethics years later with the words: "Theirs not to make reply, / Theirs not to reason why, / Theirs but to do and die."[79] The British command resolved to follow King George's prime minister's instructions that "harsh measures" were "the only sure means of subduing rebellion."[80] Unethical rules of war became governmental policy as well as a military point of duty.

During most of the American Revolution, the prime minister of England was Lord Frederick Lord North, second earl of Guilford. He entered a lifetime of politics after graduating from Oxford. By 1780 he was forty-eight years old and had been leader of the House of Commons for thirteen years. His financial and budgetary knowledge was excellent, as were his abilities as a debater. Given time, he could convince Parliament about anything with proof of numbers. The House of Commons usually bent to his reasoning. Lord North had a close relationship and friendship with the king. He ran the cabinet at Whitehall by consensus except when managing the war, which he mostly delegated to Lord Germain. North's lack of decisive leadership was an ongoing weakness in the unity of effort required from the chain of command to conquer America. He never really understood that the American rebellion was more a war of ideas than taxes and gunfire. He tried to solve American disenchantment with intellectual concepts underpinned by tax mathematics few understood. North was unwilling to allow Americans to control their economy or trade, but he was adamant about America contributing to discharging the public debt. He viewed America's economic responsibility to the Crown as a supplier of raw materials to Britain's value-added manufacturing and as an inexpensive food and commodity source.

Adam Smith, the father of modern economics, was a consultant to the Crown when North was prime minister. In February 1778, he wrote to North with recommendations about ending the war entitled "Smith's Thoughts on the State of the Contest with America."[81] Smith's recommendations included settling the matter of independence with only a part of the thirteen colonies or offering a constitutional union to keep all of America within the empire. Imperial control of trade and industry was no longer the answer to growing the wealth of Britain, so loosening government control of America's economy would theoretically place "the invisible hand" of supply and demand in Britain's pocket minus traditional regulatory expenses. But Lord North was an accountant and great convincer, not a free-market economist, visionary, or top-line moneymaker. His finances were frequently in arrears. He dismissed Smith's laissez-faire trade recommendations designed to grow commerce between America and the British while keeping them within the empire. North believed that Britain would best prosper by simply restoring American colonial relations to the political and economic model of 1763. North held steadfast to the old trade-control model where America supplied raw materials to the Crown at fixed prices, and Britain made the finished goods to sell at the highest prices with the king's blessing. Lord North resigned from office in March 1782 after Congress turned down his offer to stop the war if America returned to their 1763 political and economic relationship.

Lord North could never catch up to the present. As an accountant, he was focused on looking at the past. In 1780, he would not adjust his war strategy with America, even though France, Spain, and the Dutch had enjoined the fight. He was not a military man, so he continued to believe that one or two substantial battlefield triumphs would win back America, not winning territory with the consent of the governed.

Lord North was convinced that the route to victory would be paved by conducting the Southern Strategy campaigns in the same cruel way that had successfully extinguished the rebellion in Scotland years before.[82] He empowered Lord Germain to get the job done the king's way while he minded budgets.

Lord George Germain was Lord North's war minister. His office was alternatively referred to as the American secretary or the secretary of state. Germain had authority over military conduct in the American war, which morphed into a global conflict in 1778. He was about sixty-four years old and had a tarnished military career stemming from his actions as commander in chief of British forces at the Battle of Minden in 1759. He was convicted of disobedience, although most believed the charge should have been cowardice in the face of the enemy. He avoided execution by one vote. He was elected to the House of Commons some years later. Germain aligned himself with the right coalitions that advocated coercion and harsh military measures to stomp out the colonial rebellion in America.[83]

After hearing of the news of Lexington and Concord, King George, through Lord North, sought Germain's advice about how to handle the situation. They liked what they heard from Germain about overwhelming the rebels with military strength and harsh punishment until they were repressed like Scotland had been successfully handled years before. Lord North appointed him as American secretary in his cabinet ministry despite Germain's notorious military record and lack of political support.

A product of European wars, Germain believed in the theory that one extensive campaign would extinguish the rebellion: "The Southern Strategy." In 1780, "he advocated a piecemeal conquest of the colonies with imperial government being reestablished as each colony was conquered."[84] Germain failed to understand that the ministry's insistence on punishment and subjugation of the populace would undermine the end goal of colony reannexation after the military conquest. Nonetheless, Lord Germain vigorously pursued the harshest measures to put down the rebellion and teach the king's American subjects a lesson they would never forget.

In the field, the British commanders had different ideas of ethics. They held the perspective that it was dishonorable for an enemy not to appear on a formal battlefield to fight. Colonel John Watson, the commander of the Third Regiment of Guards (the magnificent "Buffs"), bitterly complained that Francis Marion's men "will not fight and sleep like gentlemen, but like savages are eternally firing and whooping around us at night, and by day waylaying and popping at us from behind every tree."[85] Watson responded under a flag of truce to this perceived ungentlemanly behavior by taking Marion's messengers prisoner, burning homesteads, and raping women in the surrounding area. The British regulars set the example for Provincial and Loyalist militias to know no boundaries.

In contrast, Marion allowed the safe passage of Colonel Watson's wounded to Camden after an engagement. Fort Watson surrendered to Marion on April 23, 1781, because the defenders believed they would be treated honorably and granted amnesty. Like Watson, British frustrations often turned into the butchery of Patriot combatants and civilians suspected of providing aid and intelligence. British duty to ruthlessly put down the rebellion in the King's name trumped all ethics of conscience. That duty would be pushed to a vicious extreme when they struck back at Charlestown in 1780 and fanned out to conquer the entire South in the king's name.

IV.
THE BRITISH SOUTHERN STRATEGIES TO WIN THE WAR

They make a desert and call it peace.
—-Calgacus, in defending Britain against the Romans (AD 85)

Almost four years after General Henry Clinton's failed invasion of South Carolina, he successfully captured Charlestown on May 29, 1780. The next thirty-one months of British occupation during their offensive to conqueror the South was *total war.* The Southern Strategy, as the British named their conquest offensive, spiraled into a civil war within a rebellion accompanied by a brutal occupation featuring shock-troop mercenaries, fast-attack cavalry dragoons, and Native American atrocities. Besides combatants and citizens, the enslaved population, refugees, and orphans suffered terribly. Few were spared from the out-of-control war, where depopulation favored the Crown. The British mission was clear: conquer the South by slaying or converting the rebels using whatever means necessary.

Britain's prime minister, Lord North, clearly understood King George's desire to crush the rebellion and punish his subjects just as the king's father had done in Scotland. The secretary of state responsible for prosecuting the war was Lord George Germain. Lord Germain demanded

General Cornwallis employ brutal measures as the "sure means of subduing rebellion."[86] As a result of this policy of punishment, many residents in South Carolina and Georgia experienced violence, displacement from their homes, or both in the years 1780 through 1783. General Nathanael Greene would refer to the war he would inherit in the Lower South as "nothing but blood and slaughter."

The horrors did not end there. Continental currency was rendered useless by widespread British counterfeiting. British troops confiscated guns and powder, destroyed printing presses and spinning wheels, and scorched large tracts of land. Crop burnings, livestock slaughters, plundering, rape, murder, torture, scalping, and church burnings were commonplace.[87] Starvation, dysentery, smallpox, typhoid fever, yellow fever, and malaria raged in extreme heat. Death from wild animals, poisonous snakes, disease, dehydration, shock, and exposure far exceeded combat deaths. The subjugation of the South through war conducted in the most extreme manner was the primary objective of the Southern Strategy to extinguish the rebellion. Insurrectionists would be shown no mercy. "For King and Country," harsh martial law, absent of ethics for life, liberty, or justice ruled the land. Everything and everyone was a target.

Charlestown, South Carolina, was the key to the British Southern Strategy. Taking it and successfully conducting southern offensive operations from headquarters there meant winning back America for the British and holding on to the wealth-generating Lower South. Lord George Germain made clear to Sir Henry Clinton what the commander's intent was for the first phase of the Southern Campaign. "It is the King's intention that an attack should be made against the Southern Colonies with a view to the *conquest* and possession of Georgia and South Carolina." King George was explicit about keeping South Carolina and Georgia within his empire. Moreover, negotiation toward reconciliation was off the table.

Britain launched their opening war offensive against Charlestown and the Carolinas in June 1776, but failed. Charlestown would not serve as their base of operations to prosecute the War. Alternatively, the British successfully captured New York and established that city as their primary base of operations. In January 1777, they called off another amphibious assault on Charlestown before disembarkation from New York. Then the British launched an offensive to isolate New England by capturing the Hudson River but were stopped when their troops surrendered at Saratoga, New York. Next, another army occupied Philadelphia, the seat of Congress, in September 1777. The following June, that army evacuated Philadelphia after the French entered the war and prepared to blockade their support fleet. Another army captured Savannah, Augusta, and the Savannah River in Georgia in early 1778 and reinstalled the royal governor in the process. That same army prepared to attack Charlestown from outside the gates but abandoned the effort. Still, the revolution would not collapse. The fact that the British attempted their first amphibious assault against Charlestown in their 1776 opening grand offensive to extinguish the rebellion emphasized the city's economic and strategic importance to the Crown. That same defeated army and navy were augmented and captured New York, New Jersey, and Pennsylvania. After the British lost an army at Saratoga and had to evacuate another army occupying Philadelphia to reinforce New York, the British Northern Strategy to put down the rebellion sat in stalemate in autumn 1778. The British could militarily control lower New York state but little else in New England. What became clear was that the British could not hold territory while Continental armies remained in the field.

Before the stalemate in the North, General Charles Lee's handpicked replacement, Continental General Robert Howe, created havoc in the Lower South. Howe conducted two failed offensives in Florida, one in 1777 and another in the first half of 1778, intended to capture the British fortress at Saint Augustine and check the British from raiding Georgia. Howe alienated the Georgia state militias in both efforts, and his armies were decimated from disease and illness, not from combat or from achieving his missions. In withdrawing back to South Carolina, Howe dismissed his North Carolina Continental troops, leaving Georgia vulnerable to attack.

Continental General Christopher Gadsden challenged Howe's reassertion of Southern Continental headquarters command when General Howe returned to Charlestown in 1777 without an army. Gadsden wrote to Congressional president Henry Laurens demanding an investigation of Howe's activities while asserting his command seniority rights—offering his resignation if this did not occur. Rather than conduct an investigation into Howe's activities, which could threaten the budding French alliance, Congress accepted Gadsden's resignation. Personal insults between Gadsden and Howe ensued, culminating in a duel on August 30, 1778. On the field of honor, Howe grazed Gadsden's ear, and Gadsden was left to fire with an unhurried aim. Gadsden turned his pistol at a right angle and fired, likely sparing Howe and the French alliance in the making. British intelligence officer Major John Andre published a satirical poem about the event in the nationally distributed *Rivington's Gazette* to unsettle the French and demoralize Patriot forces. The "Affaire of Honor" poem publicly lampooned Continental Army leadership but did not dampen the French commitment. Assuming that Andre's poem did not also serve as an encrypted message to field operatives, how Major Andre received such detail of the "private" event in Charlestown while sitting in New York is unknown.

Congress would rue their mistake in backing General Howe instead of Gadsden. Howe would unsuccessfully defend Savannah against a British land attack in the months to follow. He was responsible for leaving a trail into the walled city undefended, enabling a small British force to capture Savannah. His failures to capture Saint Augustine enabled the British to launch an attack against Savannah from there by land and sea. As a result of these defeats, General Charles Lee's handpicked successor, General Robert Howe, would have his loyalties and competence questioned. He was relieved of Southern Continental Army command by Congress to face a court-martial and replaced by General Benjamin Lincoln. In contrast, Christopher Gadsden would refuse to surrender Charlestown in 1779 to the same British army that captured Savannah.

The empire struck back to take Charlestown in 1780 by land with overwhelming force. Charlestown was essential to enlarging the British economy as a hub for their world trade supply chain. Military possession of that capital port city was also strategically crucial to reannexing the South and for winning the colonial war, which had gone global. Charlestown was the trade terminus for a network of river "superhighways" and trading posts reaching far into the densely forested interior of both Carolinas and Georgia. Charlestown was also a key hub for trade with England, the West Indies, the western American frontier, and Native Americans. Rice, indigo, raw materials, and animal pelts were in high global demand. British aristocracy invested heavily in trading companies that depended on Southern trade. Lord Germain emphasized the economic importance to General Henry Clinton in no uncertain terms: "Charlestown is the seat of commerce for that part of America."[88]

Charlestown was also the key to controlling the Carolinas and Georgia because of its military logistics. Britain's sea power brought armies and supplies directly into the capital port city, where they could be quickly sent upriver to a network of forts spread throughout the state and along the rivers. From these fortifications, the British could extinguish the rebellion and control the commerce downriver to Charlestown. Each fort was eventually turned over to the Loyalist and Provincial militias to manage. This enabled the flower of the British army to march northward and subjugate each successive state or simply wait in place for each state's resolve to collapse before moving in.

Sir Henry Clinton, the commander of British Expeditionary Forces; Lord Frederick North; and Lord George Germain, secretary of state, were responsible for prosecuting King George's war in America in 1780. Lord Germain was the hands-on point man for running the war to crush the rebellion. These men realized that taking and holding the South was essential to extinguishing the uprising. Charlestown was ideal as the logistical hub and command and control center to operationally execute the Southern Strategy. Britain could pour troops and supplies into Charlestown, which could then flow to the upcountry forts. They would establish a network of forts to control the rivers, river crossings, the Charlestown Road running into allied Native American lands, the Great Wagon Road running from Augusta to Philadelphia, and the King's Highway, which traversed north into Virginia near the coast. After it appeared that both Georgia and South Carolina were subdued entirely in June 1780, Clinton turned over command in the South to Lord

Charles Cornwallis. He then returned to his Northern Army and mistress in New York. Clinton had fulfilled the king's intent of conquering Georgia and South Carolina. Believing the collapse of North Carolina and Virginia was just a matter of time, he left ahead of the insufferable Charlestown summer. At the same time, the Southern British military machine under Cornwallis prepared to march northward. Unfortunately for his vision, Clinton left the wrong person in charge of the Southern theater of operations.

Reminiscent of General Howe's overconfidence that the war was won after subduing Long Island in November 1776, most of the British high command except Cornwallis settled back to take tea after occupying the South Carolina Low Country in 1780. Thus, the next phase of the Southern Campaign was never adequately planned or agreed upon across the chain of command. Chuffed with their success in South Carolina and Georgia, the British war ministry became convinced that the rebellion was dissolving. Loyalists throughout America were reportedly flocking to the king's standard to complete the job. British newspapers constantly echoed these sentiments while repeatedly lionizing Charlestown's "glorious" capture as one of the most outstanding military achievements in the empire's history. General Clinton believed himself redeemed from his failure in 1776 when he wrote in June 1780, "I may venture to assert, that there are very few men in South Carolina who are not either our prisoners, or in arms with us." Shortly thereafter, he moved his command back to New York , leaving General Charles Cornwallis in command. Lord Germain believed that leaving the South in Cornwallis's capable hands was a sure bet to fulfill His Majesty's goals of conquering and punishing America. Subjects, like children, require punishment so they do not misbehave again.

Punishment, promoted as justice, would be their undoing. Atilla the Hun was one of the greatest conquerors in history. Atilla's successful barbarian policy of conquest was to commit all atrocities at once. He would kill all those who opposed him after conquering an area, then gather all who remain and explain his reasons, ask for forgiveness and invite the rest to join in his common quest to conquer and unite. Cornwallis missed this lesson at Eton. He continued rewarding atrocities throughout the British occupation of the South even when it became apparent his methods were turning Loyalists into Patriots.

Pride is a cruel master. Things began to unravel when Cornwallis abandoned his British Southern army headquarters in Charlestown and Camden in the fall of 1780 to campaign in North Carolina and afterward Virginia, believing South Carolina was secure. He did nothing to arrest the internecine war he left behind. If Cornwallis had stayed put to chaperone the installation of royal authority throughout the region, supervised the mop-up of stray rebel militias, and not pursued an aggressive policy of terrorizing Southern inhabitants, the Southern Continental Army and eventually the Northern Continental Army would have likely dissolved from lack of support, money, and food.[89] The populace would have ultimately been not-so-happily reunited with their mother country. The War for American Independence would have been a footnote in British-American history, and "Charlestowne," as the British spelled it, would still be nicknamed Little London instead of the Holy City.

Fortunately for the declared "United States," Cornwallis's impatience opened America's path to independence. His decisions to invade North Carolina changed the complexity of the war in the South by proving he was not as invincible as his nom de guerre of "the modern-day Hannibal" would imply. His Lordship's first attempt to invade North Carolina failed in October 1780 at King's Mountain when the Overmountain Men destroyed his left-wing army under the boisterous Major Patrick Ferguson. With one thousand–plus angry mountain men on his flank, the vulnerability of Cornwallis's main army at Charlotte became untenable when Tarleton became stricken with malaria. Cornwallis's light cavalry screening force was leaderless. His main forces were suffering from unrelenting militia bushwhacking, disease, and lack of supplies. Sharpshooting mountain men were filling the giant chestnut forests around Charlotte, North Carolina, named after King George's wife, Queen Charlotte. After the complete loss of his left wing at King's Mountain, North Carolina, Loyalists wavered in joining His Lordship as planned. Cornwallis was compelled to retreat to the garrison in Winnsboro, South Carolina, near

Camden, to recuperate. Simultaneously, word of the Overmountain Men's victory at King's Mountain and the British retreat spread across the countryside. Hope sprang anew among oppressed Carolina Patriots.

After retreating to South Carolina and recovering his strength, Cornwallis repeated the same operational mistake three months later. In January 1781, he lost his left wing again at Cowpens, South Carolina, under Lieutenant Colonel Banastre Tarleton, not far from his previous mistake at King's Mountain. In both cases, his left wing was operating too far away for his main army to provide support. The loss at Cowpens was only the beginning of losing over four thousand crack troops over the next seventy days.[90] Cornwallis had acted with glory-seeking impatience without establishing a reliable supply line, reconnaissance operation, or area intelligence network. Also, he committed multiple preparation errors: not coordinating with his Cherokee allies to the west, not taking time to organize Loyalist militias in North Carolina to prepare the ground before his invasion, not training and arming Black runaways following him to scout and screen on his flanks, not integrating select militia forces into his regular ranks, and not coordinating his offensive in North Carolina with Generals Phillips and Arnold operating in Virginia. "The great Hannibal" acted alone.

Glory was not to be shared among the king's military leadership. Instead of behaving rationally by staying put in Winnsboro and securing the South Carolina upcountry after Tarleton's defeat at Cowpens, Cornwallis abandoned the South Carolina mop-up. Instead, he chose to chase General Nathanael Greene's ragtag army across North Carolina to Greene's supply base in Virginia. He substantially degraded his professional army in the process while boosting hope for the Patriot cause and inspiring recruits to join Greene. He allowed his prideful emotions to direct his actions. As a result, Cornwallis's abrupt decision to reinvade North Carolina opened the door to the eventual expulsion of all His Majesty's armies from the South and laid the cornerstone for America's independence.

Cornwallis knew better. He knew not to begin an extensive campaign without at least six months' provisions and a prearranged supply line. The Southern Command was Cornwallis's first independent theater command. With no previous experience in widescale civil affairs, he was a man of action who disliked civil administration required of a military governor. He was tactically trained, not strategically insightful. He followed the king's orders, through his ministry, without question. General Cornwallis was provoked into launching an unsupported offensive through deep forests in the dead of winter that ultimately destroyed his army's fighting capability.

His tactical accomplishments as an aggressive regimental commander serving in the Seven Years' War in Germany earned him the king's commission as a general when the American Revolution broke out. He was at the Battle of Minden in 1759 as a regimental captain when Lord Germain refused to execute a flanking charge, resulting in Germain's court-martial and a dishonorable discharge. Cornwallis lacked strategic vision, which would often cause him to lose focus during a prolonged operation. The weeks-long immobility across from Sullivan's Island in 1776 bore out this characteristic. By 1780, his relationship with his commander, General Clinton, had soured because Lord Germain communicated directly with Cornwallis rather than following the chain of command through Clinton. Cornwallis's effectiveness in short-term field operations was more than offset by his lack of strategic insight into why he was fighting a battle in the first place. His failure to establish royal authority and civil administration after conquering an area to develop "protective trust" would turn civilians against British political reunification for want of protection and justice. However, he was a lion on the battlefield, and he completely subscribed to Germain's two-pronged war of conquest and punishment. He chose Lieutenant Colonel Banastre Tarleton, Lord Rawdon, and Lieutenant Colonel Nesbit Balfour as his inner circle to fulfill Lord Germain's punitive directive in the South. Neither Lord Germain nor Cornwallis considered more practical methods to reunite America with Britain short of total subjugation. At forty-two years old, Cornwallis served two masters doing a job beyond his ken.

Cornwallis's other master, at least on occasion, was General Henry Clinton. Unlike Cornwallis, Clinton knew military strategy and the conciliatory civilian policies required after battle to win the war. About fifty years old, Clinton had attended school on Long Island in his youth, so he knew the American culture. Clinton served extensively in Britain's foreign wars as a British regimental commander and an aide-de-camp to various headquarters commands. He became friends with Charles Lee during the 1760s. Clinton was promoted to general and sent to co-command the first major offensive against America at Charlestown, South Carolina, in 1776, which ended in a defeat that sent shock waves across Europe. Reassigned to assist General Howe with the New York offensive, Clinton developed the attack plan on Long Island, which commenced on August 27, 1776. His well-executed plan destroyed the American Army and secured the capture of New York for the remainder of the war. The New York offensive occurred six months after Clinton had a "coincidental" meeting with Continental General Charles Lee at New York governor William Tryon's estate. Charles Lee was developing the entire plan for the American defense of New York when he met with General Clinton in early 1776.

After the conquest of South Carolina and Georgia in 1780, Clinton did not want to risk any British gains by launching unnecessary offensives into North Carolina. After securing South Carolina and capturing Wilmington, he felt that his offensive operations in Virginia would eventually cause North Carolina to capitulate. Clinton was a man of thought, strategy, and patience whom Cornwallis rarely listened to once he received his independent command. Lord Germain outranked Clinton, so Cornwallis would follow Germain's direction more closely regardless of strategic inconsistency.

While both armies employed compound warfare strategies during the Southern Campaign, the Patriots mastered it. Compound warfare is a military strategy that synergistically combines regular and irregular forces to compound, or complement, each other's effects.[91] The almost daily changes in war-fighting dynamics and alliances in the Carolina wilderness alongside waterways and crossroads were the key to controlling territory and supply logistics. Spies delivered constant streams of coded messages, by fast horse and on foot, that provided steady streams of intelligence of enemy activities. Commanders used operational intelligence to coordinate and direct troop marches and countermarches, often through oppressive weather, dangerous swamps, and swollen rivers. Timely intelligence, properly applied, was used to synchronize Continental and militia forces to meet near a particular target. Patriot spies and enslaved Black persons collected and delivered troop-movement information to General Greene's chain of command. When reliable intelligence was acted upon quickly, joint militia and Continental forces would outnumber or equal British troops at a particular location enabling the combined force to liberate territory.

Timely intelligence often kept Patriot forces one step ahead of the well-equipped British troops operating from their forts. The primary American strategy was to use fast-attack cavalry forces to harass, intercept, and pin down British forces to prevent them from aiding sister forts under siege. The local militias would then join the main Continental Army from all points to outnumber an isolated enemy, skirmish by skirmish, battle by battle, fort by fort, and town by town, to drive the British back into their coastal city bastions. In between investitures and battles, the state militias were constantly harassing British troops, intercepting enemy communications and supplies, and making the forests dangerous for the British forces to move between forts and fortified towns. The overall effect of these compound warfare tactics "compels a superior enemy to both amass and disperse forces simultaneously, thereby diluting their strength."[92]

Wars are often won or lost based on the treatment of civilians. The Southern Continental Army was the nucleus of the occupation counterforce, with dragoon cavalry detachments operating on the periphery and beyond between significant battles. The cavalry was also essential in reconnaissance, force screening, and delaying operations against the king's forces. State militia units often complemented Continental light cavalry forces in their missions. They isolated British forts, dispersed Loyalist militias, won over the population, established intelligence networks, and provided Greene intelligence. Militias were charged with disrupting and destroying enemy supply lines and depots within their assigned geographic areas. The key to successful compound warfare boiled down to the willingness of the local inhabitants to support the side they most trusted to ensure their safety and future happiness. The British needed local support to sustain their occupation of a conquered area, yet their oppressive tactics did little to curry favor.

The Continental Army had to show better ethical conduct than the British Army to generate more trust among residents to win and hold territory with its insurgent operations. Once they won territory, the Continental Army would have to provide residents protection from British and Loyalist retaliation for their support. At its core, the American Revolution was an ethical revolution, and victory in the Lower South would depend on practicing those values of humanity.

In 1778, after about three years of war, the American and British armies in the Northern Colonies were at a stalemate. British planners in London modified the Southern Strategy, first initiated against Charlestown in 1776, by making strategy, operations, and tactics changes. "Southern Strategy 4.0" called for land and sea attacks against Savannah, Georgia, so that British troops could get a foothold in the South. After capture, the British would use Savannah and Fort Saint Augustine as their bases to launch a joint land and sea attack on Charlestown.

This modified strategy to capture the soft underbelly of the South and work northward could be sustained by utilizing Native resources. Inhabitants loyal to the Crown and their Native American allies could be conscripted to operate on the periphery of the leading British and Hessian regiments during concentrated offensives. Loyalist militias and Provincial troops would be directed to roam the backcountry on horseback to burn out rebels and terminate rebel resistance without regular British troops. When areas became pacified, forts would be constructed by the enslaved Black population and manned primarily by Loyalist and Provincial troops. The chain of mutually supported fort clusters would be positioned to control the conquered towns, rivers, crossroads, and countrysides, not unlike the firebase camp strategy of the Vietnam War. With these operational changes, overtaking the South could be managed piece by piece from south to north until the rebellion was entirely extinguished.

British regulars would militarily overwhelm each state, using Charlestown, South Carolina, as their Southern army headquarters and logistics supply depot. As these armies progressed northward, the system of forts left in their wake would enable the British Empire to establish a formidable supply line, control commerce, and enforce the king's authority. Once British forces secured Virginia, they could build a superport along the Chesapeake Bay. From there, Britain's navy could rapidly transport regular troops along the eastern seaboard to maintain control over Southern-held provinces and launch new offensives against any state that did not submit. When the conquest of the Southern colonies was complete, Washington's army in the North would be weakened due to the interruption of supplies from the South, putting his army in an undersupplied and vulnerable position exposed to a two-pronged attack. If well executed, the British Southern Strategy 4.0 would break apart the "United States" and eventually extinguish the rebellion.

While being held captive in 1777, Continental General Charles Lee provided a Southern Strategy plan to then British commander in chief General William Howe. Lee's treacherous plan detailed how the British could win America by splitting the Southern states from the Northern states and building a superport along the Chesapeake.[93] Building a superport along the Chesapeake River was the centerpiece of the plan. The British and Americans referred to the South as the area stretching across Delaware and Maryland then southward down through Georgia. Congress sometimes included Philadelphia, Pennsylvania in the South, listing it as part of "The Southern Department," headquartered in Charlestown. The success of Lee's plan hinged on two things: (1) restoring "protective trust" among the neutral and Loyalist populations to bring hearts, minds, and militiamen to the king's standard, and (2) capturing and holding Virginia and the Chesapeake, preferably while occupying the rebel capital of Philadelphia.[94] As academically gifted as he was, General Lee was not educated in macroeconomics or logistics; therefore, his original plan did not emphasize capturing South Carolina's economic and logistical infrastructure centered in Charlestown.

In 1777, General Howe's operations to capture Philadelphia and areas around the Chesapeake resembled the plan Lee provided. Lee's plan convinced the ministers at Whitehall; General William Howe; his brother, Admiral Richard Howe; and General Clinton that to win the war, the British Armies must cut off the Northern colonies from the Southern colonies. The success of this plan depended on conquering Annapolis, Maryland, and Alexandria, Virginia, and establishing bases along the Chesapeake, mutually supported from Philadelphia and a neutralized Pennsylvania. The British needed to gain control of the central north–south road, the Great Wagon Road, running from Philadelphia to Augusta, Georgia if conquering the South was to be achieved. Howe and then Clinton and then Cornwallis appeared to pursue Lee's Southern Strategy in fits and starts, without mutually supported, coordinated effort. There is a good argument that the absence of a unified operational plan to pursue Lee's strategy prevented the British from conquering or splitting America or extinguishing the Continental armies. The British had three ways to win; the Patriots only one—united, sovereign independence. Marching and sailing all about America stretched British resources beyond their limits and enabled the growing ranks of persecuted civilians turned Patriots to exploit their follies.

After the First Battle of Charlestown, fought at Sullivan's Island, Lee convinced then-president Rutledge of South Carolina to write Congress on his behalf to pay for his real estate holdings purchased on credit in America. Congress did so, considering his service defending the South from invasion, ostensibly to replace his property confiscated in England when he joined the American cause. As the most well-educated professional military officer in North America, Lee could convince almost anyone about anything except King George.

Another Lee curiosity involved his defense plan for New York. Washington tasked Lee with this responsibility in January 1776. Charlestown and New York City on the island of Manhattan were remarkably similar peninsulas. They both had narrow passageways into their harbors, where ships and invasion forces were the most vulnerable to cannon fire. Lee had seen firsthand that the Fort Sullivan and Fort

Johnson gauntlet defending the narrow passageways into Charlestown harbor had successfully repulsed the British fleet despite the defenders being undersupplied, outmanned, and outgunned. After the First Battle of Charlestown, Lee knew that the Continental Army had an advantage in preparing city defenses to keep the British out because of these similarities. In Lee's defense plan for New York, the blueprint that Washington and Greene would follow, there were no plans to fortify either side of the Verrazano Narrows with impregnable forts, as Lee had seen at Fort Johnson and Fort Sullivan. Lee's defense plan for New York involved deploying scarce Patriot forces across Long Island and Manhattan Island to oppose British ground forces by constructing a series of "bunker hills" or elevated entrenchments. Lee's plan afforded the British uncontested landings, two months of military buildup, and a restful encampment after long sea voyages and their humiliating defeat at Charlestown. The British were expected to march up to each entrenched Patriot position and endure withering rifle and cannon fire without adjusting their tactics or flanking Patriot entrenchments. In actuality, the well-supplied and rested British forces quickly skirted Lee's series of works and sliced across Long Island in two days. The British navy easily sailed up to Manhattan Island and deployed along the East River, effectively splitting the Patriot army, controlling the waterways, and ending the Battle of Long Island with ease. Washington's army escaped only by a clever evacuation during a foggy night. Lee's defense plan of New York was unprofessional if not enemy friendly.

Lee had learned firsthand at Charlestown that the key to protecting harbor peninsula-cities was not to allow the British fleet into the harbor in the first place. Yet Lee did not try to correct his glaring mistake in his July 1, 1776, after-action report to Washington. Howe landed unopposed at Staten Island with ten thousand weary troops in early July, where a super fort or at least an unfinished Fort Sullivan–like battery should have been vigorously repelling British ships with deadly cannonades and sharpshooter crossfire.[95] Like the professional he claimed to be, Lee had time to correct his planning mistake by urging Washington to immediately oppose Howe's then outnumbered army as they were landing near the

Narrows. Instead, the British comfortably built up their forces around the Narrows' beaches before launching a massive blitzkrieg across Long Island with rested troops eager to avenge their embarrassing defeat at Charlestown. During the War of 1812, the Narrows was fortified, and a formidable British invasion fleet tasked with capturing New York was turned back rather than risk sure destruction. Whether the front door to New York was left open in 1776 by the careless oversight of a professional general can only be guessed.

Lee's consistently curious behavior and communications continued throughout the British invasion of New York. Washington requested Lee join him there as quickly as possible after the Charlestown victory to assist him with installing the New York defense plan Lee devised. Lee finally arrived months later after first making a trip to Philadelphia and collecting 30,000 Spanish dollars (about $900,000 today) from Congress to settle his debts. While Lee was collecting his 30,000 Spanish dollars, Washington and Greene were being chased across Long Island by about thirty thousand British and Hessian regulars due to Lee's puzzling defense plan. After the Patriot disasters on Long Island, Lee joined Washington at Fort Lee, New Jersey, named in his honor. Lee promptly criticized the situation created by following his plans but offered no solutions other than platitudes to conduct a full retreat and wage a partisan war.

Soon after that meeting, the British forced Washington into full retreat. Fort Washington fell on November 16, and Cornwallis launched a surprise attack on Fort Lee on November 19. After the fall of both forts, Lee wrote the following to the president of Massachusetts: "There are times when we must commit treason against the laws of the State for the salvation of the state. The present crisis demands this, brave, virtuous kind of treason."[96] Whether Lee was laying the groundwork for commandeering the Continental Army, surrendering his army, or encouraging the Massachusetts Assembly to separate from the confederation can only be speculated. Lee also exchanged secret correspondence with Colonel Joseph Reed, Washington's adjutant on his senior staff. In this letter, Lee criticizes Washington's leadership while seemingly jockeying for command of the entire Continental Army: "That fatal indecision of mind which in war is a much greater disqualification than stupidity."[97] Without consulting Washington, Joseph Reed encouraged Lee to act independently in direct contradiction to Washington's orders to Lee. Reed assured Lee that he and all of Washington's staff had confidence in him, possibly as a nod for Lee to unilaterally assume command over Washington without congressional permission. Certainly, Lee was playing undermining politics when he should have been showcasing the military skills he so eloquently touted.

Lee was the most revered general in the Continental Army then. He styled himself "the Hero of Charlestown" and ensured Congress knew he was right about everything. Washington was convinced and gave Lee command of his left wing at White Plains with about four thousand troops. When Washington's force was in a pell-mell retreat to Pennsylvania, he ordered Lee to join him with his fresh troops to form a defense of Philadelphia around Congress. Lee never followed the order, repeated in writing three times. After being reenforced, he had five thousand soldiers and was in a perfect position to maul Howe's rear and cut off his overextended supply lines on his way to join forces with Washington. If Howe continued his offensive to Philadelphia, Washington's army could be annihilated defending Congress and the capitol. If Washington were captured or killed, Lee would automatically assume command of the Continental Army and obey Congress at his pleasure. Lee could assert authority in peace negotiations and unilaterally recognize the king and Parliament, rather than a scattered Congress, in exchange for a general's rank in the British army, a lordship, and possibly more. All it seemed Lee had to do was wait for Washington's army to dissolve.

Instead of following Washington's explicit orders to join him, Lee slowly brought his army to Morristown at a snail's pace of three miles a day. He watched as Gates's army passed him on their way to reinforce the commander in chief. General Greene, who was with Washington, wrote, "General Lee['s] slow motions distrest us amazeingly."[98] Not only did Washington need Lee's troops desperately to make a stand against Howe, but their enlistments expired in twenty days. As Lee well knew, if he continued to drag his feet, Washington's army would evaporate as their enlistments ran out.

Finally, on December 11, Lee ordered his second-in-command, General Sullivan, to lead the troops and march them toward Pennsylvania. Despite being in an active theater of war, Lee spent the next night about three miles away from his army's camp at a tavern in Basking Ridge along with his entourage. Lee then penned a letter to General Gates condemning Washington "entre nous, a certain great man is damnably deficient." About 10:00 a.m. on December 12, a detachment of the British Sixteenth Light Dragoons surrounded the tavern house where he was staying and ordered him out. One of the four officers leading the mission was Coronet Banastre Tarleton, the boisterous junior officer from Liverpool who publicly promised Lee's head on a pike at first sight after learning of his desertion from the British Army. Fortunately for Lee, Tarleton was not in command of the operation.

Renowned English historian George Trevelyan described Lee's capture as an event of divine intervention for America.[99] He maintained that day in history should be marked by the Americans, who are "a people observant of anniversaries," with "a white stone in their calendar." Trevelyan states that Lee's capture and Howe's decision on that same day to cease offensive operations short of crossing the Delaware, capturing Philadelphia, and occupying New Jersey, marked the turning point in an otherwise outmatched contest. Interestingly, Lee correctly predicted that Howe would stop short of crossing the Delaware River into Pennsylvania to finish off the rebellion. Trevelyan saw Lee's removal from Continental command by his "capture" as instrumental to Washington's success at Trenton and Princeton. He was also aware of Lee's treacherous plan to come, diverting Howe from marching up the Hudson to link up with Burgoyne, which would have prevented the British surrender at Saratoga. Dr. Trevelyan was an esteemed regius professor of history at Cambridge with access to first-person archives housed at the University of Cambridge detailing the "War of the American Rebellion." He opined that Lee's capture changed the course of the war to one the Americans could win.

Lee surrendered quite ingloriously at White's Tavern if one believes British newspaper propaganda or cover stories, whichever the case might have been.[100] Some of his captors had served with Lee in Portugal and conceivably would not have been pleased about his desertion while still on army half pay. If Lee had a secret arrangement with General Clinton, Sir Henry was conducting an offensive in Rhode Island, out of vouching range. Cornwallis, who initiated the special operation, might have been instructed by Clinton to "bring in" Lee to demoralize the rebellion and position him to negotiate a general surrender. Americans across the colonies believed that Charles Lee was the only general who could lead the rebellion to victory over the empire or, at least, negotiate American representation in Parliament. Whether Lee's "lucky" capture was a prearranged defection or if Lee was manipulated into staying apart from his troops by invitation of the "tavern lady" is anyone's guess without being privy to the British intelligence book. In either case, the coincidence of Tarleton and Lee's former Portugal comrades being on the same mission to capture or collect Lee has a very low probability. The mission staffing that resulted in Lee's capture was certainly British Intelligence tradecraft, if not humor.

Lee was indirectly taken back to then British-occupied New York. Word got out to General Washington that Whitehall had ordered Howe to send Lee to England to stand trial. After Washington's miraculous victory at Trenton on Christmas Day, he had a letter delivered to General Howe stating in no uncertain terms that he had five Hessian officers he was holding to ensure Lee's safety. Whatever happened to Lee would happen to the Hessians. The British version was that the letter came just in time before Lee boarded a ship to England. If Lee's capture was genuine, Washington's letter made Lee's return to England an international incident. If Howe ignored Washington's letter by sending Lee to England, Britain's contractor agreement and friendship with Prussia, who supplied Hessian soldiers, would be jeopardized. Throwing the predicament to London would, at best, publicly embarrass King George across Europe.

On the other hand, Lee might have arranged to defect. He might have logically concluded that the war was nearly over, and his capture would be the tipping point for him or Congress to negotiate terms since they had no other competent commanders at that time to carry on the war. As they say in intelligence language, maybe "it was time to bring him in." Enlistments would expire on New Year's Day, so there would be no Continental army to oppose Howe anyway. Washington's unexpected Christmas Day victory at Trenton and his letter to Howe probably changed British thinking about Lee's future if he was fairly captured and on his way to the Tower of London gallows. Whether Lee's capture was staged or special operations luck as the British newspapers professed, he was treated as a VIP prisoner of war subject to a future exchange. If Lee was legitimately captured rather than arranging himself to be captured, Washington's fidelity to his insubordinate subordinate saved Lee's life.

Cover stories aside, Washington was rewarded for his fidelity by Lee writing out a plan for Admiral Richard Howe and Sir William Howe to crush the rebellion and conquer America. When Lee became a traitor will always be a subject of debate, like Benedict Arnold, but there is little doubt about his betrayal written in his own hand. That he might have been a British intelligence agent tasked to infiltrate the coming rebellion from the start cannot be ruled out. Lee wrote a military plan for the enemy proposing separating the Southern colonies from the Northern colonies. "Mr. Lee's Plan—29th March 1777," as Lee himself titled it, was discovered in 1858, verified to be in his handwriting and endorsed by Henry Strachey, who was the official secretary to Lord Howe.[101] This letter would serve as the core Southern Strategy plan the British Ministry and war planners would adopt for the rest of the war. Fortunately for the proposed "united States," the devil was in the details.

After Lee shared his plan with the Howe brothers, he sent a secret letter to George Germain, the British war strategist in London. In that letter dated April 2, Lee purported that General Burgoyne's mission to isolate New England by bringing a British army down from Canada and fortifying Lake Champaign, Lake George, and the Hudson River along the way was a waste of time and resources. Lee asserted that the isolation mission would do little strategically to end the war. A New York river line would be difficult to defend if established and would serve no logical purpose. Burgoyne's offensive could only offer value if he captured the rebel capital in Albany and seated the New York royal government there. Britain could rip a star off the Betsy Ross flag and establish a solid claim on that province by taking Albany and holding New York City. Lee proposed leaving Burgoyne on his own and redirecting Howe's link-up force to take Philadelphia. Burgoyne had been Lee's commanding officer in Portugal about fifteen years prior, and they had corresponded recently when General Burgoyne arrived in America with his army. Amazingly, Lord Germain agreed to Lee's plan, and Howe discontinued his plans for a link-up with Burgoyne. The result of this decision not to send reinforcements was an American victory at Saratoga and French recognition legitimizing the thirteen United States soon to follow.

Only months before, Lee was a dishonored deserter from the British army on his way to a public hanging at the Tower of London. Suddenly his credibility was second to none throughout the British Empire. As a result of Lee's recommendations outlined in his Southern Strategy plan, Howe recalled General Clinton, who was on his way to save "Gentleman Johnny" Burgoyne from his upcoming surrender at Saratoga. Ironically, by consorting with the enemy, Lee changed the war's course in favor of the United States. Howe's reinforcements to General Burgoyne would have made Burgoyne's army invincible, the capture of West Point inevitable, and France's entry into the war unlikely.

Mr. Lee's Plan, adopted as the British Southern Strategy, would repeatedly inform British offensives throughout their war against America from then on. Lee's plan centered on the Chesapeake area, but he proposed that the operation be conducted out of British headquarters in Philadelphia once it was captured. Lee knew capturing Philadelphia was the apple in Howe's eye. From a practical perspective, the British could use their vast fleet to move troops and supplies from that location to a newly built Chesapeake "superport" since the United States had no navy to challenge them. The prideful Burgoyne did not request any assistance in his attempt to conquer the Hudson River, and Whitehall liked the idea of capturing Philadelphia quickly to keep Parliamentary funds flowing. Lord Howe executed Lee's plan with grand ambitions of glory while leaving General Burgoyne to his solitary surrender. Continental General Charles Lee would unintentionally cause the mighty British war machine to begin its slow slide to defeat.

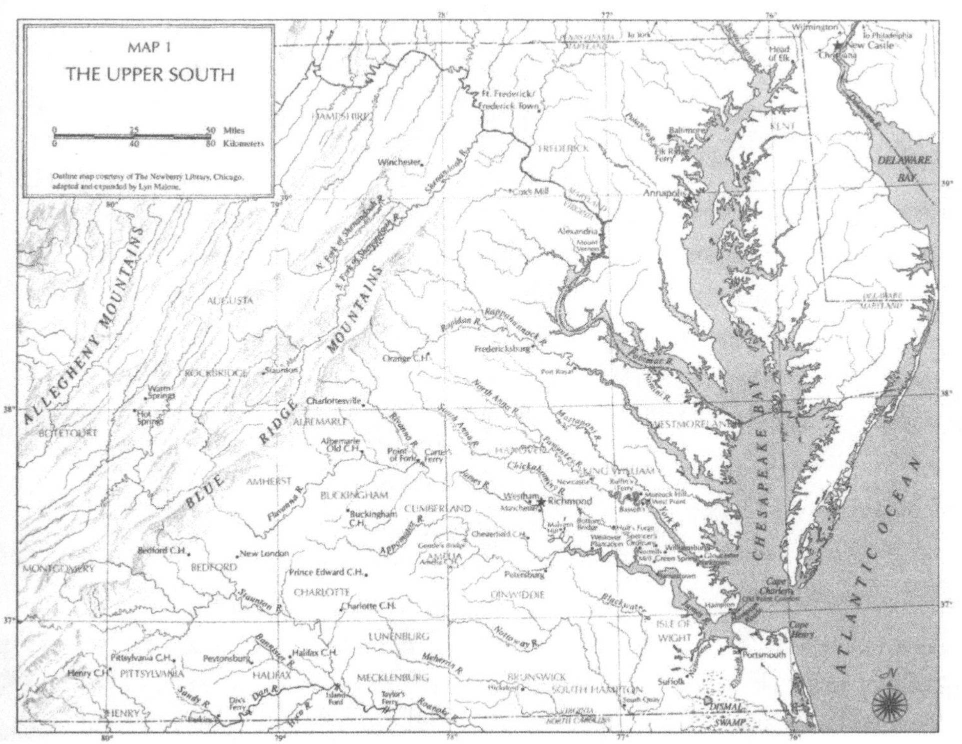

UPPER SOUTH, 1780, MAP COURTESY OF THE *NEWBERRY LIBRARY*, CHICAGO, ILL, AND UNC PRESS ADAPTED BY LYN MALONE.

In December 1777, with Howe in possession of Philadelphia and Burgoyne's army having surrendered to General Gates at Saratoga, Lee returned with another dubious pursuit, a political scheme to separate the states disguised as a peace conference. The British had concluded that the unity of the thirteen states was their biggest enemy. With France now in the war, contingent on Britain meeting America's "outrageous" demand for independence, Lee told Howe that he rejected the Declaration of

Independence. Lee advanced another treacherous plan sure to upset the unity cart in Britain's favor. This plan had a distinct air of intelligence engineering from the brilliant British intelligence officer Major John Andre. Lee sent a letter to Washington with a copy of sorts addressed to Congress urging an ambiguous conference with the Howe brothers.

Not to be taken in, Congress instructed Washington in February 1778 to tell Lee that his request was improper. Congress would not send any representatives to confer with the Howes, who they deemed did not have the authority to negotiate anything except pardons. Undeterred, Lee made another attempt in a March 1778 letter to Congress, urging that body to pass a formal resolution for the public record judging the request to negotiate improper, presumably to enlist public sentiment into reversing the decision. John Adams wrote to General Nathanael Greene explaining Congress's perceptions of the matter with the following summarized observations: Why would the Howes not make the offer in writing directly and state the purpose of the meeting? Anything relevant to peace discussions "might have been relayed by letter." The Howes' (via Lee's letters) object was "to distract and divide the Whigs at a critical moment." The last conference "did us great injury at the French court [which]… Lord Howe knows it and wishes to repeat it." John Adams concluded that Lee's "invitation to conference" was designed to weaken the power of Congress. Picking a few representatives to negotiate directly with the Howe brothers would likely create dissent between the states not involved in the direct discussions. France would probably abandon the alliance because of Congress's unilateral negotiations without their involvement.

Lee was trying to drive a wedge between any states or France or both. All he needed was one fracture or side negotiation with one renegade state for the Confederation or Congress to unravel. If Congress had chosen to send representatives to Howe's unauthorized and secretive conference, that act would have likely had disastrous results for the French alliance and the prospects for collective bargaining American independence. Judging by Congress's deliberation period, Lee's duplicitous wedge almost succeeded. Fortunately, John Adams smelled a rat and convinced Congress to reject the ploy.

With Lee's months of living in furnished apartments in New York with his servants and dogs at the king's expense, one must wonder why he did not continue with the British. He gave them a plan to win the war they adopted. He almost tricked Congress into meeting directly with the Howe brothers, which would have caused France to abandon the United States and doomed independence.[102] When Lee was captured at Basking Ridge Tavern, the revolution appeared to be within days of being over. It was likely to dissolve without him to lead half of the Continental Army as the end of enlistments came nearer. Under Washington's command, the other half of the Army was in complete evaporation with General Howe at Philadelphia's doorstep and the hangman's noose for Congress not far behind. According to Lee's correspondence, his capture disrupted his apparent plan to supplant Washington, which was proceeding well at the time. Maybe he could be exchanged and pick up where he left off, steering the Continental Army and Congress his way. Indeed, he had done his duty to get back into King George's good graces, so why risk going back to lead the army he had betrayed only to risk discovery? His exalted situation in New York brings one to consider Lee's true mission in returning to the Continental Army. Was it to cripple the army; replace Washington, possibly with the intent of turning the Continental Army over to the British; provide intelligence and expose Washington to capture or total defeat; or splinter Congress and the states with his manipulative letter writing? What did the quisling, or embedded spy, expect in return?

Unsuspecting of Lee's treason, Washington kept badgering General Howe to exchange Lee. The opportunity for him to return to a Continental army command was there. Lee's old British comrade, Sir Henry Clinton, was notified of his upcoming promotion to commander in chief effective May 1778. General Clinton was instructed that his first act of command was to withdraw British troops from Philadelphia back to New York in June. If Lee could be exchanged in April, maybe he would be given a Continental command and find himself in a situation where he could expose Washington's army to entrapment by General Clinton during the upcoming British withdrawal from Philadelphia.

In Lee's mind, he would be saving many lives and championing some American representation in Parliament, which was the original intent of the colonial rebellion anyway before it became a revolution. As Major John Andre might have put it, "If you pull off any of the above missions, you will be known as the great peacemaker of the world and deliverer of American political representation of which both the Crown and provincial America will forever be grateful." Ecco homme. Lee could go down in British history as one of the greatest and brightest figures of all time: the whole show.

If that was the plan, it was not to be. After being released, Lee returned to Valley Forge with fanfare and welcoming words from Washington. There was little suspicion that he had aided the enemy during his time with the British in New York except with Congressman Henry Laurens of South Carolina, who met with Lee in the summer of 1778. Laurens wrote to his son, Lieutenant Colonel John Laurens, that he had "discovered a change" in Lee that alarmed him. Lee secretly renewed his correspondence with Clinton and refused to take an unequivocal verbal oath against the Crown, as required from the rest of Washington's general staff.[103] Always a master of words when he wanted to be, Lee humorously stated that he had no quarrel with the Prince of Wales who was named in the oath along with King George.

There was other curious behavior. The day before the Battle of Monmouth, Lee sent a message to Colonel Daniel Morgan, hero of Saratoga, that the upcoming battle would take place the day after next. This communication caused Morgan's expert rifle regiment to miss the action and the opportunity to pick off Clinton's soldiers on the march.[104] Lee also advised Washington to hold back his troops from the route Clinton might take in his evacuation from Philadelphia to New York so Clinton's "superior" army would not outmaneuver and overrun Washington's army in that terrain. Coincidentally or not, Washington's positioning almost put him out of range to strike once the intelligence arrived verifying Clinton's route.

In Washington's council of war meeting on June 27, 1778, the day before the Battle of Monmouth, Lee was offered the command of the main strike force due to his seniority. He refuted the attack plan, insisting that the Continental troops were no match for the British force, and refused the command. He reasserted his privilege after Lafayette was given the assignment and subsequently led the flower of Washington's army the next day in the attack against Clinton's rear. While no battle is easy, given the time, place, and assets Lee commanded, Clinton should have been forced to surrender at least part of his force while the rest galloped on to New York. Even a British combatant, Charles Stedman, reported that Clinton's flanks could have easily been turned and the army lost if Lee had pressed in after approving Wayne's request for reinforcements.[105] Wayne's and Lafayette's dragoons were poised to split Cornwallis's assembling front and turn their flanks before the British could respond effectively to a multifaceted attack. Instead, Lee skirmished sheepishly with their rear as the British refaced like mad hornets in the sweltering heat. He quickly ordered a retreat, allowing the British to close ranks, consolidate their forces, and attack with a vengeance. Strangely, Lee issued no other substantive orders.

Washington arrived on the scene, suspecting something amiss. He immediately confronted Lee between expletives with this interesting question of character: "My God, General Lee. What are you all about?" Washington arrived in time to relieve Lee and take command of an army in full retreat, and after hard fighting, the day was brought to a draw. According to British custom, the Americans won because they held the field at day's end. Clinton disputed that tradition because he asserted that the battlefield was of little value, that his mission was to conduct his troops to New York, which he did. Coincidently or not, General Charles Lee's and General Henry Clinton's armies met in battle on June 28, 1778—exactly two years after the Battle of Charlestown, where Clinton similarly refused to call his withdrawal from the field "a defeat." If Clinton planned the Monmouth battle date in anticipation of London newspaper headlines redeeming him for his failure at Charlestown to extinguish the revolution in 1776 before it could get started can only be speculated. Whether a victory or draw for the Americans, General Washington credited General Nathanael Greene and General Anthony Wayne to

Congress for saving the day.[106] Clinton's forces had been stopped, and they slipped away in the night. As usual, Charles Lee was spectacular with words but short on deed. He claimed the success at Monmouth as he had done in Charlestown.

The General Staff and Congress disagreed. Lee was court-martialed and charged with three offenses but not treason. He was convicted on all counts. General Lee was suspended from duty, never to return to the Continental Army. Trying him for treason could have nipped the new French alliance in the bud, a risk no one wished to take. Congress had established a death penalty for treason on November 7, 1775, but a Lee trial on that charge would have probably made the Continental command appear to the French as either naïve or incompetent. After his conviction on lesser charges, Lee insulted Baron de Steuben and publicly insulted Washington in letters to Congress and printed in a Pennsylvania newspaper during his court-martial proceedings. These actions drew two duel challenges—one from Steuben and the other from Lieutenant Colonel John Laurens of South Carolina. Lee accepted the challenge from Laurens and placated the not-so-English-fluent de Steuben with his German language fluency. After a bullet grazed Lee and Lee's usual puzzling words spilled forth, honor was satisfied. Lee was silently removed from the international spotlight about the same time British general Prevost launched a successful attack capturing Savannah, Georgia, in January of 1779.

Charles Lee had been in Savannah in 1776, so he was familiar with its defenses.[107] Whether Lee drew out the defenses of Savannah (and Charlestown) to British Intelligence major John Andre during his paroled captivity in New York is subject to debate. The official British version is that an enslaved person showed Prevost the secret way in. Lee's "period of confinement" aboard the warship HMS Centurion in New York harbor in early 1778 would have kept secret discussions and contacts out of the public eye. Normally a high-ranking prisoner would be regularly visited by the head of British Intelligence to obtain detailed information, including city-fort defenses and layouts over much flattery and many good bottles of wine. Major John Andre would have been that sophisticated and equally well-educated officer to "converse" with the cooperative Lee. Andre was hung as a spy in 1780 for recruiting another American traitor, General Benedict Arnold, into the British army and for being caught out of uniform with detailed plans of the defenses at West Point. Even though there is no evidence of specific conversations between Lee and Andre, a map of Charlestown drawn in Andre's artistic hand survived him. There are eyewitness accounts that Andre infiltrated Charlestown while it was under siege in 1780 by impersonating a Virginia backwoodsman. He could have made the Charlestown sketch without Lee's help. Irrespective of how General Prevost received the defense plans of Savannah, which showed the secret way in, the British now had their foothold in the Lower South. From Savannah, the British could conceptualize an updated Southern Strategy plan to capture the entire South and cut that region off from the Northern states as Lee had convinced them they must do two years earlier.

Southern Strategy 4.0 became the overarching operational plan to take Charlestown, then the Carolinas, and then Virginia, thereby sundering the confederated states. Remarketed as Clinton's brainchild, this new plan, informed by the others that came before it, would end the military stalemate, put down the rebellion, and reestablish royal authority throughout the South, thereby severing the Northern states from the Southern states as Lee had recommended. Since Whitehall recognized the strategic consistency, it gave Clinton everything he requested to get the job done his way.

Sir Henry Clinton had learned from past mistakes. Clinton's first invasion plan, Southern Strategy 1.0, failed at the mouth of Charlestown harbor in 1776 because it was one dimensional and an up-the-middle attempt to skirt a well-defended narrows. The 1.0 plan was conceived to conquer the Carolinas, then Georgia, and then begin the trek northward to complete the conquest of the South. General Howe abandoned the second plan, Southern Strategy 2.0, in early 1777 before it launched from New York because Washington's army was impolitely rampaging across New Jersey. The troops preparing to embark on an attack against Charlestown were retasked before embarkation to contain Washington after his victory at Trenton. The third Southern Strategy, 3.0, began by General

Prevost capturing Savannah, Georgia, in December 1778. That plan involved gaining a foothold at the bottom of the colonies, which British troops could support from their garrisons in East Florida. After subduing Georgia, British forces could move up the coast to take Charlestown by land. In May 1779, Southern Continental general Benjamin Lincoln's army moved toward Georgia to engage Prevost's forces maneuvering outside Savannah. General Prevost maneuvered around Lincoln, marched his three-thousand-man force outside Charlestown, and ordered their surrender. His gamble would have worked if not for the obstinance of Christopher Gadsden and the efforts of Continental general William Moultrie.

General Prevost withdrew back to Savannah, leaving death and destruction in his wake, and successfully repulsed a combined French and American attack in October 1779. Georgia fell under royal government control and was repatriated as a province of Great Britain. With three British trials and errors to capture Charlestown and Charles Lee's end goal in Clinton's mind to split the South off from the confederation, Lord Henry launched his Southern Strategy 4.0 campaign by landing troops on Johns Island, South Carolina, in April 1780. He would commence a proper European-type siege on Charlestown, force the surrender of the city and the Southern Continental Army, establish Southern British headquarters there, and reestablish royal authority in South Carolina. General Clinton's orders from King George and Lord Germain were clear: "I am commanded by his Majesty to aquaint you that the recovery of the Southern Provinces and the prosecution of the war, by pushing your conquests from south to north, is to be considered as the chief and principal object for the employment of all forces under your command .... until it is accomplished."[108]

The operational plan to execute Southern Strategy 4.0 worked perfectly in the beginning. In May, Continental Major General Benjamin Lincoln surrendered Charlestown and the entire Southern Continental Army. The state militia followed suit. Over five thousand Continental troops, the entire officer corps, thousands of Patriot militia forces, several Congressmen, several signers of the Declaration of Independence, arms, ammunition, and immense supplies were captured. According to a distinguished historian, "The estates of the political prisoners were sequestered. Clinton made no effort to prevent his men from plundering private property. He ordered them to chop down the Liberty Tree."[109] In June, General Clinton turned over the new Southern British headquarters and armies to General Cornwallis. Cornwallis dispatched the forces of Lieutenant Colonel Tarleton, Major Patrick Ferguson, Major James Wemyss, Loyalist Lieutenant Colonel Thomas Brown, Major James Dunlap, Colonel Nisbet Balfour, and Colonel Francis Lord Rawdon to establish a system of forts throughout the newly-rejoined province of South Carolina and "pacify" the entire state.

By September 1780, the British army had conquered Georgia, Charlestown, and South Carolina and was poised to take North Carolina and Virginia. General Phillips and newly-minted British general Benedict Arnold were in the process of softening up Virginia with a proper reign of terror, beginning with the burning of Richmond. In Georgia and South Carolina, occupied cities, towns, waterways, and crossroads had been fortified and primarily staffed by Provincials and Loyalist militia troops and complemented with regulars, Hessians, and Native Americans. Crown forces had destroyed two American armies, one under General Lincoln defending Charleston and another one sent by Congress under General Gates at Camden. General Clinton returned to New York in June with the conquest of South Carolina and Georgia secured: "I had soon … the satisfaction … to see all my measures throughout the course of this expedition crowned with the most flattering success. For, before my departure for New York … almost the whole country … had submitted without opposition." The Southern Command was subsequently turned over to General Lord Cornwallis to complete Southern Strategy 4.0 but not risk South Carolina. General Clinton made clear to Cornwallis that maintaining possession of Charlestown "is always to be considered as the principle object."[110] With that prime directive stated, Clinton also made clear that Cornwallis was to recover North Carolina, and possibly assist in Virginia operations after the Carolinas were safe from any attack.

Cornwallis had ideas of his own. From Southern British headquarters, he wrote in the summer of 1780 that resistance in Georgia and South Carolina had been broken except "for a few scattering militias."[111] The British now occupied both provinces, and they controlled an interconnected network of solid forts along all major roads, rivers, and waterway crossings. The London newspapers constantly crowed about the reuniting of "Little London" and the resounding defeat of General Gates, their nemesis from Saratoga, at a place called Camden, South Carolina, named after Lord Camden, Charles Pratt. If Cornwallis could follow his Camden victory by conquering North Carolina and Virginia, he would be in a prime position to become the ruling governor-general of the British American provinces as the rebellion crumbled.

Absolute power has a way of bringing out the beast in the prideful. Summer's intense heat in 1780 brought on an unrestrained reign of terror to punish the treacherous rebels into submission. Cornwallis was finally on his own to conduct a scorched-earth war as the king wanted. In August, General Cornwallis provided an after-action report to Lord George Germain with this synopsis: "The rebel forces being at present dispersed, the internal commotions and insurrections in the province will now subside. But I shall give directions to inflict exemplary punishment on some of the guiltiest in hopes to deter others in the future."[112] With martial law and the Southern British war machine under his complete control, he could do as he pleased to subjugate suspected rebels into total submission. Cornwallis was still smarting from the rebels keeping him from attending his wife's deathbed in 1777 and sniping his men off Sullivan's Island in 1776. He was now in authority to punish the insurrectionists just as his Uncle Edward had done thirty-five years earlier during the Scottish uprising. General Edward Cornwallis led his regiment into the Scottish Highlands to completely subjugate the population under explicit orders to "plunder, burn and destroy" and was rewarded with the governorship of Nova Scotia (New Scotland). Edward Cornwallis's commander, the Duke of Cumberland, clarified his task: "You have positive orders to bring no more prisoners to the camp." To Cornwallis, the rebellion in the Lower South was a continuation of the Scottish uprising

(Jacobite Rebellion).[113] He would ascend into the Carolina highlands and unleash the same beasts of hell and tools of barbarity to permanently put down this rebellion as his uncle had done in the Scottish Highlands.

Scots-Irish Pre-revolutionary Migration to America (QR code accessible)

Encouraged but publicly denied by Whitehall, human rights became a thing of the past in prosecuting the war in America. Lord George Germain made clear "to pursue the most vigorous measures for reducing his [King George's] rebellious subjects in North America to obedience."[114] Code words such as a "pacification" and "reduction" were used when issuing orders to field commanders. With conciliatory Clinton gone, the British occupation of the Lower South took on an unmerciful character that created widespread hostility toward Crown forces. The British military seized many estates without due process, often resulting in the enslaved exchanging one master for another.[115] In contravention of the written terms of surrender, Continental prisoners were placed on prison ships in deplorable conditions, resulting in their deaths. Empowered Loyalists and banditti, bestowed with military rank, prowled the countryside in each military district. Crimes of massacres, sexual assault, torture, murder, burnings, and plunder went uninvestigated and unpunished. Lord Cornwallis's general orders gave broad license to the ends justifying the means without being restrained by the record of written mission orders. Verbal orders would do just fine in purging the countryside. The Crown's quest "to completely pacify the country" with Cornwallis at the helm would hold no bounds.

Cornwallis's cavalry detachments would pursue suspected rebels or anyone deemed not loyal to the Crown, setting the tone for brutality across the South.[116] There would be no effort toward harmonious reconciliation, just punishment and total submission. Treason and rebellion were criminal acts exempt from the conventions of war and judicial due process Tarleton's Green Dragoons set the standard for pacification by massacring a surrendering Continental army at the Waxhaws under Colonel Buford of about 350 men. This incident became known as "Tarleton's Quarter," an oxymoron used as a motivator to inspire partisans to reenter the war and retaliate.[117] "The virtue of humanity was totally forgotten," wrote a British combatant, John Stedman, suffering from a bout of guilt after following orders to massacre the defenseless. Tarleton himself wrote in his after action report: "I have cut 170 Off'rs and Men to pieces."[118] Soldiers became murderers. Lieutenant Colonel Tarleton earned the nom de guerre of "The Butcher," just as the Duke of Cumberland had in Scotland years before. Cornwallis adopted the "bring me no prisoners" policy that conquered Scotland and made his Uncle Edward a national hero.

The Waxhaws slaughter was only the beginning of the holocaust in the South. Villages, hamlets, and homesteads across the Carolinas and Georgia saw indiscriminate murder, pillaging, rape, and burnings, not unlike those depicted in the fictional film *The Patriot.* Small Quaker towns such as Saxe Goethe ceased to exist. In addition to these atrocious acts, Cornwallis ordered Presbyterian churches burned because they were "houses of sedition," preaching rights of conscience and rebellion. British Major James Wemyss burned Indiantown Presbyterian Church as a "sedition shop."[119] Cornwallis curtailed freedom of religion by reinstituting the Anglican Church as the official state-sponsored religion with compulsory financial support (tithing) whether a person attended or not. British soldiers confiscated guns, powder, food, crops, and livestock from both friend and foe. "Reduction" and "pacification" ruled the land.

Just as everything was going Cornwallis's way, two events occurred that altered history. First, the Continental Congress appointed thirty-eight-year-old Major General Nathanael Greene from Rhode Island to the Southern Command (after first voting to send General Washington).

Greene had fought Cornwallis in the North. He was a humble yet confident Quaker dedicated to the service and well-being of others. As an excellent servant leader who brought people together, Greene had an insatiable enthusiasm for the cause of liberty and liberty of conscience. He was an expert in logistics and training raw troops in close-order drills. Greene was also Washington's best friend and chief strategist.[120]

ONE CENT STAMP OF WASHINGTON AND GREENE,
COURTESY OF THE *US POSTAL SERVICE.*

Nathanael Greene was a gifted battlefield commander. He stopped General Howe at the Battle of Brandywine and General Clinton at the Battle of Monmouth. He worked with two other Continental Generals to stop the British from conquering Rhode Island. General Greene won the critical Battle of Springfield with about one-fourth of the British and Hessian troops he faced. The British newspaper, *The Reading Mercury and Oxford Gazette* reported the following about Greene on January 4, 1779:

"General Greene who now commands in New England, is the person who the Americans look up to as their leader, if Mr. Washington [sic] should die or be rendered incapable of service. ..... he is esteemed one of the best officers living and is generally styled the American Wolfe [British hero Major General James Wolfe credited with defeating the French in Canada]." Next to Washington, Greene was America's best General.

General Washington recommended Major General Nathanael Greene to be appointed to the Southern Command in October 1780. Congress conferred the appointment shortly thereafter. Greene's assigned area of operations stretched from Pennsylvania to Georgia, half of which was under the military control of Britain. He was given complete authority to operate how he saw fit over all matters, military and civilian. Rarely in American history has one person been given so much power.

With Greene taking command of the South, trust, coordination, and communications between the Northern and Southern armies in both theaters would become optimal. Coordination with state and congressional elected officials would become optimal. This unity of effort would prove itself out leading up to the Yorktown entrapment. In addition to his experience with the Culper Code, Greene's fluency in Greek was a plus in secret messaging. In short, Greene was a match for British general Lord Cornwallis, his opposite in the Southern Command. Cornwallis condescendingly referred to Greene as "my little forge man," referring to Greene's civilian occupation as an iron foundry proprietor and status as a "nonprofessional" soldier. When Washington appointed Greene and Congress confirmed him, there was practically no organized army for him to command, just remnants of two defeated armies and a handful of revenge-minded, scattered militias. Greene was the right man, at the right time, with the right ethics to win back the South.

The second event that changed everything occurred on August 18, 1780. Two days after the British defeat of the American Army sent to the South under Gates, General Lord Cornwallis issued the following general orders to his commanders in the field occupying South Carolina. He wrote: "I have given orders that all the inhabitants of this province [South Carolina], who have submitted, and who have taken a part in this revolt, *shall be punished with the greatest vigor; they shall be imprisoned, and their whole property taken from them or destroyed*. I have likewise directed, that compensations should be made out of their effects, to persons who have been plundered and oppressed by them. I have ordered in the most positive manner, that every militia-man who had born arms with us, and had afterwards joined the enemy, *should be immediately hanged*. I have now sir, only to desire that you will take the most vigorous measures to extinguish the rebellion in the district you command and that you will obey, in the strictest manner, the directions I have given in this letter, relative to the treatment of this country."[121] This general order escalated the internecine war beyond control.

Civilians no longer had an option to remain neutral; they had to choose which side they were on. In a direct order, Cornwallis communicated the king's wish to "take the most vigorous measures to extinguish the rebellion" directly to all in his chain of command. This communication immediately intensified the political war between Whigs and Tories—Whigs supporting the Patriot independence cause, and Tories, or Loyalists, supporting the King's conquest of America as his loyal subjects. Loyalist militias sprang up with their only purpose being to murder, plunder, and burn. Cornwallis's policies placed him in a position of plausible deniability if he just sat back and let the country depopulate through internecine warfare. He awarded promotions to the most effective "pacifiers." (Tarleton went from Captain to Lieutenant Colonel in less than one year.) Doing so gave implicit license to British, Hessian, Provincial, and Loyalist troops to administer any level of punishment to suspected rebels or uncooperative civilians without having any courts of justice interfering. Terror and brutality became the sanctioned law of the land.

Cornwallis's new order replaced Commanding General Clinton's conciliatory articles of capitulation terms bilaterally agreed to at the surrender of Charlestown. Those terms encompassed all Patriot forces in South Carolina and Georgia. Clinton's terms were rendered in "the mildest spirit of moderation," granting pardons, peace, protection, and reconciliation in exchange for simply pledging allegiance to Britain and living in harmony under loyalty to the king's rule: conquest by conciliation. Cornwallis's new conditions constituted a unilateral change to the contractual agreement made with the Continental and militia regiments defending Charlestown, who accepted the British offer of "unarmed neutrality" as a condition for their surrender in exchange for the king's forces providing protection. Clinton's agreement assured Patriots throughout the South that they would not be asked to take up arms against their countrymen. In return, Patriots were required to stand down in their efforts to fight the king's forces and pledge their harmonious loyalty to the Crown so all could live in peace and prosperity under British protection.

In contrast, Lord Cornwallis's punitive new order required every parolee to take up arms with the British against their countrymen or hang as a traitor.[122] By issuing this new order, the British parole agreement (and ethics) with the neutralized Patriots was broken. Staying out of the war as a noncombatant was no longer an option. The forced choice was to fight for the king and against your countrymen, or your family would be massacred. Enforcement took place in the field at each local British commander's discretion, at each town, village, and homestead. Empowered by this order, Loyalist militias and British troops went rampaging throughout the South seeking plunder and revenge for their lost comrades. Citizens of all political leanings became victims of indiscriminate violence. Join His Majesty's forces on the spot and provide His Majesty's forces with their food and housing desires, or have your home burned, your men hung, your possessions plundered, and your women "insulted." This oppressive order and General Greene's appointment to the Southern Army command was the beginning of the end of the British occupation of the South and the defeat of their Southern Strategy 4.0 plan for winning the war.

According to General Clinton's memoir, *The American Rebellion*, "Great Britain was more inclined to reconciliation than to punishment" when Charlestown and the rest of South Carolina and Georgia surrendered. Clinton and Admiral Arbuthnot, who assisted in the capture of Charlestown, acted in the character of commissioners for restoring peace, issuing pardons to all for their past treasonable offenses to regain peace and quickly reestablish trade with English merchants. Clinton assigned

Brigadier General James Patterson, commandant of the city and civil affairs provincewide, a congenial person, to run the British civil administration, thereby "restoring tranquility and order to the country." In June 1780, Patterson was transferred to New York and replaced by Lieutenant Colonel Nisbet Balfour, a "proud, haughty Scot" who subscribed to Lord North's objective of treating the inhabitants and prisoners as insurrectionist rebels, repressing them entirely by using the harshest of means. Cornwallis's new policy was the king's preferred method of completely extinguishing the rebellion and permanently reannexing the Southern provinces. In one fell swoop, Clinton's plan to effect a harmonious reconciliation and reunification with Southern Patriots was superseded by Balfour and Cornwallis's capricious policy of vengeful oppression without respect to civil rights or due process.

But Cornwallis knew that policy had worked in Scotland thirty-five years earlier, and from what he could see, the Lower South was just a continuation of the war between upper and lower Scots. Assisted by the American High Treason Act, introduced to Parliament by Lord North, Cornwallis could ignore the traditional articles of war stipulating humane treatment of adversaries and use whatever necessary means to crush the rebellion. His subordinates filled the basement of the Exchange Building in Charlestown with men and women of influence who would not sign the new oath of absolute loyalty and submission to the king's forces. Over sixty Patriot leaders in the city were arrested and sent to the dungeons at Saint Augustine. Suspected sympathizers were banished to Philadelphia as their homes were confiscated. Loyalists and Provincial British troops were given wholesale license to terrorize as they saw fit to pacify the countryside. Britain's Habeas Corpus Act and the rule of law were canceled to empower the military to silence dissenters and seize food, shelter, and any plunder they might fancy. The instant loss of civil rights, property, and life or limb were at the whim of British and Loyalist officers.

The future president of the United States, Andrew Jackson, witnessed this treatment firsthand in 1780 and 1781. He and his brothers assisted their mother in May and June 1780 at the Waxhaws meeting house to treat the wounded survivors of Banastre Tarleton's Waxhaw Massacre. Andrew saw the hacked bodies of over 150 Patriot soldiers taken to the meeting house to spend their dying hours in agony. He heard their testimony describing the hundreds of Patriots cut down after they surrendered and abidingly threw their weapons to the ground. Jackson would experience the same British "bring me no prisoners" cruelty in later months.

In early 1781, as the British were wrecking the home of a neighbor Whig (Patriot sympathizer) in the Waxhaws, Andrew, thirteen, and his brother Robert, fourteen, were discovered hiding in the house. The British officer in charge ordered Andrew to clean his boots, to which he replied, "Sir, I am a prisoner of war and expect to be treated as such."[123] The officer responded by swinging his sword at Jackson's head, and Andrew parried with his left hand, leaving him with a severe injury to his fingers and a gash across his head. These scars would remain with him throughout his life. Robert was likewise hit with the officer's sword, which "sprawled him across the room." His brother later died from his wounds and the smallpox he contracted while imprisoned among the infected prisoners at Camden jail. Andrew barely survived after his negotiated release by his mother and the cold trek home.

Some months later, his mother traveled about 160 miles to Charlestown harbor to care for relatives held aboard prison ships suffering from starvation, smallpox, and cholera. She contracted cholera nursing Patriot prisoners in Charlestown and died, leaving Andrew an orphan at age fourteen. (A granite marker memorial to Elizabeth Jackson may be found on the College of Charleston campus today.) The British would rue their inhumanity to the Jacksons in the next war with America. At the Battle of New Orleans, General Andrew Jackson destroyed their great army sent to claim the Mississippi and middle America. But Jackson still had the Revolution to get through.

One thing was clear about Southern Strategy 4.0: it featured terror and punishment for all when Cornwallis took over. Cornwallis likely remembered his humiliating defeat on South Carolina's Long Island in June 1776, trying to get his regiment across Breach Inlet to assault Fort Sullivan. After King George and his ministers learned of the capture of Charlestown in 1780, Whitehall's official British military policy was to apply indiscriminate fire and sword to completely extinguish the rebellion, just as Britain had done to crush the Scottish Jacobite Rebellion of 1745. The British press would print an editorial cartoon depicting British soldiers lashing a bound rebel with "13 stripes" for treason. Lessons must be taught for disloyalty to the benevolent king so revolution would never enter the minds of "his beloved subjects" again. These extreme policy changes took effect in June 1780 after Clinton's departure to New York.

In August 1780, Cornwallis appointed John Cruden, commissioner of sequestered estates, to carry out these orders and formalize property confiscation. Cornwallis empowered this office "to seize the estates real and personal of all such rebels and adherents to, and abettors of, rebellion… For the publick benefit and advantage." Cruden used his broad authority to confiscate about four hundred estates and more than five thousand enslaved laborers to provide food, land, and housing to the British army while displacing, imprisoning, or executing their "rebel" inhabitants.[124] Property confiscation was another punitive measure to compel renewed oaths of loyalty to the Crown, enlistment into the king's forces, and to compel the population to service the whims of His Majesty's officers, contrary to the original articles of surrender.

Conversely, several months later, in November 1780, the strategy Greene developed on his ride down to Charlotte from West Point was based on winning over the hearts and minds of the Southern population. Greene had inherited an internecine war out of control, fueled by British policy: a civil war within a colonial rebellion within a ruthless occupation by a foreign government. Indiscriminate British and Loyalist atrocities were reported throughout the reclaimed provinces, with whole villages, hamlets, and homesteads slaughtered and plundered. With Loyalists, Provincial troops, and Native American allies doing the lion's share of the slaughtering, Cornwallis maintained an official position of a civil war beyond his control and the wanton violence throughout the South not of his doing. Officially, he was a lord and gentleman who would never approve of such outright inhumanity.

Cornwallis's harsh subjugation policy would soon immobilize his northward blitzkrieg. Cornwallis's army had occupied Charlotte, North

Carolina, briefly in September 1780 but withdrew back to Winnsboro, South Carolina, after his left wing was destroyed at the Battle of King's Mountain. Cornwallis's left-wing commander, Colonel Patrick Ferguson, had openly bragged that his Provincial regiment would be coming to the western Carolina mountains to lay waste to the mountain men by fire and sword, and ravage their women "as he had done in the South Carolina Backcountry."[125] Ferguson's admissions and threats resulted in over a thousand mountain men forming an army that destroyed the Colonel's forces, killed him, mutilated his body, and hung his men who had committed the worst atrocities.

With these angry mountain men on Cornwallis's flank and his Provincial cavalry commander, Banastre Tarleton, bedridden with malaria, Cornwallis was compelled to withdraw from Charlotte back into South Carolina, leaving central and western North Carolina unconquered. Tar Heel Loyalist militias were left waiting at the altar. His first attempt to conquer the state ended in failure.

Cornwallis's setback illustrated to Greene the importance of treating inhabitants respectfully and the penalty of being oppressive. If Greene's reconstituted forces could provide hope and "protective trust," as Charles Lee recommended to the British, maybe he could turn the oppressed against their oppressors. Cornwallis's terror war left inhabitants with nothing but fear and nothing left to lose.

Cornwallis's temporary absence in western North Carolina gave Greene the needed time to attract local recruits and patch together a credible army. The British withdrawal from Charlotte and Greene's arrival in Hillsboro showed that the American army had retaken central North Carolina with the Overmountain Men allies controlling the western mountains, keeping the Cherokee and Creek British allies at bay. Although Georgia and South Carolina had been conquered by the British, Greene's presence just across the border gave South Carolinians hope.[126] "While I breathe, I hope" became their underground motto (and eventually their state motto). Rebellions are won by hope and a commitment to liberty or death after fear loses its power to control. With hope on the rise, urgently needed recruits and scattered units from past defeats began coming in at Continental army headquarters in Hillsboro and Charlotte.

Upon taking command of the Southern Army, Greene had a critical ethical situation that had to be dealt with immediately, setting the tone of his command. General Horatio Gates, Greene's predecessor, had abandoned his army under attack at the first Battle of Camden in late August 1780. Gates was accused of cowardice and had requested a court of inquiry to clear his name. General Washington requested that Greene conduct the investigation using specified officers upon his arrival.[127] Gates would be the fourth senior officer in Washington's inner circle to face a court-martial since 1777 (Benedict Arnold, Robert Howe, and Charles Lee were the other three). After taking command on December 3, Greene formally thanked Gates for the polite manner in which he introduced Greene to his new command and polled his officers, who unanimously agreed that a court of inquiry was impractical at that time. The officers Washington had requested were "not available." Gates was informed of the decision, and the tense situation was defused. Soldiers siding with Gates would stay on with Greene. Gates would quietly retire, allowing the focus to be on Cornwallis rather than punishing suspected cowardice. Greene's skillful handling of the situation earned the allegiance of many of Gate's followers to his command.

Patriots in the Lower South were desperate for a trustworthy and competent leader. When Greene took over the "so-called Southern army," he described it to General Henry Knox on October 29, 1780, as "rather a shadow than a substance, having only an imaginary existence."[128] The situation was grim. "The men had little or no clothing, there were no wagons or other means of transportation, there was but little ammunition, there was no organized medical department, and there was no money to purchase supplies; the men were dispirited by defeat, and they were in the habit of going home when they felt so inclined and returning at their pleasure." With no gunpowder manufactured in the United States, the few soldiers with arms had little or none. Those with reliable gunpowder had little or no shot or a working bayonet to put them on equal combat terms with the British. Soldiers had inadequate clothing to keep them warm in the onslaught of winter. To top matters off, Greene was responsible for coordinating with state governors from Delaware southward to have their states send men and supplies. General Washington's orders to Greene were, "I give you no particular instructions…but I rely upon your abilities and exertions for everything." Southern Continental soldier numbers were few and scattered, and their organization, equipment, discipline, and training provided no evidence of a force capable of offensive or defensive operations. Shadow Patriots and abused inhabitants of all stripes throughout the South had no one to lead them out of hell.

Major General Nathanael Greene would change all that. He immediately began to set up his intelligence operations to acquire situational awareness and enemy intentions. Simultaneously, Greene began to build an army from scattered elements and novice volunteers. Greene had to obtain supplies, organize and train a core combat-ready force, and coordinate with detached state militia commanders. He wrote to Colonel Francis Marion on December 4, 1780, requesting that Marion stay in place to keep up a "Partizan War and preserve the tide of sentiment among the people as much as possible in our favour."[129] Greene enlisted Marion to set up and run a spy network in the low country, including Charlestown. "Spys are the eyes of an Army, and without them, a General is always groping in the dark and can neither secure himself or annoy his enemy. It is of the highest importance that I get the earliest information of any reinforcements which may arrive at Charleston or leave the town to join Lord Cornwallis." Greene further instructed Marion on training spies, maintaining secrecy, and getting reimbursed for spy payments or expenses.[130] Greene needed the state militia groups in the Carolinas and Georgia, like Marion's men, to gather intelligence and harass the enemy to buy precious time.

General Francis Marion was one of the most important regiment militia leaders of the war. Known today as "The Father of US Army Special Forces," Marion held a colonel's commission in the Continental Army as well as a general's commission in the South Carolina state militia. When Charlestown fell to the British in 1780, Marion was forty-eight years old with a lifetime of successful military leadership experience. General

Marion conducted a partisan, or guerrilla war against the British occupation of South Carolina, operating primarily in the Cainhoy-Santee-Pee Dee-Georgetown regions north of Charlestown. (The more modern term of "guerrilla war" is similar to the terms "partisan" or "partizan war" used to describe an irregular military force not incorporated into a regular army which opposes control of an area by a foreign power, lives off the land, and disperses when confronted by a larger, opposing regular army.) His knowledge of the great cypress swamps and giant live oak and pine forests enabled his "flex force" to prevent the British from securing territory above the confluence of the Cooper and Wando Rivers to North Carolina. Operating from hidden swamp base camps, Marion and his men would strike enemy columns moving up from Charlestown along the King's Highway and northwestward to the Great Wagon Road that were tasked to man and supply British forts. As a result of Marion's efforts, the British were hampered in their efforts to "pacify" or control these areas throughout their occupation; they had to keep scarce regulars in the Low Country on security details rather than marching with their invasion forces northward. Clandestine food production to supply the Continental Army and state militias continued from farms (plantations) located along the Santee River, and General Marion became known as the Swamp Fox. Lieutenant Colonel Banastre Tarleton, who gave Marion the name, admitted that "the devil himself could not catch him" after failing in his mission to destroy him.

General Francis Marion had a wealth of military experience. He was a veteran of a Cherokee War, a French-Cherokee War, the First Battle of Charlestown at Fort Sullivan, and the joint French-American operation against Savannah in 1779. General Marion was a superb horseman and trainer of troops in dragoon fighting, hit-and-run attacks, night fighting, and ambushes. He was an expert in the use of marsh tacky horses, which enabled his men to navigate swamps and strike the enemy when they least expected it. Marsh tacky horses paled in size to the massive cavalry horses employed by the British, but they withstood the heat and humidity well and ate much less. Tactically they were perfect for riding silently through swamps and forests while sensing their way through shallow water at night without becoming spooked. His men were rumored to chew Pinckneya tree bark to prevent and treat malaria and carry yarrow to treat battle wounds. Also, Marion knew how to keep his men healthy by limiting alcohol use, subsisting on vegetable and fish diets, and using apple cider vinegar for purifying drinking water and treating injuries.

All in all, Marion was a proven military servant-leader. He knew the area of operations intimately, had the respect and confidence of Low Country residents, and had extensive knowledge of Native American fighting tactics and classic European warfare principles. Marion's men consisted of a rainbow of races, including free and enslaved Black men and Native Americans, as depicted in the famous *Sweet Potato Painting*. His famous motto was *Always Surprise Your Enemy*. Marion was a master of the swamp, living off the land and surprise attacks that hurt the British in many ways. Plus, he was a daring, ethical warrior, opposed to plunder and self-enrichment but totally committed to the cause of independence.

Getting Marion's spy network established was imperative for Greene's information and intelligence flow. Marion knew which people could keep a secret. British offensive operations originated from their Southern headquarters in Charlestown. The outlying areas were dominated by rain forest–like cypress swamps where Marion operated. Marion's network of spies, working in and around Charlestown, obtained advance knowledge of enemy intentions, strengths, plans, locations, and weaknesses. Messengers and messages between Charlestown, Camden, and Winnsboro, Cornwallis's command centers, had to be intercepted. This information would enable Greene to balance a lopsided British force and supply superiority equation.

Greene's trusted Third Regiment Cavalry Commander, Lieutenant Colonel William Washington, had just captured Rugeley's Fort in South Carolina on December 4. This support post for the Camden garrison was located thirteen miles north along Lynche's Creek and was assigned to running patrols and interdicting Patriot supplies. Washington captured the fort by fashioning a log to look like a cannon and ordering Rugeley to surrender or be destroyed by cannon fire. After their surrender, Lieutenant Colonel Washington interviewed about a hundred prisoners who provided valuable intelligence for Greene on British troop locations, strengths, intentions, assignments, orders, and leadership. Upon their surrender, prisoners received treatment with such dignity that their commander, Colonel Rugeley, agreed to become a double agent if exchanged and sent back to Charlestown.[131] Greene's intelligence network began taking shape.

General Greene had decided that fast-moving light cavalry forces would be the centerpiece of his plan to defeat the British Armies in the South. Lieutenant Colonel William Washington was one of Greene's best cavalry commanders. At twenty-eight years old, William had four years of experience as a combat leader covering six states and numerous battles. Among his many heroic exploits before forcing the surrender of Fort Rugeley, he saved dozens of men and possibly a Hessian turnabout during the Battle of Trenton. At a critical moment, he charged the enemy's line on foot toward a lit cannon to render it harmless, burning his hands in the process but saving his men and possibly the revolution. General Greene referred to Lieutenant Colonel Washington, a second cousin of George Washington, as "my right arm, my sword of Marcellus" William was an expert equestrian, horse trainer, dragoon trainer, and swordsman. According to his Charlestown girlfriend, Jane Elliott, who stitched his regimental flag from crimson drapes, William was a "dashing cavalryman." Washington figured prominently in Greene's plans to take back the Lower South in surveillance, screening, infantry support, cavalry charges, and joint operations with state militias.[132] Lieutenant Colonel William Washington would lead numerous special missions for Greene and become an essential resource in turning popular support to the Patriot cause in the Lower South.

Lt. Col. William Washington signed 18th century lithograph, author's private collection.

Greene knew that instilling and keeping public confidence by insisting on ethical conduct was crucial to victory. "Everything here depends upon opinion. If you lose the confidence of the people, you lose all support," he would emphasize.[133] The revolution depended on public trust, voluntary allegiance, turning Loyalists, and gaining the support of as many people as possible. Support was imperative for food, clothing, guns, powder, hard money, horses, passive resistance, and intelligence. Greene's army had few supplies.

By contrast, the British operated two hundred plantations to supply their forces with food; plus, they received daily shiploads of war supplies into Charlestown. These supplies would be dispersed to their forts and garrisons in the field via the rivers and main roads. Greene knew that the success of Cornwallis's strategy depended on His Lordship's army (1) conquering and fortifying an area, (2) raising a local militia to hold the area, (3) rooting out suspected rebels and obtaining the full cooperation of residents, and (4) moving on to take another area with the supply line behind him secured. Interrupting any of these four tactical objectives in each area of operations would eventually make holding territory impossible. Each area of operations was a link in the chain of British occupation. For Greene to have a chance of breaking apart that chain, he had to protect as many inhabitants as possible from British terror, limit Loyalist recruitment, interrupt supply lines, and limit the area the British could conquer or control. In essence, Greene and the Southern Continental Army had to win public confidence to make it impossible for the British to occupy land irrespective of battle outcomes.

The British reign of terror was everywhere. Cornwallis's regulars, Provincials, and Loyalist militias were looting indiscriminately, making little distinction between Loyalist or Patriot. However, the British lust for plundering diverted their attention away from completing their mission to secure the Lower South. Captain John Peebles of the infamous Black Watch wrote that the officers of the Royal Army and Navy "did not agree so well" about how the spoils of war would be divided, thereby creating a source of continuous contention and distraction. Captain Peebles wrote about "Carolina Crackers" offering "their services" to take revenge "against the rebels…the Hessians plunder methodically to a great distance in the Country."[134] British plunderings produced widespread misery and slaughter.

Allied Creeks and Cherokees were also committing atrocities against Patriot homesteads throughout the western regions of the Southern colonies. British commanders and their Indian superintendents were outsourcing scalping and torture to these tribes for intimidation, intelligence, revenge, and pacification. However, those atrocities caused many Loyalists to switch sides and join the Patriots to counterattack Native American incursions and undo British gains. Native American atrocities, ignited by the British with rum and weapons, also hardened Patriot resolve to fight both enemies as a matter of survival. General Andrew Pickens's brother was tortured at the stake as revenge for him rejoining the Patriot cause. Still, this act and others like it galvanized upstate militias to rout both enemies.[135] Rank barbarity was the fate awaiting Patriots who had surrendered under the Charlestown capitulation terms but did not comply with the Crown's new set of conditions.

South Carolina State General Andrew Pickens was one Patriot who would not subscribe to Cornwallis's new rules. Pickens was among the greatest militia commanders of the Revolutionary War. His ethics and accomplishments were rivaled only by General Francis Marion. After serving under the British in the Cherokee War of 1760–1761, Pickens wrote: "I learned something of british cruelty which I always abhorred."He was given the name of Skyagunsta (the Wizard Owl) by the Cherokee Nation after his reconnaissance platoon defeated a large force of warriors at Tomassee, South Carolina, in what became known as the Ring Fight, locally known as the Ring of Fire Fight. On August 10, 1776, approximately two hundred Cherokee warriors allied with the British surrounded Captain Andrew Pickens, leading about twenty-five expert riflemen. Pickens immediately formed his men into two defensive rings in the high, dry cane field, one ring inside the other. Seeing that the wind was at his back, Pickens ordered his men to ignite the dry cane with their flints at the outer ring. As the field fire moved toward the surging warriors, every other man within each circle would rise and fire at the attackers in successive sequence so that a steady and deadly barrage of six rounds was continuously traveling downrange. The loud popping of the burning cane sounded like gunfire, which added to the enemy's confusion caused by the heavy smoke in their eyes. Elements of the outer ring went to hand-to-hand combat just as Andrew's brother, Lieutenant Joseph Pickens, arrived with reinforcements and the warriors withdrew.[136] After-action reports listed seventy-five Cherokee dead and eleven militia killed in the battle. Captain Pickens was promoted to colonel for seeing clearly, acting wisely, and striking quickly—like a wizard owl. In December 1780, at forty-one years old, Andrew Pickens was made a South Carolina state general when he rejoined the cause after the British harassed his family in Long Canes without provocation while he was away. He and his men would join Greene's left wing under Continental general Daniel Morgan at Catawba River.

In contrast to the British policies of indiscriminate violence, widespread plundering, and "bring me no prisoners," General Greene issued orders to treat prisoners with respect and cease all plundering. "Repeatedly I urge militia commanders to put an end to plundering and promise severe punishment," he ordered.[137] He considered the practice wrong and damaging to the public support essential to success. Plundering led to retribution, which led to more plundering and retribution, which diverted attention away from mission assignments and liberating territory.

While Greene had direct control of his Continentals to prevent plundering and punish plunderers, he had to work through state militia commanders to stop the practices in their commands. For example, Greene wrote State General Francis Marion granting him the authority under a military court proceeding to prosecute marauders who had been caught plundering. If the offenses were of a capital punishment nature, Greene offered to send him a commission to hold such a court.[138] When impressment was necessary, Greene instructed all officers and militias that "the best compensation should be made them that our circumstances will permit." Loyalists and Patriots were equally compensated with certificates for horses and food. Impressment with compensation vouchers was to be used only as a last resort.

Greene made clear his standing orders regarding plundering to his officers: "You will exercise such discipline as well to effectually prevent plundering. If nothing else to stop this horrid business punnish every person who is detected in this scandalous practice by flogging them without further ceremony, and you have my authority for doing."[139] Protecting civilians not under British control while obtaining forage and supplies from them was imperative to winning hearts and minds. Greene's methods would lead the Lower South out of a continuous cycle of robbery, retribution, and genocide.

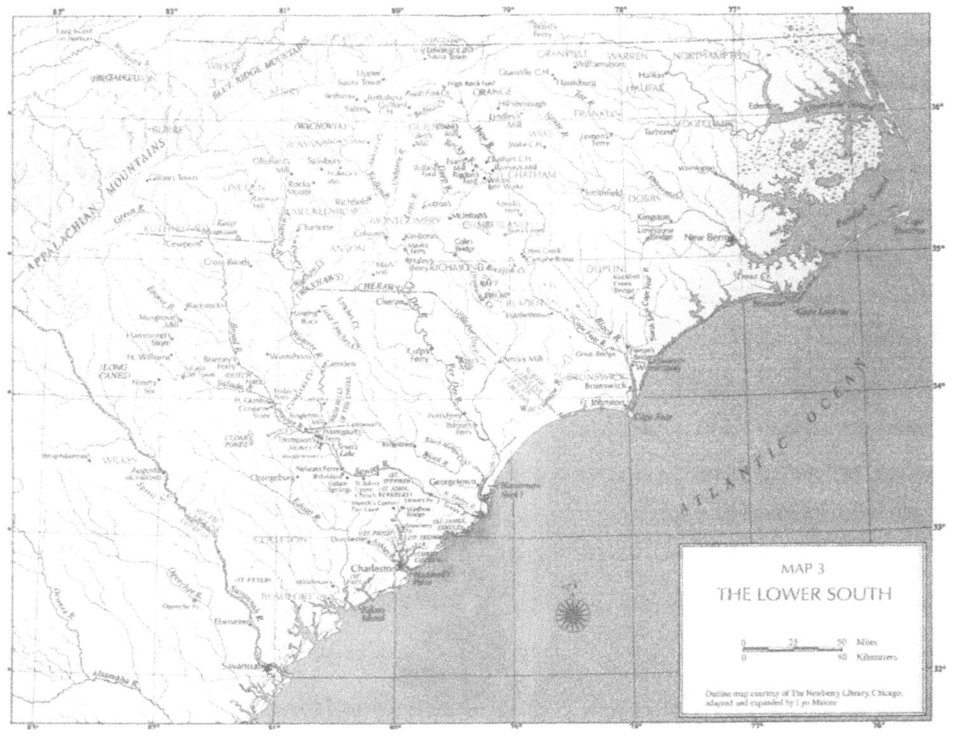

Lower South, 1780, map courtesy of the Newberry Library, Chicago, Ill, and UNC Press, adapted by Lyn Malone.

V.
TAKING THE INITIATIVE

Victory is the result of action.
—Sun Tzu, The Art of War

Once Greene became organized, he took the initiative. Crown forces would converge and crush his bedraggled army if he waited in place. On December 15, 1780, Greene received intelligence that General Cornwallis would renew his invasion of North Carolina and then Virginia.[140] To stop British barbarity and shine a light on their war policy, Greene wrote to Cornwallis to protest the house burnings of inhabitants who had been assured protection and security if they observed neutrality. Greene also protested the open bounty offered by Lord Rawdon, Cornwallis's second-in-command, for "bringing in the head of a deserter" and for Rawdon's circulars promising to whip any civilians helping deserters. Greene also protested Cornwallis's sending of South Carolina's congressional leaders to the Saint Augustine dungeon, contrary to the signed articles of capitulation. Then Greene acted.

In December 1780, Greene split his army, with General Daniel Morgan commanding his left wing, forcing Cornwallis to do the same. Cornwallis took the bait after a daring joint-force raid by Lieutenant Colonel William Washington deep behind enemy lines at Hammond's Store that destroyed a Loyalist militia plundering homesteads throughout the upcountry.[141] Washington's troops subsequently destroyed Fort

Williams near current-day Clinton, South Carolina, after the British and Loyalists abandoned the fort upon approach, despite their superiority in numbers and weaponry. Lieutenant Colonel Washington's attack appeared to Cornwallis to threaten the nearby British super-fort at Ninety-Six along the Charlestown Road supply line intersecting with the strategic Great Wagon Road.

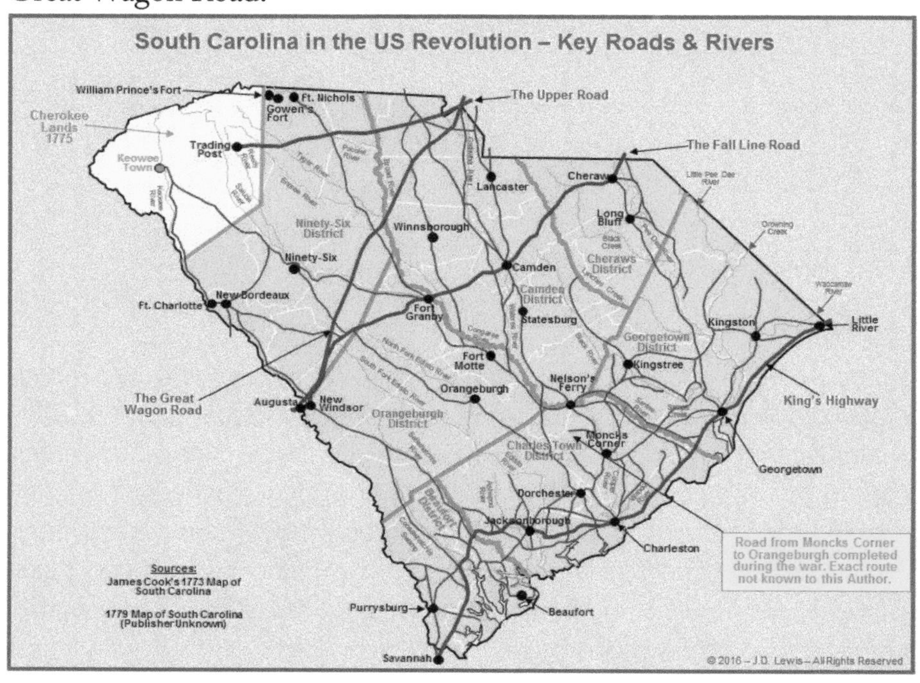

South Carolina in the US Revolution – key roads and rivers, courtesy of J.D. Lewis, www.carolana.com.

The raid on Fort Williams captured desperately needed arms, powder, wagons, ammunition, and horses to bring General Morgan's army up to full fighting capability. Lieutenant Colonel Washington's surprise attacks also provided a diversion for General Andrew Pickens and his two hundred Patriot followers in Long Canes (present-day Abbeville) to escape British house arrest and join Morgan's army after moving their families to safety. Washington's raid angered Cornwallis into splitting his army, assigning Lieutenant Colonel Tarleton to command his left wing. At the same time, Cornwallis and his main force waited for General Leslie to march up from Charlestown with fresh regulars. Cornwallis ordered the notorious Lieutenant Colonel Banastre "Bloody" Tarleton to track down and destroy Morgan. Instead, Morgan's Continental and militia forces destroyed Tarleton's army at Cowpens on January 17, 1781, with the help of General Pickens's men, Washington's Cavalry, and the weapons captured in the Hammond's Store-Fort Williams special operation.[142] Lieutenant Colonel Washington's enslaved orderly and regiment bugler, Collin, saved Washington's life by shooting one of Lieutenant Colonel Tarleton's officers as he was about to cut down Washington. Colonel Washington then struck Tarleton's sword, slicing off several of his fingers. (This scene is depicted in several famous paintings, including one by William Ranney.) Morgan prevented his men from massacring the surrendering British soldiers in retaliation for Tarleton's Quarter at the Waxhaws. In keeping with the Articles of War, the Patriots took over eight hundred prisoners even though their capture would put Morgan's army at a higher risk of interception by Cornwallis. So far, Greene's initiative was working.

Cowpens Battle Flag

With Cornwallis's defeated left wing taken prisoner and the possibility that Morgan could turn south to attack Fort Ninety-Six, Morgan had to be intercepted. Ninety-Six was the strategically located super-fort on the South Carolina frontier, serving as the central British forward operating base. It was also the strategic nexus for controlling the Lower South. This well-engineered, star-shaped fort stood at the intersection of the main road to Fort Granby and Charlestown going east and the road to Fort Rutledge and Fort George going west, connecting with the Cherokee Nation. The east road also intersected with the Great Wagon Road, which ran north to the Saluda River, Charlotte, and Philadelphia. Going south, the Great Wagon Road ran to the tri-forts at Augusta, Georgia, which guarded the Savanah River trade route straddling the South Carolina border. The Wagon Road ran along the fall line and terminated at the falls of Augusta. Control of the Great Wagon Road was imperative for the British to complete their conquest of the Southern states. They could move troops up along the Charlestown Road to Ninety-Six, then turn northward on the Wagon Road and progressively build a chain of forts and posts to Philadelphia as they conquered each state going northward. Fort Ninety-Six's span of control covered about a one-hundred-mile radius in the upcountry of South Carolina that stretched into the Appalachian Mountains, connecting them with their Cherokee and Creek allies. Fort Williams nearby and Fort Granby on the Congaree River were close support forts, while the British tri-forts at Augusta provided longer-range support in large numbers. These forts mainly were staffed with a cadre of British regulars, Provincial troops from New York and New Jersey, Loyalist militias from the Lower South, and Cherokee and Creek warriors supplied by various tribes. Fort Ninety-Six was the backbone of the British Southern Strategy because it enabled them to control the Georgia, South Carolina, and North Carolina mid-country. The Great Wagon Road was the logistical key to victory for the British conquest on its way northward. Fort Ninety-Six was the key to controlling the Great Wagon Road and the Lower South.

After Tarleton's defeat at Cowpens, Cornwallis was reinforced by General Alexander Leslie's 1,500-man force to help chase Morgan's army.

Morgan's army turned north rather than south toward Ninety-Six, so Cornwallis knew that Morgan intended to march his prisoners to the Winchester, Virginia, prison camp that held Saratoga survivors. Morgan reunited with Greene's main Southern Army in North Carolina one step ahead of Cornwallis intersecting him. With both armies reinforced, a flat-out chase ensued northward to the border of Virginia over about one month. This grand chase resulted in the degradation and isolation of Cornwallis's army, while Greene's relatively untrained "pickup" army became competent, reinforced, amply supplied, and disciplined. This forced march through the giant chestnut forests of North Carolina was slow going and debilitating for a British army untrained for such maneuvers and without a supply line.[143] Greene had planned for an all-out chase from river to river through North Carolina. Colonel Tadeusz Kosciuszko waterproofed Conestoga Wagons to rapidly cross rivers without unloading—a trick Greene learned as an anchor maker who shipped product across Rhode Island's many rivers. The chase also trained his cavalry regiments under Lieutenant Colonel Harry Lee and Lieutenant Colonel William Washington to become expert skirmishers, recon and intelligence units, screeners, and combat dragoons, using the immense forests to their advantage. On February 14, 1781, Greene's army made it to the swollen Dan River bordering Virginia and crossed, leaving no boats on the opposite shore for Cornwallis's army in the chase. Cornwallis could only watch like Captain Ahab watching his obsession slip away, knowing that General Greene would return on his terms to sink him one day. Virginia would provide Greene with safety, supplies, rest, and recruits. The great chase and on-the-job training mission were successful. Greene had built himself an army.

The hunted was soon to become the hunter. After being resupplied and receiving recruits, Greene crossed back into North Carolina to undermine Cornwallis's proclaimed conquest of that state. Cornwallis had been busy announcing the return of King George's rule throughout middle North Carolina along the Great Wagon Road, calling for Loyalists to join his forces. Greene's immediate operational concerns were to prevent Cornwallis from being reinforced by North Carolina Loyalists, prevent his control of the Great Wagon Road, and neutralize Lieutenant Colonel Tarleton's reconstituted cavalry from harassing the countryside. While the two armies were marching and countermarching for advantageous position, Greene tasked Lieutenant Colonel Harry Lee and General Andrew Pickens to cooperate in a joint operation locating and destroying Tarleton's reconstructed cavalry.

On February 23, in advance of Pickens's troops, Lee's Legion encountered scouts from a Loyalist force headed to reinforce Cornwallis near Hillsborough. The scouts mistook Lieutenant Colonel Lee for Bloody Tarleton because their uniforms were a similar green color. The Loyalist pickets offered to bring Lee's Legion to the Loyalist commander, Colonel John Pyle, so Lee devised a quick plan to capture the entire British force reminiscent of his 1779 operation at Paulus Hook, New Jersey. Lee told the scouts to ask Colonel Pyle to have his men stand to the right side of the road so Lee, posing as Tarleton, could review the troops as Lee processed to the end of the column where he would pay his compliments to Colonel Pyle (and demand his immediate surrender). As it happened, the plan only half worked. Pyle set his troops on the right side of the road, and Lee's Legion processed down the road reviewing his troops with Pickens's dragoons following. Just as Lee came to the end of the column of troops where Pyle stood, Pyle's militiamen "discovered their mistake on the near approach of our militia & commenced action." [144]Fighting ensued, which quickly spread from the front to the rear of the column, where Lee and Pyle had just aligned. Pickens's troops responded to the Loyalists commencing the action, and the fighting rapidly progressed up along the single-file Legion to Lee. The Patriots completely routed the Loyalist militia by being in a superior position on horseback with pistols and swords at hand. Although there were no reports from either side of Pyle's troops attempting to surrender, the British press characterized Lee's and Pickens's joint operations victory as a "massacre." This propaganda was an attempt to offset the horrendous political effect of Tarleton's publicized massacre of Buford's surrendering troops at the Waxhaws months before. According to Pickens's after-action report to Greene, "This Affair ...has been of infinite service. It has knocked up Toryism altogether in this part." Pickens meant that Loyalists thinking about stepping forward to join Cornwallis in the area were now not of that mind. The British army had not conquered the state as they asserted or provided the protective trust they had promised. Like the Battle of Hammond's Store, which enabled the victory at Cowpens in January, the effect of Pyle's defeat is often mischaracterized and understated. This resounding defeat stopped Loyalist militias from forming up and reinforcing Cornwallis at a critical time when North Carolina hung in the balance.

War and the conduct of war are not pretty. Sometimes if special operations are correctly planned and luck comes a detachment's way, a strike force catches the enemy unprepared and has a narrow window to destroy it before the enemy can regroup or launch a counterattack. Surprise is a soldier's best ally, but that moment can turn in a flash. It is, therefore, the duty of a soldier to take the initiative, act in unison, and destroy the enemy unless the enemy surrenders. To do otherwise puts one's fellow soldiers, the operation, and their army at risk. To conduct a surprise attack well is to strike a lingering fear into the enemy—brave men become afraid of "ghosts." The success of a surprise attack is not ruthless barbarism; it is the violent nature of ethical war.

The news of Pyle's defeat raced across the countryside. Cornwallis's field ministers assured North Carolinians that the royal government had returned to the province and that loyal king's subjects should flock to the Crown's standard. The British captured the capital at Wilmington in January, and the royal governor was seated and holding court.[145] According to Cornwallis, his army had conquered the state. He counted on the king's subjects throughout the region, augmenting his army, harassing Greene's army, and establishing forts along the Wagon Road and key riverways. Pyle's demise, along with Lieutenant Colonel Tarleton's defeat at Cowpens, stymied Cornwallis's design of reannexing North Carolina for Mother Britain with the help of Loyalists.

On March 1, 1781, Tarleton made matters worse. His reconstituted Legion destroyed another armed group of Loyalists in the vicinity of Guilford Courthouse, answering the call to join Cornwallis. According to Greene's correspondence with Baron Steuben, "the British Legion…

cut them to pieces."[146] This "friendly fire" rout compounded the harmful effect of Pyle's defeat on Loyalists stepping forward to join Cornwallis's ranks. As a result of both events, Cornwallis was left without a sufficient Loyalist flanking force when meeting Greene at Guilford Courthouse. Both Greene and Cornwallis knew the upcoming battle at Guilford would decide the fate of North Carolina and possibly the war.

Two weeks later, on March 15, the two armies finally met face to face. The Guilford battlefield sits within the present-day city of Greensboro near the strategic Wagon Road into Virginia. About two hundred miles away near Portsmouth, Virginia, British General Phillips was reinforcing General Arnold's troops. If Cornwallis could scatter Greene's forces, he would have control over the Wagon Road. He could link up with Phillip's 3,500-man army to complete a chain of British forts extending from Charlestown through the heart of the Carolinas and Georgia to the Chesapeake. This British supply circle would link Portsmouth, Virginia, to Wilmington, North Carolina; Charlestown, South Carolina; Savannah, Georgia; Augusta, Georgia; Fort Ninety-Six, South Carolina; Charlotte, North Carolina; Hillsborough, North Carolina; and back to Portsmouth. Cornwallis would conquer the South if he could destroy Greene.

Meanwhile, in Europe, the French were ready to accept mediation by Russia and Austria. The implied offer was for France and America to trade British-occupied South Carolina, Georgia, and possibly North Carolina and Virginia for New York City and its surrounds. Vergennes, the French secretary of state, affirmed to John Adams that independence was not negotiable provided there was a US dependence on France. John Adams would not agree to participate in mediation, putting the French in a position to unilaterally begin mediation without an American representative or put it off. Adams thought that the United States had become a French client state. He foresaw that the European nations would disallow sovereign independence, resulting in Britain and France forging a separate peace deal dividing up America. He was probably right. Unless a victory occurred soon, the French would abandon the alliance, leaving America without an ally, a navy, gunpowder, money, and independence.[147]

Greene gave the French renewed confidence with his strategic victory at Guilford Courthouse, stopping the cream of the British Army from conquering North Carolina. Cornwallis avoided a tactical battlefield defeat only by repeatedly firing cannon grapeshot into the backs of his ranks engaged with the Americans, despite protests from his officers.[148] His Lordship's forces were in the process of surrender, something Cornwallis could not have. This unethical act of betrayal presumably would not be forgiven by his men. Greene withdrew, unwilling to subject his men to indiscriminate slaughter and risk his entire army to keep the field. He had stopped Cornwallis and had to keep his army combat effective to fight another day against two more British armies across two more provinces.

As a cold rain fell, Cornwallis's decimated army camped in place on His Lordship's "victory field" among their dead, dying, and wounded brothers. Lieutenant Colonel Tarleton recounted in his memoirs that Greene had the opportunity to claim the battlefield at Guilford if he had ordered a brigade to take possession of the "eminence on the edge of the wood." [149]Greene had released Pickens's crack brigade a week before the battle to protect Patriot-leaning inhabitants in South Carolina, which likely kept him from winning the field but kept South Carolina from being completely conquered. Greene had devised his battle plan based on Pickens's riflemen opening the battle as they had at Cowpens. Pickens's forces' substitutes performed poorly; therefore, what could have been a complete tactical and strategic victory was not. But Greene's army had saved North Carolina and had devastated Britain's finest army, rendering it incapable of conquest or offensive operations. Retaining possession of the contested state of North Carolina was more important than risking the entire Southern Continental Army to pursue his personal glory. Cornwallis was left with the field to claim a European-standard victory when the battle was over, but his troops could not move. Speaking in Parliament about Cornwallis's military disaster, Lord James Fox commented, "Another such victory would ruin the British army." Cornwallis and the European community were aware of the symbolic importance of Guilford Courthouse, named after Lord North's father. Lord Fox's published comment and Cornwallis's retreat abandoning North Carolina was a public relations disaster that reinvigorated the French alliance at a crucial time. With the French putting off mediation, America's quest for independence still had hope.

On the seventeenth, the shattered British army loaded seventeen wagons of their wounded and moved toward the New Garden Quaker settlement a few miles away. Contrary to military custom, the dead and severely injured, some with British grapeshot in their mutilated bodies, were left behind. Their abandonment spoke volumes about the army's tenuous security situation. In the middle of nowhere and wholly devastated with no supply line, Cornwallis did the only thing he could do short of surrender. The following day he "distributed a proclamation… in which he published an account of his victory, exhorted the Loyalists to join him, and offered pardon to the Americans who had taken part in the rebellion if they would surrender their arms and ammunition on or before the 20th day of April and retire to their homes to live peacefully until civil government was restored."[150] Interestingly, this proclamation did not require able-bodied men to report for the king's duty under the threat of hanging and property confiscation as Cornwallis had ordered in Georgia and South Carolina when his occupation armies dominated the countryside. His proclamation had Clinton's conciliatory tone used to entice Charlestown and South Carolina to surrender the year before. Nonetheless, residents and diplomats knew who had really won the battle for North Carolina and who was now on the run.

Without supplies and the residents' trust to gain recruits or adequate support, Cornwallis's shattered army retreated from Greene's grasp toward Cross Creek (current-day Fayetteville).[151] Loyalists would not willingly serve a British commander who would fire cannon shots into his soldiers' backs to claim a Pyrrhic victory for himself. Nevertheless, back in the occupied provinces of South Carolina and Georgia, residents were ordered to place lit candles in their windows to celebrate the king's glorious "victory" at Guilford Courthouse over the "rebel army" in a pish-posh show of things.

Despite his claims of victory, Cornwallis now faced saving his army from complete dissolution or destruction. On the withdrawal march, the death of beloved Lieutenant Colonel James Webster brought even more despair to his men. In addition to his high casualties, Cornwallis reported to Clinton, "a third of my army sick and wounded...The remainder without shoes and worn down with fatigue."[152] Greene had a vital choice to make: chase Cornwallis's broken army to finish them off or rest and refit his army to secure the interior of North Carolina and then take back South Carolina and Georgia. Fortunately for the liberation of the South and independence, he wisely used this precious time to pursue final victory rather than pursue the personal glory of forcing Cornwallis's surrender. Greene turned his army south.

On April 13, 1781, Cornwallis's decimated army finally found refuge at Wilmington after their March 15 mauling at Guilford Courthouse and ensuing two-hundred-mile trek to safety. What remained of his once-mighty army that had precipitously invaded North Carolina in January 1781 was shoeless, exhausted, and incapable of combat.[153] Cornwallis had launched his second invasion to conquer North Carolina with over 3,168 first-rate British and Hessian troops, more troops than it had taken to capture Savannah and all of Georgia two years before. In the past three months, he had lost at least 48 percent of his army, totally failed to conquer the state, failed to reestablish a royal government or reliable Loyalist army throughout North Carolina, and he had exhausted his equipment and war chest entirely. In Lieutenant Colonel Banastre Tarleton's Southern Campaign book, ghostwritten by his girlfriend, Cornwallis's strategic failure was highlighted. Bloody Ban uncharitably noted that, given the "comparative situations" of the British and Continental Armies, Cornwallis's failure to return to Fort Camden, South Carolina, after Guilford doomed the British in the Lower South.[154] The flower of the British army under Cornwallis embarked on one of the longest military marches in the history of Western civilization, about 1,500 miles, only to achieve total failure. General Henry Clinton lamented that Cornwallis's actions caused "the ruin of a fine army and the ultimate loss of an opulent and important province." By taking the tattered remnants of his once-formidable army out of North Carolina into Virginia, he left South Carolina and Georgia open for the Continental Army to launch a sustained insurgency and counteroffensive against the British armies occupying those states.

Near the first of May 1781, the remainder of Cornwallis's army that could walk left Wilmington for Virginia while his unfit troops sailed to Southern British headquarters in Charlestown. Joseph Martin, the North Carolina royal governor whom Cornwallis was tasked with protecting, subsequently lost confidence and sailed for England, abandoning the unconquered province. The British troops remaining at Wilmington, Fort Johnston, and Cross Creek would have to fend for themselves. In two invasions of North Carolina, British combat and noncombat losses amounted to over five thousand first-rate troops. Cornwallis was defeated militarily, politically, and strategically in his second attempt to conquer the lynchpin Tar Heel State.

On May 10, 1781, Cornwallis and his remnant army finally made it to the safety of Virginia to be resupplied and reinforced. The resentful remains of his once-proud army terrorized the defenseless towns and families along their way north from Wilmington. Cornwallis never returned to the North Carolina he claimed to have conquered, leaving British forts isolated in the eastern part of the state. His boss's family namesake, Guilford Courthouse was left to the enemy. Most importantly, the Americans had won control of the Great Wagon Road through the state's heart. They also controlled the headwaters of the strategic rivers that flowed into South Carolina down to Charlestown. Cornwallis's men never forgot leaving their dead and wounded brothers behind at Guilford Courthouse or the grapeshot fired into their backs while fighting for a leader they had once trusted. During the critical point of the battle when the British were entangled with the Virginians and beginning to surrender, General Charles O'Hara begged His Lordship not to fire cannon into his own men. O'Hara's brother, in charge of the artillery that fired the fatal grapeshot, was reportedly "killed by the enemy" after also protesting the order. After gaining the field, Cornwallis's men knew that the chase to destroy the "little forge man's" army had failed. Their lingering feeling of betrayal and extreme sense of loss likely contributed to his men's unwillingness to fight it out to the end six months later when under siege at Yorktown. Cornwallis did not appear with his men at the Yorktown surrender, but his soldiers' trusted advocate, General Charles O'Hara, did. The will to fight had depreciated with every failure of leadership.

Upon entering Virginia, Cornwallis would get fresh troops as he took over the British offensive from General Benedict Arnold. Cornwallis's plan to restore his reputation was to conquer Virginia, not just terrorize it, and establish an impregnable fort-port in the Chesapeake just as the duplicitous Charles Lee had recommended in 1777. Cornwallis, Clinton, Lord North, and Lord Germain planned to efficiently manage troop logistics along the Southern seaboard from this new superport. Cornwallis was convinced that "the Carolinas could be subdued only when Virginia was securely under British control." From a Chesapeake base, he would crush insurgent Patriot forces in the Carolinas by sending a massive army from Virginia by water to destroy them in concert with local Provincial and Loyalist forces.[155] The network of forts he had established throughout the Carolinas and Georgia would maintain British control until he returned—or so he assumed.

General Nathanael Greene had other ideas. With the Regular British army offensive to conquer North Carolina defeated, the Patriot militias could keep the middle and western part of the state free. As Cornwallis's strategy became apparent, Greene wrote to General Baron de Steuben in Virginia on April 2 to coordinate Continental strategy. In his message, he stated, "Their [Cornwallis's Army] advance northward secures their possessions Southward [therefore] I think it will be our true plan of policy to move into South Carolina…This will oblige the enemy to follow us or give up their posts there." Greene discovered the fatal numerical flaw in the British compound strategy: the British would lose Loyalist militia as the numbers of regulars decreased. The war planners did not plan to keep enough regulars in the Lower South to hold conquered territory, and there was no plan to professionalize Loyalist militias.

Based on Cornwallis's manpower predicaments, Greene resolved to return to South Carolina to begin his liberation offensive there. "I will recover South Carolina or die in the attempt," he proclaimed to rally his troops, local militias, and inhabitants.[156] Greene now planned to take all the enemy posts in South Carolina and Georgia to win back conquered territory in Cornwallis's absence. He planned to offer protection to inhabitants as his troops and detachments invested, or placed under siege, each British fort in the occupied region while separating British forces from their Native American allies in the west. He would offer Loyalists not guilty of genocide amnesty to get them to switch sides. As each post in the British chain of forts would fall, the recovered territory would come under the protection of Congress and his Continental Army. Greene planned to gradually force the British back to the coast by breaking every link in their occupation chain of forts and retaining the liberated areas by protecting the populaces, thereby earning popular consent.

VI.
THE WAR FOR THE FORTS

Breaking the Chain of Oppression

In April 1781, as British General Lord Cornwallis was leaving North Carolina with the remnants of his battered army to assume command of the king's forces terrorizing Virginia, a new strategic phase of the war in the Lower South began. Conceived and directed by General Greene, the "war for the forts" commenced in earnest to win South Carolina, Georgia, and eastern North Carolina. The strategic intention of capturing enemy forts was to force the British back to the coast and bottle them up in the overcrowded, disease-infested port cities. Greene would commence operations by taking the offensive, augmenting his forces with state militias, and being everywhere at once: disrupt, confuse, isolate, exhaust, and demoralize the enemy into seeking protection in their coastal garrisons. The psychological intention of taking the forts was to destroy the symbols of British oppression that stood over the towns, rivers of commerce, and crossroads. The tactical purpose was to reclaim the British territory controlled from these forts and liberate the people oppressed by their presence. The war of the forts marked a strategic and operational shift away from a defensive war halting British conquest to a war designed to methodically win back territory from the British, fort by fort, area by area, river by river, crossroad by crossroad, from west to east.

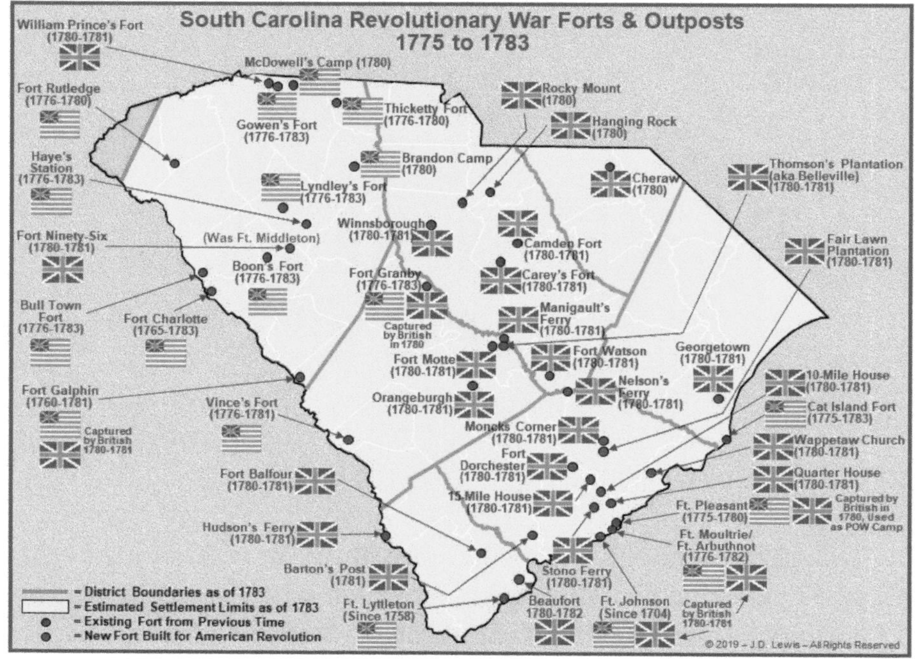

South Carolina Revolutionary War Forts and Outposts, 1775-1783, courtesy of J.D. Lewis, www.carolana.com.

For their first target, Greene assigned a fellow Mason, his cavalry commander, Lieutenant Colonel "Light Horse" Harry Lee, to link up with General Marion's partisans and capture Fort Watson near Camden, South Carolina.[157] Lieutenant Colonel Lee had been awarded a Congressional Gold Medal for capturing the British fort at Paulus Hook on the Hudson River across from New York City in August 1779. Congress commended him in that action for not putting a single prisoner to death despite the great concern for his men's safety given the disproportionate number of enemy prisoners captured. "Humanity was shown…corresponding to the noble principles" stated in the Declaration of Independence.[158] As an ethical and effective commander, Lieutenant Colonel Lee was frequently employed by Greene as a detached Continental Cavalry commander to operate in conjunction with state militia forces in executing Greene's offensive strategy while promoting Congressional rules of war. During his joint operations with both militia commanders, he became close friends with state Generals Francis Marion and Andrew Pickens. Harry Lee was twenty-four years old and the battle-hardened commander of Lee's Legion when he joined General Greene's Southern Continental Army in 1780.

Fort Watson was the primary support post for the strategic British garrison at Camden, located near the center of South Carolina. To threaten the mega-fort at Camden, Fort Watson had to fall first. Lee and Marion's combined forces laid siege to Fort Watson in April 1781. Together they forced the fort's surrender by building a sharpshooter's tower (Maham tower) and then offering capitulation terms that assured surrendering prisoners would be unharmed. Fort Watson surrendered, prisoners were not harmed, and the first link in the British chain of forts in South Carolina was broken.

Greene's next target was Lord Francis Rawdon, stationed at Camden, marking the third British army Greene had opposed since taking the Southern command. As Cornwallis's deputy and second-in-command, Rawdon was responsible for holding South Carolina and Georgia. At the same time, his theater commander, General Cornwallis, endeavored to conquer Virginia and established a port in the Chesapeake region, as Charles Lee had recommended. The new Chesapeake port would enable the rapid movement of troops between New York, Charlestown, Wilmington, and Savannah, thereby tightening the British grip on the Southern colonies—"doing more with less," so to speak. Rawdon's responsibility was to hold South Carolina and eliminate rebel resistance until Cornwallis completed a Chesapeake superport and returned to tidy things up.

Irish-born Frances, Lord Rawdon was another of Cornwallis's ruthless "boy wonders." Tall, athletic, slender, and self-promoting, the twenty-six-year-old was a former Clinton mentee who distinguished himself during the bloodbath at Breed's Hill (Bunker Hill). As a lieutenant of a grenadier company, Rawdon had the reputation of leading the final assault and executing a mortally wounded General Warren after the battle. He followed the typical path of a high-born British military officer, first taking his family's seat in the House of Lords, then entering Oxford before joining the King's Army by paying for an officer's commission.[159] Rawdon was at Oxford, where he became friends with Lieutenant Colonel Banastre Tarleton. Putting down the rebellion in America by finishing off the last pockets of resistance in the Lower South would be a tremendous career boost for Rawdon. Spiced with a bit of military fame, Rawdon's postwar appointments would be guided by the king's hand.

He and his Volunteers of Ireland started well in the spring of 1780 by capturing the Patriot fort on Haddrell's Point, Mount Pleasant, before the siege of Charlestown commenced. Less than a year later, the young regimental commander was elevated to, in effect, the Carolinas theater command position over both military and civilian matters. This de facto appointment might have been the biggest British mistake of the war. Rawdon had neither the experience nor the temperament to manage such an enormous military and civilian command. An aggressive assault captain cannot become an effective theater force commander and regional governor-general overnight. Even so, as a fellow lord, Rawdon was Cornwallis's "proper class" choice as commander of British forces in the Carolinas in his absence.

In April 1781, Lord Rawdon's tactical command center was located at Camden, South Carolina. This positioning gave him control of the east branch of the Great Wagon Road and the Wateree River down to Charlestown. He was about three to four days march to Wilmington, Ninety-Six, Augusta, and Charlotte. He was also perfectly positioned to counter a Continental land attack on Charlestown. Rawdon operated out of a strong garrison adjacent to the town of Camden, where he was well-supplied and well-situated to run the war in the Carolinas while his mentor and commander, General Cornwallis, was attempting to conquer other states.

With Cornwallis and his battered troops recuperating in Wilmington, Rawdon took the offensive in South Carolina to eliminate Patriot resistance. On April 9, 1781, he sent a British force from Fort Camden to burn Old Waxhaw Presbyterian Church and homes in Lancaster in retribution for General Andrew Pickens destabilizing British control over South Carolina.[160] As a teenager, Pickens's family had lived in the Waxhaws before relocating to Long Canes. Andrew Jackson, the future US president, witnessed Rawdon's men burn Lancaster. Rawdon's troops also burned the homes and crops of the Patriot-allied Catawba Nation nearby. Lord Rawdon subscribed to indiscriminate terror tactics to completely subdue the "rebels" as the designated theater commander.

While Rawdon's forces were preoccupied with terrorizing the Waxhaws, Lieutenant Colonel Henry Lee and General Marion captured Fort Watson. With the fall of Fort Watson on April 23, Rawdon's mega garrison at Camden was cut off from his Wateree River supply route coming up from Charlestown. Word of the fair treatment by the Patriots of surrendering British troops at Fort Watson raced across the countryside. At the same time, Greene's main Continental army moved into position to isolate Fort Camden and force the British commander to attack or come under siege. On April 25, 1781, Lord Rawdon chose to launch a preemptive attack on Greene's army at Hobkirk's Hill outside Camden.[161] While he temporarily occupied the battlefield and scored a tactical "win," he lost a third of his army and retreated to Fort Camden before Greene could counterattack. According to Greene's official report to Congress, "We should have had Rawdon and his whole command prisoners in three Minutes if Col Gumby had not ordered his Regiment to retire; the greater part which was advancing."[162] Isolated and surrounded by Patriot forces, and with no other British force able to come to his relief, Rawdon was forced to abandon this key British garrison halfway between Charlotte and Charlestown. Before leaving behind his sick and wounded, Rawdon ordered his men to destroy the fort and burn every public building and area home in an extreme act of vengeance to friend and foe. Greene could have chosen to attack Rawdon on his retreat from Fort Camden, but his objective was achieved. He did not want to lose men to unnecessary combat and become burdened with guarding prisoners. Camden could no longer support Fort Winnsboro or protect the Wateree River transports from North Carolina into Charlestown or reverse. The central British fort in South Carolina had fallen, and public confidence in the Patriot cause skyrocketed throughout the Carolinas. Cornwallis was gone, and Rawdon was responding to Greene rather than the other way round. Combined Continental and militia forces proved they could successfully converge offensive operations to outnumber and best British forces to capture a fort and liberate conquered territory.

General Greene's tasking of the partisan militias to operate in concert with his Continentals was working. With the assistance of South Carolina's exiled governor in Philadelphia, John Rutledge, he divided South Carolina into three districts with state militia generals Francis "Swamp Fox" Marion in charge of the low country, Thomas "Gamecock" Sumter in command of the Midlands, and Andrew "Wizard Owl" Pickens responsible for the western upcountry. Greene also coordinated assigned operational areas in Georgia, working with Elijah Clark, Benjamin Few, and John Twiggs, and similarly in North Carolina with the militia leaders there. These partisan commanders were to constantly disrupt and destroy the enemy and capture supplies en route to the British chain of forts while gathering and providing intelligence. When it came time for battles, Greene would call in the state militias to participate in the siege or battle. (General Thomas Sumter would be the only militia commander to disobey orders and not participate in collective battles.) After capturing a fort, the state militias, with the guidance of Continental officers, would be responsible for holding it and protecting the civilian population from British or Loyalist reprisals. This strategy was the essence of Greene's compound strategy to liberate the Lower South.

Greene coordinated siege operations to be simultaneous, unanticipated by the enemy, rapid, and constant, thereby completely reshaping the strategic operating environment in the Patriots' favor. Superior British numbers were effectively neutralized by simultaneously keeping troops isolated within their assigned forts, unable to assist one another effectively. Maintaining communications between forts became impossible for the British forces as General Greene coordinated militia and Continental cavalry movements based on information from a broad network of spies, shadow Patriots, and the quick application of superior operational intelligence. Greene often knew more about British troop locations, size, strength, and psychological condition in the field than their commanders.

As a result, British forces were compelled to switch from offensive conquest and security operations to defensive reactions in response to constant, coordinated Patriot attacks. State militia commanders harassed isolated and invested British forts of occupation, in concert with Greene's movements and detachments, which enabled combined Patriot forces to break the British chain of forts, one by one, region by region.

The all-important battle for hearts and minds in the Lower South became centered in South Carolina. Which side could the population trust to ensure their protection and fair treatment? Both General Pickens and Marion were in complete agreement about their troops following the Congressional Articles of War, particularly in the treatment of prisoners and civilians. General Thomas Sumter, however, employed a contractual recruitment system referred to as "Sumter's Law," which promised a share of the booty and captured enslaved people while exercising extreme retribution against surrendering Loyalists and British forces.[163] His practices of severe punishment intensified the internecine war between Patriots and Loyalists, the civil war within the rebellion's amorphous battlefront. The British well knew that no peace or liberation could occur while these vengeful raids ensued. Plunder, slaughter, revenge, and depopulation worked to their benefit.

On the contrary, Greene realized that there would never be peace without forgiveness. But forty-six-year-old militia general Sumter did not see things that way even though wanton acts of revenge played right into the British justification for brutality. Sumter was seething with the desire for revenge from Bloody Tarleton burning his home and store and molesting his infirm wife as he was living a somewhat neutral life in May 1780. Vengeance is often a reaction to grief. From June until November, General Sumter and Francis Marion's "on-the-run rebels" were the only armed resistance to the British occupation in South Carolina. On November 20, 1780, Sumter was seriously wounded but slowly recovered and returned to the field in February 1781. During his recovery, he refused to order "his men" to join General Morgan for the Cowpens battle that would change the trajectory of the war. Sumter's commitment to independence was subordinated to his personal interests.

Sumter's regiment had initially been a magnet for men who had likewise suffered brutality from Crown forces and Loyalists. To enlarge his partisan army, he moved to attract a type of land pirates, or poltroons, interested primarily in enriching themselves and persecuting others. In January 1781, Greene wrote Sumter appealing to him to stop his plunder and depredation when he returned to the field: "I persuade myself though you may set a just value upon reputation, your soul is filled with a more noble ambition." Nonetheless, in March, Sumter's men killed surrendering British troops near Fort Watson, which was repaid when some of Sumter's men were captured by the British soon afterward. Greene was adamant about stopping this constant cycle of retribution violence and property theft. He formally requested that the South Carolina governor-in-exile, John Rutledge, write to Sumter to order him to cease these unlawful practices, which ran counter to values embraced by the confederation. Governor Rutledge, Sumter's civilian commander in chief, wrote Sumter in July 1781 when popular opinion and the war hung in the balance, declaring Sumter's Law to be "illegal and reprehensible."[164] Rutledge ordered Sumter to stop his unethical practices, to which he begrudgingly complied. Rutledge and Greene systematically reduced and reorganized Sumter's militia to end "share of plunder" and slave payment contracts to make the orders stick. State General Andrew Pickens would eventually assume the bulk of Sumter's command. Sumter did not comport with the American virtue ethics until ordered to do so. Greene's and Rutledge's ethical code enforcement interrupted the internecine cycle of violence and wholesale plunder of civilians, which helped change people's minds toward the Patriot cause to oust the British. As a result of this protective trust policy, the Patriot cause gained the ethical high ground. With Sumter reeled in and Greene aggressively pursuing the role of comportment enforcer, Patriot forces increasingly became the side inhabitants could trust.

Meanwhile, Greene continued his strategy of taking forts and swaying allegiance toward the Patriot cause. When word got out that the Patriots treated prisoners honorably, Provincial and Loyalist defenders did not fight to the last man. Surrender, parole, and an escort to Charlestown were preferred to a slow death of isolation and starvation. The roads and riverways between forts became dangerous for small British forces to traverse. Insurgent ambushes made it impossible for British couriers to deliver orders between forts or for the British to shift troops. Supplies could not get through the river systems and roadways due to the constant attacks of the state militias and shadow Patriots. The wilderness, the rivers, and the countryside turned against the British occupiers and Loyalists.[165] Forts of occupation became isolated prisons for the British.

In May 1781, the combined forces of the Swamp Fox and "Light Horse" Henry Lee began a siege on Greene's next target, Fort Motte. Fort Motte protected the Congaree and Wateree Rivers' apex and the road to and from Charlestown, above the Santee. It was a central supply depot between Charlestown and Camden and a logical fallback position if Rawdon was forced to abandon Fort Camden. Capturing it would place the entire Wateree River supply line under Patriot control and break the British Congaree River supply line leading up through the midlands and then branching northward up to Charlotte. Rebecca Motte was the Patriot owner of the house seized by the British and then fortified. She provided Lee and Marion with an African bow and arrows to set her home on fire and force the British occupiers to surrender before Lord Rawdon's retreating army from Camden could come to the fort's rescue. The house was set afire by flaming arrows but the fires were extinguished by the British soldiers as they waved a flag of surrender. The prisoners taken were not harmed despite their having burned many homes in the area. Fort Motte and the house were kept intact, and the prisoners provided extensive intelligence.[166] With the abandonment of Forts Camden, Watson, and Motte, the British were deprived of a fixed supply line from Charlestown necessary to reinvade North Carolina. The reputation and trust of the allied Patriot forces began to flourish.

Fort Granby was the next link in the South Carolina chain of forts to be taken. This fort, among other things, was used as a supply depot for British forces garrisoned at the super-fort of Ninety-Six. Fort Granby, located across from modern-day Columbia (which did not exist at the time) was adjacent to the ravaged village of Saxe Goethe. It controlled the upper Congaree River trade route, which flowed down to

Charlestown. Goods could be floated down from North Carolina and also transported overland from the western frontiers to Fort Granby to be traded or purchased. From there, these goods could be floated down a series of rivers to Charlestown to shipment anywhere in the world. Before the British invasion, Fort Granby was one of America's the most significant trading posts. Furs, mink, and skins from all points west streamed into Fort Granby to be floated down to Charlestown. On May 14, 1781, Lieutenant Colonel Henry Lee surrounded the fort and negotiated guaranteed free passage of defenders if they surrendered the next day.[167] The defenders' only demand was to take the booty they collected by plundering homesteads. Besides gaining control of a strategic fort and intact trading center, an immense amount of desperately needed rifles, muskets, powder, and shot were captured.[168] The entire midlands of South Carolina subsequently became Patriot territory under Continental army protection, inspiring the oppressed throughout the province to join the Patriot cause and Loyalists to switch sides.

With the Fort Granby link broken, the British forts at Augusta and Ninety-Six became the next strategic targets. At Augusta, Georgia, the tri-forts controlled trade along the Savannah River stretching up to Cherokee lands in Oconee near modern-day Clemson, South Carolina. These three forts, Galphin, Grierson, and Cornwallis, supported one another at the south end of the Great Wagon Road. Trappers could float their skins down the Savannah River to Savannah, Georgia, or unload part of their load at Augusta or hire wagon teamsters to take their goods northward. Armed British river galleys also supported these multipurpose Augusta forts, which served as supply depots and trading posts. Occupying the Savannah River at Augusta was imperative to controlling trade from the American interior and interrupting the British supplies pulled upriver from Savannah along the towpath. Most importantly, these forts had been recently supplied with rifles, ammunition, and powder to arm British Native American allies. These arms had to be intercepted before they could be used against Patriot forces.

At the end of May, Greene instructed Lieutenant Colonel Lee's Continental Cavalry Legion and Pickens's State Militia dragoon forces to conduct a joint operation to capture the forts at Augusta. The tri-forts at Augusta supported Fort Ninety-Six and vice versa. If any location was attacked or came under siege, reinforcements from another fort could come to the rescue. Greene's strategy was to lay siege to all four forts simultaneously so they could not come to each other's aid. Colonel Elijah Clark's Georgia Militia and Colonel Isaac Shelby's King's Mountain Men joined Lee and Pickens in the siege of the Augusta tri-forts. The overall commander of these forts was Loyalist colonel Thomas Brown, a merchant from England who had organized a force of rangers that operated jointly with Cherokee and Creek warriors. Brown and his regiment had become notorious for horrendous acts of wanton violence, including murder and torture of prisoners.

Despite Brown's best efforts, Forts Galphin, Grierson, and Cornwallis were captured in sequence.[169] Fort Galphin (British-named Fort Dreadnought), situated twelve miles below Augusta on a bluff commanding the Savannah River, was taken on May 21 by Continental major John Rudolph and Georgia State Colonel Elijah Clarke. Clarke's troops paraded in front of the fort enticing the garrison forces to give chase and leave the gates to the fort open. The fort was captured by Rudolph's troops rushing in after the British took the bait. Over 126 redcoats were captured, and an immense amount of much-needed powder, arms, and food were captured in addition to wagons and horses. Boosted by these supplies, Lieutenant Colonel Henry Lee's and General Andrew Pickens's men laid siege to and captured Forts Grierson and Cornwallis. The notorious Loyalist Colonel Thomas Brown was captured and protected against slaughter after his surrender of Fort Cornwallis on June 5. Capturing these tri-forts liberated the town of Augusta and prevented British gunboat patrols from navigating up from Savannah to control the Savannah River and from controlling the Savannah River trade route originating in north Georgia. General Pickens personally ensured the safe passage of those surrendering. A Loyalist prisoner was killed in custody, so Pickens and Greene issued an order for the offender's arrest. The rest of the prisoners, including Colonel Brown, were given parole and escorted under Continental protective guard to the British lines around Charlestown.

With the surrender of these forts, no British troops remained in Augusta to reinforce Fort Ninety-Six if that garrison came under attack.

On May 14, 1781, General Greene wrote the president of Congress to update his civilian boss on significant gains in South Carolina and Georgia. Territory possession in South Carolina was changing quickly, and the remnants of Cornwallis's army were dragging into Virginia. General Greene provided Congress with the following summarized progress report: Fort Camden was evacuated after an enemy loss of 300 men or more. The area was now in Continental hands. Fort Orangeburg and Fort Motte were taken along with arms, ammunition, and cannon. Also, 120 British and Hessian regulars were taken prisoners. The forts at Augusta and Ninety-Six were under siege. The fort at Friday's Ferry (Fort Granby) will be under siege tomorrow. Enemy forces are now in a position where if they divide their forces, "they will fall by detachments, and if they operate collectively, they cannot command the Country."[170] Greene's compound warfare strategy was working to perfection.

If Cornwallis was reinforced and renewed the British offensive in Virginia, Greene planned to go to Virginia and command Patriot forces there. General Isaac Huger would remain in the Lower South to complete the capture of the remaining forts. But that remained to be seen. In the meantime, Greene's territory control updates were essential to keep Congress informed. When back-door negotiations commenced, Greene's reports would be passed on to American negotiators in Europe to make the most of the progress. Continental Army military control over territory would decide which states would be granted independence during treaty discussions.

General Marion continuously attacked British and Loyalist troops in South Carolina's Pee Dee and low country regions to contest territory.[171] He attacked Loyalist militias at night on only three sides, allowing escape rather than obliteration. The enemy did not fight to the last man. Those who chose to escape could return to their homes and reflect on putting down their weapons. Loyalist militias gradually began to disband or switch sides as they lost their trust in the British Army regulars to support them, protect them, or promote peace. Marion's tactics encouraged Loyalists to lay down their arms or switch sides.

Besides Marion's continuous attacks against Loyalist militias and British columns, he developed a network of spies that provided constant information streams about British troop activities. Timely and actionable intelligence was essential to direct military operations against superior British forces. Shaping operations around intelligence information enabled Patriot forces to attack points of vulnerability and identify numerical mismatches. Greene described this field strategy as follows: "intelligence to an army is like the soul to the body it directs all motions." Between Marion and Greene's efforts, they were able to recruit a double agent in Charlestown, General Andrew Williamson. He was a former senior militia officer who unilaterally surrendered all the South Carolina state troops after the British captured Charlestown. Williamson provided important troop movements and enemy intentions intelligence from inside the city as a double agent. Residents throughout the countryside, such as eighteen-year-old Emily Geiger, and enslaved Blacks, such as Antigua and Prince, gathered intelligence and ran messages between militia commanders and Greene.[172] Captain Wilmot oversaw Greene's intelligence operations, supported by General Thaddeus Kosciusko, to seek out, collect, verify, and organize constant streams of incoming intelligence. Orders would go out from headquarters to exploit enemy vulnerabilities and avoid concentrated enemy offensives. Lookout posts along the many "superhighway" rivers monitored British movements and weaknesses. Foragers, sent out from isolated British forts, were captured and interrogated. Deserters were debriefed.[173] Patriots constantly ambushed British messengers between posts along the heavily forested roads, making communications between forts dangerous if not impossible. Residents routed captured communications and information through the militia commands up to Greene. Intelligence activities became the lifeblood of Greene's insurgency offensive.

As British manpower numbers and operational plans became known, Greene moved undetected to surround more prominent forts while having his cavalry forces act in conjunction with militia forces to cover the smaller support forts in the region. His chief scout, Captain C. K. Chitty, became a surveillance expert collecting vital intelligence to guide Greene's operations.[174] This operational strategy prevented British forces from reinforcing their networked forts, and it diluted their superior manpower numbers in each geographic area, so each fort became vulnerable. As each fort was surrounded, communications and supplies were cut off. Abandonment or surrender became a matter of time. This operational strategy would enable Continental forces to liberate large areas in South Carolina and methodically push British forces to the coast.

In May of 1781, the central British super-fort in South Carolina, Fort Ninety-Six, was surrounded by Greene's forces. This British engineering marvel, also known as a "star fort," was the critical fixed fortification near the Great Wagon Road fork into North Carolina located on the Charlestown Road. This fort was essential to the British Southern Strategy of progressively conquering the Southern states by moving northward from this front-forward garrison and logistics center. Fort Ninety-Six became isolated after their support forts of Fort Granby and Fort Williams were captured. Fort Granby, which controlled the Congaree River across from modern-day Columbia, was one of the highest-volume trading posts in the world before the war. Lee's Legion effected a surrender of that important fort earlier in the month. Fort Williams was captured and made unusable by Lieutenant Colonel William Washington's forces on December 31, 1780. To take Fort Ninety-Six, Greene had to put the British tri-forts at Augusta, Georgia, about a three-day southward march down the Great Wagon Road, under siege simultaneously. Detachments from Ninety-Six had come to the relief of the Augusta tri-forts, located along the Savannah River, the previous year. On May 22, Lee's Legion and Pickens's dragoons surrounded the three British forts on the same day Greene's main Continental army surrounded Fort Ninety-Six. On June 5, the last fort at Augusta surrendered.

The siege of Ninety-Six lasted for twenty-eight days. On June 20, Greene withdrew just before a two-thousand-man relief force consisting of three regiments of Irish Guards under the command of Lord Rawdon arrived. Rawdon had quick marched his troops up the Charlestown Road in the searing heat and soon found himself in the same situation he had experienced in abandoning Fort Camden the month before. He had decimated his powerful army by the forced march and exhausted his supplies. Given his situation, the critical operational post to hold the Lower South had to be abandoned. Rawdon's nearest support was over 179 miles away at British Southern headquarters in Charlestown.[175] He could not link up with Cherokee and Creek warriors to the west because his go-between Indian superintendent (Colonel Brown) had been captured at Augusta. Pickens and Lee had captured the quid pro quo arms destined for his Native American allies. Rawdon was faced with either dissolution from lack of supplies or marching back to Charlestown at four miles per hour with another train of Loyalist refugees to screen his retreat. Lord Rawdon burned the village and demolished Fort Ninety-Six just as he had at Fort Camden the month before, leaving friend and foe with ashes. He retreated again to Charlestown with another spent army and a load of Loyalist refugees who would have to camp outside the city and fend for themselves. Rawdon returned to Charlestown thoroughly defeated in his attempt to hold Britain's strategic forward operating base in South Carolina and destroy Greene in the process.

Earlier in the year, on January 25, 1781, General Francis Marion's militia forces and Lee's Legion launched a surprise attack deep behind enemy lines against British fortifications at Georgetown. Georgetown was a British ship and boatbuilding port city surrounded by indigo plantations. Marion and Lee's attack occurred days after the Battle of Cowpens to distract General Leslie's British forces marching from Charlestown to reinforce Cornwallis in the upstate. Marion and Lee's forces successfully breached the fortifications and captured the garrison's commander, but the British defenders retreated to the safety of the citadel, which was impregnable except by cannon. Marion and Lee withdrew before reinforcements arrived. Marion would not make the same mistake again.

General Marion began to lay siege to Georgetown toward the end of May. Patriot forces desperately needed this port to supply Greene's army from the sea because Generals Phillips and Cornwallis had interrupted the overland supplies from Virginia. The British garrison decided to evacuate their post, considering the strong Patriot forces on its doorstep.

Fort Georgetown fell to Marion, but the British burned forty-two houses before sailing away.[176] Instead of seeking retribution against the Loyalists remaining behind, General Marion took the opportunity to negotiate a one-year cease-fire with the leader of a large Loyalist regiment operating in the area commanded by Major Micajah Gainey. This act of statesmanship significantly stabilized the low country; plus, it ensured the town's security and Greene's supply line from the sea going forward. The Patriots would keep the invaluable Georgetown port for the rest of the war.

General Thomas Sumter also achieved critical military success. On May 11, his forces captured Fort Orangeburg, and the retreating British burned the countryside. Orangeburg protected the Charleston Road that connected to Fort Ninety-Six.[177] By July 4, 1781, the fifth anniversary of the Declaration of Independence, the Americans controlled the middle and upper regions of South Carolina above Camden, Orangeburg, and Augusta. They could receive reinforcements overland from liberated North Carolina and precious gunpowder supplies transported up from the Patriot-controlled port at Georgetown. For the first time since General Henry Clinton's capture of Charlestown, the British army was retreating and on the defensive in the Lower South.

But General Thomas Sumter was a "loose cannon" in Greene's plan to liberate the Carolinas and Georgia. Sumter would not respond to Greene's request for assistance in major battles and sieges. His actions were routinely insubordinate and unilateral.[178] No one except Sumter knew what he would do next despite General Greene's orders that he conduct specific missions in coordination with the sequencing of fort sieges and territory repossessions. Sumter received orders to maul Rawdon as he marched up from Charlestown to relieve Fort Ninety-Six. He disobeyed orders, exposing Greene, the Continental Army, and other state troops to defeat. General Sumter reportedly was furious that Lieutenant Colonel Harry Lee had captured Fort Granby in May. Sumter wanted the booty the British were allowed to take away, and he was in the habit of hanging Loyalists after their surrender. If Sumter had unilaterally captured Fort Granby with its abundant supplies and established his headquarters there, he would have controlled a major American trading post and the

Congaree River in the center of the state. In the extreme, Sumter could have declared himself the head of state from this strategically located fort.

Sumter was someone who needed careful handling. He did not participate in the defense of Charlestown in 1780 and only entered the war after his home and store was destroyed by British forces. Sumter and his militia officers had never signed the Congressional Articles of War. His men had signed up for "Sumter's Law," which rewarded those who joined with a share of the plunder and enslaved people they captured—a practice that was later legally prosecuted.[179] Sumter kept the British off balance and the Loyalists on the defensive in the center of the state as much as he kept Greene and other Patriot forces in the dark. His eyes were more often fixated on plunder targets than strategic military targets.

Nonetheless, Sumter unwittingly confused the British by not following leaked or intercepted orders from Greene. Rarely was he where he was supposed to be. Sumter's noncooperation with Greene often resulted in British forces futilely chasing his anticipated movements. Sumter unintentionally enabled General Greene's joint forces to capture forts and secure territory made possible by the enemy's presence elsewhere (dispersion of forces). Despite the absence of Sumter's cooperation, the British chain of forts had been broken throughout South Carolina.

The British command in Charlestown responded to their fort capitulations with harsh revenge. Lord Rawdon was outraged by massive defections of former parolees rejoining the Patriot militias, his humiliating retreats from Camden and Ninety-Six notwithstanding. In May 1781, he posted a reward of five guineas for each live deserter brought in, ten guineas if only their head.[180] On August 4, after his inglorious retreat from Fort Ninety-Six, Lord Rawdon resorted to making a public spectacle of neutrals rejoining the Patriot cause. His troops captured Lieutenant Colonel Isaac Hayne, who conducted a daring raid to capture the presumed turncoat General Williamson. Unbeknownst to Hayne, Williamson was an American double agent working alongside the British in Charlestown.[181] Hayne was well-respected and well-known across the province by both sides.

Rawdon and the Charlestown garrison commandant, Lieutenant Colonel Nisbet Balfour, charged Hayne with espionage and conducted a public street hanging outside the Exchange Building, without trial, that shocked the world.[182] (This event could be compared to the televised shooting of a Viet Cong prisoner on the street in Saigon during the Vietnam War almost two hundred years later that produced moral outrage in America.) Rawdon's example had the opposite effect he had wished. Outraged citizens reacted by pouring into the Patriot militias while shocked members of Parliament called for an investigation. One London newspaper printed a graphic cartoon depicting the atrocities (and corruption) committed in America that was broadcast across Europe.[183] Public confidence in the British army's methods to bring Americans back into the Empire throughout England and America collapsed. Widespread belief in the moral superiority and civility of the British collapsed. Americans of all political stripes lost confidence in the king's officers to provide protection and justice toward reconciliation. British barbarity stood starkly on the world stage for all to see. General Greene sought to have Rawdon hanged for the heinous act of hanging Colonel Hayne without trial.

In response, Lord Rawdon blamed (non-Lord) Commandant Nesbit Balfour and resigned his post shortly after that, citing health problems. The well-connected gentleman aristocrat wanted nothing to do with a documented hanging atrocity that would interfere with a future in the king's court and House of Lords. While en route to England, a French privateer captured Rawdon. Curiously, Rawdon's detailed notes concerning the Hayne hanging were "thrown overboard" before his capture. Whether the French destroyed the incriminating messages or the letters went to Davy Jones's locker by the British commander's hand, their disappearance likely saved Rawdon from extradition, trial, and a Patriot noose, if not an ostracized political future. Even though Lord Rawdon did not receive justice, the summary hanging of Colonel Hayne was a tipping point in changing public attitudes across America and among European diplomats who would decide America's fate with pro or no independence sentiments.

With Rawdon out of the fight, Colonel Paston Gould was appointed commander of the Lower South under Cornwallis. Lieutenant Colonel Alexander Stewart would continue serving in the field under Gould's command. Gould was a weak placeholder more than a commander, which proved to be a blessing for Greene and the Patriot cause. According to the historical records of the Third Regiment, or Buffs, "The English leaders at this time were without a plan and could not agree on one. Hence a succession of orders and counterorders, which resulted in nothing done... The injudicious act [of hanging a popular citizen, Colonel Isaac Hayne], and certainly alienated many from the English party."[184] In the middle of July, about three thousand British regulars were marching aimlessly around Orangeburg, near the center of the state, without a plan, a fort, or a reliable supply line.[185] Greene's forces amounted to no more than two thousand, even adding in the screening militias. Both sides were suffering from the extreme heat and rampant disease, but the Patriot forces had little gunpowder and ammunition. Instead of launching a sustained, decisive attack on massed Patriot forces on their doorstep, General Gould allowed Greene to rest his main army at the High Hills of the Santee, post Sumter at Friday's Ferry on the Congaree River, post Pickens at Ninety-Six at the western frontier, and post Marion at Nelson's Ferry on the Santee River.[186] Amazingly, Greene had dislodged entrenched enemy forces from their garrisons and forts in the upstate and the center of South Carolina in less than four months. British newspapers claimed victories at Ninety-Six and Camden while Greene's forces held both forts, the center of the state, and the most important strategic areas of South Carolina. The "victorious" Lord Rawdon could only watch his commander surrender at Yorktown while a prisoner of war aboard an enemy warship in the Chesapeake Bay preventing Cornwallis's escape.

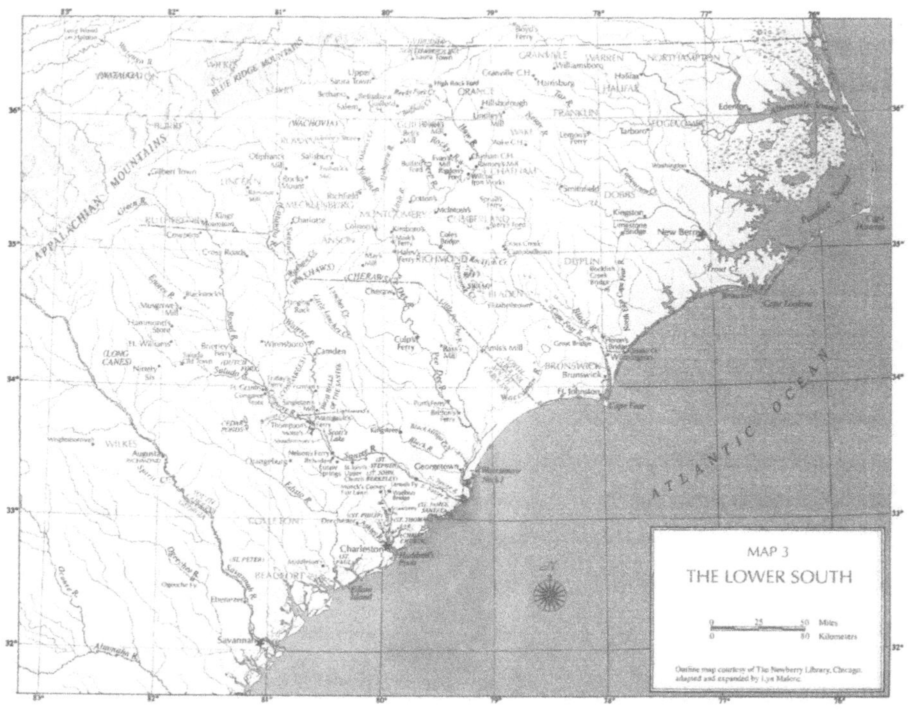

South Carolina 1780, map courtesy of the *Newberry Library*, Chicago, Ill, and UNC Press, adapted by Lyn Malone.

Another British army, commanded by Lieutenant Colonel Alexander Stewart, was encamped at Eutaw Springs, about sixty miles northwest of Charlestown about the first of September. While this was Stewart's first independent command, he had one of the best field officers in the British army as his second, Major John Majoribanks. The career military officer from Scotland was about forty-two years old. Stewart's estimated two thousand troops received massive supplies brought from Charlestown by wagon and from the Santee River by boat. He was well-equipped for battle.

The month before, on August 3, Stewart was positioned at McCord's Ferry on the Congaree River, about thirty miles north of Orangeburg.

He withdrew to Eutaw Springs (which placed him about thirty-five miles east of Orangeburg) after Greene ordered Lieutenant Colonel Harry Lee's Legion to disrupt his supply line and prevent Stewart's force from becoming ensconced at McCord's Ferry near Thompson's Plantation. Lee's forces dispersed about thirty-two supply wagons and captured about twenty of the wagon train's escort soldiers en route to Stewart. Lee reported to Greene that Stewart was fighting a mutiny in his ranks and "there is a general inclination to desert."[187] Stewart likely precipitated his desertion problems by ordering "the Loyalists to enlist for three years or forfeit their rations" to solve supply shortages.[188] Simultaneous with Lee's mission to disrupt enemy supplies, Greene tasked General Sumter and state militia Colonel William Henderson to harass the strong contingent of Loyalists operating around Orangeburg. The Loyalist militias coordinated with Stewart's regular forces to maintain a north–south battle line between the Santee and Edisto Rivers. The most populated areas of the state were behind this British front. Deprived of his supply wagons, Stewart was forced to retreat forty miles downriver to Eutaw Springs adjacent to the Santee River. There he could secure his supply line while coordinating with the Hessians and Loyalists in the Orangeburg area. Stewart's retrograde move relinquished control of the confluence of the Wateree and Congaree Rivers and a large triangle of territory mid-state.

Meanwhile, General Alexander Leslie was reassigned from Cornwallis's offensive in Virginia to join Clinton in New York to advise him on the Chesapeake Campaign. Leslie knew the ground and Clinton probably wanted more information than Cornwallis was sharing. Leslie had already been announced as the new Southern British commander, adding more confusion to an already disorganized command structure resulting from Cornwallis's absence from South Carolina. Subsequently, unified British decision-making in the Lower South theater of operations stalled at a crucial time.

On September 5, the Battle of the Chesapeake left Cornwallis stranded at Yorktown, so the high command center's job in New York was to figure out how to get reinforcements to Cornwallis by land. Clinton was sure that Washington's forces would attack New York rather than

Yorktown. Therefore, he would not consider sending any New York troops to reinforce Virginia. The next practical alternative was to order Stewart in South Carolina to fall back to Moncks Corner, about twenty-six miles below Eutaw Springs. From that location, Lieutenant Colonel Stewart could rendezvous with the Thirtieth Regiment and the Hessians and Loyalists roaming around Orangeburg and then lead a forced march up the King's Highway through North Carolina to relieve Cornwallis. General Leslie was in Clinton's command center in New York at this time. Leslie had marched the King's Highway with Cornwallis from Wilmington to the Yorktown peninsula in April, so he knew the potential relief route.

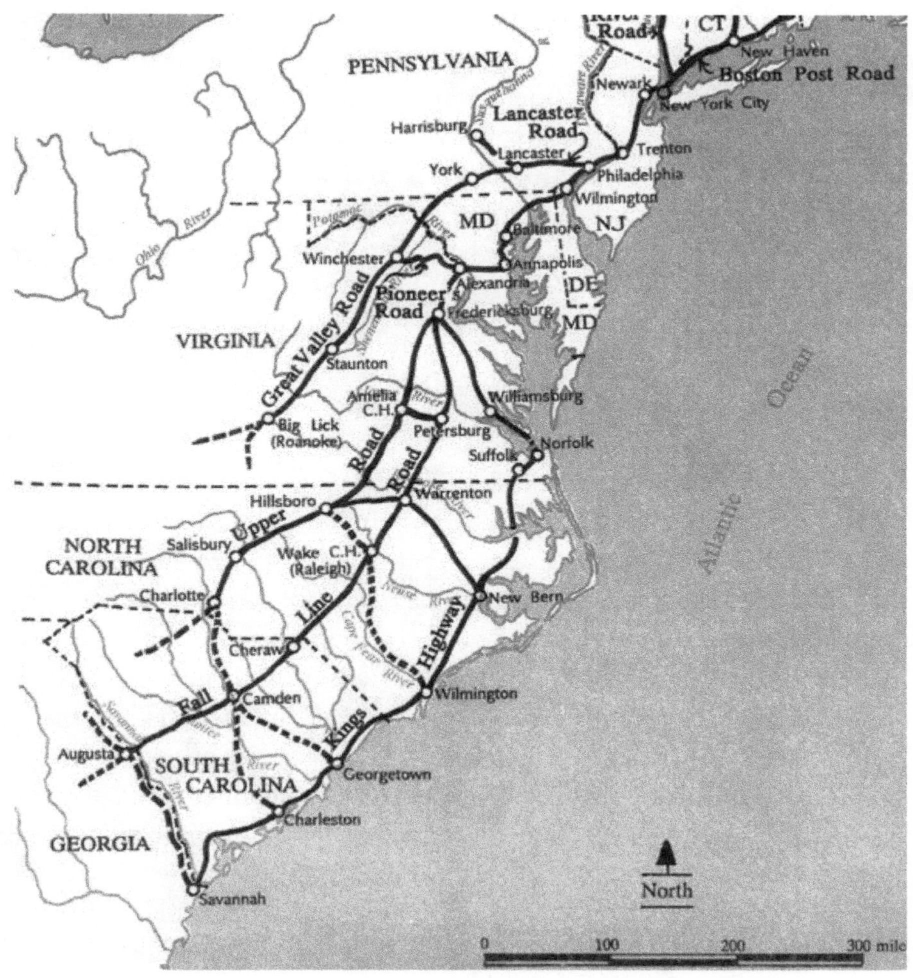

Colonial Roads 1735-1815, by William Dollarhide.

Lieutenant Colonel Henry Lee had received intelligence that Stewart had been ordered to fall back to the post at Moncks Corner, about thirty miles northwest of Charlestown near the Wadboo Bridge and the road to Virginia.[189] Simultaneously, Hessian lieutenant colonel Ernst Leopold von Borck was withdrawing from the Orangeburg District with about seven hundred men, including a large company of Hessians and about a hundred Loyalist dragoons. Greene wrote Marion on August 10 with instructions to combine forces with Colonel Harden and ambush Leopold's army in a secret operation. Lieutenant Colonel William Washington had reported that Leopold's forces were beset with malaria and yellow fever, leaving behind three hundred sick and wounded from their post in Orangeburg. On August 30, Marion and Harden's combined forces decimated Leopold's advance Loyalist force under Major Thomas Fraser at Parker's Ferry as Fraser approached the Edisto River, inflicting more than two hundred causalities. Marion's successful ambush likely prevented Lieutenant Colonel Leopold von Borck's forces from linking up with Stewart at Eutaw Springs. Von Borck's decimated forces retired instead to Charlestown and left the fight.

Greene did the opposite. After resting and resupplying at the High Hills, he began marching a circuitous route to attack Lieutenant Colonel Stewart at Eutaw Springs. There is some question whether Stewart's troops at Eutaw Springs were being repositioned for a mission to reinforce Cornwallis at Yorktown or if Stewart's mission was to establish a new British fort at either Eutaw or Moncks Corner. A garrison at either location would likely prove the preponderance of control of South Carolina in anticipation of treaty negotiations because the majority of the province's population was in the low country. From a war planners' perspective, establishing a solid fort at Moncks Corner and sending a large relief force to Cornwallis from that location up the King's Highway would satisfy both urgencies. Stewart's force consisted primarily of regular offensive troops complemented with garrison soldiers evacuated from Fort Ninety-Six. His second-in-command, Major John Majoribanks, had recently led Rawdon's two-thousand-man forced march up from Charlestown to relieve Ninety-Six, so the experience and firepower to conduct a relief mission were present. Stewart had many supplies at Eutaw Springs, enough to commence a march to aid Cornwallis at Yorktown.

Whatever British mission was unfolding, the importance of the Battle of Eutaw Springs cannot be overstated. Both armies had about two thousand men, and the battle was hard fought on September 8, 1781.[190] The state song of South Carolina refers to the Battle of Eutaw Springs as a fight to be a state rather than a British province. The battle could have been more appropriately named "the battle for the state of South Carolina." A post-battle theater play was produced, emphasizing this battle's importance while honoring the heroes who fought in it. The best militia leaders from South Carolina and the best Continental officers in the Lower South came together to dislodge the mostly professional British army under Stewart. Marion, Pickens, Taylor, Lacey, Thomas Polk, Horry, Middleton, and Hampton bravely led South Carolina state troops and militia in concert with the North Carolina Militia under William Polk. The Continentals included the North Carolina Brigade under General Sumner, the Virginia Brigade under Campbell, the Maryland Brigade under Otho Williams, the North Carolina Dragoons under Malmedy, Lee's Legion under Harry Lee, and the First and Third Legionary Corps under William Washington. Greene field commanded the entire force. The British had some of their best troops present: The Third Regiment of Foot (The Buffs), the Sixty-Third, the Sixty-Fourth, the Eighty-Fourth, plus some of their best provincial soldiers from New Jersey and New York. The British sent their best, and Greene showed up with America's best. European negotiators' eyes were on who controlled what territory in South Carolina after the fighting. The flame of independence for South Carolina would either die or brighten as a result of this battle.

Both armies claimed the field at separate times. Stewart's perimeter security was nonexistent, so Greene completely surprised his detached foraging forces and gained the field, where he assembled his main army. The two armies clashed, and the Patriot forces had the British in full retreat before being stopped at Stewart's brick-house headquarters. This fortress like house at the field's edge was protected on its flank by blackjack miniature oaks impenetrable by human or horse and Eutaw Creek at its rear, making it an ideal defensive citadel. After hours of fighting, Greene withdrew but sent a mounted force to reclaim some portion of the field afterward. Stewart ungraciously called Greene's after-action report to Congress "full of lies." Stewart showed bitterness after the battle when he refused Greene's proposal to tend to the wounded under truce, yet he had no compunction about abandoning his wounded on the battlefield the next day to Greene's care. Stewart's unbecoming behavior aside, Greene's strategic mission was to dislodge Stewart's forces, cripple his offensive capability, and claim the entire Eutaw area for the allied Congressional forces.[191] In this, he entirely succeeded and was awarded a Congressional Medal.

Stewart withdrew the next day after destroying substantial guns and supplies. He left his wounded and about four hundred of his men captured by Greene in a disorganized retreat. The Thirtieth Regiment came up from Moncks Corner to cover his retreat as Lee's Legion and Marion's men nipped at their heels. As a result of the battle, Stewart's fractured army no longer could relieve Cornwallis by land at Yorktown, nor could the British build a fort between Nelson's and Murray's Ferries to control the Santee River and the road to Charlestown. Both possible missions were defeated before either could be started. The indecisive Colonel Paston Gould, Cornwallis's Lower South commander in Charlestown, was no help. Control of the riverways from King's Mountain and Oliphant's Mill, North Carolina, connecting through the middle of South Carolina to Georgetown, was in the Patriot's hands. The major rice- and indigo-producing areas of the Pee Dee and the Santee River region also fell into the Patriot's hands. British land access to Wilmington from Charlestown via the King's Highway was cut. Internationally, the news of this British dislodgement and Patriot territory acquisition likely assured the French court that Greene could take back the Carolinas without foreign assistance. After consultation with John Adams, French foreign minister Vergennes put off a mediation proposal that would have likely acquiesced the Carolinas and Georgia to Britain.

Greene's victory at Eutaw Springs dislodging Stewart's army combined with Marion's mauling of the British force at Parker's Ferry degraded a possible three-thousand-plus man relief force to Yorktown to below offensive combat capability. The French fleet's successful containment of the British army at Yorktown on September 5, sealing off a relief effort by sea, likely stimulated war planners in New York and Cornwallis in Virginia to begin organizing a relief force by land. Expecting a full-on attack in New York by George Washington, Clinton was not going to part with any troops to reinforce Cornwallis until he knew for sure the intended target of the French fleet. General Alexander Leslie, who was advising Clinton in New York, had traveled the King's Highway with Cornwallis from Wilmington to the Yorktown area in April, so he was familiar with the road Stewart could take (which roughly followed present-day Highway 17). If Stewart's prize regiments encamped at Eutaw Springs had remained intact after September 8, one can only speculate what mission he would have been assigned. For sure, Stewart's and Leopold von Borck's combat capabilities were destroyed, and the American lines moved forward toward the coast after Stewart's post-battle retreat to Moncks Corner. With the decimation of those forces, Cornwallis's and Clinton's contingency option to order Stewart's southern army to the rescue evaporated. There were not enough combat-ready British troops left in South Carolina to spare without sacrificing Charlestown. Deprived of Stewart's possible three-thousand-man relief force, an encircled Cornwallis surrendered his army to French and American troops about five weeks later at Yorktown.

VII.
THE FINAL PHASE

"The talent of the strategist is to identify the decisive point and to concentrate everything on it."
—Carl von Clausewitz, On War

The launch of a full-scale Southern Strategy offensive became possible after the British successfully captured Savannah and the remainder of Georgia. This relatively small-scale operation involving about 3,100 men was completed in early 1779. Lieutenant Colonel Archibald Campbell, commander of the operation, fulfilled his promise to be "the first to [strip] a star and stripe from the flag of Congress." The Betsy Ross Flag was reduced to twelve stars.

In July of 1779, the control of Georgia was formally returned to the Crown with the installation of Royal Governor James Wright. A combined French and American attack to retake Savannah failed in October of that same year. Thus, Sir Henry Clinton, commander of all expeditionary forces in America, now had a foothold in the South from where he could safely land troops and supplies. From Savannah, Clinton could launch his massive Southern Strategy 4.0 Campaign to capture the entire South and "possibly more," according to him.

Having failed to capture Charlestown in June of 1776, Henry Clinton gave Lord Germain a long list of ships, troops, equipment, and supplies he thought necessary to conduct a successful conquest. Clinton received everything he wanted, and British forces captured Charlestown in May of 1780 after about a six-week siege. The timespan between Charlestown's capture and Cornwallis's surrender at Yorktown in October 1781 constituted approximately seventeen months of lighting war across the South. The general sequence of British operations during those seventeen months consisted of the following: (1) South Carolina was conquered, and an interconnected chain of forts was established to maintain control; (2) Loyalist militias throughout the Lower South were organized and armed; (3) Cherokee and Creek tribes were armed and coordinated to attack Patriot settlements along the Piedmont and Appalachian foothills and eastward to current day Spartanburg, South Carolina, and Augusta, Georgia; (4) the first major offensive to conquer middle and western North Carolina was launched (unsuccessfully); (5) the invasion of Virginia was launched by the combined forces of General Benedict Arnold and General William Phillips with an initial mission to terrorize inhabitants, destroy General Greene's primary source of supplies, and reestablish royal authority; (6) eastern North Carolina was occupied, including Fort Johnston, Fort Wilmington, Fort Cross Creek, and the strategic Cape Fear River; (7) the second major offensive to conquer middle and western North Carolina was launched (unsuccessfully); and (8) the British chain of forts throughout South Carolina were captured by the allied Southern Continental Army, and a containment zone had been established in the lower third section of the province.

Nonetheless, in November 1781, the British still had the upper hand in the Lower South. British forces controlled most of Georgia and had an operating royal government in place. Their occupation of South Carolina had been rolled back to the low country; the North Carolina occupation consisted of the coastal areas from the port capital Wilmington to Cross Creek. The British had lost all their military forts in the mid and western Carolinas but still controlled the low country coastal regions and the all-important capital-city garrisons. Occupying the capital cities provided compelling claims to those provinces at the negotiating table. The allied Patriot forces led by General Greene had driven most of the Carolina Loyalist militias and Tories down to the low country and the coastal plain. Most of the remaining Loyalists who did not desert to the Patriot cause followed Lord Rawdon in his retreats from Forts Camden and Ninety-Six down to the Charlestown neck outside the city's gates. This massive Loyalist refugee camp was derisively nicknamed Rawdon Town. Despite their setbacks, British forces held most of Georgia and the capital port cities in the Carolinas and Georgia. If treaty negotiations began in November 1781 after Yorktown, Britain had the capital city trump cards and the lion's share of the low counties' populations necessary to claim the Lower South.

Momentum was on the Patriot side, but territory possession and operating state governments were lacking. Greene had appointed a commission to negotiate a treaty with the Cherokees and Creeks, which was making progress.[192] He hoped to detach the Native Americans from the British and stop attacks on the backcountry and his rear. So far, Greene had won the trust of the Carolina people outside the British-occupied coastal regions by protecting the formerly oppressed inhabitants and preventing plundering. With sentiments favoring the Patriots, liberated areas remained in American hands and gave hope to the Georgians.

When Cornwallis marched to Virginia, his goals were to cut off supplies from that state to Patriot forces elsewhere and establish a central naval base there. His immediate campaign plan was to conquer Virginia and build a superport along the Chesapeake. He planned to locate the British provincial capital in Williamsburg to replace the rebel capital in Richmond, which turncoat Benedict Arnold had reduced to ashes. Cornwallis could efficiently protect their reinstated British capital twenty miles away in Williamsburg and rapidly sail troops to support Wilmington, Charlestown, Savannah, Saint Augustine, and New York from a Yorktown superport garrison. Offensives could be quickly launched to snuff out Patriot armies and rebel resistance anywhere along the East Coast. The British had become experts at moving troops rapidly up and down the coast with their powerful navy as conditions warranted. The ability of Virginia to supply the Southern and Northern Continental Armies was devastated by Lieutenant Colonel Tarleton's and Simcoe's love of the torch. Now Cornwallis could take his well-supplied Virginia army to the Yorktown peninsula to build a British superport, arsenal, and center of military operations for British America, just as Charles Lee had recommended in 1777. Once that was accomplished, Cornwallis would sail from there to destroy Greene's forces and repair his tattered reputation.

But there were flies in the ointment. Unexpected French troops and supplies arrived to join Generals Lafayette and Wayne in sealing off the Yorktown peninsula, trapping Cornwallis. Lieutenant Colonel John Laurens of South Carolina arrived there almost simultaneously with money loaned from the Dutch and two ships filled with military supplies. The French fleet under Comte De Grasse intercepted and defeated the British fleet coming to support or withdraw Cornwallis's army. Washington's Northern Continental Army, joined by Rochambeau's army, made a rapid march to lay siege to Yorktown and seal Cornwallis's fate. With Cornwallis's surrender on October 19, 1781, he British plan to conquer Virginia and establish their main operations base along the Chesapeake ended.

While Greene's army was recuperating at the High Hills of the Santee after the siege at Fort Ninety-Six, French admiral de Grasse sailed from the West Indies in early August to the Chesapeake Bay. Count Rochambeau, commander in chief of French troops in America, approved this movement. Washington learned of the French fleet sailing to Virginia. On August 18, the Northern Continental army began moving alongside Rochambeau's French army to join Lafayette and Wayne at Williamsburg and command the joint siege operation.[193] After de Grasse defeated the British relief fleet on September 5, French ships began offloading the cannon and war materials necessary to conduct a successful siege.

Washington decided to move against Cornwallis on the Yorktown peninsula in conjunction with the French in part because of Nathanael Greene's situational briefing letter of 6 August. Greene wrote about Lafayette's and Wayne's forces being kept in place to compel "Cornwallis to take a position and fortify himself; and if the supplies to his army could be cut off by water…he would be obliged to surrender in a fortnight or three weeks at most, for want of provisions, for I believe he has none laid at this point nor in expectation of being obliged to act on the defensive. At least I am persuaded he has no apprehension of having his water communication intercepted," Greene reported.[194] Cornwallis had to be stopped in Virginia if South Carolina and Georgia were to be liberated. Greene had received a European intelligence report that Cornwallis would evacuate his troops from Virginia "and attempt to recover the entire possession of the two [Carolina] Southern states."[195] Virginia was under Greene's Southern Department, and Lafayette and Wayne were under his command at this time.

In late August, Greene began amassing troops from across both Carolinas to attack Stewart at Eutaw Springs. The grand expectation was that after neutralizing Stewart's force, de Grasse or Rochambeau or both would join Greene in a combined land-and-sea attack on Charlestown, South Carolina. According to Greene's letter to Colonel William Henderson, he was ordering all available militia troops to rendezvous at Camden to "give [Colonel] Stewart a dressing [so] we can lay siege to Charles Town immediately," in time to coordinate with a French fleet.[196] Stewart was encamped at Nelson's Ferry and Eutaw Springs. Greene would have to displace Stewart's force before laying siege to Charlestown in coordination with the French fleet. As it turned out, the French chose Yorktown as their first target and ran out of time afterward to send their fleet and troops to coordinate with Greene against Charlestown.

On August 29, 1781, the French fleet arrived just off Jamestown, Virginia, and began offloading supplies, weapons, and troops to support General Lafayette's army at Williamsburg. The goal was to seal off the Yorktown peninsula until Washington's and Rochambeau's troops could arrive from New York to begin the push-in. Meanwhile, the French ships of the line would blockade Cornwallis at Yorktown to prevent reinforcement or withdrawal. Washington would be taking over the Southern Command in his home state of Virginia as soon as he arrived. On September 5, a British fleet under Admiral Thomas Graves attacked the French fleet supporting the siege at the Battle of Virginia Capes.[197] Sir Thomas was attempting to relieve Cornwallis and disrupt the combined French and American entrapment operation. The battle fought between the British and French navies lasted only two and a half hours but was decisive in preventing assistance or supplies to the British army isolated at Yorktown. The British fleet disengaged and returned to New York before eight more French ships of the line under de Barras arrived to support de Grasse, bringing the total French ships of the line to thirty-six. The result of the battle prevented Cornwallis from receiving relief and ensured the safe use of the Chesapeake Bay for the French to support the combined American and French ground forces laying siege to Yorktown.

Three days after the Battle of the Chesapeake, on September 8, 1781, Stewart's forces were enjoying a hearty breakfast when Greene's forces eliminated any chance of a Yorktown relief operation by land. The Battle of Eutaw Springs eviscerated the combat capability of the British to mount a sustainable offensive campaign again in the Lower South. With the fighting capability of Stewart's and Leopold von Borck's armies destroyed and Greene's so-called defeated army on the offensive again in the low country, Clinton's and Leslie's option to order Stewart and company to Cornwallis's aid evaporated. Defending Charlestown and South Carolina, the crown jewels of the British American empire, took priority over rescuing Cornwallis's stranded army on a nonstrategic peninsula in Virginia. Cornwallis's distraction with building a superport on the Chesapeake before destroying Greene would sink him.

The successful siege of Yorktown on October 19 was a tremendous allied military achievement. Baron Ludwig von Closen's eyewitness report stated that of the six thousand American soldiers observed, about fifteen hundred, or 25 percent, were Black persons. The Rhode Island Regiment, who participated in the key redoubt attack led by John Laurens and Alexander Hamilton, was "three-quarters" Black persons, "merry, confident and healthy in appearance," Closen reported. The capitulation of Cornwallis's army at Yorktown, precipitated by the storming of the strategic redoubt by the Rhode Islanders, shattered British expectations of conquering America. The momentous event reassured Americans that they could defeat Britain's finest armies with France's help by remaining united. On the other side of the pond, King George remained resolute about continuing the war upon hearing news of Cornwallis's surrender.

General Clinton replaced the captured Cornwallis with General Alexander Leslie for the Southern British command based in Charlestown. Leslie was expected to hold North Carolina, South Carolina, and Georgia under British occupation to retain those provinces under status quo or uti possidetis requirements if a cease-fire or mediation commenced or a treaty was signed.[198] Without further military action by Congressional forces, three or four of the thirteen American colonies would likely be retained by the British, plus the thirteen Canadian provinces the United States had contested. The British army in Virginia might have been lost, but the Lower South was not.

Thus, the War for American Independence did not end with General Lord Cornwallis surrendering the British army via his proxy at Yorktown on October 19, 1781. While a great American and French success, few leaders on either side, including George Washington, John Adams, the Count of Vergennes, and King George III, regarded Yorktown as the end of the war. Warfare continued in the prospective United States for another fourteen months in an all-out effort to control territory in the Lower South and settle the question of independence.

On January 2, 1782, Lord Germain was crystal clear about the Crown's post-Yorktown mindset. He stated, "that all existing British posts were to be retained on the Atlantic coast."[199] If Congress wanted peace with independence, the Continental Army and their allies must dislodge the British armies from their garrisons. The more considerable work of pushing several British armies out of the Lower South, without French naval support, remained to claim American control of the region in the eyes of the European community. After Yorktown, the job of liberating the capital cities in both Carolinas and Georgia and expelling the British armies entirely from the South was hard work yet to be done before the king and Parliament would seriously consider a peace proposal that included sovereign independence.

Greene knew he could not let up military pressure after Eutaw Springs and Yorktown; otherwise, he risked the British regrouping and retaking the offensive in South Carolina. The British War Office listed almost 10,000 troops ready for battle in South Carolina in November 1781 after

Yorktown: 5,024 British regulars, 1,596 Hessians, and 3,155 Provincials. These numbers do not reflect an estimated 5,000 Cherokee and Creek allies, renegade Loyalist militias, or enslaved Blacks involved in defense of the Charlestown garrison. In contrast, Greene's effective forces amounted to fewer than 1,500 men. The British held a commanding five-to-one force superiority ratio in addition to their well-supplied troops in South Carolina being among the best in the field. If Greene waited for reinforcements from troops reassigned after Yorktown to arrive at his encampment on the Santee while General Leslie took over command in Charlestown to organize an offensive, he risked everything his army had gained in the Carolinas. South Carolina and Georgia would be lost for sure at the negotiating table if Leslie were given time to recapture territory. General Leslie was no indecisive Paston Gould; he was an experienced British general who knew how to organize large commands to fight well to win a planned campaign. If Greene waited for Leslie to unify his command and seize the initiative, Greene would be on the defensive and likely destroyed-the Southern British army would prevail. .

Instead, Greene chose to renew his offensive during the British transition of command by making his army appear much larger than it was. His radical plan was to appear everywhere around Charlestown at once to panic the British field commanders into retreating to the walled city of Charlestown and its surrounding islands. He would use false intelligence and mobility to deceive the enemy into making duplicate counts: the enemy would overestimate his strength and positions. If Greene could get the separated British regiments to withdraw in a panic from their dispersed low country fortifications to form a defensive perimeter around Charlestown, he had confidence his meager forces could lock them in. Charlestown would become their prison.

But first, he needed to disconnect eastern North Carolina from the equation. Greene had prevented Cornwallis from completing his military conquest of North Carolina. Still, the British held the port city capital of Wilmington, Fort Johnston, Cross Creek, the Cape Fear River, and surrounds. The threat of regular British troops stationed at Wilmington, the roving North Carolina Loyalist regiment of David Fanning, and the South

Carolina regiment of Micah Gainey operating between Georgetown and the Carolina border had to be resolved. Greene's army, supported by Marion's regiment, could not close in on Charlestown without risking entrapment between the British forces north of the city and the large enemy army deployed around the city. Upon receiving the news of the surrender of the British army at Yorktown in October, Greene accelerated the wheels he had in motion to oust the British from the North Carolina capital at Wilmington. Patriot governor Burke had been kidnapped by David Fanning's Loyalist militia the month before. Therefore, from a negotiating perspective, the British claims on that state were enhanced. Burke's kidnapping decapitated the flimsy state government in North Carolina, and the British still held the recognized state capital.

Wilmington was a deep-water port guarded by Fort Johnston on the Cape Fear River and supported by a garrison at Cross Creek. Greene corresponded with then-acting Governor Martin of North Carolina in planning a joint Continental and North Carolina militia operation against Fort Wilmington.[200] General Griffin Rutherford's militia, General Anthony Wayne's dragoons, and General St. Clair's Virginians were assigned that task. Rutherford could isolate the target areas while awaiting the Continentals' arrival from Virginia to commence an assault jointly. Not long after Greene's plan was put in motion, General Leslie became aware that Continental troops from the Yorktown Campaign would soon march down the King's Highway from Virginia to Wilmington and join North Carolina forces to attack Craig's forces at Wilmington. Leslie knew firsthand the marching route the Continentals would take from his experience marching that route into Virginia with Cornwallis in May. He was aware of the commander's (Major James Craig) and Fort Wilmington's capabilities, vulnerabilities, and resources, having retreated there after Cornwallis's debacle at Guilford Courthouse. Major Craig had terrorized the area into a mass militia uprising of sorts. Leslie was also aware that a reinforced Greene would likely attack his weakened garrison at Charlestown if he shifted about two thousand troops plus river galleys and warships to defend the North Carolina capital.

Craig's forces at Wilmington risked isolation and freezing through a Cape Fear winter dependent on a vulnerable supply line. Greene would then have him on numbers when the combined troops of Rutherford, Wayne, and St. Claire linked up. Facing this prospect, Leslie promoted Craig to lieutenant colonel in the British show of things and ordered him to abandon Wilmington "to augment Southern headquarters in Charlestown." Wilmington was liberated on the fourteenth of November, bringing North Carolina closer into the Congressional confederation in the eyes of the diplomatic world. Lieutenant Colonel Craig was reassigned to protect Leslie's important food source across the Ashley River from Charlestown at John's Island.

With the Wilmington garrison on his flank eliminated, Greene initiated possibly the boldest military operation of the war at the end of November.[201] He broke camp and proceeded down the banks of the Edisto River toward Charlestown with a mixed cavalry and infantry force of only four hundred men. The British had a strong outpost of about two thousand men at Goose Creek Bridge, fifteen miles north of Charlestown, and a major fort at Dorchester eight miles south of Goose Creek, manned by nearly one thousand troops composed of infantry and cavalry. Greene's cavalry and infantry force consisted of selected elements of Lee's Legion, Washington's Cavalry, and Sumter's militia. On December 1, his strike force arrived at Dorchester. En route, he positioned himself to be seen by British scouts, to promote the thinking that he was leading his entire Southern Army, possibly accompanied by just-received Yorktown troops, to surprise attack Charlestown. Aided by planting false reports about the size of his forces and capitalizing on the shock of that morning's *Charlestown Royal Gazette* headline reporting Cornwallis's surrender at Yorktown, Greene's attack completely surprised Major John Doyle at the Dorchester garrison. After Greene's forward elements routed Doyle's cavalry, Doyle panicked. He ordered his cannons thrown into the Ashley River, the destruction of all supplies, and a full retreat in haste to the Quarter House several miles outside Charlestown. Lieutenant Colonel Stewart, at Goose Creek Bridge, thinking he, too, was about to be overwhelmed by his "defeated" foe, also retreated to the

Quarter House to make a stand against Greene's army together with Doyle's forces. General Leslie, now in Charlestown in command of all Southern forces, called out the entire garrison at Charlestown, and "the most active negroes were called to arms and enrolled" in manning the walls. Greene's four-hundred-man force dislodged over three thousand top British troops from entrenched, strategic fortifications with cannon, thereby securing about twenty square miles of territory. George Washington wrote to Colonel John Laurens expressing his approbation of Greene's successful blitz: "He compelled the enemy to abandon their outposts…though hopelessly [out]…numbered. This brilliant maneuver is another proof of the singular abilities which General Greene possesses." Amazingly, Greene's "mad dash" pushed the British occupation inside a perimeter of about a dozen miles outside Charlestown plus the surrounding islands in less than two days.

This brilliant operation sought to achieve other military and political results. Greene's main army had dwindled to about eight hundred effectives with only four rounds of ammunition per man. If attacked, his army would quickly run out of ammunition, and the Southern Continental Army would likely be destroyed. He could wait for a combined attack by Stewart and Doyle with their two to three thousand seasoned soldiers he was sure to lose, or he could pool his ammunition and powder to equip a four-hundred-man strike force and take the offensive with a "mad dash" to panic the enemy. Once Leslie understood Greene's strength, he was sure to order an offensive to finish him. But Greene took the fight to them and made his little army look undefeatable in the process.

Yet there was another dimension to his attack strategy. After the Battle of Eutaw Springs, Greene's convalescing army had consumed most of the food around their High Hills camp. He had to move them to a place with plentiful food supplies without being subjected to attack by a much larger force while en route. The site he selected to relocate was Jacksonborough, South Carolina, on the Edisto River, an ideal place to reassemble the state legislature and governor under the protection of the Continental Army. The town had a tavern and Masonic hall to accommodate the state government and the governor's office. Greene's mad dash toward Dorchester would divert British attention away from his main army repositioning there. Once Greene's main army was repositioned in Jacksonborough, Governor Rutledge could leave the safety of the Waxhaws to reside there and call in state representatives for legislative sessions. Greene would then supervise elections and thus establish a sound basis for John Adams and Benjamin Franklin to argue that South Carolina was an operating state within the Confederation of the United States, not a Britain possession, despite the redcoat occupation of Charlestown and its surrounds. After the safety of the state government in Jacksonborough was on sound footing, Greene could press in his main force to encircle the British in Charlestown. He would then begin land embargo operations designed to slowly suffocate the British into surrendering the city.[202] If the British army was pressured to evacuate, the elected state government confederated under Congress could move into the capital city, making possession of South Carolina indisputable at the European negotiating table.

However, the Patriots still had much to do to make this plan work: militarily, politically, diplomatically, and economically. Greene wrote Governor Rutledge on December 3 and 9, providing situational reports, making requests, and proposing the future concept of operations. General Greene had established his headquarters at Round O near Jacksonborough, about thirty-five miles from Charlestown. This positioning enabled him to cover the temporary state capital at Jacksonborough, which was taking up government business and organizing elections with his companionship. Francis Marion was assigned Saint Stephens and Saint Thomas parishes to patrol and protect. Sumter was assigned Orangeburg to cover Greene's rear and the Four Hole Bridge; John Barnwell was given the southern border area. General Pickens was appointed to the upstate of South Carolina to solve Native American, Tory, and banditti attacks. Greene then established a fast-attack cavalry unit from choice militia elements he tasked to keep the British bottled up by patrolling the areas between the Santee and Edisto Rivers west of Charlestown. In Greene's letters, he explained that the British were busily fortifying Charlestown by incorporating Tories and Blacks into their ranks and activating the

Cherokees and Creeks in his rear to attack en masse. He reported his current mission was to "cover this country" he had liberated and "drive the enemy from their strongholds." He encouraged Rutledge to begin taking measures to restart the economy. "The cultivation of the country is so important an object, and so much dependent upon trade and commerce, and both so connected with the possession of Charlestown...the people are deeply interested in this measure." Greene also outlined his plan to force the British to evacuate Charlestown without the assistance of the French or Spanish navy through a policy of containment and denying resources. There was no military precedence of a land army successfully forcing a port-city evacuation of a numerically superior army without naval force assistance or siege cannon.[203]

Nevertheless, he formally requested that he be allowed to recruit Blacks. "They would make good soldiers," enabling General Greene to repel the expected British offensives and eventually dispossess the enemy of Charlestown. They "should have their freedom...and treated in all respects as other soldiers," he urged. Rutledge followed Greene's advice and supported his requests except for the formal recruitment of Blacks. Greene would have to make do.

Meanwhile, the military situation in Florida was affecting the British province of Georgia. After the Spanish took Fort Pensacola in May 1781, the Spanish began putting pressure on Fort Saint Augustine (Castillo de San Marcos), where South Carolina congressional leaders and several signers of the Declaration of Independence were imprisoned. In July, a prisoner exchange agreement between Cornwallis and Greene was consummated. In August, the released South Carolina leaders went to Philadelphia, the location of the state government-in-exile. As authorized by Congress, Greene had written the Spanish general commanding Spanish forces in Florida back in June proposing a joint operation to liberate Savannah. General Bernardo de Galvez's forces had captured the British fort at Pensacola in May and had driven the British and their allies out of West Florida.[204] Galvez did not take Greene up on his proposal and instead sailed to conquer British-held islands in the West Indies. By November 1781, the Spanish forces Galvez had left in Florida controlled most of the state except Saint Augustine and strips of East Florida. British troop movements between Saint Augustine and Savannah by land became perilous, preventing rapid ground support between the two British garrisons. The Spanish installed their government throughout much of west and into east Florida, banishing Loyalist forces that had relocated to Georgia. Florida was no longer a haven from which Loyalist forces could launch attacks on insurgent Patriot forces. Additionally, British troops in Savannah and throughout Georgia could no longer rely on British military support from the Fort Saint Augustine garrison. British Georgia became isolated, with Greene's army to their north, the Spanish army to their south, and the Spanish navy to their southeast.

Near the end of October 1781, General Alexander Leslie arrived in Charlestown as the new Southern British army commander to replace Cornwallis. Leslie's use as an adviser to Clinton for the Chesapeake (Yorktown) campaign had become superfluous since Cornwallis had surrendered his army there on the nineteenth. Although he had no theater command or government experience, Leslie's leadership skills plus his two tours of duty in South Carolina made him the best man for the job out of the few British generals left in America. General Clinton's orders to Leslie were clear: "preserve as many of our posts in that province as you can, consistent with the safety of Charlestown."[205] This order clarified the British mission to continue occupying South Carolina, specifically the British Southern headquarters and the capital city port of Charlestown after Yorktown.

Direct orders to hold Charlestown at all costs would prove difficult to execute. Leslie inherited a Southern command that had seen at least four different commanders since the capture of Charlestown in the spring of 1780. The low country was recovering from a long, hot summer that brought smallpox, malaria, yellow fever, typhoid, and dengue fever in 1781. Matters were further complicated when the weather turned cold. There were about eighteen thousand mouths to feed daily, including troops, refugees, enslaved people, civilians, and the Loyalist camp outside Charlestown named Rawdon Town. Acquiring and distributing food, potable water, and firewood required constant foraging details and logistics management. Waste disposal, care of the sick and wounded, and horse livery and feeding compounded the density problem. Notwithstanding the British naval monopoly, as long as Greene kept Leslie's troops confined to the Charlestown environs, the walled city would be a humanitarian disaster in the making, preoccupying Leslie's time and prohibiting him from launching substantial offensive operations to attack Greene.

Greene's camp at Round O was ideal for restoring his army. His army was in the middle of the rice-growing region with abundant game, fowl, and fish. He could receive daily spy and intelligence reports from Charlestown and issue orders and communications via horseback throughout South Carolina.[206] He could await reinforcements, supplies, and ammunition from there while maintaining a roving offensive posture to keep the British bottled up. Round O was an excellent location to manage the containment of British forces around Charlestown while he strengthened his forces and launched his next offensive in Georgia.

Greene selected General Anthony Wayne to lead the offensive to take back Georgia. Wayne was one of Greene's closest friends. They had fought together at Brandywine, Germantown, and Monmouth and had the deep trusting friendship that only soldiers who defy death together can have. General Charles Lee abandoned Wayne on the battlefield at Monmouth, but Wayne nonetheless held his position against a numerically superior British force until Greene could reinforce him. Their gallant stand likely saved the Northern Continental Army.

Like Greene, Wayne was an expert trainer of soldiers. Wayne's specialty was light cavalry, dragoon training, and "Indian fighting." Before the war, he was a surveyor, like General Washington, so he knew how to locate his position and navigate efficiently to attack or avoid the enemy through dense forests and open terrain. At thirty-seven years old, he was battle hardened and skilled in attacking larger forces and winning. He was awarded a Congressional Medal for his special operations capture of the British garrison at Stony Point, New Jersey, where he assured General Washington before the attack that "he would storm hell, if he ordered it." After that, his nom de guerre became Mad Anthony, perhaps a psychological advantage. The enemy might have pondered whether his moniker was earned because he fought ferociously or took unorthodox gambles in attacks that only a crazy person would undertake. Wayne was neither angry nor crazy; he was the right man for the job. Native Americans referred to him as "blacksnake"—a snake that hunts rodents and rattles and strikes when cornered. Wayne and the General Marquis de Lafayette's light infantry and cavalry forces were responsible for successfully trapping Cornwallis's superior forces on the Yorktown peninsula. General Wayne would be assigned a similar mission in Georgia: trapping the British in Savannah until they surrendered the city.

Gen. Anthony Wayne equestrian statue, appreciation to the city of Philadelphia, PA, Benjamin Franklin Pkwy, John Gregory, artist.

Wayne reported for duty at Round O, South Carolina, on January 4, 1782. After a heartfelt reunion with General Greene, he was briefed and given an independent command with the commander's mission intent to take back Georgia and liberate Savannah by controlling the countryside. Georgia was named after King George II, so the British were inclined to fight hard to keep it. Wayne needed to figure out how to accomplish his primary directives while Greene worked political channels to get the itinerant state governor to embrace a policy of rewarding British and Loyalist defections over to Wayne. Greene would also take care of tasking state militias to cover Wayne's rear and flank from the Georgia upcountry and South Carolina Orangeburg district. With his briefing done, Greene sent Wayne on his way to Georgia to recapture the state.

General Wayne got right to work setting up insurgent operations in Georgia. Around the nineteenth of January, Wayne's "flying army" of about 570 light dragoons was secretly encamped fourteen miles outside of Savannah. At the same time, 100 of his artillerymen and artillery stayed ready to move at Sisters Ferry on the South Carolina side of the Savannah River.[207] The Georgia military commander, General Alured Clarke, had about 1,300 British and Hessian regulars and about 500 Loyalist troops plus an undetermined number of Loyalist refugees from East Florida and at least 300 Creek and Cherokee Native American warriors in and around Savannah. Many more Native Americans were being organized and tasked by the British Indian superintendent, Provincial colonel Thomas Brown, to conduct coordinated attacks against Augusta and other Patriot targets. General Clarke was about thirty-seven years old and had overall command of Georgia and East Florida Crown forces, enabling him to move troops from Fort Saint Augustine to Georgia as needed. Clarke coordinated his activities with James Wright, the Georgia provincial governor seated in Savannah. All told, the British enjoyed well-manned and well-supplied garrisons and a supportive Crown government in Georgia, while Wayne's insurgent force was outnumbered about five to one.

To support Wayne's military efforts, Greene wrote relocated Rhode Islander and recently elected governor John Martin of Georgia in Augusta to coordinate strategy. Augusta, located on the South Carolina–Georgia border, along the Savannah River, was the terminus of the Great Wagon Road originating in Philadelphia. General Andrew Pickens and Lieutenant Colonel Harry Lee captured Augusta in August 1781. After the town's liberation, Greene skillfully encouraged Georgia's representatives-in-exile to make their way back to South Carolina from Philadelphia. He would provide them with a protective escort to Augusta and security after that so Governor Martin could reestablish the state government within the congressional confederation. Greene was credited with the "reestablishment of civil government in this state." In his letter to Governor Martin, Greene laid out his strategy for returning the state to the union.[208] He acquainted Martin with Wayne's presence in Georgia and requested complete cooperation by assigning state militias to Wayne. Greene also asked the governor's cooperation in issuing an executive order to all militias that plundering and deprivations were not legal and would not be tolerated: "The preservation of morals, and an encouragement to honest industry should be the first objects of Government." Martin replied with assurances of total support.

Shortly after that, Wayne met with the Georgia legislature in Augusta to discuss the general strategy for taking back Georgia. Besides preventing militia plundering and revenge killings by strict enforcement, the cornerstone of the plan was to entice British troops and Loyalists to defect to the Patriot cause. In support of this aim, on February 20, Governor Martin proclaimed that he would pardon all who pledged their allegiance to the state. He would also allow them to "atone for their past conduct by assisting their fellow citizens in rescuing their country from British tyranny and oppression."[209] As the congressional military authority in the state, Wayne issued two proclamations that supported Martin's statement. The first was similar to Greene's statement in South Carolina: Loyalists who joined the Patriots would be pardoned and protected if they faithfully served in the Patriot forces until Georgia was liberated from British occupation. Loyalists who had committed atrocities would not be eligible for the repatriation program. The second proclamation was designed to entice the Hessians to desert by offering them citizenship and protection for their faithful service until liberation was complete. Buttressed by a now-operating government in Augusta offering amnesty and the presence of an experienced Continental army in Georgia, Wayne's proclamations enticed many Hessian and Loyalist troops to defect to the Patriot cause.

Simultaneously, Greene was working to stop the steady stream of Native Americans joining the British in Georgia. In the late summer of 1781, he established a multistate commission drawn from leaders in the Carolinas to begin treaty negotiations with the Cherokee. These negotiations aimed to win Cherokee neutrality, thereby countering the efforts of British agents living among them to unite the tribes and begin an all-out offensive against Patriot forces and upstate homesteads. While the negotiation efforts progressed among some tribes, Cherokee raids and massacres coordinated by embedded Loyalist militia elements increased in western South Carolina in early 1782. General Leslie had sent Loyalist major William Cunningham to the South Carolina upstate with about three hundred idled men residing in the shanty confines of Rawdon Town to conduct terror operations and coordinate Cherokee attacks from the west. Cunningham was to link up with the Loyalists who took refuge in the lower Cherokee towns after the fall of Fort Ninety-Six. These operations were to be coordinated with the Blue Ridge Cherokees and the warriors from the Creek towns near Augusta to drain Greene's forces away from Charlestown or attack Wayne's rear in Georgia after uniting forces. Cunningham's irregular troops operated in bands, working jointly with Cherokee warriors from upstate villages. Among their deprivations was the massacre of Colonel Wade Hampton's brother, his brother's family, and General Andrew Pickens's brother John, who was tortured, scalped, and burned at stake.[210] In early 1782, General Andrew Pickens partnered with militia forces from Georgia to destroy Cunningham's forces and defeat the Cherokees and Loyalist militiamen in their village strongholds, "saving this country from total ruin." It was essential to arrest these joint Cherokee and Loyalist attacks before they grew into a massive, unified effort to recapture the South Carolina upcountry and attack Wayne's rear in Georgia.

To counteract Loyalist and Cherokee terror operations, a Georgia militia unit under John Cunningham joined General Pickens to seek out and destroy their camps.[211] On February 6, Wayne reported an encounter with about three hundred Choctaws near Ebenezer, Georgia, on the Savannah River, whom the British were attempting to supply with arms.[212] He took twenty-six prisoners while a renegade militia unit destroyed a small party of Chickasaws operating in his rear. On February 19, Wayne was operating near the Ogeechee River inside enemy lines when "he learned that a considerable number of Creek chiefs were coming down the river trail" to entreat with General Clarke in Savannah. Many of these chiefs were promised the guns, powder, ammunition, blankets, and gifts captured by Greene's forces when they took the Augusta forts in June 1781.

Wayne devised a plan to capture the chiefs by dressing some of his men in British uniforms and greeting them on the Ogeechee trail. With Wayne's men posing as a guard of honor, the chiefs were brought to Wayne's camp without a fight. There Wayne addressed the multilingual leaders, pointing out the military failures of the British against Patriot forces in America. He requested they stay neutral to avoid unnecessary bloodshed on behalf of the British losing cause. Wayne sent the chiefs back to their homes without harming them, asking them not to return. Linguists were sent with the chiefs to repeat Wayne's appeal to their village tribesmen. In a letter to his wife Polly, he wrote: "I am satiete of this horrid trade of blood, & would much rather spare one poor savage than destroy twenty." [213]About the same time Wayne addressed the captured Creek chiefs, one of his detachments intercepted a party of Loyalist and Native American traders on their way to Savannah with ninety-three horses loaded with furs. Not only did Wayne benefit from these prime horses, but he also prevented another warrior group from linking up with the enemy and trading their goods for arms. Wayne's success in the "preventative delinking" of the British and Native Americans in Georgia was worth more than a regiment of infantry to fight them after they united.

Wayne's insurgency was producing results. At the end of January, he reported to Greene that his army had "maneuver'd the Enemy out of their posts at Mulberry Grove & Mrs. Gibbon's & Ogeechee."[214] Wayne had successfully invested the British forts throughout Georgia, forcing the garrison troops to withdraw to Savannah. In February, General Clarke received about 116 Hessians and 122 Choctaw reinforcements at the British garrison in Savannah to further increase his offensive capability. Wayne had to keep his insurgency operations on the move to avoid destruction: "It is now upward of five weeks since we entered this State, during which period not an officer or soldier with me has once undressed... nor do the enemy lay on beds of down."[215] To counter Clarke's increasing strength, Wayne had to pull off a sabotage operation near Savannah to stymie British confidence in their ability to leave the city lightly defended while pursuing Wayne. General Clarke was positioned to deploy a large force to destroy Wayne's army, reopen the Savannah Road and River, and recapture Augusta with his reinforcements. Wayne had to act first.

Wayne's attack occurred near the end of February on Hutchinson's Island across from the Savannah after a perfectly timed diversion. In Wayne's after-action report to Greene on February 28, he described the destruction of horse forage stockpiles and a "considerable magazine of clean rice." British supplies were set ablaze and brightly illuminated the town "at the expense of [Royal Governor] Sir James Wright."[216] This operation, conducted right under the cannons of Savannah, psychologically spooked the city residents and soldiers who had experienced relative security there since 1779. Tactically, this raid immobilized the British cavalry, who depended on the stored forage to feed their horses in the dead of winter, and it created a food scarcity for the Savannah garrison that would limit the taking in of additional reinforcements. With their horses underfed, British cavalry operations became hampered. Despite superior numbers, British forces became confined and less mobile, enabling Wayne's dragoons to roam Georgia unchecked.

The British addressed Wayne's threat by calling in their Native American allies across the rainbow of tribes in the Carolinas and Georgia. Wayne's forces controlled the road along the Savannah River, and they patrolled the Great Ogeechee Road, which connected the Creeks and Choctaws with British forces in Savannah. With Wayne blocking the way, warriors could not get to Savannah in force. The British could not deliver their arms, ammunition, and "gifts" to tribal leaders, fulfilling the terms of alliance and bringing them into a coordinated fight. General Clarke wanted warriors in his ranks and operations rather than have them continue to conduct indiscriminate raids and continue taking scalps for rewards. These terror tactics drove Loyalists and neutrals away from the British and destabilized Crown rule throughout the province. Clark needed to change the Creek and Cherokee mode of small terror operations to achieve the large force unity of effort necessary to defeat Wayne.

In March, General Clarke was dealt a significant setback with his reinforcement and coordination plan. White Fish, a powerful Creek Chief, was captured on the Savannah River Road after being assured by Tory guides the way to Savannah was open. White Fish escaped from capture, located his three hundred well-armed warriors, and returned to his home on the Altamaha River. On his way back, he massacred "a number of tories who acted as guides" because they had wrongly assured him the Savannah Road was open.[217] This event caused a break between the Creeks and British at a critical time in the war for Georgia.

Preventing Native Americans from augmenting British forces in Georgia was also on General Greene's mind. Wayne was outnumbered badly enough without the British receiving more help. On March 2, Greene ordered General Pickens to occupy the Patriot post at Orangeburg, South Carolina "to guard the frontireers [sic] against the inroads of the savages" while requesting that South Carolina governor Matthews call up one-third of the militia to supplement his forces.[218] Pickens had successfully ended Loyalist colonel Bill Cunningham's joint terror operations with the Cherokee in the South Carolina upcountry after the latter bragged about having "made hundreds of widows." Pickens's mobile dragoons were needed to prevent Cherokee infiltration into the area between Orangeburg and Augusta, to protect both Greene's rear in the South Carolina low country and Wayne's rear between Augusta and Savannah.

Wayne's military insurgency in Georgia and his political and diplomatic efforts destabilized the entire British province by March. Governor Martin had turned down Greene's proposal to allow Wayne to recruit Blacks, offering their freedom for satisfactory service, but the "forgiveness" proclamations directed at turn coating Loyalists and Hessians produced positive results.[219] For example, Sir Patrick Houstoun and his brother William, both prominent Georgia Loyalists who had immigrated from England, surrendered with their forces to Wayne in February due to the amnesty program. Royal Governor Wright expressed much concern about these defections in official correspondence. To compound Wright's problems, Clarke made an ill-advised consolidation of British military units about the same time, resulting in many Loyalist officers receiving reduced rank and pay as his regulars had more direct authority over them. The consolidation caused some Loyalist officers to defect to "the rebels,"[220] as reported by one of the commanders of Hessian troops in Savannah.

The Hessians were also deserting. Wayne enlisted spies to circulate offers of amnesty printed in German to Hessian soldiers if they joined his ranks. Governor Martin sweetened the offer to defect by promising two hundred acres of land to any Hessian who would depart British service and "become an inhabitant, citizen and member of this country."[221] These efforts produced such a steady stream of desertions that the Hessian commander, Friedrich von Porbeck, hired Blacks and Native Americans to patrol the forests outside Savannah to prevent them. He offered the patrols two guineas for every deserter brought "back dead or alive." Despite British attempts to stop desertions, many "reclaimed citizens" and Hessians joined Wayne's ranks. Georgia frontiersmen, or "crackers," whose companions had been murdered by Native Americans, also joined Wayne's army. By the end of March, Wayne's ranks were steadily increasing while British forces in Georgia were shrinking.

General Clarke and Royal Governor Wright resorted to punishment and rank barbarity. One of Wayne's men was captured during a running firefight outside Savannah. The captive was taken back to town where he was "scalped in a most barbarous manner, under the eye and Inspection of a British officer, cut off his upper lip and nose, and cut his face… in the public square."[222] His scalp was paraded "through the city with Governor Wright and General Clarke…cheering [his assassin] on and giving a ball in his honor."[223] The dragoon's mangled body was ordered to remain unburied as a stark warning for anyone thinking about joining Wayne's army.

Wayne was outraged by this act of barbarity. He regarded scalping and torture as savage crimes against humanity. Wayne was shocked that the practice was institutionally promoted and rewarded by the British government against all civilized conventions and the Articles of War. Moreover, he would not relegate his men or Patriot-leaning citizens to the inferior psychological condition that they should fear being victimized by British torture. He wanted his men to have the psychological edge of avenging angels determined to purge war crimes from Georgia by protecting those who could not defend themselves against such heinous crimes. General Wayne resolved to stop the practice of scalping. From that point forward, Wayne asserted his martial law authority by issuing standing orders that anyone caught with scalps on their person would be put to death.

The scalping and terror strategy was not helping General Clarke's manpower needs. He had to keep enough regulars at Fort Saint Augustine to defend it against Spanish attack, and he had to man at least one post near the border between East Florida and Georgia. General Leslie could not send him additional troops and still have enough manpower to man posts around Charlestown and conduct daily foraging operations to feed his army and refugees. Winter made manpower matters worse since wood-cutting operations were necessary to keep people warm. Clarke had not planned on Wayne's Continental army and militia attachments coming to Georgia, closing the Savannah and Ogeechee roads, and attacking his forces and allies attempting to go in or out of Savannah. Wayne was operating in an arc between Ebenezer northwest of Savannah and the Great Ogeechee Road south of the city, far enough away to make it difficult to be attacked in force but close enough for him to intercept people and supplies. Clarke's plans to destroy Patriot forces in Georgia and retake Augusta, at the constant urging of Royal Governor Wright, became impossible to execute without reinforcements.

Clarke pressed their Native American allies to gather in Savannah to augment his ranks. By doing so, he could conduct multiple offensive operations to drive Patriot insurgents out of the state and recapture the strategic forts at Augusta. Besides making a questionable choice bringing Native American terror warfare to the public stage in Savannah, he made another poor leadership mistake that would precipitate the British downfall in Georgia. General Clarke elevated the much-hated Loyalist Colonel Thomas Brown to Indian superintendent of the Cherokee and Creek nations while increasing Brown's command authority. Most British regulars and Hessians wanted nothing to do with Brown, Brown's Loyalists, or his Native American terrorists. Clarke thought he would get his needed reinforcements from the many Creeks who resided within 150 miles of Savannah and the many Cherokees who lived along the Appalachian Mountains' foothills if he used Brown to organize them for offensives. Wayne skillfully prevented this from happening.

As the weather turned warmer, Wayne's spies in the city alerted him to the offensive he knew was coming. General Greene had sent Wayne Continental reinforcements from Virginia under Colonel Thomas Posey, which arrived in April. These veteran troops included infantry and the First and Fourth Continental Dragoons. Colonel Brown left Savannah on May 21, leading about 1,000 British soldiers composed of cavalry and infantry from the Seventh Regiment, the Hessians, Fanning's and Brown's regulars, Choctaws, and Loyalists (the *Royal Gazette* British-Charlestown newspaper reported postbattle a force of only 350). Their mission was to link with about 300 Creeks along the Great Ogeechee Road with a high likelihood that Colonel Brown would then have the discretion to seek out and destroy Wayne's forces.[224] To counter Brown's operation, Wayne conducted a night march of cavalry and infantry through four miles of tangled swamp to intercept him. (This likely took place with a native guide leading a single column of dragoon horses while mounted on a marsh tacky horse, one that could instinctively locate dry and shallow areas to navigate through the swamp. Dragoon horses performed poorly in swamps without being walked and protected from wolves, jaguars, panthers, alligators, wild boar, and snakes by soldiers with fixed bayonets in front.) The vanguard of Wayne's troops emerged from the swamp at midnight to find themselves facing Brown's army marching along the road causeway in good order. Before his rear troops could emerge from the swamp, Wayne immediately charged the column while Brown's front troops froze in dismay: "This small vanguard put to route the whole of the enemies force without the use of [scarce] powder."[225] Wayne's surprise charge worked perfectly. Most of Brown's force jumped off the causeway into the dark swamp to avoid Wayne's ghostlike dragoons charging them with their swinging swords and bayonets while likely screaming a terrifying yell. "Many" were killed, and "a number of Prisoners" were taken. Brown's "best dragoon horses" and arms were left behind on the causeway so as not to burden his spooked soldiers in their frantic escape through the swamp. According to Wayne's after-action report to Greene, Colonel Brown "did not find his way back to town until the second night after the action." Brown's handpicked army suffered a complete defeat at the Battle of Ogeechee Road.

Tactically, Brown's mission to link up with the Creeks to augment his force was defeated. No one knows if Brown's ultimate mission was to collect more Creeks and recapture Augusta or if his mission was to hunt down Wayne's inferior insurgent forces, who did not have enough powder to make a good fight. Colonel Brown's intentions did not make British-American newspapers or General Clarke's after-action reports to General Leslie. Strategically, Brown's attempt to open the Great Ogeechee Road so Creeks and exiled Loyalists from Florida could reinforce the British garrison in Savannah was totally defeated. Wayne's swamp army suddenly appeared in front of them at the stroke of midnight along a deserted causeway and charged them like banshees from hell. After learning about the battle from survivors, Savannah likely became psychologically infected with a superstitious fear of their ghostlike enemy, who could move through swamps at night undetected. Besides exposing the unpopular Colonel Brown as an incompetent infantry officer, the name "Mad Anthony" must have haunted British heads from then on.

Governor Wright was flummoxed but not deterred. He would attempt to use trickery to preserve Savannah and Georgia for the Crown. On May 29, he wrote General Wayne in a joint letter with General Clarke to offer a cessation of hostilities and to "promote a speedy and happy reconciliation and peace."[226] Wright's offer was an attempt to persuade Wayne to lift the siege of Savannah in exchange for the assurance that Clarke would no longer pursue offensive action against Wayne's forces. Clarke implied that he would cease franchising Native Americans to conduct terror operations against innocent civilians if Wayne accepted his proposal. Wright did not offer Georgia independence. He had no authority to do so, nor did he mention that in his letter. He knew that Britain would likely retain Georgia, and his royal governorship would be preserved if he could hold out until European peace negotiations began. Wright's letter was a thinly veiled attempt to trick Wayne into acting unilaterally.

In response, Wayne politely stated that he did not have the authority to agree to such a proposal but would refer the letter to General Greene, the commander of the Southern Department, who would forward it to the Continental Congress. When Wright's ruse did not work, he took another approach. Sir James threw a party to spirit up the troops in Savannah into offensive action to break Wayne's siege. On June 4, 1782, King George's birthday, the royal governor threw an elaborate dinner for all the officers in the garrison. The grand affair spurred Clarke's command to attempt an offensive breakout in coordination with the Creeks expected imminently.

Fortunately for the Patriots, two sets of reinforcements needed for the offensive never arrived. In mid-June, about five hundred Native Americans under the command of British Provincial Colonel Black were attacked en route by militia Patriots Colonel Elijah Clarke and Colonel Robert Anderson, who wholly routed and dispersed them.[227] A few days afterward, about three hundred Coweta's were likely intercepted by Wayne's forces to prevent a junction with the British. While roughly eight hundred Native American reinforcements were intercepted, one party of well-armed Creeks got through, led by their nation-chief.

On June 24, an unknown British officer and Creek warriors under Emistisiguo attacked Wayne's main body from their rear while most in the camp were asleep.[228] At about one-thirty in the morning, Wayne's encampment at Sharon, five miles from Savannah, was penetrated en masse by about 150 Creeks. The warriors immediately overran Colonel

Posey's artillery and attempted to get the pieces into firing position against Wayne's rallying troops. Wayne was up quickly and shouted orders to charge after mounting his horse. According to Wayne's after-action report to Greene, "the whole was performed with such irristable [sic] fortitude, as soon to terminate in the total route of the Savages." Mainly the fighting was hand to hand, and "many Indians and two white men were left dead in the field…including several Cheifs [sic], and the famous Emistesego… principle Warrior of the Creek Nation." Emistisiguo shot Wayne's horse from under him with his last dying gasp, unable to aim higher. The rest of the warriors escaped through Pipemakers Swamp and made their way to the city garrison. The British regulars from Savannah attacked Wayne's front at sunrise but were driven back to their fortifications after sustaining losses. Unwilling to fight Wayne's "banshees" at night, the British missed an opportunity to launch a simultaneous surprise attack from two sides to crush Wayne's army. The Creek warriors could not pull it off alone. With the principal Creek Chief dead, the British lost their best chance to bring their remaining Creek Nation allies into an organized fight to preserve their province. They had lost all credibility. The Battle of Sharon decided the fate of Savannah and spelled the end of the British Empire ruling Georgia.

Besides their failures to collect reinforcements to conduct strategic offensives, the British were not holding out well in Savannah. Under Wayne, the Continental and state militia forces had taken possession of all of Georgia except the royal capital by mid-June. With summer's heat, the confines of the garrison accelerated the spread of malaria, smallpox, and other diseases, further eroding morale and slowly breaking the collective will of the besieged British to resist capitulation. Wayne's siege had turned the Savannah garrison into a smelly, sweltering prison for the British.

Meanwhile, the new commander of British forces in America, Sir Guy Carleton, was taking a fresh look at the situation in the Lower South. Carleton, who replaced Sir Henry Clinton in early May, was a crack British general with a reputation for high ethics, which rubbed contrary to King George's preferred treatment of "rebels." Carleton came out of retirement at the request of King George after Lord North's resignation at the end of March.[229] His return occurred five months after Yorktown and shortly after Congress rejected North's feeble peace proposal to end taxation in exchange for America ending the rebellion. Carleton worked out a discretionary operating framework with the new king's minister, Charles Watson-Wentworth (a.k.a. the Rockingham Ministry), for settling military and political matters in America. At the same time, Wentworth pursued back-door peace proposals with French secretary Vergennes to keep the United States within the empire by soliciting a wink from France. General Carleton immediately saw the situation in Savannah as unsustainable given a likely review of shipping supply reports, combat and noncombat deaths, desertions, desperate letters from Governor Wright, troop strength, West Indies' troop priorities, marginal leadership profiles, the Florida situation, and the operational environment in Georgia. Carlton had faced Wayne at the Battle of Trois-Rivieres in Quebec six years earlier and knew firsthand Mad Anthony's ability to outlead and defeat superior forces. Lord George Germain publicly criticized Sir Guy for not overrunning Wayne's outnumbered troops and destroying General Schuyler's entire American army after the Quebec battle.[230] Carleton further angered the king's ministry by releasing many Continental prisoners of war for humanitarian reasons during his charm offensive to recapture the hearts and minds of disaffected Americans. Lord Germain forced Carleton to resign one year later, in part for his ethical generalship—or, put another way, his failure to carry out Whitehall's policy of ruthless punishment to crush the rebellion by allowing the prisoners to expire. With Germain's resignation in February 1782 and North's resignation in March, King George and Parliament were ready to pursue a less punitive approach to ending the war with America. Barbarity and punishment were not working to retain their conquests, and peace with America was the lynchpin to ending the world's war against them. Maybe attracting bees with honey rather than poison might work. Carleton became the man of the hour to keep things from getting worse for the empire.

However, Sir Guy Carleton inherited a mess. He had a good plan worked out with the Earl of Rockingham to take care of military, congressional, and humanitarian matters in America satisfactory to the king. At the same time, the earl would handle the parliamentary politics and European back-channel negotiations based on Carleton's recommendations. Time, distance, and situation caused the plan to fall apart after Carleton arrived in New York. The most pressing military matter was that Britain's Lower South capital city forts were simultaneously under siege: Saint Augustine by the Spanish, Charlestown by Greene, and Savannah by Wayne. Troops could not be shifted to beat back besiegers without risking capitulation of the one fort left short. Another surrender of a British army on American soil would not be tolerated at home, and Savannah was teetering in that direction, with Charlestown not far behind. General Clarke's wholesale activation of the Creeks, Cherokees, and Choctaws in Georgia to conduct terror operations had discredited the British government in Georgia and driven their staunchest supporters and best troops to the Patriot cause. With no local support except counterproductive Native American terror raids, Savannah's collapse was imminent.

Carleton acted in time to prevent disintegration. In mid-June, General Francis Marion intercepted orders from Sir Guy Carleton to General Clarke to evacuate Savannah.[231] General Clarke received a duplicate set of orders to evacuate, presumably after the Battle of Sharon on June 24. When General Wayne received news of the impending evacuation, he ordered artillery in position and his men at arms to be prepared to launch a full-scale assault if the British attempted to fire or sack the city before departure. With that in mind, British forces withdrew with their plunder without incident. Colonel Thomas Brown and his terrorist friends slipped out of Savannah before the evacuation, aware of Wayne's policy of dealing with scalpers and known terrorists under his martial law authority. Wayne designated Colonel James Jackson, a highly regarded state hero and Patriot leader, to receive the keys to the city as the official representative of the elected Georgia state government confederated with the United States.

Savannah ceased to be a British province at noon on July 11, 1782. Wayne's Light Cavalry Continentals took possession of the city along with Jackson's state troops. Both the state of Georgia and the national congressional forces had representatives present to reclaim the state for

America. Wayne oversaw a peaceful transition while providing police protection to all remaining citizens. The Georgia government was reinstalled in Savannah under the Georgia state flag and the Betsy Ross flag. Wayne immediately negotiated Loyalist merchant agreements to resurrect the economy and reopen trade. Against tremendous odds, General Anthony Wayne's insurgency mission to liberate Georgia and restore the state to the confederation was accomplished against an entrenched and superior enemy.

While Wayne was busy returning a star to the Betsy Ross flag, General Greene was working to do the same in South Carolina. Operating from his army's headquarters at Round O, Greene detached Lieutenant Colonel Henry Lee to a front-forward position near Johns Island to harass the enemy posts there. As of late December 1781, the British held Johns Island, James Island, Daniels Island (presently named Daniel Island), and Mount Pleasant, which all stood off the river waters around Charlestown's garrisoned peninsula. These fortified posts protected shipping throughout the Cooper, Wando, and Ashley Rivers. In addition, these areas provided much of the food and potable water to troops, civilians, and the enslaved living in Charlestown. A network of canals on these islands and occupied areas enabled the efficient tidal flow of goods to and from Charlestown. Throughout the day and night, small boats transported their livestock, fowl, fruits, vegetables, wood, potable water, and a host of other goods into the town's system of canals using the incoming and outgoing tides as their source of power under the watchful eye of armed British galleys and ships. Greene began working to militarily control these canals and river routes to deny the enemy local goods and sustenance.

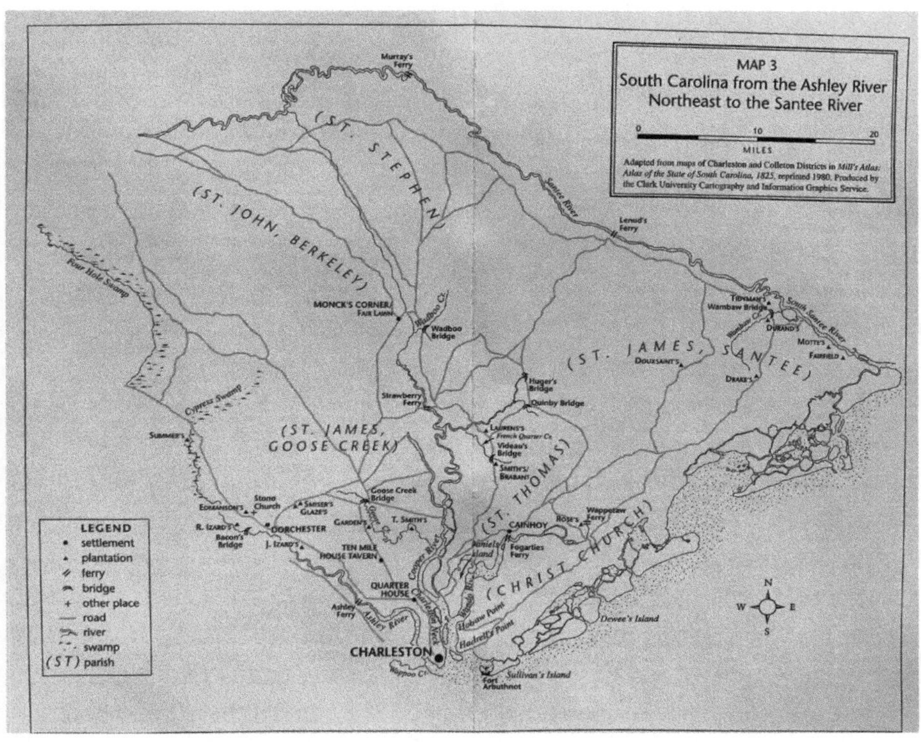

Charlestown from the Ashley to the Santee 1780, map courtesy of the Newberry Library, Chicago, Ill, and Clark University Archives, adapted by Lyn Malone.

But Greene was still substantially outnumbered and outgunned. If he could keep the British from massing, he could limit them to raids, foraging expeditions, and small battles. Loyalist militias were operating out of the Orangeburg swamps and north of Charlestown to the North Carolina border. David Fanning's notorious gang controlled the Carolinas common border area. Greene sent Andrew Pickens to destroy the Loyalists in Orangeburg and sent Francis Marion to Cainhoy to keep the British out of Saint Thomas Parish. Loyalist Micajah Gainey's regiment was operating north of Charlestown, and Gainey was soon due to come off parole. If Gainey and Fanning's Loyalists became able to coordinate operations with Leslie in Charlestown, the British could break out of the encirclement and overwhelm both Greene's and Marion's forces.

In December 1781, Greene wrote Governor Rutledge recommending that the state authorize him to recruit enslaved persons for his army as the first order of business when the legislature convened in January. In late December, sixty artillerymen reinforced the British in Charlestown, and British newspapers reported that two thousand more troops from Cork, Ireland, were en route. On January 4, 1782, Greene received badly needed Pennsylvania and Maryland Continental reinforcements under General Arthur St. Clair from the Yorktown siege. He was still substantially outnumbered, but now he had more experienced veterans to buttress his containment cavalry patrols, repulse a full-scale attack, and tighten the noose around Charlestown. While Greene's appeal to recruit the enslaved was denied, General Saint Clair's troops arrived just in time to prevent disaster.

On January 2, General Leslie ordered Major William Brereton to invade Saint Thomas Parish. Saint Thomas Parish, consisting of Daniels Island and Cainhoy, was assigned to General Francis Marion's Brigade.[232] During the frigid winter, food, forage, and shelter had become scarce for British troops and their charges.[233] Leslie ordered the slaughter of two hundred horses, which temporarily alleviated all three problems. Leslie needed a more permanent solution, so he dispatched Brereton, a veteran of the Battle of Monmouth, to secure Saint Thomas Parish and eliminate a regiment of Marion's Brigade commanded by Colonel Richard Richardson. Brereton's strike force consisted of Cavalry, Falk Corps, the Volunteers of Ireland, and the Black Dragoons. The Sixty-Third Regiment of Foot, stationed at the Fort on Haddrell's Point between Sullivan's Island and Mount Pleasant, was to join and help lead the strike or occupation force. The Sixty-Third was intercepted by a Patriot force before they could junction due to advance intelligence. Lacking these troops' fortification expertise hampered the ability of the British joint forces to garrison their intended targets to establish a permanent and dependable supply line. The British landing area was the fortified post at Scott's Ferry at the south end of Daniels Island. This critical post was supported by heavily armed galleys, which patrolled the apex of the Cooper and Wando Rivers. These galleys covered the victual vessels and Brereton's ground operation from the rivers as both tracked northward. The British post at Scott's Ferry was under constant surveillance by Richardson's men to repulse foraging efforts in the parish for cattle, game, and stored crops. Marion ordered Colonel Richard Richardson to combine his forces and oppose the British supply operation.

The British considered Saint Thomas Parish to be a critical strategic area for the control of Charlestown and South Carolina. Less than two years earlier, on April 5, 1780, a regiment of Virginia Continentals boarded riverboats on the Cooper River at Monck's Corner and successfully reinforced Charlestown while still in Patriot hands, underneath the noses of the British forces under General Clinton surrounding the city. Clinton knew he had to close off this gaping hole in his siege, so he sent Lieutenant Colonel Tarleton, Major Patrick Ferguson, and Lieutenant Colonel James Webster with 1,500 troops into Saint Thomas Parish. Their mission was to ravage the area and set up outposts at Strawberry Ferry, Moncks Corner, and the numerous local plantations. Charlestown fell less than a month later, and the rest of the state soon followed. General Leslie remembered the strategic importance of Saint Thomas Parish when he ordered Brereton to capture the region, eliminate Richardson's regiment, conduct massive foraging operations, and establish a reliable supply line.

Major Brereton and about 360 troops, led by Regulars, grenadiers and light infantry, were landed by riverboats on Daniels Island on January 2, 1782. As Brereton marched across Daniels Island, he encountered sporadic sniping until he came to his first target at Brabant Plantation, the home of Reverend Robert Smith, where his troops camped. Brereton set up security and placed troops at Videau's Bridge to guard the approach. On January 3, Richardson and his men attacked Brereton's troops from the north above Videau's Bridge, and after much intense fighting in a series of moving battles, Richardson withdrew. After taking causalities, Brereton reduced his operation to cattle raiding and evacuated his exhausted troops from Saint Thomas Parish before Marion or General

Saint Clair's Continentals could assist Richardson with a reinforced counterattack.

In an after-action report to General Clinton, Leslie put on a good face for the mail readers back in London. He described the operation as one against "General Marians" to defeat him, not one to establish foraging posts or as an attempt to capture and hold Saint Thomas Parish plantations.[234] Leslie goes on to assert that they "cut to pieces and took near 100 of the Rebels" with "the whole [his troops] returning to their different stations," meaning posts. (Battle reports list no more than thirty Patriots total killed, wounded, and captured, with the British total at nineteen.) There was no mention of the dire need for fresh meat to relieve Charlestown hunger, although Clinton would be keenly aware of such since he was shipping Leslie tons of salted meat regularly from New York. Most importantly, there was no mention of the urgency of capturing Saint Thomas Parish to secure Charlestown and claim the area for peace negotiations. General Leslie had conducted a major offensive in the dead of winter to secure his food resource supply line and control the upper Cooper River to Monks Corner, which failed.

The Charlestown garrison received fresh food, potable water, and wood supplies from Johns Island, James Island, Sullivan's Island, Long Island (Isle of Palms), and Mount Pleasant. These areas became the object of Greene's attention in January 1782. On January 11, Lieutenant Colonel Henry Lee and Lieutenant Colonel John Laurens spearheaded an offensive on John's Island with their light cavalry, supported by Greene's entire army. This operation was designed to dislodge approximately five hundred British soldiers from John's Island, commanded by Major James Craig. He had previously overseen the capital port city garrison at Wilmington, which he was forced to abandon the previous November after being surrounded by North Carolina militia units. Craig was known for his cruelty and extreme violence, starving prisoners to death and creating regional instability by encouraging and leading Loyalist raids against civilian targets. Lee's and Lauren's mission to dislodge the British from John's Island was aborted after the cavalry and infantry forces missed the timed rendezvous point from where the surprise attack would commence.[235]

Two days later, the British abandoned its garrison and posts throughout the island, reportedly due to fear of becoming trapped and poor morale. Nonetheless, John's Island was liberated, and along with Saint Thomas Parish, two British food sources were eliminated while Greene's containment circle tightened.

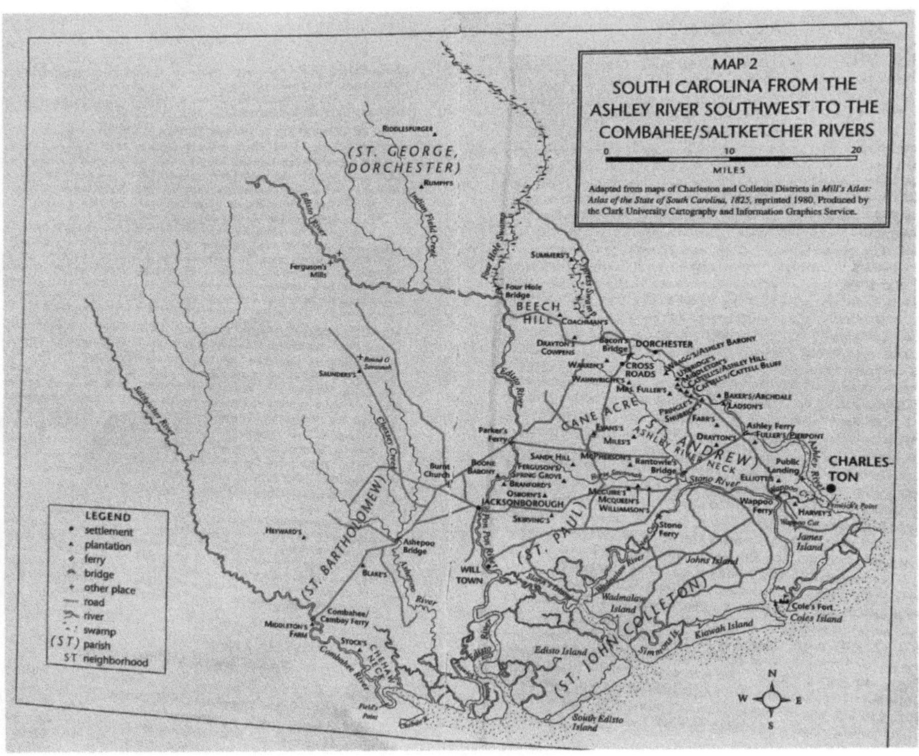

Map of Charlestown Ashley River Southwest to the Combahee/ Saltketcher Rivers 1780, map courtesy of the *Newberry Library*, Chicago, Ill, and Clark University Archives, adapted by Lyn Malone."

On January 28, Greene wrote John Adams, America's lead diplomat in Europe. Adams contacted Greene through the Count de Noel Jourda de Vaux, presumably to get a firsthand account of the war on the ground in the Lower South (rather than routed through Congress). Greene acquainted Adams with the territory repossession in the Lower

South and the earnest desire of the people there to continue to fight for independence—across generations if necessary. As part of Greene's direct situational report, he wrote, "Let it suffice to say that this part of the United States have had a narrow escape. I was seven months in the field without taking my clothes off one night. I have now more compleat (possession of t)he country and the in(habitants in)finitely more determined (to free themse)lves from british (Dominatio)n than ever they have been."[236] Greene impressed upon Adams to keep the Lower South in the independence negotiations until he finished ousting the British.

Toward that end, significant political progress was made in Jacksonborough on January 29. Greene had established Continental headquarters at a nearby plantation in Jacksonborough to provide security for a gathering of exiled South Carolina General Assembly members so the state body could become reconstituted and hold elections. John Matthews, a former delegate to Congress, was elected governor of South Carolina as the first act of the reconstituted legislature. Greene sent a letter to Washington informing him of the upcoming development accompanied by a personal letter from Matthews to Washington affirming his commitment to the union and independence. Matthews's written allegiance to the confederation was imperative for qualifying his candidacy. Greene now had organized state governments confederated with the union in both Carolinas and Georgia. However, the British still occupied the preponderance of Georgia and its capital, the populous Low Country of South Carolina and its capital, and North Carolina's governor had been kidnapped and the state's legislators were unable to meet due to Loyalist militias. American negotiators did not have a good argument for those provinces not to be retained by the British at the peace talks in January 1782.

General Leslie was not about to give up the large plantations around Charlestown. British containment encountered a breakthrough at the end of February, which would last for a couple of months. Leslie would revert to Cornwallis's mantra of "bring me no prisoners" extreme violence to achieve this. On February 24, Leslie sent his best shock troops onto Daniels Island under Colonel Benjamin Thompson to march on

Tydiman's Plantation on Wambaw Creek, connecting to the Santee River.[237] Massive flocks of birds, including the now-extinct Carolina parakeet, foretold the large movement of troops as they were frightened from their habitat and blackened the sky in flight. General Leslie sent British regulars of the Thirtieth Regiment and Royal Artillery supported by his top Hessian Jager Korps to lead the mission. Elements of the notorious Queen Rangers, the British Legion, the Black Dragoons, and "Bloody" Bill Cunningham's dragoons would lead the tour de force across Saint Thomas Parish, cutting down anything in their paths. Their operation was entirely successful in that it decimated two of Marion's regiments, and the British established a post at Tydiman's and on the Santee River as planned. These posts enabled the British to use the northern part of Saint Thomas Parish as cattle ranches, agricultural food production, and woodcutting, which could be transported down the Santee River and over to Charlestown under the protection of British galleys and coastal warships. The British held Tydiman Plantation until early April but could not expand their presence or establish permanent posts in Saint Thomas Parish. Capturing an area is easier than keeping it.

With many confined soldiers and sailors in the city, morale had to be improved before the situation got out of hand. In February, the British officer corps financed an "Ethiopian Ball," where numerous elaborately dressed enslaved females "danced with officer escorts until four o'clock in the morning."[238] The "ball" was held at an elegant townhouse. Three Black women presided over the affair in the attire of their mistresses. The affair was widely publicized and cost "some eighty pounds sterling," or about $19,000 today. Lieutenant Colonel Balfour had the authority to license "houses of public entertainment," which increased under his watch. Like the Ethiopian party, these houses exploited Black women and kept soldiers and sailors off the streets at night. The enslaved had no choice.

Soon afterward, another major foraging operation commenced. On March 4, Loyalist commander Major Andrew Deveaux captured Beaufort, South Carolina, in a mission launched from Charlestown.[239] His forces occupied the town for three weeks, gathering stored rice and other supplies loaded onto his two galleys and large sloop. Major Deveaux attempted to recover a couple of ships in the area, probably to add to his transport capacity, but his salvage crews were ambushed during the attempt. He returned to Charlestown near the end of March with loaded transports.

Meanwhile, General Greene was assigning and tasking his available forces as effectively as possible. General Barnwell and his militia kept Major Deveaux's troops confined to Beaufort. The *Charlestown Royal Gazette* of March 2, 1782, reported King George's speech from the opening of Parliament: "It is said the ministry are determined to push the war to the southward in America" under a board of war who would direct operations.[240] Greene sent General Wayne in Georgia another hundred men, clothing, and fifty Guineas while acquainting him with the king's speech. He jokingly encouraged General Wayne to be prepared for an offensive onslaught: "Thus, you see the enemy is opening new fields of glory for you." Greene was still hopeful that the legislatures of Georgia and South Carolina would authorize the recruiting of Black regiments to equalize his forces with the British. He made clear to Wayne what his commander's intent was: "Everything depends on us holding our ground." In his April 13 letter to General Washington, Greene reported: "Our force is much inferior to the Enemy's, and they are daily threatening us with an attack."[241] Nonetheless, Greene countered any efforts by the enemy to break out with tireless energy and continuous cavalry movements.

British resentment for their confinement to Charlestown showed in their treatment of Patriot prisoners. On April 12, Greene wrote General Leslie about the inhumane treatment of prisoners held aboard ships in the Charlestown harbor. The prison ship *Esk* reportedly oversaw the deaths of about 180 prisoners from exposure, disease, and starvation in a short time.[242] Prisoners, by convention, were entitled to half the rations of a British soldier. Still, with food and potable water shortages creating high prices, there were many temptations for Lieutenant Colonel Nesbit Balfour and friends to sell those rations on the black market, leaving prisoners with only rancid scraps. Balfour was a remnant of General Cornwallis's inner circle responsible for feeding and housing prisoners in the "bring me no prisoners" culture General Leslie had inherited. Balfour had a record of unilaterally committing atrocities from mass hangings to extrajudicial executions, such as his leadership in the hanging of Colonel Isaac Hayne. Commodity food prices had increased substantially due to Greene's land blockade of the city, so there was money to be made in the minds of the corrupt.[243] Balfour's fellow Scotsman, General Leslie, would not acknowledge any mistreatment of prisoners to Greene or offer any reasonable explanation of how hundreds of Patriot souls had perished over the winter in British custody. Leslie preemptively accused Greene of turning a blind eye to a Patriot militia hanging Loyalist prisoners, which Greene credibly denied. Greene hoped that by him putting the atrocities in writing, Leslie would stop them instead of covering them up or trusting reports from Balfour.

Being surrounded by an enemy and constantly being on the defensive are debilitating for combat troops. The Charlestown peninsula in 1782 was no exception. Men trained to fight are at their best conducting offensive operations—taking the fight to the enemy. Performing endless garrison and redoubt duty interrupted by alarms and protective missions for foragers grinds good men down into disobedience, gambling, drinking, drug use, womanizing, or crime. Idle time causes men to relive unspeakable orders faithfully carried out and see the faces of those they killed when they try to sleep. They wonder what became of the moral self they once knew. Others feel the ghosts of their dead brothers and become racked with merciless guilt of why it was not them whom Death caught. Their eyes cannot focus on what they see, their ears cannot hear the words from moving mouths, and their bodies seem detached from their minds. There was no private place to get away from the darkness of it all.

With the city's population inside the walls swelled to over sixteen thousand and Loyalist refugees from all over the South living in squalor in camps on the Charlestown Neck, just feeding everyone every day was an enormous task. On March 27, General Leslie wrote Clinton begging to be relieved of command. He cited, "the perplexity of civil matters here, independent of Military ones, is so much beyond my abilitys to arrange, that I declare myself unequal to the Task."[244] Clinton could not spare Leslie, so he denied the request. It would be up to him to hold the army, the Loyalists, the freed and enslaved blacks, the refugees, and the civilians together the best way possible or find a way to break out.

The misery of war and the oppressive occupation spared no one. When the British conquered South Carolina, John Cruden was appointed commissioner of sequestered estates to deal with the enslaved population, totaling about ninety-seven thousand people or 54 percent of the province's residents. Enslaved Blacks were the economic engine of the low country economy—on the plantations working rice, indigo, and farm fields and performing domestic work. They supplied both manpower and expertise in the production of rice and indigo, South Carolina's main export crops. The enslaved population also made tabby and brick and built the buildings. They built schooners, boats, and river galleys. They loaded and unloaded ships and moved the river barges full of goods up and down South Carolina's vast network of waterways stretching to the Appalachian Mountains. They tilled the soil, planted the crops, harvested them, transported them, and cooked them. They ranched the cattle and tended the livestock. The enslaved population experienced more than its fair share of horror and death during the war.

After the British captured Charlestown, John Cruden confiscated all enslaved persons of "unfriendly persons," meaning Patriots, while the Loyalist plantations retained their enslaved people. Loyalists were given Patriot plantations, and some enslaved people who worked on the sequestered estates were promised to be freed at war's end if they performed their duties faithfully.[245] If Patriots would sign an oath of allegiance to the king, they could avoid repossession of their estates—at least at the beginning of the occupation while General Clinton was in command. The British used enslaved labor extensively in Charlestown's engineering and ordnance departments and military operations to fell trees, build bridges, build houses, build defensive works, cook, clean, and perform hard labor. Most British officers appropriated enslaved people for themselves. The royal lieutenant governor of South Carolina, William Bull, wrote Lord Hillsborough of Parliament that the enslaved had become "'ungovernable' because of their absence of masters and the difficulty in enforcing 'the Code of Laws calculated for the Government of that class of People'" under British law.[246] The Board of Police, operated by Lieutenant Colonel Balfour, was responsible for maintaining order among the Black population in Charlestown, estimated to be about one-half of total persons. His involvement likely contributed to the persistent illegal exportation and resale of the enslaved during the occupation. As commandant of Charlestown, Balfour was the only authority who could authorize the sale or passage of the enslaved.[247] An estimated twenty-five thousand enslaved people disappeared from South Carolina during the British occupation.

The British also used the enslaved in their military forces. Those recruited into their ranks were assured of their emancipation for faithful service. In Charlestown, a militia group of Blacks was formed to keep order and to assist in defending the city if attacked. Additionally, the British raised a cavalry unit known as the Black Dragoons, which conducted terror raids and patrolled outside Charlestown to apprehend or kill escaped enslaved persons and deserters. The unpopularity of the Black Dragoons on both sides stymied further efforts by the British to gain approval to raise additional Black regiments.

The institution of slavery had been undergoing significant changes in the world since the beginning of the war. Adam Smith, author of *The Wealth of Nations*, proposed in his best-selling 1776 book that enslavement was "a bad economic decision" besides being absent of justice and morality. He maintained economically that the condition of enslavement resulted in perpetual maintenance (cost) and lower productivity and innovation than that of a free person.[248] His fellow Scotsmen agreed and prohibited the owning of enslaved people in 1778. Motivated by the Declaration of Independence's assertion that "all men are created equal," some northern states passed laws to abolish or phase out slavery. While Congress did not have the power to force emancipation upon individual states, they supported state efforts to foreclose the institution of slavery.

Greene desperately wanted to raise Black regiments with the state's approval. The Black troops raised in his former home state of Rhode Island had served with bravery and distinction, likely saving Rhode Island from British conquest in 1778. The First Rhode Island Regiment, composed of Blacks, Native Americans, and Whites, repulsed seasoned

Hessian and British troops against three assaults under the leadership of Colonel Christopher Greene, a relative of General Greene. In a letter to Governor Rutledge, General Greene expressed that the natural strength of South Carolina "appears to be much more in the blacks than the whites." He asked pointedly to be allowed to assemble Black regiments who upon faithful service would be given their freedom and treated "as other soldiers."[249] Greene was repeatedly requesting the same permission from the governors and legislatures of Georgia, North Carolina, and South Carolina.

Lieutenant Colonel John Laurens, a strong advocate for abolishing slavery in America, had received a resolution from Congress authorizing Black regiments. He joined Greene in the Lower South to sell the idea out of both necessity and in keeping with the values of the revolution that "all men are created equal...with certain unalienable rights...of life, liberty and the pursuit of happiness." Thomas Jefferson had included Blacks in the Declaration of Independence. Regrettably, the paragraph was omitted to entice all the states to ratify the document: "He [King George] has waged cruel war against human nature itself, violating its most sacred rights of life & liberty in the persons of a distant people who never offended him, captivating & carrying them into slavery in another hemisphere or to incur miserable death in their transportation thither. This piratical warfare, the opprobrium of infidel powers, is the warfare of the Christian King of Great Britain. Determined to keep open a market where Men should be bought & sold, he has prostituted his negative for suppressing every legislative attempt to prohibit or restrain this execrable commerce. And that this assemblage of horrors might want no fact of distinguished die, he is now exciting those very people to rise in arms against us, [Dunmore Proclamation] and to purchase that liberty of which he has deprived them, by murdering the people on whom he has obtruded them: thus paying off former crimes committed again the Liberties of one people, with crimes which he urges them to commit against the lives of another." If this passage had been left in the declaration, the institution of slavery in America would have logically met its end. Jefferson wrote later in his life that Northern delegates who were involved in the horrid trade and delegates from South Carolina and Georgia would not approve the passage.

Lieutenant Colonel Laurens was determined to include Blacks in the fight for liberty. After successfully negotiating Cornwallis's surrender at Yorktown, Laurens attended a manumission ceremony for a Black enslaved Patriot, James Armistead Lafayette, who faithfully served the American cause supplying intelligence during the siege.[250] (James Armistead served under General Lafayette's command, and his espionage efforts made the surrender possible. Later in 1782, Virginia passed a manumission act allowing for the freedom of any enslaved person who fought in the Revolutionary War). In 1781, John had temporarily converted his father, Henry Laurens, to the emancipation cause through his dogged letter writing. Lieutenant Colonel Laurens joined General Greene's army in South Carolina in late 1781 to serve in Lee's Legion and lobby his home state to manumit Blacks who would enlist in the Patriot cause.

With General Greene's coordination and support, Lieutenant Colonel Laurens made strong presentations to the South Carolina and Georgia legislatures requesting they authorize Black recruitment into the Continental Army. "Property owners" would be provided with a profitable reimbursement of $1,000 per recruit as authorized by Congress.[251] About fifty-two years later, the British government would emulate this "buyout program" with similar reimbursements as provided in the Slavery Abolition Act of 1833. John Lauren's friend, Lewis Morris, who was an aide to General Greene, wrote that "blacks…are subject to every species of oppression while we are contending for the rights and liberties of mankind." The rights Morris spoke of were the same universal rights General Lafayette, Alexander Hamilton, John Laurens, and other young Continental officers had dreamed about becoming a reality during their long, cold winter nights together at Valley Forge years before. They believed that the United States would never be truly free until all those Black persons in bondage had the same rights as Whites. John Laurens vigorously pursued officially enlisting Blacks into the Continental Army as a pathway to ending slavery.

After the British captured Charlestown in 1780, the South Carolina government in exile relocated to Philadelphia. Philadelphia was the seat of the United States Congress and the capital of Pennsylvania. Pennsylvania had just passed An Act for the Gradual Abolition of Slavery, which many hoped would become a model for other states to adopt voluntarily.[252] Thomas Paine, General Greene's former aide-de-camp, was the clerk of the state general assembly when the act became law. Despite being offered what Greene described "a most generous bounty" to go to the slaveholders for enslaved persons recruited into a Black regiment, as authorized by Congress, the South Carolina General Assembly did not approve John Laurens's proposal. Lieutenant Colonel Laurens would not get his Black regiments. The door to emancipation would not budge.

General Greene found other creative ways to enroll Blacks. He requested and received five hundred blacks to serve as waggoneers, laborers, and aides to be paid like regulars.[253] Given Greene's Quaker upbringing and his commitment to the founding values, one could surmise that Greene and Laurens figured out unofficial ways to have enslaved Blacks serve as soldiers with a path to freedom that never made the public record. Greene could not alienate the resurrected state legislatures by forcing the issue and risk having them break away from the confederation. Case-by-case manumission would have to do.

Besides advocating for the enlistment of Blacks, April 1782 was a busy month for General Greene. Frustrated by contested foraging operations around Charlestown, General Leslie sent a large Loyalist force to capture Continental warehouse food and other supplies in Beaufort, North Carolina, above Wilmington. Arriving on one warship and two schooners, the Loyalist troops occupied the town from April 4 to April 10, during which time they stripped the town of all supplies and took away the enslaved. Greene dispatched a relief force of four ships and about 250 men, which arrived after the raiding party left.[254] The operation provided Leslie with much-needed food and additional manpower but deprived the Continental army of a reliable supply source that could be shipped to Georgetown.

On April 4, Catherine Greene, Nathanael's wife, arrived to join him in South Carolina. As her social peers called her, Caty was considered by many to be one of the most beautiful women in America, along with militia General Andrew Pickens's wife, Rebecca. Caty had not seen Nathanael in almost two years due to his constant duty in combat zones. Her arrival was viewed as a sign that British capitulation was on the horizon and that a return to peace was not far off.[255] She became an instant morale builder and, like Martha Washington in the North, was regarded as the first lady of the South.

Caty arrived in time to see General Leslie twice attempt to kidnap her husband. Greene had picked up intelligence that Leslie was initiating plots to kidnap or kill him.[256] The respected General Charles O'Hara, doing most of the day-to-day troop management, was scheduled to leave Charleston to Jamaica the first week in May with a top regiment, leaving Leslie without sufficient troops for a potential offensive. Leslie had to fix his containment predicament before his right-hand man left town or face a summer of steady physical and mental troop deteriorations. Leslie had likely concluded that if Greene were no longer in command, no one else would be capable of pressing in the sieges in Georgia and South Carolina. No one else could hold together the Lower South state legislatures and their governors and militias, or effectively coordinate with Washington and the other states, or keep American diplomats informed about the situation on the ground. The Patriot armies and legislatures in the Carolinas and Georgia would likely disintegrate. No one else had trusting relationships with General Washington, Congress, French general Rochambeau, John Adams, French diplomats, the state governments, the state militias, and the northward state governors. No one else could keep together an unpaid Continental army serving outside their home states. If Leslie could kidnap or kill Greene, the Continental containment campaign would likely evaporate. General Leslie could still win in the Carolinas and Georgia.

From the British perspective, Greene was the key man they must neutralize. On April 20, Sergeant George Gosnell of the Pennsylvania line was arrested for mutiny after an informant revealed a plot to kidnap

Greene. The cover story was that his wife informed on him, but a secret double agent inside Charlestown likely exposed Gosnell. Gosnell and four other noncommissioned officers were arrested before they could execute their plan of kidnapping Greene and his key officers to deliver them to the British or have them meet their end. One hundred and fifty British cavalrymen waited in Dorchester for Greene and company to be handed over by Sergeant Gosnell and his men.[257] Before he transferred south to Greene's command, Gosnell was a deserter from the British army and a participant in the January 1781 mutiny while under George Washington's command. Gosnell was tried, convicted, and executed in front of the entire headquarters camp two days later.

But Leslie had another plan. Days later, Caty received and graciously accepted an invitation to dinner at a society home on the Ashley River that also included General Greene and his two aides-de-camp. Soon after arriving, a note was given to General Greene notifying him of a plot to kidnap him while he was dining.[258] The group left immediately, and about twenty minutes later, the house was surrounded by "a number of the British Horse" with the officer in charge demanding that General Greene be sent out. Instead, the lady of the house came out to inform them that General Greene, his wife, and his security entourage were gone. Leslie's second attempt to kidnap or kill Greene had failed.

Spies and timely intelligence saved Greene. Unbeknownst to General Leslie, Lieutenant Colonel Nesbit Balfour's secretary fed information to Greene's intelligence group about British plans, operations, and plots.[259] Greene had many well-placed spies throughout Charlestown constantly feeding him information. The encirclement of the city had become a game of chess moves rather than epic battles. North Carolina, the Orangeburg area, and the Native American frontier area were still actively contested by Loyalist militias and terror warriors. The struggle over the capital cities of Georgia and South Carolina had become a game of which side had the best intelligence to move and countermove chess pieces correctly. With Greene's imperfect embargo in place, time was working against the surrounded garrison. Leslie was constantly looking for breakout opportunities and a quick checkmate; Greene was methodically maintaining and shrinking the containment perimeters with just enough dedicated pawns and a handful of swift knights informed by a few well-placed spies. Victory would likely go to the general who made the next-to-last mistake.

Greene needed to respond to the British kidnapping attempts to keep Leslie in check. With the arrival of much-needed ammunition on May 4, Greene was ready to make a show of force to dare the British out of Charlestown to fight or have them put aside the thought of mounting an offensive to eliminate Greene's army.[260] General O'Hara embarked with about 1,200 British regulars to Jamaica on May 6, leaving 5,877 British troops to defend the city. Greene was now only facing one British general, not two, and 1,200 fewer troops. The day after O'Hara's departure, Greene ordered the North Carolina Continental Brigade to fire three rounds into the air for the enemy in Charlestown to hear. Leslie had likely picked up intelligence that Greene's troops were dangerously low on powder and ammunition, so Greene wanted to discourage any mass offensive against him and have Leslie doubt his intelligence sources. On the tenth of May, Captain William Wilmot, Greene's head of intelligence, reported that the Hessians were massing at the outer British lines at the Quarter House. Two days later, Greene responded by ordering his "Light Infantry and all the Cavalry of the Army," totaling about one thousand troops, to march to the outer works and form for battle with himself in the lead.[261] Greene paraded the army in front of their works, capturing nine enemy soldiers, but the Hessians and British troops would not come out for battle. Greene encamped with his troops near Dorchester for the next few months to keep the British in check below the Quarter House. The point was made: "We are ready to battle if you dare to come out."

Unable to break out, forage sufficiently, or kidnap Greene, General Leslie offered a cessation of hostilities on May 20. Sir Guy Carleton had taken over command of North America, and one of his first actions was to get General Leslie to switch his tactics from belligerence to conciliation. Leslie deliberately misrepresented the facts when he wrote in his proposal to Greene: "a suspension of hostilities has taken place in the North-ward, and that a treaty to conclude the War is now carrying on."[262] Recognizing a fraud guaranteeing nothing but giving Leslie everything, Greene wisely declined any cessation of hostilities short of Leslie's surrender. There is a high probability that if Greene had agreed to Leslie's truce ploy, British diplomats would have been under no pressure to grant independence to the Lower South since there was a de facto peace already in place. In addition, Greene's embargo on Charlestown would likely disintegrate, alleviating the pressure on Leslie to evacuate. Greene immediately wrote the president of Congress and General Washington advising his bosses of the proposal and requesting guidance. After hearing from both, he wrote Leslie that admitting to neutrality with the British Southern Army under threat impugns "the honor and dignity of United States" to acquiesce to a foreign power "who refuse obedience to the Laws of the State, and think themselves at liberty to join in any future attempt to overturn the Government."[263] Washington dismissed Carleton's and Leslie's proposals as the same offered "by former Commissioners [of peace] in the year 1778"—a promise by the British to suspend offensive operations against America with little for "their United Colonies" to gain. The truce would not provide Congress with official or binding consent to collective or sovereign independence or removal of British troops. Greene knew that accepting a verbal end to hostilities would enable the British to likely retain both Charlestown and Savannah and kill any chance of collective independence. The European peace deciders would likely view an American agreement to a national cease-fire as a weakness of both political will and military strength to see the war through to settle the matter of British occupation. The United States would appear as if it lacked the intestinal fortitude to stand alone as a nation capable of taking care of itself without a monarch. The bully still had to be forced from Southern shores.

General Carleton had cleverly calculated that a verbal agreement to end hostilities in the field would save his armies from a forced withdrawal and undercut independence. While Leslie was writing Greene about ending hostilities, he planned to have one of his most notorious Loyalist commanders lead a sneak attack on a prisoner camp at Dean's Swamp near Orangeburg, hoping that the guard would be relaxed. On May 24, four days after Leslie's "end hostilities proposal," Major "Bloody"

Bill Cunningham attacked a Patriot-guarded prisoner camp at Dean's Swamp that held as many as 150 British and Loyalist troops. Leslie had rewarded Cunningham's record of wholesale genocide with a promotion to major after taking command of the Southern British Army. Cunningham's 80-man force attacked Captain William Butler's men guarding the prisoners.[264] A spirited countercharge ensued, and with a much smaller force, the Patriots defeated Cunningham. General Leslie had duplicitously authorized an attack as he petitioned Greene to accept a cease-fire agreement in a classic "art of the feint" maneuver. Carleton was likely not pleased with Leslie's deceit tactics, which doomed any hope of stimulating reconciliation-within-the-empire discussions in the southland.

At the same time, British General Guy Carleton was working his own trickery from New York. He attempted to commence diplomatic discussions directly with Congress, deliberately leaving France and Congress's authorized diplomats out of the proposed negotiations. British press cartoons urged Carleton to drive a wedge between the United States and France to upend the alliance and end the war yet keep America within the empire. However, Congress did not entertain any back-door diplomacy theatrics from a military commander who had no authority to negotiate independence or make it stick or push a preliminary deal through the European peace approval gauntlet. The king or Parliament would censure and overrule him even if he went outside his authority to provisionally offer sovereign independence. Sir William Howe and turncoat Charles Lee had tried that dangling-carrot trick before with Congress in 1778 under the backdrop of the Carlisle Commission. Even though Carleton was temporarily appointed peace commissioner and commander in chief of all British forces in North America, he did not have the power to negotiate nationhood. The king had not authorized him to put complete independence on the negotiating table, and Congress knew it.

Simultaneous with Carleton's shiny ploy, General Leslie offered a verbal cessation of hostilities to General Greene in the Southern theater of operations. Carleton had craftily synchronized these proposals expressed in Greene's words to the president of Congress: "to detach us from our alliance [France]; to relax our [military] exertions and if we do neither Carleton will report to the King's ministers our refusal to which Parliament will unite against America to vigorously renew the war..... . They have offered us Independence [within the Empire] if we renounce our alliance with France." Britain knew the French would abandon the alliance with the United States if Congress made a treaty directly with Carleton. One post peace proposal account, printed in the Charlestown Royal Gazette, maintained that if Carleton's (and Leslie's) treaty proposals had been accepted, the colonies would have returned to their political status before the war and that the purpose of the proposals was only "to quiet the minds of the people of England."[265] (This propaganda piece was written to convince people that Britain was not in a disintegrating military situation where they had to negotiate.) Carleton's peace talks strategy to kill the Confederation or America's alliance with France, thereby squashing any possibility of genuine independence, was masterful if not deceitful. But gaining an advantage is what war and negotiating peace is all about. Fortunately, neither Washington, Greene, nor Congress took the poison bait.

However, General Leslie's letter, crafted to gain a military advantage by asserting the war was over, would not be wasted. To Leslie's chagrin, Greene used his letter to persuade two potent Loyalist regiments to switch sides, virtually surrendering the low country of the Carolinas. Greene provided Leslie's cessation-of-hostilities letter to General Marion to negotiate with Loyalist militia leader Major Gainey and Colonel Fanning's militia representatives, operating north of Charlestown up to Cape Fear. Fanning had wholly disrupted the North Carolina government by kidnapping Governor Burke from Hillsborough and making conditions unsafe for the Legislature to meet. Fanning's forces roamed at will along the southeastern North Carolina border area. This circumstance created an argument in diplomatic circles that North Carolina was without an operating government and should be retained by Britain when peace negotiations commenced. Gainey had a competent Loyalist force operating in the Georgetown area, along the Pee Dee River just above the North Carolina border. His temporary cease-fire with Marion was due to expire soon. Marion met with Gainey and critical representatives from Colonel Fanning's regiment on June 3 to negotiate their surrender with Leslie's letter in hand.[266] Gainey's and Fanning's men were offered full pardons if they lay down their arms, turned in their booty, agreed to be peaceable citizens, switched sides to serve in the South Carolina militia, and delivered up anyone who persisted. General Greene and Governor Matthews endorsed the offer. Those who could not agree would be escorted immediately to Charlestown. No deal was offered to Fanning and some other men known to have committed atrocities. General Leslie's duplicitous letter and General Marion's conciliatory manner effectively switched two Loyalist regiments to the Patriot cause, stabilized the government of North Carolina, and brought a wide swarth of territory into a state of peace under Patriot control. This large area could no longer be argued as "British controlled territory" in peace talks. General Leslie likely discovered his mistake when Colonel Fanning and his notorious confederates arrived in Charlestown with their scalps and booty but no army. Colonel Fanning could only respond that he would see the Swamp Fox dead for his peace work.

Just as Marion wrote his after-action report to Greene enclosing the signed Loyalist treaties, one of Marion's spies learned of Leslie's order to evacuate Savannah in July.[267] The bad news for Greene was that General Leslie would get a reprieve from his food and manpower predicament. Leslie would inherit Savannah's massive rice supplies and replenish the troops General O'Hara had taken to Jamaica.

While Greene was having success containing the British on land in both Savannah and Charlestown, the French were not having the same success on the sea. In April, the French were soundly defeated in the Battle of the Saints in the West Indies, which Greene was informed about in mid-May.[268] Greene was counting on the French fleet, under Admiral Comte de Grasse, to coordinate with him by sea to force the Charlestown and Savannah British garrisons he had under siege to surrender. With de Grasse's fleet destroyed and Jamaica no longer threatened, General O'Hara could return, if so ordered, with his troops to recapture the

Lower South. One thing was for sure: if Greene were going to dislodge the British, he would have to do it without French help.

The British once again ruled the southeastern coast, so Greene would have to compel Leslie to surrender or evacuate by tightening the land blockade. In early June, Lieutenant Colonel Laurens reported to Greene that one of his well-placed spies had confirmed that peace talks had subsided and that no evacuation of Charlestown was on the horizon. Greene had previously served as quartermaster of the Continental Army; therefore, he arithmetically knew what it took to feed and maintain troops. Supplying a force projection army over large distances and constantly overcoming food, water, and fuel constraints depend on host nation support. Greene was compounding Leslie's enormous logistics problems by intensifying his land blockade, mobile patrols, and military confrontations, which all seemed to be working: "In one instance, British soldiers reported subsisting on alligators and oysters…."[269] Colonel Thaddeus Kosciuszko was the officer in charge of preventing fresh food from getting to British troops in Charlestown as well as intelligence activities. "Greene's army controlled the country and its resources wile the British were confined to Charlestown and James Island."[270] British foraging operations became hampered by Laurens, Wilmot, and Kosciusko attacking their covering galleys around the islands near Charlestown. Lauren's Legion captured the river galley *Alligator* earlier in the year. Foraging operations became dangerous and debilitating for the British.

Depriving Leslie of host nation forage was the best method Greene had at his disposal to prevent sustained offensive operations against him. "Armies move on their stomachs," as a future French general would proclaim. Britain's commissary general, Daniel Chamier, was routinely short "by an average of 4,000 rations" that "failed to account for officers, wives, children, refugees." Leslie was burdened with the immense task of making up the daily difference while being confined to a peninsula and outposts on James Island, Sullivan's Island, Long Island, and Mount Pleasant.[271] Collected under duress, foraged items were loaded and shipped by boat to Charlestown for warehousing, distribution, or both. Adding to these daily challenges was the institutionalized corruption and profiteering in the collection and distribution of food by Leslie's quartermaster department that distributed the food, potable water, and wood. Standard British doctrine prescribed that before an offensive campaign could begin, at least six months food supply had to be in reserve. In addition, their doctrine also stipulated that once food supply reserves fell below the two-month level, withdrawal or evacuation of forces would commence.

British food shortages also diverted combat troops from their primary mission. Sustained offensive operations could not be launched if combat troops were busy foraging. Contesting foraging operations was creating a death of a thousand cuts for Leslie. Besides destroying morale, foraging often led to lootings, atrocities, injuries, and desertions, if not deaths. On October 16, Colonel Kosciusko took eighty British prisoners involved in a foraging operation near Monks Corner, which was most likely a mass desertion in disguise.[272] Adding to Leslie's frustrations, foraging operations rarely produced enough to go around. Greene's effective intelligence network obtained target details beforehand to move stored food supplies before the foraging expeditions arrived. Foraging details also exposed seasoned combat soldiers to snipers and ambushes. With the islands and the countryside full of enormous live oak trees, dense swamps, and Patriot rifles, foraging parties were severely hampered. According to one source, "British losses in these types of skirmishes soon equaled those suffered in larger pitched battles."[273] For Leslie to achieve a victory in the South, he would have to launch a sustained offensive to seek out and destroy Greene's forces, or as he had already tried, he would have to kidnap or assassinate Greene. All told, keeping Britain's army of occupation from living off host nation land was the key to forcing General Leslie's superior forces to capitulate or evacuate from Charlestown.

In July, Leslie received a significant boost to his low food supplies. With the evacuation of Savannah, Leslie inherited their large rice stores and armed riverboats. About 846 provincial troops trained in garrison duty reinforced him while the regulars and Hessians were sent to reinforce New York and Saint Augustine. Leslie's new troops held the prospect that he could initiate an offensive operation against Greene while his new troops stood post.[274] Leslie was undercut in this potential by Greene's successful recruiting campaign of Loyalists who joined the Patriot effort in exchange for the legislature not seizing their estates and declaring them persona non grata. One move offset the other.

Meanwhile, attempts by both sides to pursue preliminary peace negotiations became more complicated. On July 1, the king's prime minister, Charles Watson-Wentworth, the Earl of Rockingham, died suddenly from influenza at fifty-two. His death plunged the British government into another political crisis with little agreement between the king and politicians on what to do with America. General Carleton was left without his ranking political advocate back home who could secure enough unified agreement to support his local negotiation efforts to keep America within the empire. Lord Shelburne was appointed to fill the empty prime minister's post, and another two months would drag by before Carleton could exchange communications with the new ministry to get direction. In the meantime, the British situation in Charlestown was growing desperate, with the summer's disease season taking its toll on British troops and their commander while food supplies ran below requirements. General Leslie became stricken with a disease resembling acute meningococcal or parasitic meningitis, which confined him to dark rooms and caused mental confusion. Congress was not willing to negotiate directly with Carleton without France's permission or without including American diplomats in Europe in the discussion. Leslie could not trick Greene into lifting his embargo to alleviate his situation. Carleton abandoned his direct peace negotiations and concentrated on Charlestown's declining military and humanitarian crisis.

After sorting his reinforcements and the food supplies from Savannah in July, Leslie was ready to step up the action in August. Although summer's diseases had decimated his garrison, he intended to make something happen to his advantage. He sent the infamous Black Dragoons to Whitehall plantation to capture distinguished persons and attract attention north of Charlestown. Captain Capers of Horry's Cavalry met the dragoons on their return to Charlestown near 16 Mile House Tavern and defeated their force.[275] The prisoners were freed unharmed. After this distraction, on August 27, Leslie sent a large force of British Regulars under Major William Brereton to a massive foraging operation south of Charlestown. About four hundred to five hundred combat troops from the Sixty-Fourth, Seventeenth, and Eighty-Fourth, supported by eighteen armed river vessels, including three brigantines, two galleys, a sloop of war, and ten empty victuals sloops, proceeded to Combahee Ferry for an extended foraging expedition.[276] They were opposed by General Mordecai Gist and the First Marylanders and light infantry with approximately four hundred to five hundred troops. The British expedition was thwarted, but tragically, Colonel John Laurens was killed in the engagement. Arguably, his demise was the death knell for Black emancipation in the South, a quest to which he had dedicated his life. Rebuffed at Combahee, the British force moved down to Beaufort to conduct their foraging operations there again.

Two days later, on August 29, Leslie launched another foraging operation to the north. Their target was Colleton's Wadboo Barony on the Wadboo River. Commanded by Major Thomas Frasier with about 160 to 250 Provincial troops and mounted Black Dragoons, their intentions were likely to occupy Mulberry Castle and conduct extensive foraging operations in the twelve-thousand-acre barony.[277] Frasier's intelligence had advised that the barony was lightly defended, and General Marion's troops were busy protecting Georgetown. The likely plan was to capture the barony and use the slaves to load the vast amount of food, crops, and livestock on private boats on the Wadboo River for a trip to Charlestown while British troops held off any possible counterattacks. Unfortunately for their plan, the Swamp Fox was nearby with scattered security elements totaling about sixty men. General Marion quickly organized an ad hoc force consisting mainly of the former Loyalists who had switched sides a couple of months prior. He set up an ambush along the Avenue of the Cedars leading to Mulberry Castle and the cabins of the enslaved. The capture of both was key to the foraging operation's success. Marion's ambush worked perfectly, killing or wounding at least ten and possibly up to thirty of Frasier's men – stopping them in their tracks. To Leslie's frustration, another large forage-in-force was defeated.

All was not completely lost. Leslie's Beaufort expedition succeeded in securing enough rice, livestock, poultry, and game in the rice fields, pastures, and storage areas around Port Royal Ferry to hang on. At least one British galley, ironically named the *Balfour*, was captured by General Gist and the Delaware Regiment and now could be used against the enemy. British causalities from this extended foraging operation have not been found.

Greene began his land embargo on the British troops corralled in Charlestown in late 1781, just after General Leslie took command of the British Southern Army. The Lower South was on its fourth or fifth commander in less than two years, depending on how one counts. As the encirclement around British headquarters in Charlestown became tighter, Continental Army headquarters relocated to Bacon's Bridge and then Ashley Hill. Daily containment patrols were tasked to various field commanders to challenge British foraging efforts within assigned areas of responsibility. Leslie repeatedly requested to be relieved of his command, without avail, due to multiple illnesses. General Henry Clinton, Leslie's boss and overall commander of British expeditionary forces in America, had been replaced by Sir Guy Carleton in May 1782. Faced with a sickly commander, disease epidemics, constant desertions, scarce food, and total confinement, Carleton was looking for a way to avoid evacuating the South while preventing another Yorktown-like surrender in Georgia or South Carolina. Carleton's path-to-reconciliation diplomatic plan failed, and his king and government could not agree on much of anything to provide direction to him. Lord Shelburne, the new prime minister, was authorized to negotiate on his own with American diplomats in Europe.

Meanwhile, by the fall of 1782, the British occupation of Charlestown became unsustainable. After a devastating summer disease season and dangerously low food supplies, an immediate reduction of "mouths to feed" became necessary. In October 1782, with winter's cold coming on fast, General Carleton sent General Leslie orders to organize the phased withdrawal from Charlestown.

That same month, General Charles Lee, father of the original British Southern Strategy plan, fell sick and died at age fifty while staying in

Philadelphia. Coincidently or not, a relative of the principal British peace negotiator, Richard Oswald, visited Lee at his hotel before his death about the same time Oswald was finalizing the preliminary peace proposal. Eleazer Oswald was Lee's artillery officer at the Battle of Monmouth who withdrew his cannons in the face of the enemy without orders to do so. He disgruntledly resigned his commission after the battle and later published critical articles about George Washington in his Baltimore newspaper.[278] After the war, Eleazer vigorously opposed the ratification of the US Constitution, left America, and went on to spy for the British in Ireland.

When Lee was selling his Southern Strategy plan to the Crown hierarchy five years before, he bet his life the plan would work. Charles Lee asserted in writing, "If it [the Plan] is adopted in full, I am so confident of success that I would stake my life on the issue." He went as far as to double down on his proposal: "I will answer with my life for the success."[279] Subsequently, Lee's Plan ("Mr. Lee's Plan—March 29, 1777") was adopted at Whitehall as a British war strategy, arguably costing Britain their America and possibly costing Lee his life. At the least, Lee's timely death saved the British Empire from suffering future embarrassments from Lee contradicting postwar remembrances by the Howe brothers, Henry Clinton, Lord North, and Lord Germain. At the most, Lee's demise saved King George from having to explain his ministry's seedy collaboration with Lee and from Lee collecting on financial promises or a generalship that the ministry might have pledged in exchange for his erstwhile duplicity. Even if any possible guarantees were satisfied by the Crown in exchange for his aiding and abetting them, Lee could never be silent about how British leadership made so many mistakes losing their Empire in America. His sardonic mastery of the English language and penchant for publicizing his priggish views in newspapers would make them all look like fools. Such prospects were untenable to the Crown, especially if Lee was adding insult to embarrassment by pushing for his longed-for British generalship and financial security like Benedict Arnold received for turn coating. Pride does not take the prospect of humiliation lightly.

With Carleton's order to Leslie in Charlestown to begin evacuation, there were loose ends to tidy before the British left America. Assassinations during war happen all the time. Assassinations during peacetime are criminal acts. Timing is important. Lee died suddenly "of a fever" during his mysterious mission to Philadelphia "to settle financial matters" while staying in a discreet tavern much below his standards. Apparently, the 30,000 Spanish dollars he received from Congress in 1776 to compensate him for his seized estates in England were insufficient to fulfill his expectations of retirement wealth. Anyone's guess is whether he was lured to Loyalist-haven Philadelphia under false pretenses to meet his maker. He signed a document to sell his home in Virginia while passing through Baltimore on his way there. There is no record of where he planned to live. When his will was executed, his estates in England had not been liquidated as he had claimed. One can only speculate if Lee was planning on sailing back to his native country from Philadelphia to live with his sister before meeting his end.

Two days after his death, Lee was buried in a poorly marked grave in a Philadelphia churchyard rather than his home in Virginia, despite his will specifying that "I may not be buried in any church or churchyard."[280] Intended or not, the churchyard burial provided convenient protection from exhuming his remains. His grave and body became lost, and any possible physical evidence of foul play with his disappearance. No record of inquest survives, and his servants returned to his estate in Virginia and were married.

Luckily for King George, Lee would not be around to contradict the Crown's characterization of the war as a noble attempt to rescue lukewarm American Loyalists from a civil war. Lee would have had something to say about Britain's punishment-obsessed leadership spoiling Lee's perfect Southern Strategy plan that hinged on providing protective trust to the king's subjects. The "hero of Charlestown" and master of puzzling disinformation would not live to tell his side of the story. After Lee's convenient death, General Leslie completed the first phase of the evacuation of the last British garrison in the South at Charlestown—the conclusion of which would end the war.

VIII.
VICTORY DAY

Victory belongs to the most persevering.
—French general Napoleon Bonaparte

America's Victory Day, or as the British referred to it, "The Evacuation of His Majesty's Troops from Charlestown," began in October 1782. It ended on Saturday, December 14, 1782, when the last of Britain's finest troops in the Lower South were escorted to their longboats in the harbor that took them aboard their navy's powerful frigates, standing ready for battle. Until that final moment, the diplomatic issue of South Carolina possession and the political question of collective independence favored the British.

In August 1782, a British military withdrawal from Charlestown appeared unlikely. On August 2, General Carleton discovered that his advocate boss, the Earl of Rockingham, had died suddenly. William Petty Fitzmaurice, the second Earl of Shelburne, became the new prime minister. Lord Shelburne quickly began to undercut Rockingham's plan to have General Carleton negotiate directly with Congress while romancing Generals Washington and Greene into winding down the war and staying within the empire. Carleton's strategy to deal directly with Congress was designed to take immediate military pressure off New York and Charlestown and drive a wedge into the French-American alliance. If Carleton succeeded in either, time or peace negotiations would turn to favor the British. Instead, he was undermined back home. The new ministry under Shelburne began negotiating quietly with American diplomats in Europe. For the first time since the rebellion had begun, the king's ministry agreed to begin direct talks with congressionally appointed representatives under the pretext "that the issue of American independence be a subject of negotiation."[281]

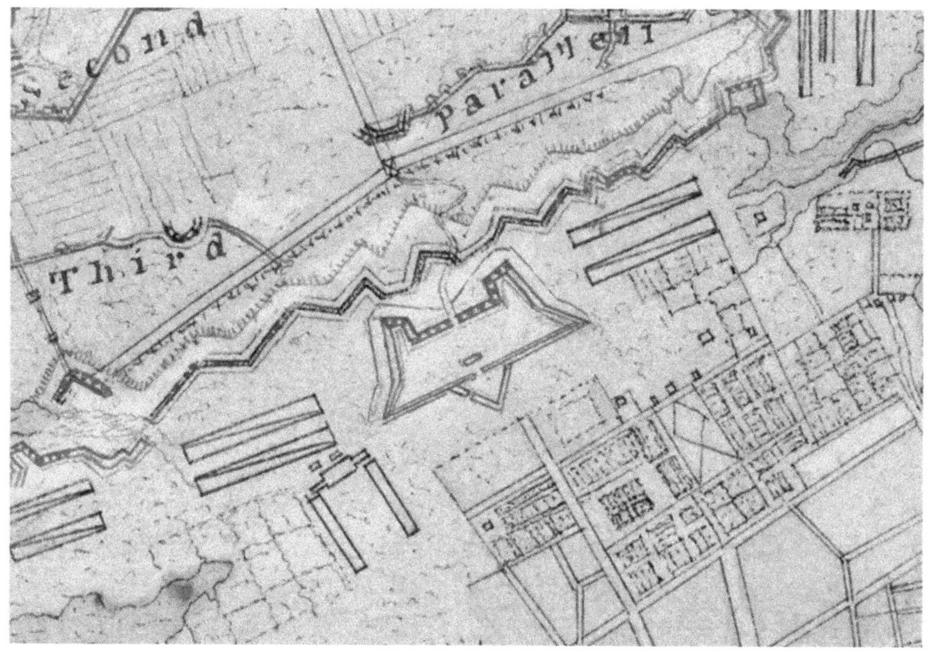

Charlestown Horn Work and Citadel 1782,
drawing courtesy of *Library of Congress.*

Carleton adjusted his stateside strategy to fit with Lord Shelburne's. If Carleton could get any states tired of war to trust his pronouncements of fait accompli peace, some states would likely recall their soldiers from Washington and Greene's Continental armies. The depletions would leave the South Carolina and New York countryside open to lightly contested territory repossession by British forces and Loyalists eager to get back in the fight to retain America. In his August letter, Carleton advanced a seductive logic that it was time to deescalate: "By authority that Negociations for a general Peace have already commenced at Paris" and that the "Independency of the Thirteen Provinces" was to be offered "instead of making it a condition of a general Treaty,"[282] Carlton's letter proposed that Washington exceed his Congressional authority by doing two things: (1) restoring Loyalists their possessions and providing them total compensation for confiscations, and (2) commencing a (lopsided) exchange of all British prisoners captured at Saratoga, Cowpens, Guilford, Eutaw, Yorktown, and elsewhere. General Washington wrote to Greene on August 6 acquainting him with Carleton's ruses. He advised Greene as follows: "Whatever the real intention of the Enemy may be, I think our strictest attention and exertion which have ever been practiced on our part, instead of being diminished, ought to be increased thereby." Greene's intelligence network had picked up information that the British were preparing to evacuate Saint Augustine and shift troops to reinforce Charlestown.[283] Adding to Washington's heightened vigilance was a credible report that British cavalry and infantry from Carleton's headquarters in New York City were preparing "to relieve part of [the] Garrison of Charlestown," not evacuate it.

Carleton's letter was very assertive and very clever—"the art of the feint." He realized that the war had entered a complex political and diplomatic phase centered around military territory possession, prisoner-of-war ratios, and economic expectations. He wanted the empire to retain New York, Charlestown, and Saint Augustine at a minimum. Still, with the toll of disease and desertions and the desperate need for reinforcements in the British posts in the West Indies, the math became impossible for him to hold all three port capitals. Carleton's solution to all his problems was to promote a separate peace deal with America to break the French alliance.[284]

But neither Washington nor Congress was biting. According to General Washington, the "species of Independence" Carlton was likely referring to in his letters was "that the Legislatures of America should be independent of the Parliament of Great Britain, but that the King of England should have the same kind of supremacy here as in Ireland."[285]

In other words, Carleton was advancing "fake independence," not the sovereign independence specified in the Declaration of Independence. Ireland had recently won their local political independence while remaining within the empire. Carleton attempted to reframe Congress's definition of independence in hopes that Washington and some states would accept the lesser and cooperate with him to wind down the war, leaving the nonmilitary details of peace to British diplomats' goodwill after an insulted France abandoned the United States. General Carleton had practiced such deceptive arts when he broke out of Quebec, Canada, in May of 1776 when the Continental army had him surrounded.[286] If Congress or Washington became lax by thinking the military war was over, Carleton could quietly reinforce Leslie and launch a "friendly" offensive from Charlestown to recapture undefended territory and substantiate Britain's claim on South Carolina. He could recapture the South in the same way he had captured Canada in 1776. Alleviating Patriot military pressure on either New York or Charlestown was the key to Carleton saving pieces of Britain's American Empire.

British army leadership was known the world over for their tactical feints. Getting the opposing army to believe they were doing one thing while doing something else was their hallmark. For example, Guy Carleton's stalling defense of Quebec in 1776 bought time for his reinforcements. Once reinforced, he launched a counteroffensive that drove the American army out of Canada. His defense of Quebec and Canada was one masterful feint after another. He had pulled a successful defense of Quebec "out of the hat" to save Britain's empire in Canada, for which he received the Order of the Bath and knighthood.[287] Sir Guy was picked to perform the same magic trick in America operating from the last British garrisons in America: New York and Charlestown. The master magician did it in Quebec with fewer resources.

General Carleton was probably Britain's most gifted general possessing governor-general political and military genius. He was taken out of the North American theater command in 1777 because Lord Germain disliked him, and his high ethical standards did not square with Whitehall's policy to ruthlessly crush the rebellion and oppress the population off the record. Germain was the only minister to vote against Carleton's knighthood. Once Lord Germain resigned at the end of February 1782, General Carleton was the obvious choice to replace General Clinton as the British military commander. He was also given the authority to act as a peace commissioner to keep America within the Empire. Carlton sent three truce ships to Philadelphia on July 4, hoping to negotiate a separate peace with the United States.[288] The king trusted him implicitly. Given enough time and political support, Carleton had the talent to pull off a victory to keep America British as he had done to win Canada back from the jaws of defeat.

To that end, Carleton attempted to get Washington involved in a diplomatic issue involving the unbalanced exchange of General Lord Cornwallis for Henry Laurens's restricted parole in London. Cornwallis was already in England operating without restriction while Laurens, the American ambassador to the Dutch, was on restricted parole release from the Tower of London. Congress had called for Cornwallis's return to the United States if Laurens was not issued a general parole. Congress resolved that "it might be better accord with the peculiar barbarities which characterize the said Earl Cornwallis in his last prosecution of a war in itself the most barbarous of Modern Ages, to make him the last, instead of so early an object of indulgence." Congress wanted to enter Cornwallis's Southern Campaign atrocities into the public record and international discussions. His lordship's misdeeds, if not prosecutable in an international court, had negotiation and global relations value. Conversely, Carleton wanted to flip the script using the Cornwallis exchange situation to tempt Washington out of his military lanes and into controversial diplomatic distractions.

Washington had other plans to see the war for territory control finish well. From the American military operations perspective, the British conquest had been reduced to a two-peninsula garrison war in the colonies by August 1782. While Greene was increasing the stranglehold on Charlestown, Washington was doing the same with the British around Manhattan. The French army moved up from the Yorktown area toward New York about the same time Carleton was writing Washington manipulative proposals that would likely provide openings to short sell independence, in whole or in part.[289] The pressure of the northward French movement probably caused Carleton to reconsider his plans to detach regular infantry and cavalry units from New York to Charlestown to recapture South Carolina territory and eliminate Greene's Southern Continental Army. Such a possibility became undone when the Comte de Rochambeau's French army marched up from Yorktown to Baltimore, significantly increasing the threat to Carleton in New York. (The French did indeed add to Washington's strength along the Hudson River opposite Manhattan in September.) Faced with this new joint-force threat, Carleton's military options for relieving the Charlestown garrison and enlarging the British grip on South Carolina evaporated. If British regulars could not be reinforced to break out of Charlestown, he would alleviate General Leslie's sustainment problem by ordering the evacuation of the Rawdon Town shanties outside Charlestown's walls on the Neck. Much to General Carleton's frustration, Washington wisely stayed within his command lanes by coordinating with Greene to concentrate on territory control and increase both Continental armies' military pressure on the British-occupied peninsulas of New York City and Charlestown.

Following General Carleton's orders, General Leslie completed the evacuation of Rawdon Town in October. According to embarkation returns, the fleet evacuated over four thousand Loyalist refugees, their enslaved people, and provincial troops to the Saint Augustine peninsula.[290] General Greene believed that this withdrawal phase was a positive sign that the British would continue the evacuation, although he cautioned that "the british will practice every art to deceive us"; the art of the feint always lurked in the background. One thing was for sure—Leslie had four thousand fewer mouths to feed. Greene further expressed the importance of forcing a British withdrawal from Charlestown without outside help: "to get rid of the enemy without foreign aid. I am fond of the [French] alliance; but I wish for the honor of America that liberty may affect her own deliverance…The blessing seems to lose half it's value, received at the hands of another."[291] Notwithstanding, the governments in Europe had to agree with any bilateral peace agreement. They would see a forced

British withdrawal of their Southern headquarters in Charlestown as proof that the United States could stand on its own if granted their sovereign independence.

In October, the first phase of the withdrawal did not significantly hamper Leslie's ability to launch a breakout offensive if conditions presented themselves. The initial withdrawal took about 58 ships to remove about four thousand souls, so given that math, at least 150 ships were required to evacuate the rest of Britain's troops, depending on contraband. Carleton did not send the necessary number of ships to conduct the demilitarization phase of extraction until November. He was still publishing his correspondence with General Washington to stimulate public sentiment against the French alliance and for reunification.[292] With the refugee shantytown outside Charlestown's gates abandoned, the only road off the peninsula was clear, and operational security probably improved for Leslie. British regulars could conduct offensive operations because there was less refugee-tending activity. Starving civilians tend to pester troops to share their rations and help them survive. Initially, Greene's intelligence believed all the British forces in and around Charlestown would evacuate in October. Given the math stated above, it was never Carleton's intention to evacuate at that time simply because the required number of ships were not ordered there.[293]

However, prisoner exchanges increased, and British and Hessian forces scattered on James Island were consolidated at Fort Johnson. From an operational options perspective, the consolidated troops on James Island could be transported by water up the Ashley River to surprise attack Greene's main camp. At the same time, Leslie's regulars could march out of Charlestown and board transports to cross the Ashley River to flank him in a pincer night attack. That option existed until Colonel Thaddeus Koscuisko conducted a special-operations raid on October 10 at Fort Johnson, where he captured forty-eight prime dragoon horses, which would have been essential to the British pulling off a surprise cavalry attack on Greene's camp.[294] Greene was ever vigilant about depriving the enemy of the means and opportunity to mount an offensive.

Vigilance and containment were still the names of the game after the initial evacuation in October. Leslie had sufficient men to attack Greene. Plans to complete the evacuation could be rescinded at a moment's notice, as evidenced by Carleton's cancellation of his Saint Augustine evacuation order earlier in the year. That situation suddenly became tenable with the French naval defeat at the Saints and the Castillo de Marcos garrison reinforcement by a contingent of Savannah's evacuated Provincial troops. (Carleton's announcement of impending evacuation from Saint Augustine could have just been the art of the feint to draw off Spanish troops laying siege.) Denying the enemy the comforts of sufficient food, potable water, and wood fuel while keeping them contained was essential to having Carleton commit to sending the required number of ships for a final withdrawal of Charlestown. General Carleton had written Christopher Gadsden in June offering to transport the South Carolina leaders and their families back to Charlestown from their exile in Philadelphia at the king's expense: "Forgetting all those severities which have embittered our unhappy divisions, I shall with great pleasure fully comply in addition to that, & in doing so doing I only pay strict obedience to the King's benevolent intentions."[295] Carleton was making overtures to Gadsden of peace and reconciliation to keep Charlestown and South Carolina within the empire.

Carleton's "benevolent" appeal to Gadsden fell on battered ears. Besides Gadsden being one of the influential leaders of the revolution, Gadsden was the leading merchant and economic generator in Charlestown. His massive import-export warehouses along his premier wharf facilitated immense international trade. He was a slaveholder, but he refused to import or sell enslaved souls on his properties.[296] He had advocated against the expansion of slavery into the backcountry. Gadsden began his ascent to revolutionary leadership in November 1765 by organizing an armed assault on the British garrison at Fort Johnson. This armed insurrection contributed to Parliament rescinding the Stamp Act and Gadsden becoming known in England as a rebellious leader. Gadsden was the first member of the Continental Congress to call for independence from England. He spoke about rebellion as early as 1764 but definitely by 1766.[297].When the British captured Charlestown, they publicly burned the Liberty Tree where Gadsden held his meetings and imprisoned Gadsden as one of their first acts of establishing authority. Rumor had it that the heart of the tree was shipped to King George as a prize. They eventually moved Gadsden to solitary confinement at the Saint Augustine dungeon, where he was imprisoned for forty-two weeks. Since he was the inspirational leader of the rebellion, the British tried everything to get Gadsden to recant his calls for independence. They hoped to use a recantation as a propaganda tool to turn Patriots throughout America back to the Crown or break the spirit of the Sons of Liberty. In 1780, when British Major John Andre was hanged for spying, Gadsden was slated for hanging in retaliation but narrowly avoided the fate. Instead, he was eventually exchanged from imprisonment. Christopher Gadsden, an original leader of the Sons of Liberty, ignored Carleton's clever overture to initiate a course of peaceful reconciliation within the empire and routed Carleton's proposal to Congress for them to adjudicate.[298] Carleton showed he was prepared to exploit every opportunity to entice South Carolina and the rest of America into remaining within the empire.

But his predecessors' barbarity was unforgivable, and time ran out for Carleton to make amends. The plundering problem created by marauding British troops only subsided when the British were forced out of an area.[299] On May 23, one of Carleton's first acts upon taking command in America was writing General Leslie in Charlestown to admonish him about plundering, insult (rape), and incivility—meaning the breakdown of discipline among troops toward civilians.[300] He ordered Leslie to prepare the garrisons in Savannah and Charlestown for evacuations just in case, recognizing the tenuousness of both situations from within and without. From a command perspective, these preparation orders had a tone of focusing Leslie to cease playing to the will of the notorious officer corps and destructive Loyalists he inherited, which had inflamed the population against the British beyond repair. The ferocity of evil the British had created destroyed public confidence in their ability to govern or provide protective trust. In July, Carleton wisely transferred the chief atrocity perpetrator, Lieutenant Colonel Nisbet Balfour, to New York, but Balfour's culture of punishment and exploitation remained in his wake.

In Providence-like retribution, the summer of 1782 was disastrous for the British army cooped up in Charlestown. Disease spread throughout the ranks, killing and incapacitating many. Leslie himself came down with acute meningococcal or parasitic meningitis. It left him confused and confined to dark rooms, unable to plan, focus his troops, lead an offensive, or conduct conciliatory negotiations as Carleton wished. General Leslie was unaware that Greene had contracted the same virus (which would return and kill them both at different times after the war). Leslie kept submitting his resignation from the Southern command, and Carleton kept refusing it. Carleton had no time to replace Leslie without risking the dissolution of the British Southern Army. There had been too many commanders already.

The first withdrawal in October reduced the humanitarian burden, but it did not eliminate it. There were still over twelve thousand mouths to feed every day on a peninsula too small for farms or sufficient grazing lands. Each arriving evacuation ship or warship added to that feeding number. The disposition of enslaved and freed Blacks and merchant agreements to sell and trade goods preoccupied Carleton and Leslie between October and December.[301] Little time was left for reconciliation initiatives or organizing sustainable offensives to keep the province. However, there was time for the British army and navy to negotiate off-the-books deals involving space reservations for loot and the reselling of the enslaved. Even the bells of Saint Michael's Church, ranging in weight from about five hundred pounds to over one thousand pounds, found reservations on board ships headed for England during this time.[302] The British likely could not stand the thought of the victorious Patriots ringing the massive church bells upon the city's liberation. At the same time, their hungry troops aboard evacuation ships in the cold harbor were likely divvying up their contraband and reflecting if the thirty-one-month tour de force in the king's name was worth it. Remnants of the famed Black Watch Seventy-First Regiment of Foot might have pondered the recruiting promise that had prompted them to join the British army and leave their homeland in Scotland. "The lands of the rebels will be divided amongst you, and every one of you become lairds."[303] Fellow Scotsman Leslie could not stand in the way of his troops bringing off a few trophies and "gifts" with all that these men had been through lest he have a mutiny on his hands. Besides struggling with his health, General Leslie was preoccupied with sustaining the army, maintaining order in the city, and preventing desertions until the Royal Navy evacuation fleets could withdraw them. With the cold winter setting in, the demand for scarce firewood added to Leslie's huge sustenance burdens.

The British need for an estimated one hundred cords of firewood a day had to be opposed. On November 14, 1782, under cover of darkness, several woodcutters landed by boat on James Island to cut desperately needed wood for the besieged Charlestown garrison.[304] The woodcutters had a security escort of over three hundred heavily armed British troops with one field piece under Major William Dansey and Captain Frederick Cornwallis of the king's forces. The security troops included the remnants of the Thirty-Third Regiment of Foot, the Royal Welch Fusiliers, the Seventy-First Regiment of Foot, and the Brigade Guards—among the best British troops in America. A seventy-man Continental and militia force consisting of the Second Maryland and First Pennsylvania under Colonel Count Thaddeus Kosciusko, Captain William Wilmot, and Lieutenant John Markland attacked them. The Continentals were repulsed with casualties, including Captain Wilmot and a Black soldier whose name does not survive. British casualties were unknown, but the point was made: woodcutting was subject to attack the same as food foraging.

Greene's siege strategy of death by a thousand cuts would soon pay off. If the British wanted wood, they should prepare to send their best troops to pay for it every day. The harbor began filling up with evacuation ships before the end of November after the battle. In Lieutenant Markland's memoirs, he wrote, "This was the last battle in the War for American Independence."[305] While the first naval battle of the war between British and American forces was initiated by cannon fire from Fort Johnson on James Island on November 11, 1775, the Battle of Dills

Bluff on the same island seven years later was the last land battle between Continental and British forces in the South, if not the Revolutionary War. The slow bleeding, the confinement, and the disease had become too much for the British war machine.

After the first withdrawal in October, opportunities for the British army to break out of Charlestown or for General Leslie to finesse some type of reconciliation to keep the city with Carleton's mannerly help never materialized. General Greene and Governor Matthews kept the imperfect land embargo in place while Patriot military operations to oppose firewood and foraging operations kept the pressure on the British to leave. Leslie would not offer a written capitulation, and Greene was not authorized to sign an untethered truce. While encamped with the Continental Army along the Ashley River, Captain Walter Finny of the Pennsylvania troops, reported, "The lator end of the Month [November] our Expectations ware very Sanguin, respecting the Evacuation of Charles Town…"[306] Toward the end of November, the British evacuation fleet began assembling in the harbor, and the enormous task of loading commenced. The options for the British to hang on to South Carolina had finally run out.

The fleet of ships in the harbor told the story. Some accounts have the number of ships as low as 130 to 150, and other reports have 300 and 500. Regardless of the number, much planning and many orders were issued to get the required number of ships to Charlestown for the rescue, retreat, covered withdrawal, capitulation, extraction, surrender, or evacuation—whichever term one may choose. Undocumented private ships transferring plunder may explain the number differences between visual ship counts and lower British records. If privately contracted ships were not recorded, there would be little traceability of contraband or the enslaved taken to other shores, which could be tied to the British army. Cargo loads aside, the big unknowns about the final withdrawal were whether the British would attempt to set fire to the town, initiate a battle or bombardment before their departure, or go peaceably. They had removed structures along the harbor, so their ten covering warships armed with about 320 cannons had clear fields of fire to decimate the town.[307] The Pennsylvania, Maryland, North Carolina, and Virginia Continental troops led by Wayne's Regiment of Cavalry and Lee's Legion would prepare for every eventuality. Whatever response plan Greene and Wayne devised to breach Charlestown's fortifications to save the town from destruction while engaging the British is unknown. Sometimes the bravest course is to prepare for everything yet have the nerve to do nothing if the situation warrants.

There were still some days to go before zero hour. General Wayne provided intelligence to Greene on December 9 that the enemy intended to conduct a final foraging operation in force, so Greene should prepare the main army to counter. There was only one road out of Charlestown via King's Street, so an offensive could be observed well in advance if not informed beforehand by Greene's spies. Greene reacted to Wayne's information by issuing orders for his cavalry to get ready to move and gave the same orders to his army.[308] Greene then wrote Washington briefing him on the situation.[309] Despite presumed food and water scarcity aboard the extraction fleet, the attack never materialized, probably because Leslie had his hands full.

The security situation in Charlestown was deteriorating quickly. After issuing orders to Wayne and briefing Washington on December 10, Greene sent his best troops across the Ashley River to position for battle. He expected the British to fire the town upon departure just as they did withdrawing from Georgetown and Camden. Tensions in the city had increased with reported outbreaks of mobs and riots. General Leslie was doing his best given his health situation to "preserve order," but his underlings were slow or indifferent in executing his orders. According to Hessian state archives, "The inhabitants of the town were forbidden, under penalty of strict punishment, either to show themselves in the streets, or to open their doors and shutters, but to keep them closed" as a safeguard against rioting.[310] The poor security situation in Charlestown was causing tensions on both sides to mount.

Greene acted to prevent a disaster. General Wayne was given field command to assess and react to the situation as he saw fit. Deconfliction channels needed to be opened between commands if possible. Greene's

Continental troops were repositioned on the Charleston Neck, near the three British redoubts that comprised the first battle line protecting Charlestown. Greene then issued the following commander's intent to Wayne: "I am a little apprehensive if you move too near the enemy it may increase the confusion, and perhaps endanger the place. It is my wish to get possession without exposing the Town if possible; and I beg all your movements may tend to this purpose…should you find an agreement to suffer General Leslie's rearguard to go off unmolested is necessary for the safety of the Town and that your guard shall be introduced before his retires you may agree to it."[311] Greene gave Wayne the authority to negotiate an official truce with Leslie in hopes of avoiding a cataclysmic battle, Parliament's wrath, and a renewed war.

Executing a collapsing perimeter is one of the most difficult military maneuvers. One weak link or panicked soldier can kill many and renew a war searching for an end. General Leslie was no stranger to executing a collapsing perimeter facing an angry mob at Salem, Massachusetts, on February 26, 1775. His successful withdrawal under high stress likely prevented the American Revolution from starting months before Lexington and Concord. The Charlestown withdrawal was different in scale but the same situation. With upward of ten thousand lives at stake, Leslie had to find a way to collapse a huge perimeter without taking casualties or causing an international incident.

One asset Leslie had to work with was his opposite, General Greene. Greene had faced Leslie in battles at Harlem Heights and Guilford Courthouse. Greene sent Leslie's troops running at Harlem. Leslie made a final do-or-die assault against Greene at Guilford Courthouse. Greene chose to relinquish the field but retain the victory that prevented North Carolina from being conquered. Leslie knew firsthand what it was like to claim blood-soaked ground littered with dead and dying comrades only to leave them behind unburied. Opponents in battle get to know each other very well. The situation in Charlestown required making a truce with the enemy and trusting your opposite to honor it and manage it. Things could quickly go wrong, rekindling the world war and leaving everyone with blood and dishonor on their hands.

Double agents do their best work at times like this. General Andrew Williamson was called into town from his plantation outside Charleston to speak with General Leslie about mediating a mutually agreeable, bloodless withdrawal plan. After the British captured Charlestown in 1780, Williamson had surrendered himself and his troops in the field rather than fight a partisan war. When Greene took command of the Southern Department, his agents turned Williamson into a double agent, possibly America's first. Williamson might have been the spy who alerted Greene about the British plots to kidnap or kill him just in time. General Wayne was meeting with Williamson at his home on December 12 when Williamson proposed to Wayne "that Gen [Alexander] Leslie had it in contemplation to leave the 60th Regiment in town until we relieve them." In writing to General Greene, Wayne reported: "I took the hint, & just observed that if such a measure was thought necessary for the protection of the Inhabatants that that Corps ought to be permitted to embark inviolate; which I expect will produce an overture from Gen Leslie on this subject."[312]

General Guy Carleton had expressed his commander's intent to Leslie that he was to act with humanity for the sake of national honor in the withdrawal. According to Captain Finney of the Pennsylvania Continentals under Wayne's command: "This Day [December 12] Gen. Lessley requisted that all Hostilleties should ceass, promising to Evacate the Town with All Expodition agreeing to give us the Erliest Intillegence of that Event." In this very tense time, Leslie trusted his Sixtieth Regiment and their commanders to honor a truce and collapse the last circle of the defense perimeter without initiating battle. His other not-so-trustworthy troops and commanders would already be on board ships in the harbor under the watchful eye of the king's marines. One Hessian account states that Leslie made known that any transgressions "by firing guns and other excesses [acts of provocation] during the out-march to the water" would result in that soldier being taken into custody "and sent to Nova Scotia upon a wild, wild island, where there is no wood" to die a lonesome death. Leslie intended to obey Carleton's order to the letter.

General Greene replied to General Wayne on December 13, 1782, stating, "I perfectly approve of the convention you have made. It argues fear in the enemy and gives a superiority to us. Besides which it gives additional security to the Town which at this period of the war is a capital object." Now that Leslie's verbal overture had been accepted, the truce and withdrawal treaty had to be reduced to writing

The ideal selection to liaison the agreement was Charlestown merchant Maurice Simons. Mr. Simons was representative of the town's merchants who sought to allay Britain's fears of merchandise confiscation and a trade embargo after withdrawal. Independence would not be such a hard pill for Parliament to swallow if business continued with Charlestown's international port, the gateway to the American market. Since Greene was operating through his second, General Wayne, Leslie would officially operate through Major James Wemyss, the adjutant general of the British Army, to sign an official truce. "Wemyss wrote Simons that in order to ally fears expressed by Simons and others 'that Plundering and other Devastation may take place in the interval of time of our Evacuating, & the Enemy taking possession of the Town,'" a security process should be put into place. Gen. Alexander Leslie had authorized Wemyss to propose that "a Captains Guard [of American troops] should march tomorrow morning at Gun firing to our advanced Redoubt, which if they find evacuated to advance until our rear is seen, their movements to be then regulated by ours, taking care to keep about two hundred yards distance, and upon our rear Guard turning off toward Gadsden's Wharf, the Enemy Guard may immediately proceed into Town, & put into execution their directions toward the preservation of Peace & Good order; during the whole of this it is to be understood that no hostility is to take place until our troops have got on board their transports." General Leslie personally told Mr. Simons to tell Wayne that "if Gen Wayne did attack him he would be answerable for the Consequences, & that the best the Inhabitants had to expect would be the Destruction of the town together with their own property."[313] In advancing this addendum, General Leslie might have bitterly recalled the proud day in May 1780 he and Lord Cornwallis sat side-by-side on horses outside the Charlestown

Horn Work, accepting Continental General Benjamin Lincoln's sword of surrender, thinking that all of America would soon return to the British Empire. On December 13, 1782, Major James Wemyss, adjutant general of the British Army, and General Anthony Wayne of the United States Continental Army signed the official truce and withdrawal agreement likely to end the war if honored. Five fleets of ships were waiting in the harbor to evacuate over 10,000 British, Loyalist, and Hessian troops; their booty; their enslaved people; and their followers.[314]

The order of troop evacuation and servants was listed as follows. The first embarkation of Hessians totaling 1,571 men was to begin on Friday, December 13, at Eveleighs, Fish Market, and Beef Market Wharves at one o'clock. Next, from the same wharves, the Provincial British Prince of Wales, King's American, First and Second Battalion Regiments, totaling 2,432 men. On Saturday, the fourteenth of December, the first embarkation of the Sixtieth, Third, and Fourth Battalions and General Stewart's command, totaling 957 men, was scheduled for seven o'clock in the forenoon at Roses Wharf. The second embarkation was scheduled for nine o'clock in the morning, consisting of Artillery, Jagers, Sixty-Third Regiments and detachments of the Sixtieth, Third, and, Fourth Battalion Rear Guard, totaling 498 troops. The Buffs and ancillary detachments totaling 674 men were scheduled for withdrawal from Fort Johnson as the fleets left the harbor.[315] Infirm soldiers, Loyalist militia, civilians including 5,333 free and enslaved Black persons would board their assigned transport ships before their troops. However, in a two-sided withdrawal plan, much can go wrong.

Greene's operational plan to secure the town was clear. First, all care was taken to faithfully execute the agreement to secure the city and avoid a truce violation. Any acts of violence could trigger horrendous bloodshed during the withdrawal. Wayne would lead the town transfer part of the operation in the morning as agreed. Greene's main army would position in reserve outside the town walls, prepared to cover Wayne's cavalry and infantry if things went wrong. Wayne's first job would be to secure the Horn Work entranceway into the walled city. Then Greene's Continentals could get into the town to cover Wayne, put out fires, evacuate the remaining residents, or engage the British ground forces remaining, whatever the eventuality might be. The massive Horn Work could serve as a refuge for the town residents if British warships opened fire on the city. (The Horn Work was a broad fortress or citadel straddling King Street, which defended the single approach into Charlestown. It measured "approximately three hundred and thirty feet across" and an estimated one-hundred and fifty feet wide, covering approximately nine acres surrounded by a moat, stone bridge, and upward-hinged draw gate. The Horn Work had parapets as high as thirty feet that supported both cannon and troops.[316]) The second phase of Greene's operational plan would depend on how the first phase went. If the town was secured and the British ground forces had all withdrawn to their ships, and if the warships had moved away from the city without commencing a cannonade, Greene would then execute the next phase. But death would have to take the day off first.

The second part of Greene's operational plan was festive and ceremonial, involving a liberation procession through Charlestown composed of military troops and civilian leadership—on horseback, in carriages, and on foot proceeding down King Street to State Street. The state government confederated with Congress would be formally installed at the statehouse, and the South Carolina and the United States flags would be raised. Charlestown and South Carolina would be officially recognized as part of the independent American government.

The first part of the plan reportedly transpired as follows: "At daybreak on the 14th, Wayne's force, consisting of the light infantry, the cavalry of Lee's Legion, and two six-pound artillery pieces, marched from their camp, which was 'before the Enemy's Works.' Upon reaching the British works, they followed the British rear guard into Charleston, which consisted of the British Sixty-third Regiment, the Jagers, detachments from the British Sixtieth Regiment, and the Royal Artillery. The American march was executed with 'great order and regularity, except now and then the British called to General Wayne that he was too fast upon them, which occasioned him to halt a little.'" The British had "gallies in the Ashley and Cooper rivers dropped down in a line with our [i.e., the

American] troops, the whole length of the Neck; and in front of the Bay, as the cavalry moved in their view, the men of war and armed vessels were ranged, with lighted matches; but not a shot was fired on either side."[317] Wayne's troops "marched into town and took post at the state house" at 11:00 a.m. Leslie was among the last to leave, "having exerted himself with great care and diligence in extinguishing and preventing fires of houses which a few sailors, actuated as they said by a zeal for the honor of Old England, had set in 2 or 3 places. The rebel cavalry was at hand and came to town that morning, but General Leslie sent to them to forbid their approach to the town's waterside until his troops were gone. A few straggling sailors had remained in town who were kindly treated by the American cavalry and permitted to return quietly to their ships." General Alexander Leslie, the commander of all British troops in the South, William Bull, the royal lieutenant governor of South Carolina, and the British Southern Army of occupation were forced to evacuate the Lower South forevermore.

Given the success of the first plan, the second part of Greene's plan went into execution and was reported as follows: "At 3 o'clock, P.M. General Greene conducted Governor [John] Mathews, and the council, with some other of the citizens into town: we marched in, in the following order: an advance of an officer and thirty of Lee's dragoons; then followed the governor and General Greene; the next two were General [Mordecai] Gist [Maryland Continentals] and myself; after us followed the council, citizens and officers, making altogether about fifty: one hundred and eighty cavalry brought up the rear: we halted in Broad-street, opposite where the South Carolina bank now stands; there we alighted, and the cavalry discharged to quarters: afterward, everyone went where they pleased; some in viewing the town, others visiting their friends. It was a grand and pleasing sight, to see the enemy's fleet (upward of three hundred sail) laying at anchor from Fort Johnson to Five-fathom-hole, in a curve line, as the current runs; and what made it more agreeable, they were ready to depart from the port. The great joy that was felt on this day, by the citizens and soldiers, was inexpressible: the widows, the orphans, the aged men and others, who, from their particular situations, were obliged to remain in Charlestown, many of whom had been cooped up in one room of their own elegant houses for upward of two years, whilst the other parts were occupied by the British officers, many of whom were a rude uncivil set of gentlemen; their situations, and the many mortifying circumstances occurred to them in that time, must have been truly distressing. I cannot forget that happy day when we marched into Charlestown with the American troops; it was a proud day to me, and I felt myself much elated, at seeing the balconies, the doors, the windows crowded with the patriotic fair, the aged citizens and others, congratulating us on our return home, saying, 'God bless you gentlemen!' Both citizens and soldiers shed mutual tears of joy." The historical etching depicting the Victory Day liberation adorns the front cover of this book.

One of General Anthony Wayne's Continental officers, Captain Walter Finney, entered the following account into his diary: "After Marching Down to Ye State House, return'd to the Berracks [located at King's College now College of Charleston campus] and Announc'd our Arrival by the Discharge of thirteen Cannon and three cheers." Greene established the Southern Army headquarters at the John Rutledge house on Broad Street, which remains to this day. The tenacious Eagle replaced the Mighty Oak.

General Greene immediately notified his superiors after the massive withdrawal fleet cleared the harbor via the British-named "Rebellion Road" narrows. His first after-action report went to Elias Boudinot, president of the Continental Congress, and it confirmed the liberation of Charlestown, the clearing of all British and Hessian occupation troops from the South, the negotiated treaty between armies, the exchange of all civil and military prisoners, and the joint British-American merchant reopening of the economy. "The people are once more free," he wrote, attributing credit to the army for their perseverance, patience, dignity, patriotism, and public virtue.[318] Greene then wrote the French minister to the United States, the Chevalier de La Luzerne, to confirm the liberation and territory possession, ostensibly to aid independence negotiations and document the final removal date to leave no doubt about control of the Lower South. He then wrote General Washington, enclosing a copy of his letter to the president of Congress. He congratulated Washington for the success and outlined his plans for security and trade protection in South Carolina. With the paperwork done, united and sovereign independence was in the hands of the politicians, diplomats, and Providence.

The time had arrived to honor the victorious army. Colonel Tadeusz Kosciuszko and his staff decorated Dillons Long Room (McCrady's Tavern) under the direction of Caty Greene for a Victory Ball on January 2, 1783. Cambridge-educated Colonel John Grimke, a veteran of the Battle of Eutaw Springs, the siege of Yorktown, and Charlestown's Regiment of Artillery sent out invitations.[319] Amid festive magnolia leaves and paper flowers on the walls, Charlestown ladies danced with officers and dignitaries "to music played by the army band."[320] The general and Mrs. Greene opened the dancing likely after remarks of appreciation by General Greene. The night of the Victory Ball celebrated life and the brave Patriots who had successfully ended the war.

War rarely has a predictable ending. In official military correspondence dated January 29, 1783, General George Washington congratulated his second-in-command, General Nathanael Greene, for leading his forces to successfully conclude the ground war in the South, culminating with the liberation of Charlestown. This letter was written fifteen months after Washington's and Rochambeau's Yorktown success and less than a month before Parliament's up or down vote to end or continue the war. Washington knew Charleston's liberation would be America's best chance for winning the War for Independence when he wrote: "I am very anxious to see the King of Great Britains speech to his Parliament with the consequent Debate and Determinations, as I imagine we shall be able from these to form a better judgement respecting War or Peace than from any thing we have hitherto seen." Washington's insight of Parliament's upcoming contentious debates and a close vote turned out to be correct. "By a vote of 207–190, the House of Commons passed a resolution on 21 February [1783] accepting the peace treaties that had been negotiated and approving the grant of sovereign independence to the United States, but condemning the concessions that had been made to obtain peace."[321] War's end and the birth of an independent United

States was approved by seventeen votes, a nine-vote margin, approximately two months after Charlestown's liberation. Lord Loughborough referred to the ratified treaty as a "capitulation," while Lord Fox later stated that subsequent treaties with America involving other European parties were "superfluous." The independence deal was done: the unassisted liberation of Charlestown was the tipping point for Britain's political capitulation on the issue of sovereign independence, just as General George Washington and John Rutledge had predicted in their letters to General Nathanael Greene after the liberation of Charlestown.[322]

British Fleet in Charlestown Harbor Evacuating their last Armies from the South. (Howard Pyle painting, Delaware Art Museums/Bridgeman Art Library.)

IX.
INDEPENDENCE AT LAST!

The political object is the goal; war is the means of reaching it.
—-Carl von Clausewitz—On War

The liberation of the Lower South from British occupation was an extraordinary military and political accomplishment. This determined military campaign changed the political outcome of the war from foreign rule by a divine king to self-government elected by the people. From this point forward, the American people became their own masters. The time period from the British capture of Charlestown on May 12, 1780, to the city's liberation on December 14, 1782, could be argued as "The Thirty-One Months that Won the Revolution."

During this time, Charlestown and South Carolina became the epicenter of a world war that would decide whether authoritarian monarchies or elected governments by the people would rule western societies. The liberation of the Lower South, culminating with the fall of Charlestown, successfully settled the questions of American independence of all thirteen states, the inalienable right of government by the people, a government of laws versus capricious monarchs, residential quartering of troops, the freedom of assembly, the right of free speech, and the separation of church and state. These "rights of man" initially went from philosophy to practice in the newly formed United States via the Declaration of Independence. After the war, these rights were formalized by the unanimously-ratified

US Constitution. They became standard practice throughout the world and set America on a course to eventually recognize that all men and women are created equal and equal in their right to life, liberty, and the pursuit of happiness with equal protection under the law. The divine right of kings began a worldwide death march in favor of government by the people after America's ethical military victory over Great Britain.

During the thirty-one months of British occupation of the Lower South, peace negotiations between Britain and France shifted to recognizing at least some states as independent of Britain. The military situation became increasingly clear to European mediators and negotiators that the British would not be able to conquer the colonies in the Northeast by their Southern invasion as planned. Their Southern Strategy plan to win the war militarily had stalled at Guilford Courthouse. The British had failed to domesticate the territory they conquered in the Carolinas to support their drive northward. Instead, they became bogged down in a quagmire of resistance created by their brutality. Rather than earn civilian trust, they terrorized Loyalists, Whigs, and Patriots alike. They never woke to the fact that winning bloody battles in the European standard, killing suspected rebels absent of due process, raising body count, and terrorizing the countryside was less important than protecting the people and judiciously governing their military conquests. There was no rapprochement and earning the consent of the governed. There was no peace after a battle and territory acquisition as promised, just oppression and violence. The British chain of forts and their fortified towns eventually became isolated outposts in a hostile land because plundered residents had nothing to lose by attacking occupation troops caught outside their garrisons. Corruption and plundering in the field and in the British logistics organizations prevented the establishment of reliable supply lines and host nation's support.[323] As European diplomats saw no end to the Northern stalemate, peace negotiations shifted to offering home-rule political independence to those provinces short of sovereignty. At the same time, the Lower South was slated for a reunion with their mother country.[324]

Since the beginning of the war, the British knew that possessing Charlestown was the key to putting down the rebellion. The commander of all British expeditionary forces in America, Sir Henry Clinton, likewise believed Charlestown was the key to conquering the lower Southern colonies and maintaining trade, which would pave the road for defeating the rebellion throughout the colonies. When Sir Henry finally captured Charlestown on the third British attempt, he wrote, "I think we conquer the Southern provinces and perhaps much more." [325]The wealthy port city of Charlestown was considered the essential cornerstone for snuffing out the rebellion in the South and eventually throughout America. After four Southern Strategy plans and three expensive attempts, the British finally captured it on May 12, 1780.

General Clinton secured the rest of South Carolina after Charlestown's capitulation and, feeling confident in his conquests, turned over command to Lord Cornwallis in June. He expected Cornwallis to protect the Crown's reacquisitions of South Carolina and Georgia from British Southern headquarters in Charlestown while organizing the Loyalists in western North Carolina to secure the rest of that state. Once that ground was prepared, Cornwallis would "walk through" North Carolina, with some of his South Carolina-based regulars, complete a chain of forts there and reinstall the exiled royal governor. Cornwallis could conquer North Carolina personally, or he could send Lord Rawdon up the Great Wagon Road to accomplish the task. Meanwhile, Commander in Chief Clinton would initiate a conquest of Virginia from British-America headquarters in New York.

When Greene took over the Southern Command on December 3, 1780, the military situation in the South was grim.[326] The urgency of his army's survival trumped any thought of independence. The British occupied Georgia, South Carolina, and sections of North Carolina and had reestablished royal authority in those provinces. Turncoat Benedict Arnold and British General William Phillips had invaded Virginia en route to burning the Patriot capital at Richmond, terrorizing the population, destroying the Patriot supply heartland, and rallying the Loyalists. The British had forced the surrender of the main Southern Continental army headquarters in Charlestown and had destroyed two Continental Armies sent to stop them from conquering the South. They had imprisoned thousands of Patriot troops on prison ships in the Charleston harbor and other prisoner camps nearby. The British fortified a chain of forts across all three states at vital crossroads and river crossings from which they enforced martial law, actively hunted resistors to the Crown's authority, confiscated Whig homes and property, transferred ownership to Loyalists, forced conscriptions, plundered, and terrorized the population.[327] Their massive Southern army consisted of British, Hessian, Provincial, and Loyalist militia forces who, in contrast to Patriot forces, enjoyed professional training, plenty of supplies, and pay in the hard currency accepted everywhere. Their Native American allies included the Cherokee and Creek nations, which were armed and operationally coordinated by British Indian superintendents to conduct terror raids throughout the western Carolinas and Georgia.[328]

When General Greene took command, his intelligence put enemy Southern Army strength above eighteen thousand troops plus thousands of militia and African Americans in support and combat roles. (For size comparison, the population of Charlestown before the war was about twelve thousand.) The British had complete command of the eastern seaboard with their massive navy and enforced a strict embargo along the coast. Their armed river galleys constantly patrolled the Carolina rivers' trade network that stretched from the sea to the mountains. In short, the British controlled the Lower South, and North Carolina and Virginia were on their way to reannexation. The only problem standing in their way was one of their own making: their harsh subjugation policies stimulated partisan resistance and dampened Loyalist support.

The British conquest of the South was going well in mid-1780. Their Southern Army, commanded by Lord Cornwallis, was well-ensconced and poised to snuff out the remaining "rebel" insurgents in the Carolinas. His immediate plans were to turn over western North Carolina to Loyalist militias after conquering the area. He would then push his regular army into Virginia and unite with General Phillips and General Benedict Arnold's troops to defeat that state. Once Virginia was conquered and a superport established there, Cornwallis could continue north to join Sir Henry Clinton outside New York in a pincer movement to eliminate General Washington's disgruntled army, thus completely extinguishing the rebellion. What British General Burgoyne did not accomplish attacking from North to South in 1777, Cornwallis endeavored to accomplish by marching from South to North in 1780. General Clinton had recently written to his boss, Lord Germain, assuring him that South Carolina was secure, almost all had declared their allegiance to the king, and he expected "the recovery of the whole of the southern provinces in the course of the campaign" (Southern Strategy 4.0).[329] Clinton's correspondence set in motion a back-channel diplomatic move to force France into abandoning the Lower South and ending the war, which almost came to pass.[330] The prospect of scattered Patriot forces stopping Cornwallis and somehow achieving their independence was inconceivable in the fall of 1780. To have a chance of doing so would require retaking the Lower South with the help and consent of the population, expelling all the king's forces and all the king's men from the entire South and reseating the exiled state governments loyal to the cause in the recaptured states. These conditions might create enough political pressure in England and at the diplomatic table to force King George to concede American independence to a proxy Congress.

In contrast to well-supplied British operations, the Patriot military situation was desperate. The remnants of the defeated Southern Continental Army Greene inherited from Gates numbered approximately two thousand, scattered throughout the North Carolina foothills. This was less than one-ninth of the British strength of 18,000 effectives.[331] There was not enough gunpowder, guns, or swords for those able to fight. The army's last Continental commander, General Gates, had abandoned his troops in the midst of battle to seek his safety, leaving behind irreplaceable supplies. Inadequate arms, ammunition, food, morale, and confidence in leadership could not support offensive military operations against the British war machine. The only sparks left for the Patriot cause was that the famed Swamp Fox partisans raiding British supply lines had yet to be caught in the low country of South Carolina. In North

Carolina, there were still some capable militias in the mountains who had banded together in October to defeat a British invasion force at King's Mountain. Offsetting that victory was South Carolina General Sumter's rout at Blackstock's, which decimated his regiment and badly wounded him, removing him from the partisan field. Save for a few pockets of resistance and an unconquered western North Carolina, the Carolinas and Georgia were occupied by the British, and an unprepared Virginia was about to be invaded.

General Greene needed to change the game. "I will recover the country or die in the attempt," he espoused to rally Patriot spirits and set the tone of leadership commitment. Greene wasted no time assembling his Continentals into an insurgent "flying army" to be chased across the Carolinas by Lord Cornwallis. He united various Continental and militia elements and groups into coordinated counterforces utilizing an unprecedented light cavalry concept the British could never match. Greene coordinated with units throughout the Carolinas and Georgia to conduct simultaneous offensive operations to confuse, divide, degrade, and frighten the enemy. He established a vast spy network and horseback communications express to outsmart the enemy. Greene's light cavalry war was led by several Continental cavalry commanders: Lieutenant Colonel William Washington (George Washington's second cousin), Lieutenant Colonel Harry Lee (father of Robert E. Lee), and General Anthony Wayne. Militia cavalry forces Greene had inspired to get back into the fight created havoc on British supply lines and small outposts while providing valuable intelligence. Greene engendered cooperation between his military forces and residents so liberated areas would support the Patriot cause and welcome back their elected state governments aligned with the Confederation of the United States. This compound strategy of using several layers of military forces while wooing the hearts and minds of residents became the backbone of his mission to oust the British.[332]

Greene used his knowledge gained from fighting Cornwallis in the Northern theater of operations to his advantage. After degrading Cornwallis's army of conquest with a tactical victory at Cowpens and a strategic victory at Guilford Courthouse, Greene methodically isolated the Southern British occupation forces in their forts and town garrisons throughout the Lower South, while Cornwallis pursued his plan to conquer Virginia and establish a Chesapeake superport. Cooperating state militia forces would cut communications between garrisons, ambush patrols, and capture desperately needed supplies, so forts and towns became outnumbered and vulnerable. Greene's light cavalry dragoons would pin the British in place until his regular army arrived to decide matters. Greene offered honorable terms for the surrender of forts in keeping with ethical rules of war, while the British were still pursuing ruthless subjugation, encouraging the burning and looting of homesteads, and conscripting paroled Patriots while murdering "rebels" on the spot who refused to cooperate. Lord Cornwallis communicated his expectations when he advised his militias "to do what they please with the plantations [homes] abandoned by the rebels…if it is more convenient now and then to destroy one, I have no objection."[333] With this carte blanche in the Loyalist militias' hands, a hell storm commenced across the South. Greene changed the game with his flying army tactics, compound strategy, and protective trust that confounded the British and many historians. The strategy was not to "win" battles by the European standard of possessing the battlefield at the fighting's end. The strategy was to recapture British-held territory and keep it by ousting the British and protecting the area population from terror attacks and plundering. As Greene put it, his cavalry was "his trusted sword, his arm"; the leading edge of his strategy to divide, isolate, and defeat a numerically superior, entrenched army by increasing the tempo of operations and preventing stretched British forces from coming to each other's assistance.

After Yorktown's surrender in October 1781, Greene concentrated his efforts on ousting the other British armies occupying the Carolinas and Georgia. This final phase of the war focused on reducing the British occupation footprint by conducting simultaneous offensive operations; disrupting and destroying their logistics supply chain and local-area forage; reestablishing state governments in sanctuary towns; and encircling the British forces within a tighter and tighter circle around the capital port cities until they were forced to evacuate, dissolve, or surrender. Executing this plan to fruition would take perseverance and skill.

The British were strategically squeezed out of the Lower South coastal cities, one by one after Yorktown. Wilmington was the first city liberated in November 1781. It was a vital capital city post commanded by Major James Craig. While a good port, Wilmington could be easily blockaded by a few French warships, and it was not easily sustainable from across the Atlantic. The garrison was supported by Fort Cross Creek (now Fayetteville, North Carolina) farther up the Cape Fear River, with the sizable Tory force commanded by Loyalist Colonel David Fanning in between. Wilmington was located about 165 nautical miles from Charleston, about one and a half days sailing, 86 nautical miles from Georgetown, and about 210 nautical miles from Savannah, two days sailing. Each of these ports could quickly reinforce another. Fort Johnston, named after the North Carolina colonial governor in the mid-1700s, stood guard over Wilmington near the mouth of the Cape Fear River.

With British Regulars cleared from eastern North Carolina, Greene could concentrate on South Carolina and Georgia. About seven months later, in July 1782, British forces withdrew from Savannah under pressure, finalizing the liberation of the entire state of Georgia. Many of the evacuated British troops from Wilmington and Savannah were sent to defend Charlestown, while many Loyalist militias were sent to the West Indies. By November 1782, the only British troops left in the South were in and around Charlestown, and about 40 percent of those were ill.[334]

After Yorktown, British plans to retain the Carolinas and Georgia failed due to sustained offensive operations of Greene's Southern Army and his continued use of compound warfare. Fourteen months later, British forces equal to the size of the army besieged at Yorktown surrendered Charlestown. Perhaps their finest army in America was forced to evacuate the isolated Charlestown peninsula, thereby placing enough pressure on the British Parliament to consent to independence. General Washington wrote Greene, "It is with a pleasure which friendship only is susceptible of, I congratulate you on the glorious end you have put to hostilities in the Southern States."[335] All British and Loyalist forces had been forcibly removed from the South, and all forts and towns came under the control of the American Army and elected civilian governments. On December 14, 1782, Charlestown was liberated from foreign military occupation, effectively ending the war and placing the final negotiation for independence in the hands of American diplomats overseas.

Like Washington in the Northern theater of operations, Greene coordinated his military plans with civilian authorities in the Southern states while providing advice. His requests for the reconstituted state governments to soften amercement policies against Loyalists had a positive effect. His proposal to entice Loyalists to accept amnesty by offering them to take an oath of allegiance to the United States and serve six months' duty in the Patriot service was accepted. However, his proposals to raise Black regiments to swell his ranks while beginning the emancipation process through profitable enslaver reimbursement were not. His plan to methodically isolate the British in Charlestown was accepted and generally supported. All the British designs to stop Greene failed, and the noose around Charlestown closed tighter until there was no room to breathe.

Thirty-one months after Charlestown's capture, the British evacuation of their prized province and Southern headquarters left no question about America's claim of sovereignty. The Continental Army's complete repossession of the Lower South meant that Britain had lost the war to extinguish the rebellion as viewed in European diplomatic circles where it mattered. The issues of status quo retention of Charlestown and removing British troops from the American South became moot in British negotiation attempts to shortcut independence.[336] The order to evacuate Charlestown was underway at the time of the initial signing of the preliminary peace proposal by British diplomats. The last containment battle at Dill's Bluff outside Charlestown on James Island was fought on November 14, one month before the evacuation, making the British pay in blood for wood to keep them warm. The likelihood of the British army lasting through the winter on the isolated peninsula was a slim prospect. They had to leave or face disintegration.

The timing of American diplomats putting forward a preliminary peace proposal was critical. Henry Laurens, the president of the Second

Continental Congress from Charlestown, was the key American representative who signed the preliminary agreement in Paris on November 30, 1782, fourteen days before the massive British evacuation from Charlestown, was completed.[337] The London-educated South Carolinian Patriot leader had earlier been released from his imprisonment in the Tower of London, and the charges of treason against him by the Crown were dropped. As the former president of the Continental Congress who spearheaded the passage of the Articles of Confederation, Laurens was currently serving as the official US ambassador to the Dutch. The ambassador's signature on the preliminary agreement added considerable gravitas to the accord. The terms bound Congress. The British negotiators, led by the king's minister Lord Shelburne and Richard Oswald, provisionally agreed to abandon Britain's claim on the Lower South and grant independence to the entire thirteen United States, subject to approval by France and ratification by King George and Parliament.[338] Since Britain could not maintain possession of any significant territory in the United States except the city of New York, it was in her best interests to conciliate their European enemies. While not definitive or binding, a treaty proposal was signed by an official member and past president of Congress from Charlestown, Henry Laurens, along with the king's authorized minister, to be submitted to France and Spain for approval and then placed on the table for Parliament's consideration if the king so approved.

The diplomatic road had been long and uncertain. King George III would not entertain direct diplomatic negotiations with Congress because doing so would automatically recognize the representative body's legitimacy, which he refused to acknowledge. That situation changed when France entered the war by signing the Treaty of Alliance, formally recognizing the United States in 1778. The Treaty, among other things, assured the United States that France would not enter a peace accord with Britain unless they acknowledged the political independence of America. From that point forward, the French foreign minister, Charles Gravier, Comte de Vergennes, became the single-most important person in the world in deciding whether the United States would have their independence or any variations of it. Historian James Perkins would refer to Vergennes's importance by unequivocally stating, "He did more than any other Frenchman to secure political independence for the United States."[339] Although Vergennes wavered a time or two as the war dragged on, in the end, he remained steadfast in honoring France's commitment not to sign a treaty with Britain unless the king's diplomats acknowledged American independence.

After France entered the war in 1778, Congress would authorize Benjamin Franklin and John Adams to begin negotiations for peace and independence in Europe. However, King George was unwilling to have his ministry negotiate directly with his rebellious subjects in America. After Yorktown, in anticipation that the king's no negotiation policy would relax, Congress approved Henry Laurens and John Jay to join the overseas diplomatic team in meetings stretching from Paris to London to Madrid and more. Yorktown opened opportunities for American diplomats to discredit mediation talks from which they were excluded and, instead, be received at some European courts to finally be heard. The first job of American diplomats was to defeat the ongoing European plot to partition America well underway in 1781. Canada would be returned to France, England would retain the Southern provinces, and the remaining states would be declared independent in some form.[340] Feeling confident that the Lower South populous low countries and cities would remain under British control, Whitehall was unwilling to consider forfeiting Canada to France, so the plot could not hatch. Britain refused to come to the mediation table, which would have immediately stopped the war and recognized territory possession on the date talks commenced. John Adams went to the rescue by convincing Vergennes not to agree to mediation.[341] Adams would describe his stand as having "defeated the profound and magnificent project of a congress at Vienna, to chicane the United States out of their independence."[342]

In the post-Yorktown winter of 1781, Vergennes was eager to end the war. British territory possession in the Lower South was a stumbling block since King George was clear on keeping parts of provinces under his military control. The Comte intended to honor the alliance promise of some sort of independence for at least some of the United States. He was strongly pushing Congress to recall Adams and have that body assign peacemaking authority to him and his boss, the king of France. Vergennes considering partitioning the Lower South by negotiating a settlement with deputies from each of the thirteen states rather than with congressionally approved diplomats.[343] France stood to gain Canada in a Lower South partitioning deal. Negotiating directly with state deputies might also placate Spain, who was still dead set against American independence in late 1782.[344] The progress of the war in the Carolinas and Georgia would decide the issue of collective independence on the world negotiating stage.

By late February 1782, King George was willing to negotiate separately with American states based on territory possessed.[345] These separate negotiations would have left Georgia, the low country of South Carolina, Manhattan Island, and three capital port cities with Britain, if not more. The pursuit of direct negotiations with individual states was intended to break the French alliance and leave Congress neutered without any states to represent or united states army to oppose the king. If individual negotiations did not work to Britain's satisfaction, the ministry could negotiate a separate peace directly with France and the Dutch, leaving Britain free to renew the war with America minus her allies. After several changes of the British Ministry, direct negotiations with American diplomats authorized by Congress finally came to be in the fall of 1782.

The impending expulsion of all British troops in the South settled the matter. Prime Minister Lord Shelburne was likely counting on France abandoning the United States after the French learned of bilateral negotiations between Whitehall and American diplomats behind their backs. Direct negotiations produced a preliminary peace agreement just before the final evacuation of Charlestown. French abandonment of the alliance with America would render the preliminary agreement unfulfilled and open the door for Britain to end the war by directly negotiating with the French without recognizing American Independence.[346] The preliminary peace agreement would die from a lack of ratification. Benjamin Franklin magnificently averted that potential tragedy, coming to the rescue to soothe the insult to the French and gain Vergennes's approval.[347] With feathers unruffled, France and Spain validated the preliminary agreement by signature on January 20, 1783, after both nations learned Charlestown had been liberated and the South was free of British occupation troops.

With the fall of Charlestown in December 1782, King George finally gave up hope that the Lower South could be retained or that the American Congress would settle for anything less than collective, sovereign independence. Efforts to negotiate directly with each state had failed. Efforts to deal directly with France failed. The British VIPs withdrawn from Charlestown arrived back in London to tell the king's ministers and Parliamentarians that there were no more British troops in the Southern colonies Moreover, a cease-fire was in place, and commerce between the nations' merchants had resumed. Charlestown remained intact. The next step happened when France and Spain's signed the "provisional" peace treaty recognizing sovereign independence, making the agreement effective upon Parliament's approval.[348] The provisional treaty negotiated by the British Ministry now had enough signatures to send to the king and Parliament. If they agreed, the war would end.

Government leaders can sometimes outsmart themselves. To King George's chagrin, Congress and the confederation remained intact after Yorktown. His military forces controlled no territory in the Southern colonies. His intractability about any earlier talk of independence cost him all his former thirteen colonies.[349] France had not abandoned the American alliance, and both France and Spain had signed an international agreement of British diplomatic engineering and authorship. So crestfallen was King George that his armies were ingloriously pushed out of the South and that the alliances he expected to crumble remained intact, he drafted a letter of abdication.[350] His royal yacht was prepared to take him to Hanover, Germany, at a moment's notice. His abdication letter was finalized in March 1783 after Parliament's binding ratification of the peace proposal. The king cited the reason for his abdication as the "lack of support in the House [of Commons] for the King's preferred policy of resisting American Independence at all costs." However, his abdication letter was never submitted. In an overview of the situation, the liberation of the Lower South capital cities, culminating with Charlestown, likely prevented the breakup and partitioning of the colonies in rebellion, settled the question of "province ownership by possession," and ensured that all thirteen colonies represented by Congress would be recognized as independent by the British king, Parliament, and the world powers. The table was set at Yorktown and the American victory was served at Charlestown fourteen months later.

After a narrow vote by Parliament approving the Preliminary Treaty, Great Britain officially recognized the independence of the United States on February 21, 1783. Lord Shelburne, Parliament's prime minister responsible for negotiating the peace treaty with US diplomats, was censured and forced to resign two days after treaty ratification—ostensibly for accepting such a "bad deal" which Parliament was forced to ratify.[351] Charlestown's impending capitulation was the likely tipping point for Shelburne to sign the preliminary peace accord recognizing American independence, gambling that France would abandon the United States rather than sign the treaty.

Great historical events do not occur in isolation. The triumph at Yorktown made a complete American victory possible, but winning a joint siege on a remote Virginia peninsula led by a French protectorate would not be credible enough for the world to recognize the thirteen United States as an unaffiliated, independent nation. According to Oxford-educated historian Andrew O'Shaughnessy, King George's "fixation on winning the war at all costs was unabated" after Yorktown.[352] The Franco-American triumph halted the merciless British conquest of Virginia and opened a path toward a negotiated settlement, likely not including South Carolina and Georgia or sovereign independence. King George, the majority of Parliament, Spain, Austria, and Russia also stood firmly in the way. However, a narrow path to collective, sovereign independence was opened after Yorktown provided several events took place: (1) the French did not assert a claim that the American "provincial forces" were assisting them at Yorktown rather than the other way round, (2) the Lower South and their capital cities would be militarily liberated, and (3) elected state governments attached to the confederation could be resurrected and installed in the Carolinas and Georgia. The Yorktown triumph achieved European respect as a successful joint operation, but it presented a different threat to achieving American independence. The declared "United States" was now at risk of being broken up at the negotiating table if the war was not managed well militarily, politically, economically, and diplomatically to a successful conclusion in the final phase.

The post-Yorktown period required that American leadership politely put the French at arm's length lest the French could be entitled to claim or negotiate the acquisition of some or all the thirteen "colonies" in play. The European community was not beyond intrigue to expand their colonial empires in North America. Trapping Cornwallis at Yorktown was probably General Greene's idea. Still, it was a French plan, their navy, about 50 percent of the forces, their equipment, their gunpowder, their cannonballs, their siege guns, their siege experience, and their money that made it work.[353] The French fleet defeated the Royal Navy sent to withdraw Cornwallis at the Battle of the Capes, making the Yorktown siege possible.

To augment a potential French claim on the South, the British surrender of Yorktown was offered to the French commander Comte de Rochambeau, a veteran of fourteen sieges in Europe. Rochambeau politely directed the British sword of submission to be handed to American General Benjamin Lincoln, who had suffered the ignominy of surrendering Charlestown and the Southern Continental Army to the British the year before. Rochambeau's refusal to accept the British sword of surrender possibly saved America's quest to achieve independence, but it did not assure it. Without adroit American management of the war after Yorktown, the Lower South below Virginia was vulnerable to be claimed or traded to another king somewhere. Each colony was viewed as a single pawn on a European power chessboard subject to negotiation.

The war was not on track to end well for the declared United States if left unattended after Yorktown. Quite the contrary. The war entered a new multidimensional phase and even a higher level of sophistication. There were now four dimensions requiring management and synchronization for the war to be won, culminating with the liberation of Charlestown—the

British crown jewel. The four dimensions necessary to achieving victory at that point were military (Lower South territory and capital city possession), political (ensuring all restored state governments remained loyal to the confederation), economic (offering trade resumption with Britain to increase the benefit side of the cost/benefit equation of stopping the war), and diplomatic (fielding respected negotiators that could play European powers against one another to achieve consensus on the American independence objective). Amazingly, the threat to the future of monarchies by recognizing American independence governed by an elected Congress was relegated to the European powers' quests for other profitable colonies and future trade deals.

European monarchies erroneously assumed that a local king or kings, like Washington and Greene, would eventually emerge from the American rebellion. Luckily for America, the idea of an elected government by the people was not a sticking point among European allies after a deal was struck between Britain and America. The idea of an elected president and elected regional bodies to govern a nation had no Western precedent since the fall of the Roman Empire. Government by the people was dismissed as fanciful and unsustainable. Threats to monarchies aside, adroitly managing the final phase of the war after Yorktown would determine if peace terms recognizing sovereign independence for all thirteen provinces could be accepted by the world's colonial rulers totally against rewarding colonial rebellion. Without successful management of the final phase of the war, sovereign independence was unlikely to be conceded or awarded to all thirteen colonies by the world order.

From a negotiating perspective, the British defeat at Yorktown shifted the ongoing European peace discussions from brokered mediation to direct talks.[354] Virginia was taken off the mediation table in London, Paris, Vienna, Saint Petersburg, and Madrid. The triumph precipitated direct negotiations between Britain and American diplomats. Secretive mediator negotiations, which excluded US representatives, and roundtable negotiations with a host of European powers in which American diplomats were at a numeric disadvantage, ended. This diplomatic progression from mediation to direct negotiations misled some historians into believing that the ground war for territory control in the Lower South was irrelevant after Yorktown: the two British armies remaining in the Carolinas and Georgia simply "gave up" and retreated to Charlestown to await their final withdrawal orders. This conclusion implies that three of the most profitable ports in America, Charlestown, Savannah, and Wilmington were summarily relinquished by Britain's military leadership in America, without orders to do so, to the financial detriment of Britain's economy and many lords in Parliament. The conclusion also implies that King George would eventually concede independence to all American colonies as a result of the Yorktown surrender. George Washington himself wrote to General Greene four months after Yorktown that Charlestown had received reinforcements of both infantry regulars and artilleryman and that "The King's speech at the opening of Parliament 'is firm and manifests a determination to continue the War...'" without alliances.[355] Indirect talks to sign a peace accord where Britain would agree to stop offensive operations against America in exchange for ending taxation were being pursued after Yorktown, but only Lower South territory possession by the Continental army would open the door to serious independence negotiations which included all thirteen declared states.

In early 1782, Lord Germain sent General Clinton explicit orders that all existing British posts on the Atlantic coast were to be retained.[356] Also, in the spring of 1782, five months after Yorktown, King George had one proviso when he agreed on Lord Rockingham as the new prime minister: Britain would be "keeping what is in our possession in North America and attempting by a negotiation with any separate province [state] or even district [part of a state] to detach them from France, even upon any plan of their own provided they remain separate states."[357] Washington insisted the French army under the Comte de Rochambeau remain in Virginia post-Yorktown to prevent another British invasion there rather than march to support Greene in liberating the Lower South capital port cities. Before Yorktown, the French were actively thinking about trading New York and Long Island to Congress in return for relinquishing South Carolina and Georgia to the British or their designee.[358] Cornwallis's surrender of his forces at Yorktown did not materially change that equation because British armies remained ensconced in the New York and the Lower South provinces.

In short, the British did not give up after Yorktown, but their goals changed to keep, at least, South Carolina and Georgia. Their expectations for the complete subjugation of the South, triggering the subsequent dissolution of Washington's unpaid army, followed by the French abandoning the American alliance, were completely dissolved. Eviscerating the revolution and restoring Crown rule across the colonies was now out of the question. But the king and his ministry were not planning to abandon their British-America. General Henry Clinton wrote Lord Germain in December 1781, two months after Cornwallis's surrender of his army in Virginia, that he expected an attack on New York or Charlestown in the Spring of 1782 and that he would go to Charlestown himself if the attack was there.[359] Militarily, Britain lost their campaigns of conquest in both North Carolina and Virginia, and they lost the equivalent of two first-rate armies in the South. Politically, King George was quite clear that the new prime minister, Lord Rockingham, would keep the possessions in the Lower South and concentrate on negotiating separately with the other unoccupied states to retain them within the empire.[360] His war of punishment conducted throughout the South had turned the preponderance of residents against the Crown instead of the rebels. The British policy of conquest and compliance by promoting internecine warfare, brutal subjugation, terror, and genocide had failed miserably, but "lukewarm Loyalists" and "inferior recruits" were repeatedly mentioned in the London press to divert the blame away from the king's leadership and the actions of his chain of command. The on-the-ground war policy of brutality and punishment to bring about submission would continue as negotiations with individual states commenced. With three British armies still occupying America, the war for American independence was far from being won after Virginia was liberated at Yorktown.

Much more had to be accomplished to overcome King George's steadfast intransigence to grant independence. Until 1782, Georgia was squarely controlled by the British with an operating royal government in place, and both the Carolinas and New York were on the diplomatic trading table. Only the successful management of the final phase of the war after Yorktown would decide if America's sovereign and collective independence would become a reality. The largely unpaid Continental armies would have to stay in the field for this to happen. Loyalist militias and allied Native Americans had to be prevented from supporting regulars. British regulars would have to be pushed to the coast and slowly bled out of the Lower South. In addition, elected state governments loyal to the confederation would have to be installed and in operation if all thirteen states stood a chance of King George recognizing their independence.

Yorktown shattered Parliament's confidence in Lord North's war plan to crush the entire rebellion and conquer America as a whole. There were accounts that either Lord North or Lord Germain exclaimed, "Oh God! It's all over" when learning of Cornwallis's surrender. Those unwritten words, reportedly remembered after the war, misleadingly imply that Whitehall had the authority to decide whether the war would continue. The British kept fighting vigorously for another fourteen months in the Lower South, and the North ministry stayed in power for another five months. After Yorktown, Lord North offered a peace plan that proposed to put an end to British offensives and taxation without representation, not troop withdrawal from America or genuine independence. The British still had the numerical and strategic advantage in the Lower South. In addition to these realities, the British Ministry's job at Whitehall was to execute policy decided by the king and supported by Parliament, not unilaterally make it. The preponderance of contemporaneous sources shows that the king and Parliament were of no mind to give up the Lower South, voluntarily remove their troops, or offer "their colonies" collective independence after Yorktown.

In the parliamentary form of government of the time, the ministry worked for the king and Parliament. With a strong monarchy like King George III, step one to end the war was acquiescence by the king to negotiate or offer terms within stipulated boundaries. At the same time, clandestine operations would continue to improve the Crown's negotiating position. The king was arguably "God's regent on earth," so all power flowed from his "divine right." Parliament further empowered the king on June 17, 1782, by passing the Enabling Act, giving King George complete authority for appointing ministers to negotiate a peace or truce as he saw fit with any or all colonies.[361] Step two was for the appointed king's ministry to negotiate a provisional agreement directly with official US diplomats authorized by Congress or separately with each colony's authorized representative. Step three was for France and Spain to approve the preliminary agreement between the US colonies and Britain by signing the peace deal. Step four was for the king to appear before Parliament and formally endorse or oppose the preliminary agreement so the proposal could be debated and voted on. Step five was for Parliament to ratify the proposed peace plan by majority vote after debate. When all five steps had been accomplished, the war between the two nations (Britain and the United States) politically ended once the US Congress approved the ratified treaty. Step one, concession by the king, did not happen until all British troops departed the South, climaxed by the liberation of Charlestown, South Carolina.

The course the Provisional Peace Treaty took was unlikely. Congress accepted the consummated treaty sent to them by Parliament in April 1783. That agreement was the same *provisionally* put forward by American diplomats in September 1782, signed by the end of November between American and British diplomats, officially approved by France and Spain on January 20, 1783, and then ratified by Parliament vote in February 1783 after the king's concession speech, acknowledging independence for all thirteen colonies. After Congress ratified the treaty in April, they ordered the disbanding of the Southern Continental Army immediately. The other nations that had supported the United States—France, Spain, and the Dutch Republic—subsequently agreed to end their war against Britain in exchange for separately negotiated concessions, which occurred after the bilateral Britain–US Peace Treaty granting independence was consummated. The 1782 Preliminary Peace Proposal stipulating the recognition of American independence amazingly became the final treaty signed by all warring parties on September 3, 1783, at Versailles.

Lord North and Germain could not win the war or negotiate Britain's exit from it. The North ministry hatched an arrangement with Cornwallis to be the heir apparent to General Clinton, undermining Clinton's war strategy.[362] North's direct communications with Cornwallis violated best practice principles of chain of command and unity of effort. Clinton had ordered "Sir Charles" to stay in South Carolina to keep control of the Lower South—mopping up rebel bands, establishing law and order, and cementing royal political authority. Clinton's patient strategy likely would have succeeded if Greene had not provoked Cornwallis into splitting his supersized army into three pieces, following him into North Carolina with two of those pieces, and after two devastating battles, leave the Carolinas for Virginia with less than half of his once-supersized army still alive. Lord North likely believed Cornwallis's status report that Georgia and South Carolina would remain uncontested and that North Carolina was "with us"—ready to provide thousands of enlistments and Loyalist militias when Cornwallis showed up. There was a significant disconnect between people saying they would fight for the Crown and those who would join the fight without training, protection, or the steady companionship of the King's regular troops.

Lord Germain wanted Cornwallis to conquer each successive state from South Carolina going northward, seating a royal government in each state before he moved on to the next. Cornwallis, however, "skipped over" North Carolina, left South Carolina to a twenty-six-year-old "infantry Captain" (Lord Rawdon), and outran his planned supply line, which would have likely carried him to final victory. Lord Germain approved Cornwallis's expedition northward, with an expectation of finally getting the superport in the Chesapeake, splitting America, and taming the colonies forever. Germain's expectations were never met.

After Yorktown, Lord North's preoccupation with establishing a port on the Chesapeake to put down the rebellion was lost, but he was still not done. In a good show of things, Lord Germain was granted a peerage by the king and submitted his resignation in February 1782, ostensibly to be the "fall guy" for Cornwallis's surrender and for the British Ministry to signal a revised policy of reconciliation with America rather than one of conquest and punishment prosecuted by Germain. With that olive branch in the air, North subsequently offered a peace plan to American diplomats that would rescind the tax laws the colonies had gone to war over. Providing independence to their British-American colonies was still out of the question. The king and his ministry believed that offering to cease the prosecution of the war and offering to reembrace the colonies by conceding on their original issue about taxation would end the war, almost as if they had been living in a 1763 Stamp Act time warp. Congress rejected the offer, and North was forced out of office five months after Yorktown. For Lord North, his fixation on winning the war by splitting America and establishing a superport on the Chesapeake, as Charles Lee initially proposed in 1777, did him in.

Lord North was eventually replaced, but not before Britain plunged into a historic cabinet crisis and leadership vacuum. This crisis froze King George's power of the purse to reinvade or surge in America. The Parliament and the king intensified their power struggles with little agreement on a new cabinet and liaison minister. The Earl of Rockingham was agreed upon with provisions. One such requirement was to bring General Guy Carleton out of retirement and make him the "Commissioner for Restoring Peace" in America, as well as the Commander of British Expeditionary Forces in North America replacing General Clinton in New York.[363] This appointment gave him military, diplomatic, and policy-making power to end the war in America without granting independence. His special authority would enable him the flexibility to use whatever means necessary to diplomatically and militarily piece back together the North American British empire, not to include political separation or British troop withdrawal. He would have the complete resources of all British assets in North America at his disposal. Just as Carleton was beginning to handle the situation, the Earl of Rockingham died, and Carleton's authority to unilaterally sort things out directly in America was undermined in London. Instead, negotiations to end the war became centered in Europe. Carleton would have to figure out what to do with the surrounded British military forces in America on his own while trying to finesse the Lower South into staying within the empire. The British Ministry leadership crisis resumed at full tilt with no one having clear responsibility for negotiating an end to the war while keeping America, or at least parts of it, in the realm.

The Yorktown triumph shifted European peace discussions away from redistributing North American lands between European monarchs to discussions recognizing some vestige of nonsovereign independence of at least some colonies in rebellion. Most discussions about independence became craftily defined as a British client-state like Ireland, not independence as in sovereignty that Americans articulated in the Declaration of Independence.[364] While Britain was generally ready to stop pursuing the war and make a truce with America, neither the king nor Parliament was willing to concede the colonies to collective independence or withdraw their regular troops from America. Carleton was gifted enough to pull off such a "stick and carrot" diplomatic feat if his authority had not been undercut back home after he took command of the situation. Luckily for the United States, Britain's cabinet crisis kept the government from agreeing on a unified strategy to retain America while negotiating themselves out of a world war.

Back on the American ground war front, much was gained by the Yorktown triumph. About eight thousand British occupation troops were removed from Virginia, Virginia was able to supply Patriot forces in other states with French supplies, four British armies were reduced to three in America (New York, Charlestown, and Savannah), and, most importantly, the French decided to stay in the war. Without tentative France staying in, the war for sovereign independence was destined to die on the vine. Without France, the colonial rebellion lacked credibility on the world stage. Financially, the French voted to extend desperately needed loans that kept American armies in the field to finish the war. Psychologically, the Yorktown victory renewed Patriot hopes that the war to obtain collective, sovereign independence, while unprecedented, was achievable if all the states continued to work together and stay united. Much had been accomplished in the allied defeat of Cornwallis's isolated army in Virginia.

King George, the decider, was unbowed. According to his papers, he wrote: "I have no doubt that when men are a little recovered of the shock felt by the bad news [Yorktown defeat] ...that they will find the necessity of carrying on the war."[365] While the British plan to conquer all the American colonies by destroying both the Northern and Southern Continental armies was no longer a possibility, there were still four colonies Britain had not lost: Georgia, South Carolina, North Carolina, and New York. Granting home-rule independence of some sort to nine colonies and partitioning the Lower South as British America connected to British-East Florida was a likely prospect without further military action.

British forces still significantly outnumbered Patriot forces in the theaters of operations after Yorktown. In addition, their Cherokee and Creek allies in the South were still potent. British forces occupied the state capitals of Wilmington, North Carolina; Savannah, Georgia; Southern Army headquarters in Charleston, South Carolina; and Northern Army headquarters in Manhattan, New York, and surrounds. Their fort at Saint Augustine stretched their possessions from North Carolina down through East Florida. Supported by the Royal Navy, the king's ground forces could remain at these coastal bases, conduct offensive operations, and entice the unpaid Continental armies to dissolve or mutiny. Secretly supporting shadow governments unconnected to the Continental Congress to break the Confederation was not beyond the British. The conditions on the ground did not warrant the Crown giving up the entire thirteen colonies to an experimental confederation governed by the people. Most importantly, the king was not budging.

According to the accepted European rules of negotiated settlements at the time, the Southern provinces below Virginia and the province of New York would have likely stayed with the British Crown after Yorktown if negotiations had commenced immediately thereafter. The precedent diplomat rules of status quo and uti possidetis determined how territory would be divided between warring parties when fighting stopped.[366] Lurking in the background was the possibility that France could assert Virginia as the protectorate state they snatched from the British. John Adams feared that the United States had become France's client state after Congress directed him to follow the French minister's "advice" in armistice negotiations.[367] Fortunately for the United States, their chief negotiator at the time, John Adams, did not follow the advice of Congress or Vergennes to allow mediation that would have likely resulted in the Lower South being retained by Britain or traded to another monarch. European powers continued to propose that each state government be called upon individually to choose their preference: sticking with the United States' formal confederation, going independent as a separate state, or aligning with another European power like France. This world-order mediation convention, which split Poland apart after the Revolutionary War, would have similarly separated the American states and prevented collective independence.

The European appetite for dealing with one overarching rebel government speaking for all thirteen rebellious colonies was still not there. Britain also had a competitive concern not to allow another European country to acquire any of the thirteen colonies in rebellion to settle matters. Nine of thirteen provinces could probably show their state governments were aligned with Congress and maintaining the preponderance of control over their major population areas. North Carolina, South Carolina, Georgia, New York, and possibly Maine would have difficulty proving the same. Thus, Britain would likely retain the Lower South colonies or trade them at the European bargaining table for captured colonies in the West Indies or ports like Pensacola.[368] (Korea remains partitioned today because neither army captured all the territory in both the North and South before peace talks commenced.) A "carveout" of the Lower South and an Ireland-like recognition of the remaining "United States" within the British Empire appeared likely after Yorktown if ground conditions were left to stand.

Nonetheless, King George knew that completely extinguishing the colonial rebellion in America was now out of the question. The negotiations to return the colonies to "as they were" before the war had no legitimacy. However, King George believed that the Lower South provinces and New York could be excluded from an Ireland-like recognition. If his ministers could negotiate the partitioning of the provinces his armies occupied, he could eventually reannex his "lost" colonies when they came to their senses or after their volunteer armies dissolved from lack of French support.[369] The king's troops, still in the Lower South, would be just a stone's throw away to repossess the lost colonies when the timing was right. Further bolstering His Majesty's hopes, in the Spring of 1782, the British navy destroyed the French fleet in the West Indies that had sealed Cornwallis's defeat at Yorktown. After that, the French navy was no longer capable of assisting Generals Washington or Greene in liberating New York or Charlestown. George Washington confirmed the implications of this "disastrous" French defeat for the Lower South in a July 9, 1782, situational briefing letter to General Greene, eight months after Cornwallis's surrender.[370] Washington warned that this French defeat would prevent "the Evacuation of the Southern States" by the British unless military measures were taken to "counteract" British designs "to occupy as much territory" before "a negotiation can be entered upon." He ordered Greene to "hold your own ground, until the Southern & Middle States" could reinforce his Continentals and bring along the siege cannon and supplies sitting idle at Yorktown. In mid-summer of 1782, Washington kept the allied French troops positioned in Virginia so they could protect that state from reinvasion and also be midway between reinforcing either the Northern or Southern Continental armies depending on the target of the next British attack. His coded letter to Greene shared his efforts of actively raising troops to carry on the war.[371]

Britain was not budging. The ensconced royal governor of Georgia held a grand celebration honoring King George's birthday in Savannah on June 4, 1782, seven months after Yorktown, to show the world Britain still governed Georgia. Events like this show the situation on the ground presented no compelling reason for the king to grant absolute independence to all thirteen colonies or to recall his troops from the fortified capital cities in the Lower South in his possession after Yorktown. He could even renew conquest operations if Parliament reauthorized the power of their purse and agreed to a new war-winning Tory minister of his liking. Lord Shelburne was pursuing negotiations on the pretext that some provinces of America would be retained, based on territory British troops controlled.[372] Without being pressed militarily from their coastal garrisons, time was still on Britain's side to politically splinter the states or wait for the Continental armies to dissolve. They could even begin trading unwinnable states to France, Spain, and the Dutch, without the consultation or consent of American diplomats, to break the confederation. After all, those countries had a common interest in punishing a colonial rebellion uprising against the world order of monarchies.

General Greene was not about to let time disintegrate the rebellion or separate the states. Hundreds of battles and skirmishes were fought in the Lower South to push the British into their coastal capitals and economically suffocate them.[373] The importance of the final phase was emphasized by Washington when he wrote the Southern Continental commander, General Nathanael Greene, congratulating him on putting down a British-coordinated "dangerous Mutiny" designed to turn over Patriot forces in the South to the British. The British attempted to kidnap or kill Greene in two separate plots to end his prosecution of the war after Yorktown. Meanwhile, Loyalist and banditti militias rampaged throughout the lower provinces to blur battle lines, renew internecine warfare, and demonstrate to European negotiators that Patriots had little control over the territory they were claiming. In 1782, the Lower South Cherokees and Creeks conducted a unified offensive against Patriot forces in South Carolina and Georgia in coordination with British regulars and Loyalists.[374] Greene's forces faced defeating an entrenched enemy in three coastal capital garrisons plus winning a bitter internecine war while installing elected governments loyal to the confederation in three states and holding off the Native American insurgency. Accomplishing all these tasks was required to win collective independence.

America's political objective of sovereign independence had a long way to go after Yorktown, but a path to liberty was opened. Britain was still a military and economic superpower that regarded the American colonies as an essential link in their global supply chain, with the port of Charlestown as their "superstore" hub. The British controlled the slave trade, a prime source of direct and indirect payments before the war. They still retained the profitable ports of trade and "superstore" warehouses in the Lower South. They still had thousands of displaced Loyalists consolidated along the coast, ready to renew the offensive. Maybe Britain could not end the rebellion, but giving up their profitable ports and forking America over to an itinerant Congress in Philadelphia was not on their minds or the negotiating table. Their entrenched forces in the Lower South would have to be pushed out for thinking to change.

At the onset of the war, Britain visualized victory as militarily destroying the "rebel" army, putting down the rebellion, and hanging the ringleaders: a plan of punishment patterned after their Scottish Rebellion remedy. Later, the objective switched to conquering America and putting down the colonial rebellion in geographic sections. To accomplish this objective, the king's first major offensive of the war in June 1776 was against the most strategic, wealthiest, and most profitable city in the colonies—Charlestown, South Carolina. From Charlestown, the British would headquarter the war effort while maintaining the valuable trade routes into the American interior and out to the Caribbean and England. They would quickly subdue the Lower South and cut it off from other colonies.

Amazingly, they were defeated in their first American invasion attempt, so the king's amphibious forces went on to their secondary target, New York, which they won handily. The British victory there was, in part, due to General Charles Lee's inadequate or duplicitous defense plan not to fortify and defend the Narrows, which had succeeded at Charlestown. New York proved not to be as strategically important as Charlestown, and the war settled into a stalemate.

Due to Henry Clinton's failure to take Charlestown on his first try in 1776, he was passed over for command of the Northern army. That promotion went to "Gentleman" Johnny Burgoyne, who was inexperienced as a supreme commander of theater offensive operations. Burgoyne would pursue Lord North's and Germain's objective to break up the confederation by militarily dividing it down the Hudson River, thereby isolating New England. Although the divide-and-conquer plan was initially thwarted in the South, it might work in the North in 1777.

Burgoyne was defeated entirely in executing his divide-and-conquer mission at the Battle of Saratoga. His defeat was inadvertently caused by Charles Lee's advice to Lord North to divert the British army on their way to reinforce Burgoyne to occupy Philadelphia instead.[375] After

Burgoyne's surrender at Saratoga, the outmatched colonial rebellion turned into a world war, giving the newly formed United States instant credibility, money, and allies. France, Spain, and the Dutch Republic joined America against Britain after being inspired by Burgoyne's defeat made possible with French-supplied arms. This new four-on-one situation put the security of the British Empire at risk by a gang of resentful, colony-hungry European nations with large armies and navies. Victory for Britain suddenly shifted from simply putting down a ragtag colonial rebellion gone broke to preserving the British Empire in a global war in which they were outnumbered and outgunned. All thanks to turncoat, or embedded saboteur, General Charles Lee.

From the American perspective, the Declaration of Independence stated what America wanted to achieve—political independence. Up to that point, the war had been about achieving reconciliation with Britain by having American representation in Parliament. After the Declaration, the war's aim for America was about defending the homeland against foreign conquest and becoming a sovereign independent nation composed of a confederation of thirteen self-ruled states. The proclaimed "United States" upped their demands to be "free and independent" from Britain and conduct free trade on their own. American expectations changed, and the definition of victory changed with the Declaration of Independence.

In response, an outraged King George III launched a massive war on America with Parliament's financial approval. After the Saratoga defeat and seeing France, Spain, and the Dutch join the American cause, Britain shifted its goal to win a world war by conquering America and defeating each adversary. The objective of the United States remained focused on forcing King George to cease hostilities, expelling all British troops, and becoming globally recognized as a politically and economically independent thirteen United States. Peace, removal of all foreign troops, and independence for all thirteen of the United States constituted a complete victory for America.

After the Saratoga defeat, Britain began peace negotiations with America in 1778 to end the war by discussing the possibility of accepting American representatives in Parliament. Britain was simultaneously involved in similar negotiations with Ireland to keep them within the empire. Many historians theorize that the ministry's 1778 Peace Commission was a sham political maneuver to stop the war while "negotiations" dragged on. The pursuit was likely intended to allow time for the Continental Army and the Confederation to dissolve. The insult of direct, bilateral negotiations also held the prospect of America's new allies abandoning them. The Carlisle Commission, sent to America to make such a "let's talk" offer, did not acknowledge that American expectations had changed to one of sovereign independence for the united thirteen colonies, nor were they authorized to discuss any such independence terms. The commission was only permitted to discuss the outdated grievance from 1775 of "no taxation without representation," which was insufficient to prompt Congress to order a cease-fire or curtail Continental Army operations. Besides not having the authority to negotiate beyond the ministry's set offer, the commission was undercut by Lord Germain's order to General Clinton to withdraw Howe's army from Philadelphia in advance of their proposal to entreat. The British withdrawal order was probably politically calculated to harden the American stance on independence, thereby dooming peace negotiations before they began.

But the Peace Commission made a good show of things for the ministry. After Congress refused Britain's gracious offer to entreat, a miffed Parliament renewed financial and political support to extinguish the rebellion. Moreover, Parliament gained the political will to take on France and Spain—much to the satisfaction of King George and the North ministry. The king would show off his power of divine authority, and Lord Germain would show the world he was no coward.

After Cornwallis's surrender at Yorktown, the war and peace calculus changed again. The war for Ireland-like home-rule independence from Britain probably could not be lost for some states after Yorktown, but the war for *sovereign* independence of *all* thirteen states still had to be won. The United States still needed to show the European world they could provide for their security without client-state help and govern themselves independently. Yorktown was a small village on an isolated peninsula, not a strategically important port or capital city. It had few residents, no ships, no port, and no international economy. The combined French and American military operation there prevented the British from conquering Virginia. However, New York, Charlestown, and the other occupied Southern capital cities remained to be liberated or significantly threatened to convince King George and his ministry to cease hostilities throughout the colonies and grant political independence to all the colonies in rebellion. Giving autonomy to a collection of colonies in rebellion had no precedent; ruthlessly putting down rebellions despite temporary battlefield setbacks was the norm. The British still remembered the setbacks in Scotland before the decisive route at Culloden, which extinguished that rebellion. (Scotland is still not independent of Britain and was only recently granted representation in Parliament.) The primary goal of America achieving her sovereign independence was still a long way from being won in the fall of 1781, after Yorktown. Unpressed militarily, King George only needed to keep his remaining troops in place and wait for the money-starved rebel armies to dissolve.

It would take another fourteen months of warfare after Yorktown for Britain to entertain the thought of collective independence. Combined Continental and Patriot militia military operations had to force the thousands of British, Hessian, and Loyalist troops in the Lower South onto the Charlestown peninsula with no alternative but to wither away in the cold of winter after a disease-ridden summer or evacuate by sea. With over twelve thousand mouths to feed every day, British sustainment options had run out. The last containment circle had closed to create a situation where the "peninsula captives" were fighting sorties to obtain potable water.[376] The arduous task of maintaining the initiative, liberating North Carolina and Georgia, pressuring British forces throughout the Lower South to consolidate back into South Carolina and Charlestown, and forcing a British surrender or evacuation from their prized Southern headquarters would decide victory and independence. Completing the job begun at Yorktown would require a sustained, well-executed military, political, economic, and diplomatic effort in the Lower South. The British army was not giving up what they had not lost.

Popular support for the British "repossession" of the Lower South diminished with each act of cruelty to friend, foe, or neutral. The British military's ability to maintain strict martial law, recruit, get messages through, obtain timely intelligence, obtain regular food supplies, and enjoy the cooperation of the local "King's subjects" became more difficult with each plunder and barbaric act. The once-friendly countryside became increasingly hostile, and with that, the British military's ability to conduct offensive operations and hold territory became impossible. Conversely, the Continental Army and the Patriot militias had methodically earned popular support and the upper hand in pushing British forces into their walled fortress on the Charlestown peninsula.

In July 1782, Leslie augmented his Southern headquarters garrison at Charlestown with a regiment of soldiers evacuated from Savannah. The summer months in an overcrowded Charlestown brought disease, unbearable heat, tainted water supplies, and accumulating sewage. The collection and distribution of food supplies and medical treatment of the sick and wounded required significant manpower. To undernourished troops susceptible to disease, surviving another day became the order of the day. Illness and disease had significantly reduced his army's ability to withstand a concentrated American attack now that the Continental forces which had liberated Georgia had joined Greene's forces surrounding the city. General Carleton, who had taken command of all British expeditionary forces from Clinton, recognized the peril of the situation by summer's end. Britain could not move up troops from Florida to help Leslie because the Saint Augustine fortress was under siege by the Spanish. To make matters worse, desertions and noncombat deaths were piling up, while morale was dangerously low. Leslie had already resorted to roving dragoon patrols outside Charlestown's defenses to kill or capture the steady stream of deserters surrendering to Greene's forces. One Continental officer described the situation: "The British deserters come in now every day and may be averaged at thirty per week, and numbers more would come off but are prevented by the Negro Horse [sic]."[377] Adding to Leslie's urgent concerns, a French or Spanish fleet could seal off Charlestown from the sea that supplied them, and Leslie's undernourished army would disintegrate or surrender in short order. Carleton wisely ordered Leslie to prepare for evacuation as his logistics people ordered hundreds of ships to Charlestown to execute a covered withdrawal of five fleets. The final withdrawal became a race against time.

Politically, everything changed after the Lower South was liberated, culminating with the Charlestown withdrawal General Greene provided a military situation report to the president of the Continental Congress, Elias Boudinot, on December 19, 1782. General Greene described the military situation to General Washington as "[the liberation of Charlestown] gives us complete possession of the Southern States." [378]The British were left with no troops in America to exert their will except those remaining on the New York peninsula and its surroundings. The French had voided any potential claims to individual colonies because they were not substantially present in the Lower South to slug it out next to Greene and company for fourteen more months after Yorktown. The French lost their joint operation with the American forces to take Savannah back from the British in 1779, so there was no client-state claim on Georgia King Louis XVI could suddenly assert. The French vacated their potential argument gained at Yorktown as a rightful American protectorate to be bequeathed a few colonies in compensation when they left Virginia.

Upon Charlestown's liberation, the predominant political will in the House of Commons shifted toward supporting the preliminary agreement recognizing complete independence for all thirteen states. The political pressure on the king to agree to sovereign independence to end the American part of the global war finally reached the tipping point. Why place the British homeland at risk by renewing the American theater of war, where a cease-fire, merchant trade agreement, and loyalist amercement policy were already in place and working? The thought of reinvading America while the French, Spanish, and Dutch threatened other profitable colonies and the lightly defended British homeland had no appeal.

Britain had much more to lose if they did not stop the war after Charlestown's fall. Spies reported that Lafayette was currently in Cadis, Spain, preparing an assault army of twenty-five thousand men to capture the valuable colony of Jamaica and then assault the now-isolated British garrison in New York, in concert with a combined Northern and Southern Continental Armies.[379] Lafayette was the same capable French general who had bottled up Cornwallis on the Yorktown peninsula about fifteen months before, plus he had a written agreement with Congress to lead an expedition to liberate Canada. Moreover, the American Southern army, after liberating Charlestown, would be free to join Washington in the North to produce superior numbers in which to attack New York from the west while the French attacked by sea from the east. Canada, with thirteen more colonies, could be the next object of America's demands at the peace table, just as Benjamin Franklin desired. This urgent predicament for the Crown was made even worse by a decision-making leadership vacuum caused by one of the most significant cabinet crises in Britain's history. No one ministry was in charge, and no unified negotiation strategy was supported. The king and Parliament were not on the same page regarding peace terms. A power tug-of-war existed between an absolute monarchy and a constitutional monarchy, and no one person was trusted to carry on the global war from London. The stubby tail of America was wagging the British bulldog.

Meanwhile, the only peace proposal on the table awaiting ratification was an overly generous preliminary agreement formally ending the king's hostilities against America while granting the thirteen United States complete, sovereign independence as one nation. Economics, fear, and timing are often the basis for making war and making peace. The clock had struck thirteen. It was time for Parliament to take the dove in hand, swallow a little crow as if it tasted good, and preserve the nest.

The British resorted to their last line of defense – their mastery of words. Josiah Tucker, the influential Anglican dean of Gloucester, helped tip the scales by conceptually reframing the war as England's war of independence from ungrateful colonists. He wrote an open letter to Lord Shelburne to assuage Parliament egos into accepting the preliminary peace terms. Dean Tucker wrote, "America...ever was a Millstone hanging about the Neck of this Country, to weigh it down: and as we ourselves had not the Wisdom to cut the Rope, and to let the Burthen fall off, the

Americans have kindly done it for us." He went on to condemn continuing the war with America "for the sake of monopolizing, or exclusive trade" and emphasized continued open trade with America based on "Mutual Interest …till the End of Time; whether they are dependent on, or independent of us." Tucker's words hit their mark.

Parliament begrudgingly ratified the preliminary peace agreement on February 21, 1783, by a vote of 207 to 190 while excoriating Lord Shelburne, who had negotiated the deal. Shelburne was subsequently forced out of office. Congress received the approved treaty and ratified it on April 11 or 15, 1783.[380] Congress ordered the dissolution of the Southern Continental Army shortly after that and Washington shelved his plans to attack New York. The British war against the United States was officially over. As Lord Fox stated, the "subsequent treaties were superfluous." The entire United States had finally won its sovereign independence, a feat Washington described as "Almost a Miracle."[381] The British army completed the evacuation of their garrisons in New York City on November 25, 1783, according to the peace terms finalized by all warring parties on September 3, 1783. The effective management of the war's final phase after Yorktown, culminating with the fall of Charlestown, left no practical alternative for the British Empire other than to ratify the only peace proposal before them before things got worse.

Thus, victory in the War for American Independence was not marked by the greatest armies on earth "giving up" and simply leaving their fortified bases in four state capitals after Cornwallis surrendered one of four British armies occupying America. On December 14, 1782, the world stood still as two seasoned Southern armies squared off at Charlestown, South Carolina. This withdrawal was not a leisurely or friendly evacuation. The final movement was one of many collapsing perimeters executed by a surrounded, sickened, demoralized, and disintegrating army. Mounted Continental dragoons escorted the last of the British Army to Charlestown's harbor, where over 130 of His Majesty's ships were covering the evacuation with cannons loaded and matches lit. The most powerful army and navy in the world were forced from the South forever by citizen-soldiers from all thirteen states. The cease-fire held, the fighting ended, the "undefeated" British army sailed away, and the American flag was raised, claiming the capital of South Carolina as part of the confederated United States. Victory in the War for American Independence took place at last at Liberty Square in Charlestown when the last redcoat south of New York City stepped on board His Majesty's last ship anchored in the harbor.

Hundreds of battles and skirmishes had occurred in the Lower South in the fourteen months since Yorktown to finish the war successfully. The determined Patriot efforts to squeeze the British out of their occupied capital cities of Wilmington, Savannah, and finally Charleston paid off. Sending General Anthony Wayne's crack dragoons to royalist Georgia to face the entrenched British and their allied Cherokees, Creeks, and Loyalists intent on eradicating all Patriots paid off. The hundreds of post-Yorktown battles and skirmishes on land, sea, and rivers throughout the Lower South paid off.[382] The hundreds, perhaps thousands, of additional Patriot casualties from battles, disease, starvation, and exposure, to whom America is forever in debt, paid off. The thwarting of British efforts to bribe Patriot soldiers to mutiny en masse from the Southern Continental army surrounding them paid off. The thwarting of the British efforts to kidnap or kill the Southern Continental Commander paid off. The resolve of Patriot citizens not to provide food to the isolated British paid off. The steadfast land embargo enforced by militia and Continental forces paid off. Methodically executing a sustained final phase plan paid off.

Winning independence was not simply waiting for the fruit of the surrender of one British army on a remote Virginia peninsula to ripen. Quite the opposite. The war entered its final and most complex phase, where, if any of the four peace dimensions was mismanaged, the flower of independence would have wilted, and the United States would be broken into pieces. The victory was the result of tactical and operational goals methodically achieved with chess-like mastery, a British government in crisis, and a French ally who stuck with America until the final checkmate.

Great respect is due to those who sacrificed everything to see the War for American Independence through to its successful conclusion. If size matters, approximately the same number of British troops evacuated from Charlestown beginning in October 1782 as those who surrendered at Yorktown. The Parliamentary Register put the number of British regulars in the South as eighteen thousand men, along with four thousand Loyalist militia, Black troops, and an undetermined number of Native American forces.[383] The final phase of the war was won by stopping the British-coordinated Native American and Loyalist attacks, pushing the British, Hessians, and Loyalists throughout the Lower South back to the coast, installing operating state governments loyal to the confederation, and forcing the proud British army ingloriously out of Charlestown to their massive covering fleet. Steps had to be taken to prevent the enemy from revengefully burning the city to the ground as they did in Richmond, Georgetown, Camden, and New London. All operational components had to be adroitly managed while politely keeping American allies from staking a claim in a colony or three and keeping American negotiators in Europe apprised on the progress of territory and capital city repossession in the Lower South. Without operating state governments in place, the world powers were unlikely to concede independence. Liberty without government would create anarchy they could not endorse.

The diligent prosecution of the final phase of the war after Yorktown brought the glorious cause to a successful conclusion. If Lexington and Concord were "the shot heard round the world," the liberation of Charlestown caused that shot to finally reach the ears of King George and Parliament. Only conceding independence would end the deafening noise shaking the British Empire by a united America and her steadfast allies. Liberty Square appropriately sits adjacent to Concord Street. The beginning and the end.

The British evacuation of Charlestown, South Carolina, marked the successful end of America's long and bloody quest for political independence from Britain. Figuratively speaking, the Declaration of Independence became America's birth certificate, but the baby was not born until December 14, 1782, after a long and hard labor. The complete repossession of the Lower South, spearheaded by the Southern Continental Army of the confederated states, left no question about territory control. The military, political, economic, and diplomatic steps that led to achieving the prime objective of liberation were meticulously planned and expertly executed. As Sun Tzu once said, "The supreme art of war is to achieve objectives without fighting...the ultimate achievement is to defeat the enemy without even coming to battle."[384] The liberation of Charlestown exemplifies this paragon.

The British just wanted to get out of town without dissolving, without having another Yorktown. The Continental Command just wanted to liberate the city as the final step in a long and bloody quest to gain independence. Americans had earned the right to become citizens of a republic of their own making rather than remain obedient subjects of a faraway king bent on punishment. Continental General William Moultrie, the real hero of Charlestown, summed up the vital importance of the British evacuation: "[The liberation of Charlestown]...is the real day of our delivery and independence and ought never be forgotten." Based on their correspondence and actions, General George Washington, General Nathanael Greene, the British Parliament, and King George III likely agreed.

The most powerful army and kingdom in the world lost their popular support to restore royal authority in America and end the colonial rebellion. From the time the British Army captured Charlestown in May 1780 to the day the besieged remnants of that army evacuated the valuable city they once so proudly occupied marked *The Thirty-One Months That Won the Revolutionary War.* American support for the king turned to dust because of British barbarity and wholly unethical behavior in the form of indiscriminate violence. Through his ministers and the military chain of command, the king committed injustices contrary to "God's law," which forfeited "His divine right of absolute authority in political and spiritual matters," as Thomas Paine professed. In the eyes of most biblically minded Americans, the horrors of an unjust war were not forgivable. In the world's eyes, "life, liberty and the pursuit of happiness" and "government by the people" became reasonable expectations. The British politician and writer Horace Walpole summed up the Southern British Army's unethical conduct that cost them America. He wrote,

"Lord Cornwallis's military Excursion and cool Butcheries of defenseless People in South Carolina, irrevocably seals the perpetual Disunion between Great Britain and America." Unethical power increased until it was stopped by an outside force. Instead of cultivating a harmonious reunification and engagement of occupied provinces, the British pursued a policy of subjugation and punishment against inhabitants with their infamous Southern Strategy Campaign (4.0) plan to conquer the South. What the elite British army and their allies could accomplish on the battlefield failed them in ethical conduct, and with it, popular support, the war, and America.

In contrast, Southern Continental Army commander General Nathanael Greene, who Congress entrusted with extraordinary powers to oust the British from the South, summed up the complete victory in his farewell remarks to his men. "It is with happiness that he [Greene] has had the honor to command an army no less distinguished for its patience than bravery, and will add no small lustre to your character that you have regarded with abhorrence the practice of plundering, the excise of cruelty…urged…by the example of the enemy to the last."[385] The liberation of the South came about as he had predicted during the darkest days in January 1781 as a "contest of States dependent upon opinion." Protecting citizens, rather than subjugating them, won the territory that won independence that won the war.

A final cataclysmic battle to send off the last British troops in the South was narrowly avoided at Charlestown on that cold day in December 1782. The cease-fire negotiated before the final British withdrawal was held in place until King George III agreed to recognize American independence and unceremoniously end his war with America. After learning of the fall of Charlestown, he was so crestfallen to have lost the British economic crown jewel, he planned to abdicate the throne. Finally, His Majesty King George III put on a brave face and made a speech to Parliament, publicly conceding the point of sovereign independence: "I did not hesitate to go the full length of the powers invested in me, and offer to declare them Free and Independent States, by an article to be inserted in the Treaty of Peace."[386] This speech paved the way for Parliament to vote on the provisional treaty. Up to that point, the King could have rejected or stopped the provisional peace proposal from going forward. Still, there was no justification to tarry with no troops left in America except on a few islands in southern New York. The French and Spanish had signed the proposal already. Parliament would have to pass a 25 percent import tax to continue the war, which would cause economic hardship if not starvation in Britain. Militarily, King George's war of punishment to end the rebellion was played to its final act. When the king concedes that the war he declared is over, the war is over. Days later, Parliament ratified the preliminary peace proposal by a slim margin, formally ending Britain's war to extinguish the American rebellion. The United States had achieved its collective goal of sovereign independence.

When Congress received the official letter agreeing to a cessation of hostilities and recognizing independence from the Crown, Congress accepted the peace terms and declared an end to the war in April 1782, four months after the liberation of Charlestown and eighteen months after Cornwallis's surrender at Yorktown. Congress's act concluded the War for American Independence between Britain and the United States, subsequently acknowledged by all the other warring nations at the Treaty of Paris signing in October. Greene received the news of Congress's declaration of war's end by an express rider on April 16, 1782. Major General Greene immediately wrote General Washington upon hearing the news: "I beg leave to Congratulate your Excellency upon returning smiles of peace, and the happy establishment of our Independence."[387] The War for American Independence from Britain was formally over. The thirteen United States were victorious.

The ethics of a group are usually reflective of its leader. Major General Nathanael Greene stood before his men on June 21, 1783, to deliver his farewell address and disband the great, noble Southern Continental Army. "We found a people overwhelmed with distress, and a country groaning under oppression. It has been our happiness to relive them—The occasion was pressing, the attempt noble, and the success answerable."[388] Greene's moral compass, aligned with Congress's expressed ethics of promoting the happiness of America through rights-based self-government, comprised the living values that ultimately saved the South from conquest. Promoting the ethics of conscience and conciliation saved the revolution from becoming just another failed colonial rebellion in a world imperiously ruled by divine monarchies.

On Greene's journey to Princeton to submit his leave to Congress in October 1783, he rendezvoused with his old friend and commander, General George Washington in Trenton, New Jersey. Trenton was the site of their surprise Victory or Death attack on the crack Hessian troops occupying the town on Christmas Day 1776, following Greene and Washington's crossing of the freezing Delaware River during a blizzard in a desperate gamble to keep the revolution alive. Washington had arrived at the rendezvous point of Colonel Cox's home in Trenton before Greene. He was standing on the stairs when Greene opened the door. "Washington grasped Greene's hand and held it, not saying a word. Then Greene embraced his commander-in-chief and wept openly" as tears ran down Washington's face.[389] The moment two warriors embrace after the battles are done is the most moving in heaven and on earth. They had both committed themselves to victory or death seven years earlier in a bond no enemy could break. They had unexpectedly come out of the war alive and on the side of victory because they stuck to the ethical principles Congress had laid out for them to follow years earlier. They had trusted each other to act independently but in strategic unison. Together they delivered independence to an upstart group of colonies trapped in a mob-like rebellion with only citizen-soldiers and a set of values with which to work. Greene and Washington rode alone together the next day to Princeton and had dinner with their boss, the president of Congress of the new republic they had won together. Sometime after that, Washington obtained a lithograph of Greene, which is still displayed above his dinner table at Mount Vernon. By strange coincidence, George Washington died on December 14, 1799, the seventeenth anniversary of the liberation of Charlestown that sealed independence for America.

Gen Nathanael Greene 1783, mezzotint of painting turned into lithograph, courtesy of Mt. Vernon Ladies' Association.

General Nathanael Greene was honored throughout America as he traveled from South Carolina to Rhode Island in the fall of 1783. When he arrived in Philadelphia, the church bells rang throughout the city to greet him. After he submitted his resignation from service, Congress voted to award him two British cannons his armies captured "at Cowpens, Augusta, or Eutaw Springs." The cannons were to be a public testimony of his "wisdom, fortitude and military skill" in defeating "an Enemy greatly superior in numbers" during his "Command in the Southern Department."[390] The cannons were never delivered to the site of his final victory.

Like George Washington, Greene referred to his retired troops as "family" and endeavored to help those who sought his intervention after the war. "Whatever credit may be given to General Washington and myself, there are others no less deserving," he insisted to Henry Knox. Humble heroes take no umbrage as they relegate themselves to be minimized in history. Life, liberty, honor, and the opportunity to serve are higher rewards than fame. By order of the Continental Congress on November 1, 1783, General Greene was to be furnished with a clerk to copy his war correspondence of the history of Southern command operations into books housed in the secretary's office. This order was fulfilled in 2005, 222 years after being issued. The books of Greene describe and honor America's birth.

Right up to the final British withdrawal from Charlestown, ethics in keeping with the Declaration of Causes, the Articles of War, and the Declaration of Independence were practiced by the Southern Continental Army. Major General Nathanael Greene delivered the spirit and letter of these ethics laid out almost seven years earlier by Congress's spectacular promise to protect "life, liberty and the pursuit of happiness." Virtues and rights-based ethics won enough hearts and minds to take back the Lower South from ruthless British occupation.

While Cornwallis's surrender at Yorktown arrested Britain's military conquest of America, the liberation of Charlestown turned the world order of divine monarchy upside down and a new democratic republic right side up. By the grace of God and the bravery of many, the long war to achieve sovereign independence for all thirteen United States came to a glorious conclusion in Charlestown, South Carolina, on December 14, 1782—America's Revolutionary War Victory Day!

"The times that try men's souls are over—and the greatest revolution the world ever knew, gloriously and happily accomplished. The struggle is over...and, perhaps, never could have happened at a better time."

> —Thomas Paine, General Greene's former aide-de-camp, *The American Crisis XIII,* April 19, 1783, seven days after Congress declared war's end, four months after the liberation of Charlestown.

Greene and Continental Troops Liberating Charlestown. (Image courtesy of South Carolina Historical Society.)

Army and General Staff College Press. (2002). "Nathanael Greene's Implementation of Compound Warfare during the Southern Campaign of the American Revolution" (University of North Carolina classified). Based on Thomas Huber's *Compound Warfare: The Fatal Knot.* Fort Leavenworth, KS, Printed in Columbia, SC, on 1 May 2018. ISB 9781500748463.

Avalon Project. "Declaration of the Causes and Necessities of Taking Up Arms." Retrieved from: http://avalon.law.yale.edu/18th_century/arms.asp.

Barnwell, Joseph W. (1910, Jan). "The Evacuation of Charleston by the British in 1782." *SC Historical and Genealogical Magazine.* 11(1) p.14. Retrieved from: https://www.jstor.org/stable/27575255?seq=18#metadata_info_tab_contents.

Bartram, William. (1775). *Travels Through North and South Carolina*. Pennsylvania: Thomas Mifflin, Reprinted by Kessinger Publishing, NY.

Bass, Robert D. (1973). *The Green Dragoon*. Orangeburg: Sandlapper Publishing, pp. 170–171.

"Battle of Sullivan's Island." https://www.nps.gov/articles/battle-of-sullivan-s-island.htm

Baxley, Charles. B. (2016). "An Enterprise upon Johns Island." *Army History*, PB 20-16-1 (No. 98) Washington, DC, p. 43. Retrieved from: https://history.army.mil/armyhistory/AH98(W).pdf.

BBC Archives. (2009). *Quakers*, Retrieved from http://www.bbc.co.uk/religion/religions/christianity/subdivisions/quakers_1.shtml

Bemis, Samuel F. (1957). *The Diplomacy of the American Revolution*. Bloomington: Indiana University Press.

Blanco, Richard L. (1993). *The American Revolution 1775–1783: An Encyclopedia*, vol. I, A–L. New York and London: Garland Publishing, Inc.

Blanco, Richard L. (1993). *The American Revolution 1775–1783: An Encyclopedia*, vol. 2, M–Z. Garland Publishing.

Blanco, Richard L. and P. J. Sandborn. (eds). (1993). *The American Revolution 1775–1783: An Encyclopedia*. New York and London: Garland Publishing, Vol II.

Boyle, J. L. (ed). (1997). "The Revolutionary War Diaries of Captain Walter Finney, February 1782 to June 1783," *South Carolina Historical Magazine*, 98(2).

Brain, J., Butcher Cumberland. (N.d). https://www.historic-uk.com/HistoryUK/HistoryofBritain/Butcher-Cumberland/.

Buchanan, John. (1997). *The Road to Guilford Courthouse: The American Revolution in the Carolinas*. New York: Wiley.

Burns, Arthur. (n.d.). The Abdication Speech of George III. Retrieved from: https://georgianpapers.com/2017/01/22/abdication-speech-george-iii/.

Butler, Nic. (2017, December 14). "Charleston's Victory Day, Parts 1 & 2," *The Charleston Time Machine*, Charleston

County Public Library, Retrieved from: https://www.ccpl.org/charleston-time-machine/charlestons-victory-day-part-1; https://www.ccpl.org/charleston-time-machine/charlestons-victory-day-part-2.

Butler, Nic. (2018, Feb 2). "The Story of Gadsden's Wharf," *The Charleston Time Machine*, Charleston County Public Library, Retrieved from: https://www.ccpl.org/charleston-time-machine/story-gadsdens-wharf.

Butler, Nic. (2020, June 5). "The Rise of Charleston's Horn Work." *Charleston Time Machine*, Charleston County Public Library. Retrieved from: https://www.ccpl.org/charleston-time-machine/rise-charlestons-horn-work-part-1.

Butler, N. (5 Jul 2019). "Declaring Independence 1776." *Charleston Time Machine*, Charleston County Library. https://www.ccpl.org/charleston-time-machine/declaring-independence-1776-charleston.

Butterfield, L. H. (1961). *The Adams Papers. Diary and Autobiography of John Adams.* Volumes 2 and 3. The Belknap Press of Harvard University Press. Cambridge, Mass.

Carbone, Gerald M. (2008). *Nathanael Greene*, New York: Palgrave/Macmillan.

Clain-Stefanelli, Vladimir and Elvira Clain-Stefanelli. (1973). *Medals Commemorating Battles of the American Revolution*. National Museum of History and Technology, Smithsonian Institution, Washington, DC.

Clinton, Sir Henry. (1783). *Narrative of the Campaign in 1781 in North America*. London, England: J. Debrett Publishing.

Commanger, Henry S. and Richard B. Morris. (eds). (1967). *The Spirit of Seventy-Six: The Story of the American Revolution as Told by Participants*. New York: Harper and Row.

Conrad, Dennis M. (ed). (1998). *The Papers of General Nathanael Greene*. Published for the Rhode Island Historical Society. Chapel Hill and London: University of North Carolina Press, vol. X.

Conrad, Dennis M. (ed). (2000). *The Papers of General Nathanael Greene*. Published for the Rhode Island Historical Society. Chapel Hill and London: University of North Carolina Press, vol. XI.

Conrad, Dennis M. (ed). (2000). *The Papers of General Nathanael Greene*. Published for the Rhode Island Historical Society. Chapel Hill and London: University of North Carolina Press, vol. XII.

Conrad, Dennis M. (ed). (1997). *The Papers of General Nathanael Greene*. Published for the Rhode Island Historical Society. University of North Carolina Press, vol. IX.

Conrad, Dennis M. (ed). (1995). *The Papers of General Nathanael Greene*. Published for the Rhode Island Historical Society. University of North Carolina Press, vol VIII.

Daigler, Ken A. (2004, Spring). "Code Names, Ciphers, and Spies: General Nathanael Greene's Efforts at Espionage," *Carologue: A Bulletin of South Carolina History*, 20(1).

Danielski, John. (n.d.). "Friedrich von Steuben—Meet the Prussian Aristocrat Who Built America's First Professional Army." Retrieved from: https://militaryhistorynow.com/2019/09/05/from-prussia-with-love-how-frederich-von-steuben-shaped-americas-first-professional-army/amp/.

"Divers Account of the Battle of Sullivan's Island in His Majesty's Province of South Carolina the 28th of June 1776." The South Carolina Historical Society, Charleston, SC, 1976.

Drayton, John. (1821). *Memoirs of the American Revolution, from its Commencement to the Year 1776, Inclusive*, vol. 1. Charleston: printed by A. E. Miller.

Dull, Jonathan R. (1987). *A Diplomatic History of the American Revolution*. Yale University Press.

Duval, Lauren. (2018). "Mastering Charleston: Property and Patriarchy in British-Occupied Charleston, 1780–82." *The William and Mary Quarterly*, 75(4). Retrieved from https://www.jstor.org/stable/10.5309/willmaryquar.75.4.0589.

Edgar, Walter B. (2001). *Partisans and Redcoats: The Southern Conflict That Turned the Tide of the American Revolution*. New York: HarperCollins.

Thane, Elswyth (1972). *The Fighting Quaker: Nathanael Greene*. New York: Hawthorn Books.

"Fateful Choices—The Hanging of Isaac Hayne," Historical Marker Data Base, https://www.hmdb.org/Photos/24/Photo24557o.jpg.

Ferling, John E. (2007). *Almost a Miracle*. Oxford: Oxford University Press.

Ford, Worthington C. (ed). Journals of the Continental Congress, 13:384-88.

Gallagher, John J. (1995). *The Battle of Brooklyn 1776*. Edison, NJ: Castle Books.

George Washington Papers. (n.d.) "Timeline—Feb 14, 1776 Meeting between Lee and Enemy Clinton." Retrieved from: https://www.loc.gov/collections/george-washington-papers/articles-and-essays/timeline/the-american-revolution/

Gilbert, Alan. (2013). *Black Patriots and Loyalists: Fighting for Emancipation in the War for Independence*. Chicago and London: University of Chicago Press.

Glickstein, D. (2015). *After Yorktown: The Final Struggle for American Independence*. Westholme Publishing.

Godbold, S. and R. H. Woody. (1982). *Christopher Gadsden and the American Revolution*. Knoxville: UT Pres.

Golway, T. (2006). *Washington's General—Nathanael Greene and the Triumph of the American Revolution*, New York: Henry Holt.

Gordon, John W. (2003). *South Carolina and the American Revolution*. Columbia, SC, University of South Carolina Press.

Greene, Francis V. (1893). *General Greene, Great Commanders Army and Navy Edition*. Edited by J. G. Wilson. New York: D. Appleton. Reprinted by Heritage Books, Westminster, Maryland.

Hagist, Don N. (2020). *Noble Volunteers—The British Soldiers Who Fought in the American Revolution*, Westholme: Yardley, Pennsylvania.

Haller, S. E. (2007). *William Washington—Cavalryman of the Revolution*, Westminster, MD: Heritage Books.

Henderson, A. Scott. (n.d.). "Richard Furman." South Carolina Encyclopedia.org. Retrieved at http://www.scencyclopedia.org/sce/entries/furman-richard/.

Horry, Brig. Gen., and Weems, Parson M.L. (2000). *The Life of General Francis Marion—A Celebrated Partisan Officer, in the Revolutionary War, Against the British and Tories in South Carolina and Georgia*. Winston-Salem, North Carolina: John F. Blair Publishers, pp. 169–170.

Huber's Compound Warfare: The Fatal Knot.(2002). Fort Leavenworth, KS: US Army and General Staff College Press, 2002.

Huw, David. (2017). "A Spirit of Enterprise in Trade, Superior to Any Other State: Commerce in Wartime Charleston, 1775–1780." *The SC Historical Magazine.*

Jones, Mark. (2020). "November 7, 1775—Runaway Slaves flocked to Sullivan's Island," *Charleston Post and Courier.* Https://www.postandcourier.com/350/articles/november-7-1775-runaway-slaves-flocked-to-sullivan-s-island/article_dc6715ba-1deb-11eb-b89e-1f8275b9752d.html.

Keller, J. (28 Jun 2017). "How the Declaration of Independence Went Viral—A Brief Chronology of America's First Big Story," *Pacific Standard*, https://psmag.com/news/how-the-declaration-of-independence-went-viral.

Kerpelman, L. C. (Oct 2018), "The Slave Who Spied: James Armistead's Role in Revolutionary War." https://www.historynet.com/the-slave-who-spied-james-armisteads-role-in-revolutionary-war.htm'

Kershaw, P. M. (n.d.), "Ethics of Freemasonry." Retrieved from http://www.freemasonryresearchforumqsa.com/ethics-of-freemasonry.php.

"King George III Powers," Retrieved from: https://www.quora.com/If-th-King-has-no-real-powers-then-why-is-the-name-os-George-III-so-strongly-associated-with-the-war-for-Amercan-independence.

King, G., and B. Dobrée. (1968). *Letters of King George III.* London: Cassell.

Knight, L. (2019, April 19). "Be a King George." *Journal of the American Revolution.* Retrieved from: https://allthingsliberty.com/2019/04/be-a-king-george/.

Kyte, G. W. (1983, Jan). "Thaddeus Kosciuszko at the Liberation of Charleston." *The South Carolina Historical Magazine*. 84(1). https://www.jstor.org/stable/27567777.

Kyte, G. W. (1983, Jan.). "Thaddeus Kosciuszko at the Liberation of Charleston." *The South Carolina Historical Magazine*, 84(1). https://www.jstor.org/stable/27567777.

Library of Congress, "The Continental Congress Establishes the Articles of War." June 30, 1775, Retrieved from: http://www.loc.gov/teachers/classroommaterials/presentationsandactivities/presentations/timeline/amre/contarmy/articles.html.

Library of Liberty. (2004). *Joseph Addison, Cato: A Tragedy*. Retrieved from: http://oll.libertyfund.org/tittles/addison-cato-a-tragedy-and-selected-essays.

"Lord Charles Cornwallis's March Down the Cape Fear River." (n.d.). Www.ncgenweb.us. Retrieved October 8, 2021, from https://www.ncgenweb.us/cumberland/1776revolution.html.

McBurney, Christian M. (2020). *George Washington's Nemesis: The Outrageous Treason and Unfair Court-Martial of Major Charles Lee during the Revolutionary War.* Savas Beatie: California

McBurney, Christian M. (2020, January 20). "Top Ten Quotes of Major General Charles Lee." *Journal of the American Revolution*. https://allthingsliberty.com/2020/01/top-ten-quotes-of-major-general-charles-lee/. Moore, G. H. (1851).

McCandless, P. (2007) "Revolutionary Fever: Disease and War in the Lower South, 1776–1783." *The American Clinical and Climatological Association Magazine*, 118. Retrieved from: https://www.ncbi.nlm.nih.gov/pmc/articles/PMC1863584/

McCowen, George S., Jr. (1972). *The British Occupation of Charlestown*. 1780–1782, Columbia, SC: University of South Carolina Press.

McGee, Suzanne. (2020, Sep 9). "5 Ways the French Helped Win the American Revolution—The Marquis de Layfayette Was Only the Beginning." https://www.history.com/.amp/news/american-revolution-french-role-help, item 4.

Moore, George H. (1860). *The Treason of Charles Lee*. NY: Charles Scribner. Retrieved from: https://openlibrary.org/books/OL24345989M/Mr._Lee's_plan_-_March_29_1777.

Morgan, K. (2016, June 28). *British American Port Cities*. Oxford Bibliographies. Retrieved from: https://www.oxfordbibliographies.com/view/document/obo-9780199730414/obo-9780199730414-0094.xml.

Morris, R. B. (1965), *The Peacemakers—The Great Powers and American Independence*. New York: Harper and Row.

"Nathanael Greene Passes Away." https://www.masonrytoday.com/index.php?new_month=6&new_day=19&new_year=2016.

"Nathanael Greene's Implementation of Compound Warfare during the Southern Campaign of the American

Revolution." (University of North Carolina classified). Based on Thomas Huber's "Compound Warfare: The Fatal Knot (Fort Leavenworth, KS: U.S. Army and General Staff College Press, 2002. Printed in Columbia, SC on 1 May 2018, pp. 39, 40–41.

National Archives, Declaration of Independence. Retrieved from: https://www.archives.gov/founding-docs/declaration-transcript.

National Park Service—Yorktown Battlefield. (n.d.) "Battle of the Capes." Retrieved from: https://www.nps.gov/york/learn/historyculture/battle-of-the-capes.htm

O'Kelley, Patrick. (2005). *Nothing but Blood and Slaughter—The Revolutionary War in the Carolinas*, vol. 1. USA: Blue House Tavern Press.

O'Kelley, Patrick. (2005). *Nothing but Blood and Slaughter—The Revolutionary War*, vol. 3. USA: Blue House Tavern Press.

O'Kelley, Patrick. (2005). *Nothing but Blood and Slaughter—The Revolutionary War*, vol. 4. USA: Blue House Tavern Press.

O'Shaughnessy, Andrew J. (2013). *The Men Who Lost America*. New Haven and London: Yale University Press.

Omand, D. & Phythian, M. (2018) Principled Spying—The Ethics of Secret Intelligence, Washington, D.C. Georgetown University Press, p. 1.

Paine, T. (1780, Mar 1). "An Act for the Gradual Abolition of Slavery." USHistory.org, https://www.ushistory.org/presidentshouse/history/gradual.plp.

Pancake, John S. (1985). *This Destructive War—The British Campaign in the Carolinas, 1780–1782*. University Alabama: University of Alabama Press.

Paper 1539624917, p 96. https://dx.doi.org/doi:10.21220/s2-0thk-rc77.

Papers of John Adams, vol. 5, "Proposed Amendment to the Articles of Confederation," https://www.masshist.org/publications/adams-papers/index.php/volume/PJA05/pageid/PJA05p321.

Parker, J. C. (2009). *Parker's Guide to the Revolutionary War in South Carolina: Battles, Skirmishes and Murders*. United States: Hem Branch Publishing.

Parks, R. N. (ed). (2005). *The Papers of General Nathanael Greene*, vol. XIII. Published for the Rhode Island Historical Society. University of North Carolina Press.

Ramsay, D. (1785). *The History of the Revolution in South Carolina*, vol. II, Trenton: Isaac Collins.

Rankin, H. (1976). Greene and Cornwallis: The Campaign in the Carolinas. Raleigh: Office of History and Archives.

Reynolds, W. R. (2012). *Andrew Pickens*. Jefferson, NC, and London: McFarland.

Rimini, R. V. (1966). *Andrew Jackson*. Twayne Publishers.

Ripley, W. (1983). *Battlegrounds, South Carolina in the Revolution*. Charleston, SC: Evening Post Publishing.

Robins, E. (1921). "Charles Lee: Stormy Petrel of the Revolution." *The Pennsylvania Magazine of History and Biography*. 45(1). http://www.jstor.org/stable/20086437

Robson, E. (1951). "The Expedition to the Southern Colonies, 1775–1776." *The English Historical Review*, 66(261). Retrieved from http://www.jstor.org/stable/555586/

Ruppert, B. (2020, March 31). "An Economist's Solution to the War: Adam Smith and the Rebelling Colonies." *Journal of the American Revolution*. Retrieved from: https://allthingsliberty.com/2020/03/an-economists-solution-to-the-war-adam-smith-and-the-rebelling-colonies/.

Russell, D. L. (2000). *The American Revolution in the Southern Colonies*, Jefferson, NC, and London: McFarland.

Salmon, J. S. (1975). "A British View of the Siege of Charleston: From the Diary of Captain John Peebles, February 11–June 2, 1780." Dissertations, Theses, and Masters Projects. Paper 1539624917. https://dx.doi.org/doi:10.21220/s2-0thk-rc77

Scarlett, K. (2011, December 4). "Silent Hero Helped Save State and the Revolution." *Greenville News*.

Seymour, W. (1883). "A Journal of the Southern Expedition, 1780–1783" (concluded). *Pennsylvania Magazine of History and Biography*, 7(4). Retrieved from http://www.jstor.org/stable/20084622.

Showman, R. K. (1976). *The Papers of General Nathanael Greene*, vol. I. Published for the Rhode Island Historical Society. University of North Carolina Press.

Showman, R. K. (1980). *The Papers of General Nathanael Greene*, vol. II. Published for the Rhode Island Historical Society. University of North Carolina Press.

Showman, R. K. (1991). *The Papers of General Nathanael Greene*, vol. VI. Published for the Rhode Island Historical Society. University of North Carolina Press.

Showman, R. K. and Conrad, D. M. (1991–2005). *The Papers of General Nathanael Greene*, Volumes I-XIII Published for the Rhode Island Historical Society. University of North Carolina Press.

Simms, William G. "The Life of Francis Marion." Original 1844 text. Charleston: History Press, reprint 2007 with intro.

"South Carolina in the American Revolution." (2004). Society of the Cincinnati. Introduction. Retrieved from: https://www.societyofthecincinnati.org/pdf/downloads/exhibition_SouthCarolina.pdf

Southern, Ed. (2009). *Voices of the American Revolution in the Carolinas.* Winston-Salem, NC: John F. Blair, Publisher.

Spears, John R. (1903). *Anthony Wayne.* New York: D. Appleton.

Stacy, K. R. (2014). "The Land Battle for Sullivan's Island, Charlestown, South Carolina, June–July 1776." *Journal of the Society for Army Historical Research*, 92.

Stedman, Charles. (1794). *History of the Origin, Progress, and Termination of the American War*, vol. II. London: Printed for the Author. Reprint Bedford, MA: Applewood Books.

Stegeman, John F. and Janet A. Stegeman. (1977). Caty—A Biography of Catharine Littlefield Greene. Athens: University of Georgia Press.

Stockwell, Mary. (2018). *Unlikely General—"Mad" Anthony Wayne and the Battle for America*. New Haven and London: Yale University Press, p. 207.

Tarleton, B. (2005 Reprint Edition). *A History of the Campaigns of 1780 and 1781, in the Southern Provinces of North America*. Ayer Company.

Tattrie, Jon. (2008, January 13). "Edward Cornwallis." *The Canadian Encyclopedia*. Retrieved from: https://www.thecanadianencyclopedia.ca/en/article/edward-cornwallis/.

Thayer, Theodore. (1960). *Nathanael Greene, Strategist of the American Revolution*, New York: Twayne Publishers.

Robinson, C. A. (July 1958). *The American Historical Review*. Oxford University Press, Volume 63, Issue 4.

"The Battle of Monck's Corner." American Revolutionary War website. Accounts from various British field commanders. https://www.myrevolutionarywar.com/battles/800414-moncks-corner/.

"The Battle of Moore's Creek Bridge." No author indicated. National Park Service. http://npshistory.com/publications/mocr/index.htm

Tokar, J. A. (1999). "Logistics and the British Defeat in the Revolutionary War." *Army Logistician*, 31(5).

UK Military Archives. (n.d.) Historical Records of the XXX. Regiment, The Buffs 30th Reg., p. 46. Retrieved from: http://lib.militaryarchive.co.uk/library/infantry-histories/library/Historical-Records-of-the-XXX-Regiment/files/assets/basic-html/page46.html.

University of Illinois. "Differing Ethical Systems." Retrieved from: https://civics.sites.University of North Carolina.edu/sebauer/ethics/Basics/index.html.

University of North Carolina Civics Sites. (2012). "American Self-Government—Continental Congress, John Locke." Retrieved from: https://civics.sites.University of North Carolina.edu/files/2012/04/AmericanSelfGovtContCongress10-112.pdf .

Walsh, Richard. (1959). "The Charleston Mechanics: A Brief Study, 1760–1776." *The South Carolina Historical Magazine*. 60(3). http://www.jstor.org/stable/27566235.

Ward, C. (1952). *The War of the Revolution*, vol. II. New York: Macmillan.

"Washington, George." American Revolution Reference Library. Retrieved from: https://www.encyclopedia.com/history/educational-magazines/washington-george

Weingast, B. R. (July 2015). "Adam Smith's Theory of the Persistence of Slavery And Its Abolition in Western Europe." Department of Political Science, Stanford University, Abstract, p. 1. https://web.stanford.edu/

group/mcnollgast/cgi-bin/wordpress/wp-content/uploads/2013/10/asms-theory-of-sy.15.0725.print-version.pdf.

"William Gordon is Finally Silenced—By Himself." (n.d.). New England Historical Society. Retrieved from: https://newenglandhistoricalsociety.com/william-gordon-finally-silenced/

Zeller, Bob. (2018, June 25) *The Tipping Point*. American Battlefield Trust. www.battlefields.org/learn/articles/how-france-helped-win-american-revolution;

Yesteryearsnews.wordpress.com. (2011). "Charles Lee—The Traitor Who Threatened America." retrieved at https://yesteryearsnews.wordpress.com/2011/10/20/charles-lee-the-traitor-who-threatened-america/amp/.

York, N. L. (1993). "Freemasons and the American Revolution." *The Historian*. 55(2). http://www.jstor.org/stable/24449525.

ENDNOTES

1 Papers of John Adams, vol. 5. "Proposed Amendment to the Articles of Confederation." https://www.masshist.org/publications/adams-papers/index.php/volume/PJA05/pageid/PJA05p321.

2 Conrad, Dennis M. (ed), (2000). *The Papers of General Nathanael Greene*. Published for the Rhode Island Historical Society, Chapel Hill and London, University of North Carolina Press, Vol. XII, pp 415, 416.

3 Morgan, K. (2016, June 28). *British American Port Cities*. Oxford Bibliographies. Charleston was the focal point for ships and trade throughout the Lower South, Retrieved from: https://www.oxfordbibliographies.com/view/document/obo-9780199730414/obo-9780199730414-0094.xml; Divers account of the Battle of Sullivan's Island in His Majesty's Province of South Carolina the 28th of June 1776; Walsh, Richard. "The Charleston Mechanics: A Brief Study, 1760-1776." The South Carolina Historical Magazine 60, no. 3 (1959): 123–44. http://www.jstor.org/stable/27566235.

4 Bartram, W. (1775). *Travels through North and South Carolina*. Pennsylvania: Thomas Mifflin, Reprinted by Kessinger Publishing, NewYork.

5 Huw, D. (2017). "A Spirit of Enterprise in Trade, Superior to Any Other State: Commerce in Wartime Charleston, 1775–1780," *SC Historical Magazine*, 118(4) 264–287.

6 Huw, David. "A Spirit of Enterprise in Trade, Superior to Any Other State: Commerce in Wartime Charleston, 1775–1780," *SC Historical Magazine*, 2017. 118(4) 267.

7 Moore, G. H. (1860). *The Treason of Charles Lee*. Contains "Mr. Lee's Plan—March 29, 1777." NY: Charles Scribner, pp. 81–100.

8 Drayton, John. (1821). *Memoirs of the American Revolution, from its Commencement to the Year 1776, Inclusive*. Charleston: printed by A.E. Miller. vol. 1, pp. 44–46.

9 Butterfield, ed.= *Diary and Autobiography of John Adams*, III. 315, 357.

10 Bemis, S. F. (1957). *The Diplomacy of the American Revolution*. Bloomington: Indiana University Press, p. 194.

11 Conrad, Dennis M. (Ed.), (2000) *The Papers of General Nathanael Greene*. Published for the Rhode Island Historical Society, Chapel Hill and London, University of North Carolina Press, Vol. XI, p. 693.

12 *South Carolina in the American Revolution*. (2004). Society of the Cincinnati. Introduction. Retrieved from: https://www.societyofthecincinnati.org/pdf/downloads/exhibition_SouthCarolina.pdf.

13 Conrad, Dennis M., (ed). (1995). *The Papers of General Nathanael Greene*, published for the Rhode Island Historical Society, University of North Carolina Press, vol. VIII, p. 324.

14 Washington, George. *American Revolution Reference Library*. Retrieved from: https://www.encyclopedia.com/history/educational-magazines/washington-george.

15 *William Gordon is Finally Silenced—By Himself.* (n.d.). The New England Historical Society. Retrieved from: https://newenglandhistoricalsociety.com/william-gordon-finally-silenced/.

16 *The American Historical Review*. (Jul 1958). Oxford University Press, 63(4), pp. 924–934.

17 Butler, N. (2017, December 14). *Charleston's Victory Day, Parts 1 & 2*. Retrieved from: https://www.ccpl.org/charleston-time-machine/charlestons-victory-day-part-1; https://www.ccpl.org/charleston-time-machine/charlestons-victory-day-part-2.

18 Parks, R. N. (ed.). (2005). *The Papers of General Nathanael Greene*. Published for the Rhode Island Historical Society, University of North Carolina Press, vol. XIII, p. 397

19 Showman, R. K. (1976). *The Papers of General Nathanael Greene*. Published for the Rhode Island Historical Society, University of North Carolina Press, vol. I, p. xiv.

20 Showman, R. K. (1976). *The Papers of General Nathanael Greene*. Published for the Rhode Island Historical Society, University of North Carolina Press, vol. I, pp. xxvii–xxix.

21 Showman, R. K. (1976). *The Papers of General Nathanael Greene*. Published for the Rhode Island Historical Society, University of North Carolina Press, vol. I, pg. xxx.

22 Ford (ed). Journals of the Continental Congress, 13:384–88.

23 "Nathanael Greene's Implementation of Compound Warfare during the Southern Campaign of the American Revolution," (University of North Carolina classified). Based on Thomas Huber's "Compound Warfare: The Fatal Knot." Fort Leavenworth, KS: U.S. Army and General Staff College Press, 2002. Printed in Columbia, SC on 1 May 2018, pp. 39, 40–41.

24 www.battlefields.org/learn/articles/how-france-helped-win-american-revolution; McGee, Suzanne. (2020, Sep 9). "5 Ways the French Helped Win

the American Revolution-The Marquis de Layfayette Was Only the Beginning," https://www.history.com/.amp/news/american-revolution-french-role-help, item 4.

25 Conrad, Dennis M. (1997). *The Papers of General Nathanael Greene*. Published for the Rhode Island Historical Society. University of North Carolina Press, vol. IX, 47–48.

26 Gilbert, A. (2013). *Black Patriots and Loyalists: Fighting for Emancipation in the War for Independence*. University of Chicago Press, p.187.

27 Blanco, R. L. (1993). *The American Revolution 1775–1783: An Encyclopedia*. vol. I, A-L. New York & London: Garland Publishing, p. 333.

28 "Battle of Sullivan's Island." https://www.nps.gov/articles/battle-of-sullivan-s-island.htm

29 Jones, Mark. (2020). "November 7, 1775—Runaway Slaves Flocked to Sullivan's Island," *Charleston Post and Courier*, https://www.postandcourier.com/350/articles/november-7-1775-runaway-slaves-flocked-to-sullivan-s-island/article_dc-6715ba-1deb-11eb-b89e-1f8275b9752d.html.

30 Stacy, K. R. "The Land Battle for Sullivan's Island, Charlestown, South Carolina, June–July 1776," *Journal of the Society for Army Historical Research* 92 (2014), p. 194; *Divers Account of the Battle of Sullivan's Island in His Majesty's Province of South Carolina the 28th of June 1776*. South Carolina Historical Society, Charleston, SC, 1976, pp. 17–19.

31 O'Kelley, Patrick. (2005). *Nothing but Blood and Slaughter—The Revolutionary War in the Carolinas,* USA: Blue House Tavern Press, Volume One, pp. 115–146.

32 Southern, E. (2009). *Voices of the American Revolution in the Carolinas*. John F. Blair, Publisher, pp. 41–42.

33 *Divers account of the Battle of Sullivan's Island in His Majesty's Province of South Carolina the 28th of June 1776*. South Carolina Historical Society, Charleston, SC, 1976, p 2.

34 Stacy, K. R. (2014). "The Land Battle for Sullivan's Island, Charlestown, South Carolina, June-July 1776," *Journal of the Society for Army Historical Research* 92, p. 194.

35 Blanco, R. L. (1993). *The American Revolution 1775–1783: An Encyclopedia*, vol. I, A–L. New York & London: Garland Publishing,, pp. 910–914.

36 George Washington Papers. (n.d.) Timeline—Feb 14, 1776 meeting between Lee and enemy Clinton. Retrieved from: https://www.loc.gov/collections/george-washington-papers/articles-and-essays/timeline/the-american-revolution/.

37 Ward, C. (1952). *The War of the Revolution*, Vol. II. New York, The Macmillan Company, p 668.

38 Ward, C. (1952). *The War of the Revolution*, Vol. II. New York, The Macmillan Company, p 677.

39 Stacy, Kim. R. (2014). "The Land Battle for Sullivan's Island, Charlestown, South Carolina, June–July 1776." *Journal of the Society for Army Historical Research* 92, p. 195.

40 Stacy, Kim. R. (2014). "The Land Battle for Sullivan's Island, Charlestown, South Carolina, June–July 1776." *Journal of the Society for Army Historical Research*, 92, p. 197.

41 O'Kelley, Patrick. (2005). *Nothing but Blood and Slaughter—The Revolutionary War in the Carolinas*. USA: Blue House Tavern Press, vol. 1, pp. 123–124.

42 Stacy, Kim R. (2014). "The Land Battle for Sullivan's Island, Charlestown, South Carolina, June–July 1776." *Journal of the Society for Army Historical Research* 92, p. 189, footnote 2.

43 Stacy, Kim R., (2014) "The Land Battle for Sullivan's Island, Charlestown, South Carolina, June–July 1776," *Journal of the Society for Army Historical Research* 92, p. 189, footnote.

44 Ward, C. (1952). *The War of The Revolution*, vol. II. New York, Macmillan, p. 676.

45 Moore, George H. (1860). *The Treason of Charles Lee*, New York: Charles Scribner, p. 100. Retrieved from: https://openlibrary.org/books/OL24345989M/Mr._Lee's_plan_-_March_29_1777.

46 O'Kelley, Patrick. (2005). *Nothing but Blood and Slaughter—The Revolutionary War in the Carolinas*. USA: Blue House Tavern Press, vol. 1, p. 143.

47 Zeise, JoAnn. (2015, June 26). "Carolina Day—Celebrating since 1777." http://scmuseum.org/2015/06/26/carolina-day-celebrating-since-1777/.

48 O'Kelley, Patrick. (2005). *Nothing but Blood and Slaughter—The Revolutionary War in the Carolinas*. USA: Blue House Tavern Press, vol. 1, p. 145.

49 Ward, C. (1952). *The War of the Revolution*, vol. II. New York, Macmillan, p. 675.

50 Ripley, W. (1983). *Battlegrounds, South Carolina in the Revolution*. Evening Post Publishing, p. 15.

51 Stacy, K. R. (2014). "The Land Battle for Sullivan's Island, Charlestown, South Carolina, June–July 1776." *Journal of the Society for Army Historical Research*, 92, p 199.

52 *The Battle of Moore's Creek Bridge*. National Park Service. http://npshistory.com/publications/mocr/index.htm

53 National Park Service. "Battle of Moore's Creek, NC." http://npshistory.com/publications/mocr/index.htm.

54 Commanger, H.,S. and B. M. Morris, (ed). (1967). *The Spirit of Seventy-Six: The Story of the American Revolution as Told by Participants*. Harper & Row, p. 274.

55 Showman, R. K. (1976). *The Papers of General Nathanael Greene*, published for the Rhode Island Historical Society, University of North Carolina Press, vol. I, pp. 140–141.

56 Commanger, H. S. B. M. and Morris, (ed). (1967). *The Spirit of Seventy-Six, The Story of the American Revolution as told by participants*. Harper & Row, p. 312.

57 Blanco, R. L. (1993). *The American Revolution 1775–1783: An Encyclopedia*, vol. I, A-L. New York & London: Garland Publishing, p. 487.

58 Butler, N. (5 Jul 2019). "Declaring Independence 1776." https://www.ccpl.org/charleston-time-machine/declaring-independence-1776-charleston.

59 Omand, D. and M. Phythian. (2018). *Principled Spying—The Ethics of Secret Intelligence*. Washington, DC, Georgetown University Press, p. 1.

60 Avalon Project. *Declaration of the Causes and Necessities of Taking Up Arms*. Retrieved from: http://avalon.law.yale.edu/18th_century/arms.asp.

61 Library of Congress. *The Continental Congress Establishes the Articles of War, June 30, 1775*. Retrieved from: http://www.loc.gov/teachers/classroommaterials/presentationsandactivities/presentations/timeline/amre/contarmy/articles.html.

62 America's Homepage. *A Proclamation, by the King, for Suppressing Rebellion and Sedition*. Retrieved from: http://ahp.gatech.edu/proclamation_bp_1775.html.

63 National Archives, Declaration of Independence. Retrieved from: https://www.archives.gov/founding-docs/declaration-transcript.

64 Keller, J. (28 Jun 2017). "How the Declaration of Independence Went Viral – A brief chronology of America's first big story," *Pacific Standard*, https://psmag.com/news/how-the-declaration-of-independence-went-viral.

65 University of North Carolina Civics Sites. (2012). *American Self-Government - Continental Congress*, John Locke. Retrieved from: https://civics.sites.University of North Carolina.edu/files/2012/04/AmericanSelfGovtContCongress10-112.pdf.

66 University of Illinois. *Differing Ethical Systems*. Retrieved from: https://civics.sites.University of North Carolina.edu/sebauer/ethics/Basics/index.html.

67 Danielski, J. (n.d.). *Friedrich von Steuben—Meet the Prussian Aristocrat Who Built America's First Professional Army*. Retrieved from: https://militaryhistorynow.com/2019/09/05/from-prussia-with-love-how-frederich-von-steuben-shaped-americas-first-professional-army/amp/.

68 Kershaw, P. M. (n.d.). *Ethics of Freemasonry*. Retrieved from http://www.freemasonryresearchforumqsa.com/ethics-of-freemasonry.php

69 Blanco, R. L. (1993). *The American Revolution 1775–1783: An Encyclopedia*, vol. I, A-L. New York & London: Garland Publishing, p 587.

70 York, N. L. (1993). "Freemasons and the American Revolution." *The Historian*, 55(2), 315–330. http://www.jstor.org/stable/24449525

71 *Nathanael Greene Passes Away*, https://www.masonrytoday.com/index.php?new_month=6&new_day=19&new_year=2016.

72 BBC Archives. (2009). *Quakers*. Retrieved from http://www.bbc.co.uk/religion/religions/christianity/subdivisions/quakers_1.shtml.

73 Henderson, S. (n.d.). *Richard Furman*. South Carolina Encyclopedia.org. Retrieved at http://www.scencyclopedia.org/sce/entries/furman-richard/.

74 Avalon Project. *Declaration of the Causes and Necessities of Taking Up Arms*. Retrieved from: http://avalon.law.yale.edu/18th_century/arms.asp.

75 Library of Liberty. (2004) "Joseph Addison, Cato: A Tragedy." Retrieved from: http://oll.libertyfund.org/tittles/addison-cato-a-tragedy-and-selected-essays.

76 *King George III Powers*. Retrieved from: https://www.quora.com/If-th-King-has-no-real-powers-then-why-is-the-name-os-George-III-so-strongly-associated-with-the-war-for-Amercan-independence.

77 Ramsay, David. (1785). *The History of the Revolution in South Carolina*, vol. II. Trenton: Isaac Collins, pp. 193–194.

78 Hart, Emma. (2017) "City Government and the State in Eighteenth Century South Carolina." *Eighteenth Century Studies*, 50(2), p. 202.

79 Tennyson, Alfred. "The Charge of the Light Brigade."

80 Ferling, J. (2007). *Almost a Miracle*, Oxford: Oxford University Press, p. 475, para 4.

81 Ruppert, B. (2020, March 31). "An Economist's Solution to the War: Adam Smith and the Rebelling Colonies." *Journal of the American Revolution*. Retrieved from: https://allthingsliberty.com/2020/03/an-economists-solution-to-the-war-adam-smith-and-the-rebelling-colonies/.

82 Blanco, R. L. and P. J. Sandborn (eds). (1993). *The American Revolution 1775–1783: An Encyclopedia*. New York and London: Garland Publishing, vol. II, pp. 1249–1251.

83 Blanco, R.L. and P. J. Sandborn (eds). (1993). *The American Revolution 1775–1783: An Encyclopedia*. New York and London: Garland Publishing, vol. I, pp. 640–646.

84 Blanco, R. L. (1993). *The American Revolution 1775–1783: An Encyclopedia*, vol. I, A-L. New York and London: Garland Publishing, pp. 645–646.

85 Horry, Brig. Gen., and Parson M.L. Weems. (2000). *The Life of General Francis Marion—A Celebrated Partisan Officer, in the Revolutionary War, against the British and Tories in South Carolina and Georgia*. Winston-Salem, North Carolina: John F. Blair Publishers, pp. 169–170.

86 Ferling, J. (2007). *Almost a Miracle*. Oxford: Oxford University Press, p. 475.

87 Salmon, J. S., "A British View of the Siege of Charleston: From the Diary of Captain John Peebles February 11–June 2, 1780" (1975). Dissertations, Theses, and Masters Projects. Paper 1539624917, p 96. https://dx.doi.org/doi:10.21220/s2-0thk-rc77; Robson, E. (1951) The Expedition to the Southern Colonies, 1775-1776. The English Historical Review, 66(261), 535-560. Retrieved from http://www.jstor.org/stable/555586/

88 "The Battle of Monck's Corner." https://www.myrevolutionarywar.com/battles/800414-moncks-corner/.

89 Clinton, H. (1783). *Narrative of the Campaign in 1781 in North America*. London, England: J. Debrett Publishing.

90 O'Shaughnessy, A. J. (2013). *The Men Who Lost America*. New Haven and London: Yale University Press, p. 271.

91 "Nathanael Greene's Implementation of Compound Warfare during the Southern Campaign of the American Revolution" (University of North Carolina classified). Based on Thomas Huber's *Compound Warfare: The Fatal Knot*. Fort

Leavenworth, KS: US Army and General Staff College Press, 2002. Printed in Columbia, SC, on 1 May 2018. ISB 9781500748463.

92 "Nathanael Greene's Implementation of Compound Warfare during the Southern Campaign of the American Revolution" (University of North Carolina classified). Based on Thomas Huber's Compound Warfare: The Fatal Knot. Fort Leavenworth, KS: US Army and General Staff College Press, 2002. Printed in Columbia, SC, on 1 May 2018. ISB 9781500748463.

93 Yesteryearsnews.wordpress.com. (2011). "Charles Lee—The Traitor Who Threatened America." Retrieved at https://yesteryearsnews.wordpress.com/2011/10/20/charles-lee-the-traitor-who-threatened-america/amp/.

94 Moore, G. H. (1860). *The Treason of Charles Lee*. Contains "Mr. Lee's Plan—March 29, 1777." New York: Charles Scribner, pp. 81–100.

95 Gallagher, John J. (1995). *The Battle of Brooklyn 1776*. Edison, NJ: Castle Books, pp. 66–68.

96 Moore, George H. (1860). *The Treason of Charles Lee, Major General, Second in Command in the American Army of the Revolution*. NY: Charles Scribner, p. 50.

97 Ward, C. (1952). *The War of the Revolution*, vol. II. New York: Macmillan, p. 278.

98 Showman, R. K. (1980). *The Papers of General Nathanael Greene*. Published for the Rhode Island Historical Society, University of North Carolina Press, vol. II, p. 8.

99 Ward, C. (1952). *The War of the Revolution*, vol. II. New York: Macmillan, p. 288.

100 Blanco, R. L. (1993). *The American Revolution 1775–1783: An Encyclopedia*, vol. I, A-L. New York and London: Garland Publishing, pp. 914–917.

101 Moore, G. H. (1851). *The Treason of Charles Lee*. New York: Charles Scribner, p. 100. Retrieved from: https://openlibrary.org/books/OL24345989M/Mr._Lee's_plan_-_March_29_1777.

102 Mcburney, C. M. (2020). George Washington's nemesis: the outrageous treason and unfair, pp. 78–82.

103 Mcburney, C. M. (2020). George Washington's nemesis: the outrageous treason and unfair, pp. 90–91.

104 Mcburney, C. M. (2020). George Washington's nemesis: the outrageous treason and unfair, p. 119.

105 Stedman, C. (1794). *History of the Origin, Progress, and Termination of the American War*, vol. II. London: printed for the author. Reprint Bedford, MA: Applewood Books, pp. 22–23.

106 Blanco, R. L. and P. J. Sandborn (eds). (1993). *The American Revolution 1775–1783, An Encyclopedia*, vol. I. New York and London: Garland Publishing, pp 913-914.

107 Lennon, Donald R. "'The Graveyard of American Commanders': The Continental Army's Southern Department, 1776-1778." The North Carolina Historical Review 67, no. 2 (1990): 133–58. http://www.jstor.org/stable/23521245.

108 Clinton, Henry. (1783). *Narrative of Lieutenant-General Sir Henry Clinton, Relative to this Conduct During Part of His Command of the King's Troops in North America*. London: J. Debrett. Reprint by Kessinger's Legacy, p. 52.

109 Godbold, S. E. and R. H. Woody. (1982). *Christopher Gadsden and the American Revolution*. Knoxville: University of Tennessee, p. 202.

110 Pancake, John S. (1985). *This Destructive War*. Alabama: University of Alabama Press. Pp. 69–70.

111 Ferling, John (2007) Almost a Miracle. Oxford & NY: Oxford University Press, p. 451.

112 Tarleton, LTC. (1787). *A History of the Campaigns of 1780 and 1781, in the Southern Provinces of North America*. London: T. Cadell, p. 135.

113 Brain, J., Butcher Cumberland (n.d). https://www.historic-uk.com/HistoryUK/HistoryofBritain/Butcher-Cumberland/; Tattrie, J. (2008, January 13). "Edward Cornwallis." The Canadian Encyclopedia. Retrieved from: https://www.thecanadianencyclopedia.ca/en/article/edward-cornwallis/.

114 Ward, C. (1952). *The War of the Revolution*, vol. II. New York, Macmillan, p. 669.

115 Ramsay, D. (1785). *The History of the Revolution in South Carolina*, vol. II. Trenton: Isaac Collins, p. 109.

116 Pancake, J. S. (1985). *This Destructive War—The British Campaign in the Carolinas*. 1780–1782. University of Alabama Press, pp. 93–94.

117 Rankin, H. (1976). *Greene and Cornwallis: The Campaign in the Carolinas*. Raleigh: Office of History and Archives, pp 23–24.

118 Ferling, John. (2007). *Almost A Miracle*. Oxford and New York: Oxford University Press, p. 436.

119 Pervis, Randy A. (2018, Nov. 27). "Major James Wemyss: Second most hated British officer in the South," *Journal of the American Revolution*. https://allthingsliberty.com/2018/11/major-james-wemyss-second-most-hated-british-officer-in-the-south/.

120 Golway, T. (2006). *Washington's General—Nathanael Greene and the Triumph of the American Revolution*. New York: Henry Holt, pp. 2, 182.

121 Ramsay, D. (1785), *The History of the Revolution in South Carolina*, vol. II. Trenton: Isaac Collins, p. 157.

122 Ramsay, D. (1785), *The History of the Revolution in South Carolina*, vol. II. Trenton: Isaac Collins, p. 158–159.

123 Rimini, R. V. (1966). *Andrew Jackson*. Twayne Publishers, pp. 7–8.

124 Duval, L. (2018). *Mastering Charleston: Property and Patriarchy in British-Occupied Charleston, 1780–82. William and Mary Quarterly*, 75(4), 589–622. Retrieved from https://www.jstor.org/stable/10.5309/willmaryquar.75.4.0589.

125 Ramsay, D. (1785). *The History of the Revolution in South Carolina*, vol. II. Trenton: Isaac Collins, pp. 182–185.

126 Ramsay, D. (1785). *The History of the Revolution in South Carolina*, vol. II. Trenton: Isaac Collins, pp 192–193.

127 Showman, R. K. (1991). *The Papers of General Nathanael Greene*. Published for the Rhode Island Historical Society, University of North Carolina Press, vol. VI, pp. 518–519.

128 Showman, R. K. (1991). *The Papers of General Nathanael Greene*. Published for the Rhode Island Historical Society, University of North Carolina Press, vol. VI, p. 442.

129 Showman, R. K. (1991). The Papers of General Nathanael Greene. Published for the Rhode Island Historical Society, University of North Carolina Press, vol. VI, pp. 519–520.

130 Showman, R. K. (1991). *The Papers of General Nathanael Greene*. Published for the Rhode Island Historical Society, University of North Carolina Press, vol. VI, pp 519–520.

131 Showman, R. K. (1991). *The Papers of General Nathanael Greene*, published for the Rhode Island Historical Society, The University of North Carolina Press, vol. VI, p 529.

132 Haller, S. E. (2007). *William Washington—Cavalryman of the Revolution*. Westminster, MD: Heritage Books.

133 Showman, R.K. (1991). *The Papers of General Nathanael Greene*. Published for the Rhode Island Historical Society, University of North Carolina Press, vol. VI, p. 547.

134 Salmon, J. S. (1975). "A British View of the Siege of Charleston: From the Diary of Captain John Peebles, February 11-June 2, 1780." Dissertations, Theses, and Masters Projects. Paper 1539624917. https://dx.doi.org/doi:10.21220/s2-0thk-rc77.

135 Reynolds, W. R. (2012). *Andrew Pickens*. Jefferson, North Carolina, and London: McFarland, p. 295.

136 Reynolds, W. R. (2012). *Andrew Pickens*. Jefferson, North Carolina, and London: McFarland, p. 74.

137 Showman, R. K. (1991–2005). *The Papers of General Nathanael Greene*. Published for the Rhode Island Historical Society, University of North Carolina Press, vol. X, p. 34, 355, 443.

138 Showman, R. K. (1991). *The Papers of General Nathanael Greene*. Published for the Rhode Island Historical Society, University of North Carolina Press, vol. VII, p. 132.

139 Showman, R. K. and Dennis M Conrad (eds). (1994). *The Papers of General Nathanael Greene*. Published for the Rhode Island Historical Society, Chapel Hill and London, University of North Carolina Press, vol. VII, p. 426; Conrad, Dennis M. (ed), (1997) *The Papers of General Nathanael Greene*, published for the Rhode

Island Historical Society, Chapel Hill and London, The University of North Carolina Press, Vol. IX, p. 37

140 Showman, R.K. (1991) *The Papers of General Nathanael Greene*, published for the Rhode Island Historical Society, The University of North Carolina Press, vol. VI, pp. 508, 581.

141 Scarlett, K. (2011, December 4). "Silent Hero Helped Save State and the Revolution." Greenville News, p. 7A.

142 Ramsay, D. (1785). *The History of the Revolution in South Carolina*. Trenton: Isaac Collins, vol. II, pp. 196–200.

143 Buchanan, J. (1997). *The Road to Guilford Courthouse*. Wiley, pp. 319–371.

144 Showman, R. K. and Dennis M. Conrad (eds). (1994). *The Papers of General Nathanael Greene*, published for the Rhode Island Historical Society, Chapel Hill and London, University of North Carolina Press, vol. VII, p. 348.

145 Showman, R. K. (1994). *The Papers of General Nathanael Greene*. Published for the Rhode Island Historical Society, University of North Carolina Press, vol. VII, pp. 236–237.

146 Showman, R. K. (ed). (1991–2005). *The Papers of General Nathanael Greene*. Published for the Rhode Island Historical Society, University of North Carolina Press, vol. VII, p. 396.

147 Ferling, J. E. (2009). *Almost a Miracle: The American Victory in the War of Independence*. Oxford University Press, pp. 474–475.

148 Elswyth Thane. (1972). *The Fighting Quaker: Nathanael Greene*. Hawthorn Books, p. 218; Buchanan, J. (1997). *The Road to Guilford Courthouse: The American Revolution in the Carolinas*. Wiley. pp. 372–383.

149 Tarleton, B. (2005 Reprint Edition). *A History of the Campaigns of 1780 and 1781, in the Southern Provinces of North America*. Ayer Company Publishers, pp. 277–278.

150 Tarleton, B. (2005 Reprint Edition). *A History of the Campaigns of 1780 and 1781, in the Southern Provinces of North America*. Ayer Company Publishers, p. 279.

151 Bass, R. D. (1973). *The Green Dragoon*. Orangeburg: Sandlapper Publishing, pp. 170–171.

152 Buchanan, J. (1997). *The Road to Guilford Courthouse: The American Revolution in the Carolinas*. Wiley, p. 382.

153 "Lord Charles Cornwallis's March Down the Cape Fear River." (n.d.). Www.ncgenweb.us. Retrieved October 8, 2021, from https://www.ncgenweb.us/cumberland/1776revolution.html

154 Tarleton, B. (2005 Reprint Edition). *A History of the Campaigns of 1780 and 1781, in the Southern Provinces of North America*. Ayer Company Publishers, p. 281.

155 Pancake, J. S. (1985). *This Destructive War—The British Campaign in the Carolinas. 1780–1782*, University of Alabama Press, p. 189.

156 Anderson, L. (2002). *Forgotten Patriot*. USA: Universal Publishers, p. 305.

157 Gordon, J. (2003). *South Carolina and the American Revolution*. Columbia, SC: University of South Carolina Press, p. 148.

158 Clain-Stefanelli, V., Clain-Stefanelli, E., (1973). *Medals Commemorating Battles of the American Revolution, National Museum of History and Technology*. Smithsonian Institution, Washington, DC.

159 Blanco, R. L. (1993). *The American Revolution 1775–1783: An Encyclopedia*, vol. 2, M–Z. Garland Publishing, pp. 1375–1376.

160 Edgar, W. B. (2001). *Partisans and Redcoats: The Southern Conflict That Turned the Tide of the American Revolution*. HarperCollins, New York, p. 234

161 Conrad, Dennis M. (ed). (1995). *The Papers of General Nathanael Greene*. Published for the Rhode Island Historical Society. Chapel Hill and London: University of North Carolina Press, vol. VIII, pp. 155–157.

162 Conrad, Dennis M. (ed). (1997). *The papers of General Nathanael Greene*. Published for the Rhode Island Historical Society. Chapel Hill and London: University of North Carolina Press, vol. IX, p. 135.

163 Conrad, Dennis M. (ed). (1995). *The Papers of General Nathanael Greene*. Published for the Rhode Island Historical Society. Chapel Hill and London: University of North Carolina Press, vol. VIII, p. 67.

164 Conrad, Dennis M. (ed). (1997). *The Papers of General Nathanael Greene*. Published for the Rhode Island Historical Society. Chapel Hill and London: University of North Carolina Press, vol. IX, p. 107n.

165 Tarleton, B. (2005 Reprint Edition). *A History of the Campaigns of 1780 and 1781, in the Southern Provinces of North America*. Ayer Company Publishers, pp. 283–284.

166 Conrad, Dennis M. (ed). (1995). *The Papers of General Nathanael Greene*. Published for the Rhode Island Historical Society. Chapel Hill and London: University of North Carolina Press, vol. VIII, pp. 250–254.

167 Conrad, Dennis M. (ed). (1995). *The Papers of General Nathanael Greene*. Published for the Rhode Island Historical Society. Chapel Hill and London: University of North Carolina Press, vol. VIII, pp. 262–264.

168 Conrad, Dennis M. (ed). (1995). *The Papers of General Nathanael Greene*. Published for the Rhode Island Historical Society. Chapel Hill and London: University of North Carolina Press, vol. VIII, pp. 265–266; The Siege of Fort

Granby. (nd) American Revolutionary War 1775-1783. Retrieved from: https://revolutionarywar.us/year-1781/siege-fort-granby/

169 Conrad, Dennis M. (ed). (1995). *The Papers of General Nathanael Greene*. Published for the Rhode Island Historical Society. Chapel Hill and London: University of North Carolina Press, vol. VIII, pp. 310–312.

170 Conrad, Dennis M. (ed). (1995). *The Papers of General Nathanael Greene*. Published for the Rhode Island Historical Society. Chapel Hill and London. University of North Carolina Press, vol. VIII, p. 214.

171 Simms, W. G. "The Life of Francis Marion," original 1844 text. Charleston: History Press, reprint 2007 with intro, pp. 194–195.

172 Daigler, K. A. (2004, Spring). "Code Names, Ciphers, and Spies: General Nathanael Greene's Efforts at Espionage." *Carologue: A Bulletin of South Carolina History*, 20(1), 16–19.

173 Daigler, K. A. (2004, Spring). "Code Names, Ciphers, and Spies: General Nathanael Greene's Efforts at Espionage." *Carologue: A Bulletin of South Carolina History*, 20(1), 17–18.

174 Daigler, K. A. (2004, Spring). "Code Names, Ciphers, and Spies: General Nathanael Greene's Efforts at Espionage." *Carologue: A Bulletin of South Carolina History*, 20(1), p. 15.

175 Blanco, R. L. (1993). *The American Revolution 1775–1783: An Encyclopedia*, vol. 2, M–Z. Garland Publishing, p. 1245.

176 Conrad, Dennis M. (ed). (1995). *The Papers of General Nathanael Greene*. Published for the Rhode Island Historical Society. Chapel Hill and London; University of North Carolina Press, vol. VIII, p. 351.

177 Gordon, J. (2003). *South Carolina and the American Revolution*. Columbia, SC: University of South Carolina Press, p. 152.

178 Daigler, K. A. (2004, Spring) "Code Names, Ciphers, and Spies: General Nathanael Greene's Efforts at Espionage." *Carologue: A Bulletin of South Carolina History*, 20(1), p. 19.

179 Blanco, R. L. and P. J. Sandborn (eds). *The American Revolution 1775–1783: An Encyclopedia*. Two-volume set with 125 Contributors. New York and London: Garland Publishing, p. 1614.

180 Blanco, R. L. and P. J. Sandborn (eds). (1993). *The American Revolution 1775–1783: An Encyclopedia*. New York and London: Garland Publishing, vol. 2, p. 1376.

181 Daigler, K. A. (2004, Spring). "Code Names, Ciphers, and Spies: General Nathanael Greene's Efforts at Espionage." *Carologue: A Bulletin of South Carolina History*, 20(1), p. 16.

182 Conrad, Dennis M. (ed). (1997). *The Papers of General Nathanael Greene*. Published for the Rhode Island Historical Society. Chapel Hill and London: University of North Carolina Press, vol. IX, pp. 249–252.

183 *Fateful Choices—The Hanging of Isaac Hayne*, Historical Marker Data Base, https://www.hmdb.org/Photos/24/Photo24557o.jpg

184 UK Military Archives. (n.d.), *Historical Records of the XXX. Regiment, The Buffs 30th Reg.*, p. 46. Retrieved from: http://lib.militaryarchive.co.uk/library/infantry-histories/library/Historical-Records-of-the-XXX-Regiment/files/assets/basic-html/page46.html.

185 Greene, F. V. *General Greene*. Great Commanders Army and Navy Edition, edited by J. G. Wilson. New York: D. Appleton , 1893. Reprinted by Heritage Books, Westminster, Maryland, p. 261.

186 Greene, F. V. *General Greene*, Great Commanders Army and Navy Edition, edited by J. G. Wilson, New York: D. Appleton , 1893. Reprinted by Heritage Books, Westminster, Maryland, p. 262.

187 Conrad, Dennis M. (ed). (1997). *The Papers of General Nathanael Greene*. Published for the Rhode Island Historical Society. Chapel Hill and London: University of North Carolina Press, vol. IX, p.177.

188 Conrad, Dennis M. (ed). (1997). *The Papers of General Nathanael Greene*. Published for the Rhode Island Historical Society. Chapel Hill and London: University of North Carolina Press, vol. IX, p. 177.

189 Conrad, Dennis M. (ed). (1997). *The Papers of General Nathanael Greene*. Published for the Rhode Island Historical Society, Chapel Hill and London: University of North Carolina Press, vol. IX, p.177.

190 Gordon, J. (2003). *South Carolina and the American Revolution*. Columbia, SC, USC Press, p. 164.

191 Conrad, Dennis M. (ed). (1997). *The Papers of General Nathanael Greene*. Published for the Rhode Island Historical Society. Chapel Hill and London: University of North Carolina Press, vol. IX, pp. 328–338.

192 Showman, R. K. and Dennis M. Conrad. (eds). (1994). *The Papers of General Nathanael Greene*. Published for the Rhode Island Historical Society. Chapel Hill and London: University of North Carolina Press, Vol. vii, pp. 351–352.

193 Blanco, R. L and P. J. Sandborn (eds). (1993). *The American Revolution 1775–1783: An Encyclopedia*. New York and London: Garland Publishing, vol. 2, pp. 1807–1818.

194 Conrad, Dennis M. (ed). (1997). *The Papers of General Nathanael Greene*, published for the Rhode Island Historical Society. Chapel Hill and London: University of North Carolina Press, vol. IX, pp. 138–139.

195 Conrad, Dennis M. (ed). (1997). *The Papers of General Nathanael Greene.* Published for the Rhode Island Historical Society. Chapel Hill and London: University of North Carolina Press, vol. IX, p. 30.

196 Conrad, Dennis M. (ed). (1997). *The Papers of General Nathanael Greene.* Published for the Rhode Island Historical Society. Chapel Hill and London: University of North Carolina Press. vol. IX, pp. 234–235.

197 National Park Service – Yorktown Battlefield. (n.d.) "Battle of the Capes." Retrieved from: https://www.nps.gov/york/learn/historyculture/battle-of-the-capes.htm

198 Conrad, Dennis M. (ed). (1997). *The Papers of General Nathanael Greene.* Published for the Rhode Island Historical Society. Chapel Hill and London: University of North Carolina Press, vol. IX, pp. xi, 38–39, 183.

199 Russell, D.L. (2000). *The American Revolution in the Southern Colonies.* Jefferson, NC, and London: McFarland, p. 314.

200 Conrad, Dennis M. (ed). (1997). *The Papers of General Nathanael Greene.* Published for the Rhode Island Historical Society. Chapel Hill and London: University of North Carolina Press, vol. IX, pp. 400–401, 484n.

201 Conrad, Dennis M. (ed). (1998). *The Papers of General Nathanael Greene.* Published for the Rhode Island Historical Society. Chapel Hill and London: University of North Carolina Press, vol. X, pp. 3–5.

202 Conrad, Dennis M. (ed). (1998). *The Papers of General Nathanael Greene.* Published for the Rhode Island Historical Society. Chapel Hill and London: University of North Carolina Press, Vol. X, pp. 21–23, 294n.

203 Conrad, Dennis M. (ed). (1998). *The Papers of General Nathanael Greene.* Published for the Rhode Island Historical Society. Chapel Hill and London: University of North Carolina Press, vol. X, pp. 20–23, 228–230.

204 Conrad, Dennis M. (ed). (1995). *The Papers of General Nathanael Greene.* Published for the Rhode Island Historical Society. Chapel Hill and London: University of North Carolina Press, vol. VIII, p. 379–380.

205 Conrad, Dennis M. (ed). (1998). *The Papers of General Nathanael Greene.* Published for the Rhode Island Historical Society. Chapel Hill and London: University of North Carolina Press, Vol. X, p. 5.

206 Daigler, K. A. (2004, Spring). "Code Names, Ciphers, and Spies: General Nathanael Greene's Efforts at Espionage." *Carologue: A Bulletin of South Carolina History*, 20(1) 12–19.

207 Spears, J. R. (1903). *Anthony Wayne.* New York: D. Appleton, pp. 186–187.

208 Conrad, Dennis M. (ed). (1998). *The Papers of General Nathanael Greene.* Published for the Rhode Island Historical Society. Chapel Hill and London: University of North Carolina Press, vol. X, pp. 173–174.

209 Conrad, Dennis M. (ed). (1998). *The Papers of General Nathanael Greene.* Published for the Rhode Island Historical Society. Chapel Hill and London: University of North Carolina Press, vol. X, p. 345n.

210 Conrad, Dennis M. (ed). (1998). *The Papers of General Nathanael Greene.* Published for the Rhode Island Historical Society. Chapel Hill and London: University of North Carolina Press, vol. X, p. 345n.

211 Reynolds, W.R. (2012). *Andrew Pickens.* Jefferson, NC, and London: McFarland, p. 295–296.

212 Conrad, Dennis M. (ed). (1998). *The Papers of General Nathanael Greene.* Published for the Rhode Island Historical Society. Chapel Hill and London: University of North Carolina Press, vol. X, pp. 325–326.

213 Stockwell, M. (2018). *Unlikely General – "Mad" Anthony Wayne and the Battle for America*. New Haven and London: Yale University Press, p. 207.

214 Conrad, Dennis M. (ed). (1998). *The Papers of General Nathanael Greene*. Published for the Rhode Island Historical Society. Chapel Hill and London: University of North Carolina Press, vol. X, p. 267.

215 Spears, J.R. (1903). *Anthony Wayne*. New York: D. Appleton, p. 189.

216 Conrad, Dennis M. (ed). (1998). *The Papers of General Nathanael Greene*. Published for the Rhode Island Historical Society. Chapel Hill and London: University of North Carolina Press, vol. X, p. 423–425.

217 Conrad, Dennis M. (ed). (1998). *The Papers of General Nathanael Greene*. Published for the Rhode Island Historical Society. Chapel Hill and London: University of North Carolina press, Vol. X, p. 572–573.

218 Conrad, Dennis M. (ed). (1998). *The Papers of General Nathanael Greene*. Published for the Rhode Island Historical Society. Chapel Hill and London: University of North Carolina Press, vol. X, p. 432–433.

219 Conrad, Dennis M. (ed). (1998). *The Papers of General Nathanael Greene*. Published for the Rhode Island Historical Society. Chapel Hill and London: University of North Carolina Press, vol. X, p. 425–426.

220 Conrad, Dennis M. (ed). (1998). *The Papers of General Nathanael Greene*. Published for the Rhode Island Historical Society. Chapel Hill and London. University of North Carolina Press, vol. X, p. 398.

221 Conrad, Dennis M. (ed). (1998). *The Papers of General Nathanael Greene*. Published for the Rhode Island Historical Society. Chapel Hill and London: University of North Carolina Press, vol. X, p. 426.

222 Conrad, Dennis M. (ed). (1998). *The Papers of General Nathanael Greene.* Published for the Rhode Island Historical Society. Chapel Hill and London. University of North Carolina Press, vol. X, pp. 536–537.

223 Stockwell, M. (2018). *Unlikely General – "Mad" Anthony Wayne and the Battle for America.* New Haven and London: Yale University Press, p. 209.

224 Stockwell, M. (2018). *Unlikely General – "Mad" Anthony Wayne and the Battle for America.* New Haven and London: Yale University Press, p. 209.

225 Conrad, Dennis M. (ed). (2000). *The Papers of General Nathanael Greene.* Published for the Rhode Island Historical Society. Chapel Hill and London: University of North Carolina Press, vol. XI, pp. 244–245.

226 Conrad, Dennis M. (ed). (2000). *The Papers of General Nathanael Greene.* Published for the Rhode Island Historical Society. Chapel Hill and London: University of North Carolina Press, vol. XI, p. 264n.

227 Conrad, Dennis M. (ed). (2000). *The Papers of General Nathanael Greene.* Published for the Rhode Island Historical Society. Chapel Hill and London: University of North Carolina Press, Vol. XI, p 338n.

228 Conrad, Dennis M. (ed). (2000). *The Papers of General Nathanael Greene.* Published for the Rhode Island Historical Society. Chapel Hill and London: University of North Carolina Press, vol. XI, pp. 365–367.

229 Blanco, R. L. and P.J. Sandborn (eds). (1993). *The American Revolution 1775–1783: An Encyclopedia.* Two-volume set with 125 contributors. New York and London: Garland Publishing, p. 267.

230 Spears, J. R. (1903). *Anthony Wayne.* New York: D. Appleton, pp. 32–59.

231 Conrad, Dennis M. (ed). (2000). *The Papers of General Nathanael Greene.* Published for the Rhode Island Historical Society. Chapel Hill and London; University of North Carolina Press, vol. XI, p. 341n.

232 Conrad, Dennis M. (ed). (1998). *The Papers of General Nathanael Greene.* Published for the Rhode Island Historical Society. Chapel Hill and London: University of North Carolina Press, vol. X, pp. 161–162.

233 Conrad, Dennis M. (ed). (1998). *The Papers of General Nathanael Greene.* Published for the Rhode Island Historical Society. Chapel Hill and London: University of North Carolina Press, vol. X, pp. 177–178.

234 Baxley, C. B. (2016). "An Enterprise Upon Johns Island." *Army History*, PB 20-16-1 (No. 98) Washington, DC, p. 43. Retrieved from: https://history.army.mil/armyhistory/AH98(W).pdf.

235 Conrad, Dennis M. (ed). (1998). *The Papers of General Nathanael Greene.* Published for the Rhode Island Historical Society. Chapel Hill and London: University of North Carolina Press, vol. X, pp. 206–209.

236 Conrad, Dennis M. (ed). (1998). *The Papers of General Nathanael Greene.* Published for the Rhode Island Historical Society. Chapel Hill and London: University of North Carolina Press, vol. X, p. 273.

237 Conrad, Dennis M. (ed). (1998). *The Papers of General Nathanael Greene.* Published for the Rhode Island Historical Society. Chapel Hill and London: University of North Carolina Press, vol. X, pp. 417–421.

238 McCowen, G. S. Jr. (1972). *The British Occupation of Charlestown, 1780–1782,* Columbia, SC: University of South Carolina Press. Tricentennial Studies, Number 5, p. 104.

239 Conrad, Dennis M. (ed). (1998). *The Papers of General Nathanael Greene.* Published for the Rhode Island Historical Society. Chapel Hill and London: University of North Carolina Press, vol. X, pp. 457–459.

240 Conrad, Dennis M. (ed). (1998). *The Papers of General Nathanael Greene.* Published for the Rhode Island Historical Society. Chapel Hill and London: University of North Carolina Press, vol. X, pp. 456–457.

241 Conrad, Dennis M. (ed). (2000). *The Papers of General Nathanael Greene.* Published for the Rhode Island Historical Society. Chapel Hill and London: University of North Carolina Press, vol. XI, p. 54.

242 Conrad, Dennis M. (ed). (2000). *The Papers of General Nathanael Greene.* Published for the Rhode Island Historical Society. Chapel Hill and London: University of North Carolina Press, vol. XI, p. 34–35, 47–48.

243 McCowen, G. S. Jr. (1972). *The British Occupation of Charlestown, 1780-1782.* Columbia, SC: University of South Carolina Press. Tricentennial Studies, Number 5, p. 52.

244 Kyte, G. W. (1983, Jan). "Thaddeus Kosciuszko at the Liberation of Charleston." *South Carolina Historical Magazine*, 84(1), pp 11–21. https://www.jstor.org/stable/27567777

245 McCowen, G. S. Jr. (1972). *The British Occupation of Charlestown, 1780–1782.* Columbia, SC: University of South Carolina Press. Tricentennial Studies, Number 5, p.101.

246 McCowen, G. S. Jr. (1972). *The British Occupation of Charlestown, 1780–1782.* Columbia, SC: University of South Carolina Press. Tricentennial Studies, Number 5, 103.

247 McCowen, G.S. Jr. (1972). *The British Occupation of Charlestown, 1780–1782.* Columbia, SC: University of South Carolina Press. Tricentennial Studies, Number 5, p. 105-106.

248 Weingast, B. R. (July 2015). "Adam Smith's Theory of the Persistence of Slavery and Its Abolition in Western Europe," Department of Political Science Stanford University, Abstract, p. 1. https://web.stanford.edu/group/mcnollgast/cgi-bin/wordpress/wp-content/uploads/2013/10/asms-theory-of-sy.15.0725.print-version.pdf

249 Conrad, Dennis M. (ed). (1998). *The Papers of General Nathanael Greene.* Published for the Rhode Island Historical Society. Chapel Hill and London: University of North Carolina Press, vol. X, p. 22.

250 Kerpelman, L. C. (Oct 2018). "The Slave Who Spied: James Armistead's Role in Revolutionary War." Https://www.historynet.com/the-slave-who-spied-james-armisteads-role-in-revolutionary-war.htm.

251 Conrad, Dennis M. (ed), (1998). *The Papers of General Nathanael Greene.* Published for the Rhode Island Historical Society. Chapel Hill and London: University of North Carolina Press, vol. X, pp. 304–305.

252 Paine, T. (1780, Mar 1). *An Act for the Gradual Abolition of Slavery*, USHistory.org, https://www.ushistory.org/presidentshouse/history/gradual.plp.

253 Thayer, T. (1960). *Nathanael Greene, Strategist of the American Revolution*. New York: Twayne Publishers, p. 391.

254 O'Kelley, Patrick (2005). *Nothing but Blood and Slaughter—The Revolutionary War*, USA: Blue House Tavern Press, vol. Four, pp. 49–54.

255 Thayer, T. (1960). *Nathanael Greene, Strategist of the American Revolution*. New York: Twayne Publishers, p. 399–400.

256 Conrad, Dennis M. (ed). (2000). *The Papers of General Nathanael Greene.* Published for the Rhode Island Historical Society. Chapel Hill and London: University of North Carolina Press, vol. XI, pp. 87, 92n.

257 Conrad, Dennis M. (ed). (2000). *The Papers of General Nathanael Greene.* Published for the Rhode Island Historical Society. Chapel Hill and London: University of North Carolina Press, vol. XI, pp. 144n.

258 Daigler, K. A. (2004). "Code Names, Ciphers, and Spies: General Nathanael Greene's Efforts at Espionage." *Carologue: A Bulletin of South Carolina History*, 20(1), 16–19.

259 Kyte, G. W. (1983, Jan). "Thaddeus Kosciuszko at the Liberation of Charleston." *The South Carolina Historical Magazine*, 84(1), pp. 11-21. https://www.jstor.org/stable/27567777; Conrad, Dennis M. (ed). (2000). *The Papers of General Nathanael Greene.* Published for the Rhode Island Historical Society: Chapel Hill and London: University of North Carolina Press, vol. XI, p. 117.

260 Conrad, Dennis M. (ed). (2000). *The Papers of General Nathanael Greene.* Published for the Rhode Island Historical Society. Chapel Hill and London: University of North Carolina Press, vol. XI, p. 182.

261 Conrad, Dennis M. (ed). (2000). *The Papers of General Nathanael Greene.* Published for the Rhode Island Historical Society. Chapel Hill and London: University of North Carolina Press, vol. XI, p. 235.

262 Conrad, Dennis M. (ed). (2000). *The Papers of General Nathanael Greene.* Published for the Rhode Island Historical Society. Chapel Hill and London: University of North Carolina Press, vol. XI, p. 391.

263 O'Kelley, Patrick. (2005). *Nothing but Blood and Slaughter—The Revolutionary War in the Carolinas.* United States: Blue House Tavern Press, vol. Four, pp. 71–72.

264 Conrad, Dennis M. (ed). (2000). *The Papers of General Nathanael Greene.* Published for the Rhode Island Historical Society, Chapel Hill and London, The University of North Carolina Press, Vol. XI, p. 346n.

265 Conrad, Dennis M. (ed). (2000). *The Papers of General Nathanael Greene.* Published for the Rhode Island Historical Society. Chapel Hill and London: University of North Carolina Press, vol. XI, p. 232n.

266 Conrad, Dennis M. (ed). (2000). *The Papers of General Nathanael Greene.* Published for the Rhode Island Historical Society. Chapel Hill and London: University of North Carolina Press, vol. XI, p. 341.

267 Conrad, Dennis M. (ed). (2000). *The Papers of General Nathanael Greene.* Published for the Rhode Island Historical Society. Chapel Hill and London: University of North Carolina Press, vol. XI, p.117n.

268 Tokar, J. A. (1999). "Logistics and the British Defeat in the Revolutionary War." *Army Logistician*, 31(5), p. 45: Kyte, George; "Thaddeus Kosciuszko at the Liberation of Charleston, 1782." *South Carolina Historical Magazine*, vol. 84, No. 1 (Jan, 1983), pp. 11–21.

269 Tokar, J. A. (1999, Jan-Feb) Army Logistics—Professional Bulletin of United States Army Logistics, Logistics and the British Defeat in the Revolutionary War. Fort Lee, VA: US Army Logistics Management Center, pp 7, 41.

270 McCowen, G. S., Jr. (1972). *The British Occupation of Charlestown, 1780–1782*, Columbia, SC: University of South Carolina Press, pp. 91–92.

271 O'Kelley, Patrick. (2005). *Nothing but Blood and Slaughter—The Revolutionary War in the Carolinas*, United Stated: Blue House Tavern Press, Vol. Four, p. 97.

272 Tokar, John A. "Logistics and the British Defeat in the Revolutionary War." *Army Logistician.*

273 Conrad, Dennis M. (ed). (2000). *The Papers of General Nathanael Greene.* Published for the Rhode Island Historical Society. Chapel Hill and London: University of North Carolina Press, Vol. xi, p. 362.

274 O'Kelley, Patrick. (2005). *Nothing but Blood and Slaughter—The Revolutionary War in the Carolinas.* United Stated: Blue House Tavern Press, vol. 4, p. 81.

275 Conrad, Dennis M. (ed). (2000). *The Papers of General Nathanael Greene.* Published for the Rhode Island Historical Society. Chapel Hill and London: University of North Carolina Press, vol. XI, pp. 579–582.

276 Conrad, Dennis M. (ed). (2000). *The Papers of General Nathanael Greene.* Published for the Rhode Island Historical Society. Chapel Hill and London: University of North Carolina Press, vol. XI, pp. 606–608.

277 Robins, E. (1921). "Charles Lee: Stormy Petrel of the Revolution." *The Pennsylvania Magazine of History and Biography.* 45(1), 66–97. http://www.jstor.org/stable/20086437.

278 McBurney, C. M. (2020, January 20). "Top Ten Quotes of Major General Charles Lee." *Journal of the American Revolution.* https://allthingsliberty.com/2020/01/top-ten-quotes-of-major-general-charles-lee/; Moore, G. H. (1851). *The Treason of Charles Lee*, Contains "Mr. Lee's Plan—March 29, 1777." NY: Charles Scribner. Open Library, pp. 81–100.

279 McBurney, Christian M. (2020, January 20). "Top Ten Quotes of Major General Charles Lee." *Journal of the American Revolution.* https://allthingsliberty.com/2020/01/top-ten-quotes-of-major-general-charles-lee/.

280 McBurney, Christian M. (2020, January 20). "Top Ten Quotes of Major General Charles Lee." *Journal of the American Revolution.* https://allthingsliberty.com/2020/01/top-ten-quotes-of-major-general-charles-lee/.

281 Bemis, S. F. (1957). *The Diplomacy of the American Revolution*. Bloomington: Indiana University Press, p. 209; Blanco, R. L. and P. J. Sandborn (eds). (1993). *The American Revolution 1775–1783: An Encyclopedia*. New York and London: Garland Publishing, vol. I, p. 582.

282 Conrad, Dennis M. (ed). (2000). *The Papers of General Nathanael Greene*. Published for the Rhode Island Historical Society. Chapel Hill and London: University of North Carolina Press, vol. XI, pp. 496–499.

283 Conrad, Dennis M. (ed). (2000). *The Papers of General Nathanael Greene*. Published for the Rhode Island Historical Society. Chapel Hill and London: University of North Carolina Press, vol. XI, p. 343.

284 Russell, D. L. (2000). *The American Revolution in the Southern Colonies*. Jefferson, NC and London: McFarland, p. 317.

285 Conrad, Dennis M. (ed). (2000). *The Papers of General Nathanael Greene*. Published for the Rhode Island Historical Society. Chapel Hill and London: University of North Carolina Press, vol. XI, p. 499n9.

286 Blanco, R. L. and P. J. Sandborn (eds). (1993). *The American Revolution 1775–1783: An Encyclopedia*. New York and London: Garland Publishing, vol. I, p. 266.

287 Blanco, R. L. and P. J. Sandborn (eds). (1993). *The American Revolution 1775–1783: An Encyclopedia*. New York and London: Garland Publishing, vol. I, p. 267.

288 Conrad, Dennis M. (ed). (2000). *The Papers of General Nathanael Greene*. Published for the Rhode Island Historical Society. Chapel Hill and London: University of North Carolina Press, vol. XI, p. 583n.

289 Conrad, Dennis M. (ed). (2000). *The Papers of General Nathanael Greene*. Published for the Rhode Island Historical Society. Chapel Hill and London: University of North Carolina Press, vol. XI, p. 498–499n.

290 Conrad, Dennis M. (ed). (2002). *The Papers of General Nathanael Greene*. Published for the Rhode Island Historical Society. Chapel Hill and London: University of North Carolina Press, vol. XII, pp. 4–5.

291 Conrad, Dennis M. (ed). (2002). *The Papers of General Nathanael Greene*. Published for the Rhode Island Historical Society. Chapel Hill and London: University of North Carolina Press, vol. XII, pp. 4, 9.

292 Bemis, S. F., (1957). *The Diplomacy of the American Revolution*. Bloomington: Indiana University Press, p. 202.

293 Conrad, Dennis M. (ed). (2002). *The Papers of General Nathanael Greene*. Published for the Rhode Island Historical Society. Chapel Hill and London: University of North Carolina Press, vol. XII, pp. 24–26.

294 Conrad, Dennis M. (ed). (2000). *The Papers of General Nathanael Greene*. Published for the Rhode Island Historical Society. Chapel Hill and London: University of North Carolina Press, vol. XII, p. 51.

295 Conrad, Dennis M. (ed). (2000). *The Papers of General Nathanael Greene*. Published for the Rhode Island Historical Society. Chapel Hill and London: University of North Carolina Press, Vol. xi, p. 316.

296 Butler, N. (2018, Feb 2). "The Story of Gadsden's Wharf," *The Charleston Time Machine*, Charleston County Public Library. Retrieved from: https://www.ccpl.org/charleston-time-machine/story-gadsdens-wharf.

297 Godbold, S. and R. H. Woody. (1982). *Christopher Gadsden and the American Revolution*. Knoxville: UT Press, pp. 68–69.

298 Conrad, Dennis M. (ed). (2000). *The Papers of General Nathanael Greene.* Published for the Rhode Island Historical Society. Chapel Hill and London: University of North Carolina Press, vol. XI, pp. 315–317.

299 Hagist, D. N. (2020). *Noble Volunteers—The British Soldiers Who Fought in the American Revolution*. Yardley, Pennsylvania, pp. 157–158.

300 Conrad, Dennis M. (ed). (2000). *The Papers of General Nathanael Greene.* Published for the Rhode Island Historical Society. Chapel Hill and London: University of North Carolina Press, vol. XI, p. 63.

301 Conrad, Dennis M. (ed). (2000). *The Papers of General Nathanael Greene.* Published for the Rhode Island Historical Society. Chapel Hill and London: University of North Carolina Press, vol. XI, p. 639.

302 McCowen, G. S. (1972). *The British Occupation of Charlestown, 1780–1782.* Columbia, SC: University of South Carolina Press, p. 149.

303 Hagist, D. N. (2020). *Noble Volunteers—The British Soldiers Who Fought in the American Revolution*. Yardley, Pennsylvania, p. xii.

304 Conrad, Dennis M. (ed). (2000). *The Papers of General Nathanael Greene.* Published for the Rhode Island Historical Society. Chapel Hill and London: University of North Carolina Press, vol. XII, pp. 190–193.

305 O'Kelley, Patrick. (2005). *Nothing but Blood and Slaughter—The Revolutionary War.* USA: Blue House Tavern Press, vol. 4, pp. 97–99.

306 Boyle, J. L. (ed). (1997). "The Revolutionary War Diaries of Captain Walter Finney, February 1782 to June 1783," *South Carolina Historical Magazine*, 98(2).

307 O'Kelley, Patrick. (2005). *Nothing but Blood and Slaughter—The Revolutionary War.* USA: Blue House Tavern Press, Vol. 4, pp. 100–110.

308 Conrad, Dennis M. (ed). (2002). *The Papers of General Nathanael Greene.* Published for the Rhode Island Historical Society. Chapel Hill and London: University of North Carolina Press, Vol. XII, p. 277.

309 Conrad, Dennis M. (ed). (2002). *The Papers of General Nathanael Greene.* Published for the Rhode Island Historical Society. Chapel Hill and London: University of North Carolina Press, Vol. XII, pp. 275–276.

310 Conrad, Dennis M. (ed). (2002). *The Papers of General Nathanael Greene.* Published for the Rhode Island Historical Society. Chapel Hill and London: University of North Carolina Press, vol. XII, p. 282.

311 Conrad, Dennis M. (ed). (2002). *The Papers of General Nathanael Greene.* Published for the Rhode Island Historical Society. Chapel Hill and London: University of North Carolina Press, vol. XII, pp. 281–282.

312 Conrad, Dennis M. (ed). (2002). *The Papers of General Nathanael Greene.* Published for the Rhode Island Historical Society. Chapel Hill and London: University of North Carolina Press, vol. XII, pp. 288–289.

313 Conrad, Dennis M. (ed). (2002). *The Papers of General Nathanael Greene.* Published for the Rhode Island Historical Society. Chapel Hill and London: University of North Carolina Press, vol. XII, pp. 290, 291n.

314 Carbone, G. (2008). *Nathanael Greene.* New York: Palgrave/Macmillan, p. 215.

315 Barnwell, J. W. (1910). "The Evacuation of Charleston by the British in 1782." *South Carolina Historical and Genealogical Magazine*, 11(1), 1–26.

316 Butler, N. (2020, June 5). "The Rise of Charleston's Horn Work," *Charleston Time Machine*, Charleston County Public Library. Retrieved from: https://www.ccpl.org/charleston-time-machine/rise-charlestons-horn-work-part-1

317 Conrad, Dennis M. (ed). (2002). *The Papers of General Nathanael Greene*. Published for the Rhode Island Historical Society. Chapel Hill and London: The University of North Carolina Press, vol. XII, pp. 291, 292n, 303, 304n.

318 Conrad, Dennis M. (ed). (2002). *The Papers of General Nathanael Greene*. Published for the Rhode Island Historical Society, Chapel Hill and London: University of North Carolina Press, vol. XII, pp. 301–304.

319 Conrad, Dennis M. (ed). (2002). *The Papers of General Nathanael Greene*. Published for the Rhode Island Historical Society. Chapel Hill and London: University of North Carolina Press, vol. XII, p. 361.

320 Stegeman, J. F. and J. A. Stegeman. (1977). *Caty—A Biography of Catharine Littlefield Greene*. Athens: University of Georgia Press, pp. 101–102.

321 Conrad, Dennis M. (ed). (2002). *The Papers of General Nathanael Greene*. Published for the Rhode Island Historical Society. Chapel Hill and London: University of North Carolina Press, vol. XII, p. 608.

322 Conrad, Dennis M. (ed). (2002). *The Papers of General Nathanael Greene*. Published for the Rhode Island Historical Society. Chapel Hill and London: University of North Carolina Press, vol. XII, pp. 393, 396–397.

323 Tokar, J. A. (1999). "Logistics and the British defeat in the revolutionary war." *Army Logistician*. 31(5), 42.

324 Morris, R. B. (1965). *The Peacemakers—The Great Powers and American Independence*. New York: Harper and Row, p. 187.

325 Gordon, J. (2003). *South Carolina and the American Revolution*. Columbia, SC: University of South Carolina Press, p. 71.

326 Showman, R. K., and Dennis M. Conrad. (eds). (1991). *The Papers of General Nathanael Greene*. Published for the Rhode Island Historical Society. Chapel Hill and London: University of North Carolina Press, vol. VI.

327 McCowen, G. S. (1972). *The British Occupation of Charlestown. 1780–1782*, Columbia, SC: University of South Carolina Press, Tricentennial Studies, Number 5, pp. 43–110.

328 Reynolds, W. R. (2012). *Andrew Pickens*. Jefferson, NC, and London: McFarland, pp. 61–80.

329 Pancake, J. S. (1985). *This Destructive War—The British Campaign in the Carolinas, 1780–1782*. University of Alabama Press, p. 72.

330 Bemis, S. F. (1957). *The Diplomacy of the American Revolution*. Bloomington: Indiana University Press, pp. 181–182.

331 Conrad, Dennis M. (ed). (2000). *The Papers of General Nathanael Greene*. Published for the Rhode Island Historical Society. Chapel Hill and London: University of North Carolina Press, vol. XII, pp. 326.

332 Army and General Staff College Press. (2002). "Nathanael Greene's Implementation of Compound Warfare during the Southern Campaign of the American Revolution" (University of North Carolina classified). Based on Thomas Huber's "Compound Warfare: The Fatal Knot" (Fort Leavenworth, KS: U.S. Printed in Columbia, SC on 1 May 2018. ISB 9781500748463.

333 Duvall, L. (2018) "Mastering Charleston: Property and Patriarchy in British-Occupied Charleston, 1780–1782." *William and Mary Quarterly* 75(4), 607. https://www.muse.jhu.edu/article/707412

334 Glickstein, D. (2015). *After Yorktown: The Final Struggle for American Independence*. Westholme Publishing, p. 42.

335 Conrad, Dennis M. (ed). (2000). *The Papers of General Nathanael Greene*. Published for the Rhode Island Historical Society. Chapel Hill and London: University of North Carolina Press, vol. XII, pp. 419–420.

336 Morris, R. B. (1965). *The Peacemakers—The Great Powers and American Independence*. New York: Harper and Row, pp. 173–190, 205–206.

337 Dull, J. R. (1987). *A Diplomatic History of the American Revolution*. Yale University Press, p. 150.

338 Bemis, S. F. (1957). *The Diplomacy of the American Revolution*. Bloomington: Indiana University Press, p. 239.

339 Blanco, R. L. (1993). *The American Revolution 1775–1783: An Encyclopedia*, vol. II, M–Z. New York and London: Garland Publishing, p. 1700.

340 Morris, R. B. (1965), *The Peacemakers—The Great Powers and American Independence*. New York: Harper and Row, p. 179.

341 Morris, R. B. (1965). *The Peacemakers—The Great Powers and American Independence*. New York: Harper and Row, pp. 205–206.

342 Morris, R. B. (1965). *The Peacemakers—The Great Powers and American Independence*. New York: Harper and Row, p. 209.

343 Morris, R. B. (1965). *The Peacemakers—The Great Powers and American Independence*. New York: Harper and Row, pp. 209–210.

344 Morris, R. B. (1965). *The Peacemakers—The Great Powers and American Independence*. New York: Harper and Row, pp. 244, 306.

345 Morris, R. B. (1965). *The Peacemakers—The Great Powers and American Independence*. New York: Harper and Row, p. 253.

346 Bemis, S. F. (1957). *The Diplomacy of the American Revolution*. Bloomington: Indiana University Press, pp. 182, 212; Morris, R. B. (1965), *The Peacemakers—The Great Powers and American Independence*. New York: Harper and Row, p. 413.

347 Bemis, S. F. (1957). *The Diplomacy of the American Revolution*. Bloomington: Indiana University Press, p. 240; *The Peacemakers—The Great Powers and American Independence*. New York: Harper and Row, p. 384.

348 Bemis, S. F. (1957). *The Diplomacy of the American Revolution*. Bloomington: Indiana University Press, p. 247.

349 Bemis, S. F. (1957). *The Diplomacy of the American Revolution*. Bloomington: Indiana University Press, p. 187.

350 Burns, A. (n.d,). *The Abdication Speech of George III*. Retrieved from: https://georgianpapers.com/2017/01/22/abdication-speech-george-iii/.

351 Conrad, D. M (ed). (2000). *The Papers of General Nathanael Greene*. Published for the Rhode Island Historical Society. Chapel Hill and London: University of North Carolina Press, vol. XII, pp. 606, 608n.

352 O'Shaughnessy, Andrew Jackson. (2013). *The Men Who Lost America*. New Haven and London: Yale University Press, p. 41.

353 Blanco, R. L. (1993). *The American Revolution 1775–1783: An Encyclopedia*, vol. II, M–Z. New York and London: Garland Publishing, pp. 1807–1818.

354 Bemis, S. F. (1957), *The Diplomacy of the American Revolution*. Bloomington: Indiana University Press, pp. 185, 190–196.

355 Conrad, D. M (ed). (1998). *The Papers of General Nathanael Greene*. Published for the Rhode Island Historical Society. Chapel Hill and London: University of North Carolina Press, vol. X, p. 383n.

356 Russell, D. L (2000). *The American Revolution in the Southern Colonies.* Jefferson, NC and London: McFarland, pg. 314.

357 Morris, R. B. (1965). *The Peacemakers—The Great Powers and American Independence.* New York: Harper and Row, p. 253.

358 Ferling, J. (2007). *Almost a Miracle.* Oxford: Oxford University Press, p. 474.

359 McCandless, P. (2007). "Revolutionary Fever: Disease and War in the Lower South, 1776-1783." *The. American Clinical and Climatological Association Magazine*, 118, pp. 225–249. Retrieved from: https://www.ncbi.nlm.nih.gov/pmc/articles/PMC1863584/.

360 King, G., and B. Dobrée. (1968). *Letters of King George III.* London: Cassell.

361 1782 Public Act 22: An Act to enable His Majesty to Conclude a Peace or Truce with Certain Colonies in North America therein Mentioned, Parliamentary Archives: GB-061, https://archives.parliament.uk/collections/getrecord/GB61_HL_PO_PU_1_1782_22G3n81.

362 O'Shaughnessy, A. J. (2013). *The Men Who Lost America.* New Haven and London: Yale University Press, pp. 238–240.

363 Blanco, R. L. (1993). *The American Revolution 1775–1783: An Encyclopedia.* Volume I, A–L. New York and London: Garland Publishing, Inc., p. 267.

364 Conrad, Dennis M. (ed). (2000). *The Papers of General Nathanael Greene.* Published for the Rhode Island Historical Society. Chapel Hill and London: University of North Carolina Press, vol. XI, p. 498.

365 Knight, L. (2019, April 19). "Be a King George," *Journal of the American Revolution*, Retrieved from: https://allthingsliberty.com/2019/04/be-a-king-george/.

366 Morris, R. B. (1965). *The Peacemakers—The Great Powers and American Independence*. New York: Harper and Row, pp. 175–180.

367 Morris, R. B. (1965). *The Peacemakers—The Great Powers and American Independence*. New York: Harper and Row, p. 188.

368 Dull, J. R. (1987). *A Diplomatic History of the American Revolution*. Yale University Press, p. 149.

369 Bemis, S. F. (1957). *The Diplomacy of the American Revolution*, Bloomington: Indiana University Press, p. 187.

370 Conrad, Dennis M. (ed, 2000). *The Papers of General Nathanael Greene*. Published for the Rhode Island Historical Society. Chapel Hill and London: University of North Carolina Press, vol. XI, pp. 416-421.

371 Conrad, Dennis M. (ed), (2000). *The Papers of General Nathanael Greene*. Published for the Rhode Island Historical Society. Chapel Hill and London: University of North Carolina Press, vol. XI, pp. 416–421.

372 Bemis, S. F. (1957) *The Diplomacy of the American Revolution*, Bloomington: Indiana University Press, p. 192.

373 Parker, J. C. (2009). *Parker's Guide to the Revolutionary War in South Carolina: Battles, Skirmishes and Murders*. United States: Hem Branch Publishing.

374 Conrad, Dennis M. (ed). (2000). *The Papers of General Nathanael Greene*, published for the Rhode Island Historical Society. Chapel Hill and London: University of North Carolina Press, vol. XI, pp. 633–635; Reynolds, W. R. (2012). Andrew Pickens, Jefferson, NC, and London: McFarland.

375 Moore, G. H. (1860). *The Treason of Charles Lee*. Contains "Mr. Lee's Plan—March 29, 1777." NY: Charles Scribner, pp. 81–100.

376 Barnwell, J. W. (1910, Jan). "The Evacuation of Charleston by the British in 1782." *The SC Historical and Genealogical Magazine*. 11(1) p.14. Retrieved from: https://www.jstor.org/stable/27575255?seq=18#metadata_info_tab_contents.

377 Seymour, W. (1883). "A Journal of the Southern Expedition, 1780–1783" (concluded). *The Pennsylvania Magazine of History and Biography*, 7(4), 377-394. Retrieved from http://www.jstor.org/stable/20084622.

378 Conrad, Dennis M. (ed), (2000). *The Papers of General Nathanael Greene*. Published for the Rhode Island Historical Society. Chapel Hill and London: University of North Carolina Press, vol. XII, p. 302.

379 Conrad, Dennis M. (ed), (2000). *The Papers of General Nathanael Greene*. Published for the Rhode Island Historical Society. Chapel Hill and London: University of North Carolina Press, vol. XII, p. 416.

380 Conrad, Dennis M. (ed), (2000). *The Papers of General Nathanael Greene*. Published for the Rhode Island Historical Society. Chapel Hill and London: University of North Carolina Press, vol. XII, pp. 606–608.

381 *Washington, George*. American Revolution Reference Library. Retrieved from: https://www.encyclopedia.com/history/educational-magazines/washington-george.

382 O'Kelley, Patrick. (2005). *Nothing but Blood and Slaughter—The Revolutionary War*. USA: Blue House Tavern Press, vol. 3, pp. 380–410; vol. 4, pp. 22–145.

383 Conrad, Dennis M. (ed). (2000). *The Papers of General Nathanael Greene*. Published for the Rhode Island Historical Society. Chapel Hill and London: University of North Carolina Press, vol. XII, p. 281.

384 Tzu, Sun, 475-221 BCE. Translated by James Trapp, *The Art of War*. Reprint 2012, New York, NY: Chartwell Books, page 17.

385 Parks, R. N. (ed). (2005). *The Papers of General Nathanael Greene*. Published for the Rhode Island Historical Society. Chapel Hill and London: University of North Carolina Press, vol. XIII, p. 45.

386 Carbone, G. M. (2008). *Nathanael Greene*. New York: Palgrave MacMillan, p. 219.

387 Carbone, G. M. (2008). *Nathanael Greene*. New York: Palgrave MacMillan, p. 219.

388 Parks, R. N. (ed). (2005). *The Papers of General Nathanael Greene*. Published for the Rhode Island Historical Society. Chapel Hill and London: University of North Carolina Press, vol. XIII, pp. 44–45.

389 Anderson, L. (2002). *Forgotten Patriot*. USA, Universal Publishers, p. 343.

390 Parks, R. N (ed). (2005). *The Papers of General Nathanael Greene*. Published for the Rhode Island Historical Society. Chapel Hill and London: University of North Carolina Press, vol. XIII, p. 151.

INDEX

Printed in the USA
CPSIA information can be obtained
at www.ICGtesting.com
LVHW052235221223
767218LV00050B/1090/J